MUSLIM CHILDREN

HOW TO BRING UP ?

Vol. I

Translated By

S. Zakir Aijaz

KITAB BHAVAN

New Delhi-110002

Kitab Bhavan

Publishers, Distributors, Exporters & Importers
1784, Kalan Mahal, Darya Ganj
New Delhi - 1100 02 (India)

Phone : (91-11) 23277392/93, 23274686, 30906494
website : www.kitabbhavan.com
Email : nasri@vsnl.com
Fax : (91-11) 23263383

First Edition 1991
IInd Reprinted 2006

ISBN : 81-7151-135-X (Set)
ISBN : 81-7151-136-8 (Vol. I)
Code No. : ZZZ054

Published in India by :
Nusrat Ali Nasri for Kitab Bhavan
1784, Kalan Mahal, Darya Ganj
New Delhi - 1100 02 [India]

Printed in India at :
Nice Printing Press
Khureji Khas, Delhi-110051

CONTENTS

CHAPTER 1

MARRIED LIFE AND ITS BEARING ON THE UPBRINGING OF CHILDREN

Before setting about to deal with the basic Islamic principles of rearing children, I would like to touch on married life in its three apsects viz;

(I) As the fundamental demand of human nature
(II) As the guarantee of social welfare and
(III) As the guarantee of chastity and proof of good choice.

A correct review of these three aspects of wedlock would bring home to us the vital importance of proper upbringing of our offspring. It will make us realize not only the heavy responsibility we have to shoulder in the accomplishment of this task, but also the need to have bred and cultivated children and the significance of descent, physical health and moral excellence. It will also acquaint us with the vital role played by the mutual cooperation and affection of the parents in bringing up their offsprings, setting right th deviant among them and building their character in order that they may be able to lead a refined and civilized life. Let us now take up the three aspects of marriage in detail.

(I) MARRIAGE AS THE FUNDAMENTAL DEMAND OF HUMAN NATURE

A careful study of the basic and unambiguous principles of Islamic Shariah would reveal that the Shariah, so to speak, is a declaration of war on the cult of renunciation of life of seclusion; for renunciation is out of tune with the demands of human nature. It is in conflict with human instincts, desires and aspirations. Hazrat Sa'd bin Abi Waqqas (R.A.A.) aptly observes:

"Allah has endowed us with a propensity to the right state rather than to monkishness". (*Baihaqi*)

The HolyProphet (S.A.W.) denounces celibacy in the following words:

"I have nothing to do with the person who can afford to marry but prefers to remain single."

(*Baihaqi and Tabarani*)

It is clear from the above observations that it is unlawful for a Muslim to abstain from matrimony for the sake of devoting himself to the wroship of Allah seeking thereby to draw closer to Him or he is apathetic to it with a view to leading a secluded life. He will, according to the Shariah, be guilty of an unlawful act particularly when he remains a celebate in spite of having all the material resources to marry. The methods adopted by the Holy Prophet (S.A.W.) for the safeguard of the individuals in the society and for the discipline of the human mind lead us to the firm conviction that both these functions are based on the proper understanding of the reality of human life and are designed to fulfil human desires and aspirations. In doing this, however, care should be taken that no individual exceeds his natural limits by trying to do something beyond his means and capacity but acts with temperance, moving on smoothly with his natural speed along with others so that he may not lag behind or find himself in a predicament as a weak person surrounded by strong people. Says Allah:

"The Nature (framed) of Allah in which He has created man. There is no altering (the laws of) Allah's creation. That is the right religion but most men know it not"

(30: 30)

The practice of the Holy Prophet is the best guide to married life and the upbringing of children. The following tradition embodies his attitude to matrimony:

It is reported by Hazrat Anas (R.A.A.) that once three people called on the Prophet's wife to enquire how long he used to pray. When they were told about it, everyone of them felt that he prayed too little. They said that they were nothing as compared to the Prophet of Allah who had no sin to be forgiven. So one of them solemnly declared that he would pray to Allah the whole night; another vowed that he would keep fast all his life and the third pledged that he would abstain from women and continue single. They had been making these pledges when the Prophet (S.A.W.) arrived. He said to them:

> "Well, I know what you have just been talking about. Listen! By God, I am the most God-fearing of you all and am far more pious, too. But when I keep fast I do eat something at my fast break; when I pray I also have sleep. Also, I marry women. Whoever deviates from my practice is no follower of mine."

From what has been stated above it will be clear to every sensible person that according to Islam matrimony is the demand of human nature which enables a man to discharge the heavy responsibility of rearing children and taking proper care of them. Thus through matrimony he can fulfil the demands of his nature, gratify his desires and lead a civilized life.

(II) MARRIAGE AS THE GUARANTEE OF SOCIAL WELFARE

According to Islam there are numerous advantages of matrimony. Its collective utility, like other advantages is common knowledge. We deal herewith some of the more important advantages of marriage and then proceed to show its relationship with the upbringing of children.

Some More Important Advantages of Marriage

1. Survival of Human Race

Matrimony is necessary for the survival of mankind. The humans are multiplied as the result of wedlock. This process of human procreation has continued without a break. According to the pundits of human affairs, formulation of rules for the breeding of human-beings is as essential as for maintaining their bodily health. The Holy Quran refers to this ceaseless process of legitimate procreation through wedlock in the following words:

"And Allah has given you wives of your own kind

and hath given you from your wives sons and grandsons."
(16: 72)

Again,

"O Mankind! Be careful of your duty to your Lord Who created you from a single soul and from it cteated its mate and from them twains has spread abroad a multitude of men and women." (4:1)

2. Preservation of Lineage

Matrimony has been made lawful by Allah. It is because of matrimony that the individuals descending from common ancestors take pride in their lineage and kinships. This relationship gives them satisfaction and generates confidence among them. It is to wedlock that they owe their respectability. Had there been no custom of marriages, the community would have given birth to children devoid of human quality and moral virtues, having no family background. This state of affairs would have given rise to disruption and there would have been no criterion of legitimacy.

3. Safeguard Against Moral Deterioration

Matrimony saves the community from moral degeneration and the individual from collective depravity. Every sensible person fully realizes that if sex sublimated by conjugal ties, the community is imbued with moral excellence and social propriety and is thus capable of propagating the message of Islam and of fulfilling its respnsibility according to divine will.

The following words of the Holy Prophet express most appropriately the philosophy underlying matrimony and its collective utility. Says the Prophet (S.A.W.):

"O young people! Whoever of you can afford to marry, ought to marry; for marriage is the most effective means of keeping one's eyes downcast with modesty and preserving one's private parts. Whoever, does not have the means to marry should keep fast, for fasting is the antidote to sexual appetite."

4. Prevention of Disease

Matrimony prevents young people from all the diseases resulting from adultery, debauchery and sodomy. These are moral offences that cause the venereal diseases of reninal flux and intestinal ailment. This is a dangerous disease which threatens the reprodction of human species, makes the young people sickly lean like rakes and susceptible to epidemics.

5. Spiritual and Mental Satisfaction

Wedlock strengthens the bonds of love, affection and benevolence between man and woman. When the husband returns home after the day's toil and is surrounded by the wife and children, he is relieved of the fatigue and tension caused during the work. The wife also gets similar satisfaction as she is joined by the husband each evening.

Both the husband and wife sitting together at each other's side enjoy married life and feel psychologically satisfied. Allah describes this state of bliss in the following words:

"And of His signs is this: He created for you help mates from yourselves that you might find rest in them and He ordained between you love and mercy. Lo! Herein indeed are portents for folk who reflect." (30:21)

The spiritual and psychological satisfaction with which a married couple is blessed is fraught with the infinite urge to breed and take care of their offsprings in the best possible manner and to look after their rights.

6. Mutual Coopration of Parents in Bringing up Children and Building of Family.

The husband and wife cooperate with each other in the formation of family and the fulfilment of the household responsibilities, each discharging his or her respective duties. The woman performs her job in a befitting manner and does everything suited to the genius of her sex. For instance, she keeps the home in order and fosters and breeds her offsprings. Someone has aptly observed:

The bosom of the mother is a school. Establish this school and you will build a whole nation imbued with moral excellences."

The husband, on the other hand, accomplishes his respective function manfully. He toils and bears hardhsips for the sake of his family and protects it against adversity. This spirit of mutual cooperation in man and wife underlies in the condcut of family affairs and thus the task of inculcating manners and morals in the children is carried on. The result is that we have a well based and refined generation of believers with unshakable faith in Allah and with the spirit of Islam rooted deep in their hearts. In fact it is owing to cooperation between man and wife that the family is happy and prosperous. Each member of such a family lives happily under the unbrella of affection, security and peace.

7. Parental Affection Engendered by Marriage.

It is because of wedlock that the parents, hearts fill with love and sacred passions for their offsprings which has salutary affects on their upbringing and training with the result that the efforts of parents in this direction are fruitful. It is this sacred passion which motivates the parents to work wholeheartedly for the welfare of the children and for ensuring a bright future for them.

These, then, are some of the blessings of matrimony that have a long way in rearing and refining children, building of famly and the growth of new generation on sound grounds.

Islam does not stress the need to marry without a motive underlying therein. Says the Prophet (S.A.W.):

"A virtuous wife is only next to the fear of Allah which is the most valuable possession of a believer. If he commands her, she obeys him. If he looks at her she delights him. If he wishes her on oath to have something for him, she fulfils her wish. If she is not with him, she proves to be his well wisher in respect to herself and his property."

There is another saying of the Holy Prophet (S.A.W.) to the same effect:

"The world is an asset and the most valuable of the asset is woman (wife)."

(III) MARRIAGE AS THE GUARANTEE OF PURITY AND PROOF OF GOOD CHOICE.

A manifestation of the superiority and comprehensiveness of Islamic system is that it has laid down certain principles for the man making a proposal of marriage and the girl to whom such a proposal is made. If these principles are translated into action, marriage would prove an ideal of mutal understanding love and harmony and the family composed of the progeny of such a married couple would attain the aim of faith and would be blessed with sound minds in sound bodies as well as with the peace of mind.

Some of the Basic principles relating to marriage are as follows:

1. Faith Should Be the Criterion of Choice.

By faith is meant a proper understanding of Islam as well as adopting the Islamic way of life. Faith also includes action on the eternal principles and laws of the Islamic Shariah.

If the man making the proposal of marriage or the woman whose hand is asked for has no sense of faith in the above sense and does not translate faith into practice" will obviously be treated as wanting good manners and morals and as removed from Islam regardless of his pretensions to righteousness and his impression about himself to be living up to Islam.

Hazrat Umar Farooq (R.A.A.) has laid down the best standard for the judgment of a man's character. Once a man bore witness about another man.

Hazrat Umar Faooq (R.A.A.) asked him, "Do you really know the man?"

'Yes', Said he.

"Are you his neighbour and see him pass as he goes and comes back?" asked the Caliph.

"No."

"Did you even happen to travel with him and have thus experience of his character?"

"No, I did'nt."

"Do you ever enter into financial and commercial trans

action with him wherein he proved to be an honest man?"

The witness replied in the negative again.

"Have you, then, seen him offer prayers in the mosque, sitting and raising and bowing his head as he prayed?" demanded the Caliph raising his voice.

"Yes, I did", replied the man.

Hazrat Umar Farooq (R.A.A.) asked the man bearing witness to go away as he knew nothing about the person referring in the case. He then turned to the person concerned and asked him to bring someone who did really know him. In other words, Hazrat Umar was not taken in by th outward appearance of the man, but kept in view the standards of acquaintance by which the man's adherence to faith and character could be ascertained.

The following Tradition of the Holy Prphet (S.A.W.) means the same thing:

"Allah does not see your faces and bodies. He
sees your hearts and actions."

It is because of these considerations that the Holy Prophet (S.A.W.) exhorts persons wishing to marry that they should look for religious minded consorts who could discharge their duties towards their husbands, children and household in conformity with the injunctions of Islam. The Prophet (S.A.W.) stressed the need to have such a wife. Hazrat Abu Huraira (R.A.A.) quotes him as having said:

"There are four considerations for which a woman is contracted into marrage: her assets, the family she belongs to, her beauty and her adherence to faith. I wish you wed both woman and faith." (*Bukhari and Muslim*)

Again, Hazrat Anas (R.A.A.) reports the Prophet (S.A.W.) to have observed:

"Whoever marries a woman because of her status would be degraded by Allah. Whoever marries a woman because of her wealth would be reduced by Allah to a destitute. Whoever marries a woman because of her high ranking family would be degraded by Allah into an abject fellow; but whosoever marries a woman for the purpose of keeping his eyes downcast with modesty and his private parts immune from debauchery or for doing good to his kith and kin would be blessed by Allah with bounty through that woman."

(*Al Tabarani-al-Ausat*)

The Prophet (S.A.W.) exhorts the guardians of a marriageable girl to find for her a religious-minded and virtuous husband who could duly discharge his duty of looking after the family and the rights of his wife and bringing up children properly and who has the sense of honour and is worthy of being trusted to spend money for meeting domestic expenses.

Says the Holy Prophet (S.A.W.):

"If a man comes to you with a proposal of marriage and you are pleased with him for his good conduct and adherence to faith, then marry your girl to him. Otherwise inequity would prevail in the world and great corruption would ensue." (*Tirmizi*)

There can be no greater evil posing a threat to the religious and moral training of a family than a chaste girl coming into the grips of an immodest, immoral and ungodly husband who cares little for the sanctity of wedlock with the believing woman, who does not discharge any responsibility imposed upon him as her husband and who is insensitive to honour and civility.

There can be no greater threat to a virtuous woman than her marriage with an inequitous and adulterous man who compels her to be immodest, freely mixes with people, drinks and dances with other men and who forces her to break the shackless of religion and morality.

There are innumerable damsels who were leading a life of purity and modesty with their parents before marriage but have been turned into lewd women after they were tied with matrimonial bonds to dishonourable and shameless families and passed into the hands of inequitous husbands. They have no sense of moral values honour and modesty.

There can be no denying of the fact that children brought up in a shameless and immoral family will grow in a deviant milleu and acquire corrupt practices and inequitous traits. The choice of a wife based on religion plays a vital part in ensuring the harmonious life of sweet home. This would create a congenial atmosphere for bringing up children in conformity with the principles of Islam and thus pave the way for the formation of a happy and honourable family.

Choice of Wife in Consideration of Respectability and Noble Birth.

Islam enjoins that man and woman should choose for themselves such consorts as are of noblebirth and belonging to respectable families of noble origin. The raison d'etre of this precept is the diversity of natures and dispositions. There are people with both good and evil tendencies, apt to act subversely as well as righteously.

The Holy Prophet (S.A.W.) himself has described in the following tradition the variety of people's dispositions and has explained that some of them are naturally disposed to do good and others to do evil:

"Human beings are repository of good and evil. In the days of Pagan ignorance those who were morally better than others embraced Islam and continue to be better after embracing it."

It is for this reason the Prophet (S.A.W.) advises anyone desirous of marrying to take into account noble descent, kind disposition and moral excellence in the choice of the consort. The following sayings of the Prophet (S.A.W.) are noteworthy in this context:

Hazrat Abu Saeed Khudri reports the Prophet (S.A.W.) to have said:

"Avoid the weed growing over the dunghill."

His companions enquired what the weed growing over the dunghill meant. The Prophet (S.A.W.) replied:

"A beautiful woman at a vile place (i.e. one brought up in an evil environment)."

(*Dar Qutni, Ibn Asakir and Ibn Adi*)

Hazrat Aisha (R.A.A.) quotes the Prophet (S.A.W.) to have observed:

"Choose good consorts for your progeny and
marry in a family of equal rank."

There is another saying of the Holy Prophet (S.A.W.) to the same effect:

"Choose a good consort for your progeny, because family traits are inherited from generation." (*Ibn Maja, Daylami*)

Again:

"Choose good wives for your sons for women give birth

to children resembling their brothers and sisters."

(Reported by Hazrat Aisha, Ibn Adi, Ibn Asakir)

In yet another Tradition the Holy Prophet (S.A.W.) is reported to have said:

"Look for families akin to your own to find wives for your sons because male often take after their paternal uncles."

Ibn Adee al Kamil relates one more tradition to the same effect:

"Marry virtuous women, for family traits are transmitted from generation to generation."

The sum and susbtance of all these traditions is that those wishing to marry should choose such wives as are chaste and virtuous and brought up in an environment uncontaminated with wicked elements and are bred in families well-known for their nobility and sterling qualities. The families of the girls to be chosen should be noble in the sense that they descend from ancestors known to have born excellent moral character. The implication of this emphasis on the nobiility of lineage may be that noble girls give birth to children who are naturally ambitious of performing great deeds and endowed with sterling qualities and their character is moulded according to the teachings of Islam. Such children acquire cardinal virtues from the milk they suck from the breasts of their noble mothers.

It was for this reason that Usman bin Abul 'Aas Al Saqfi exhorted his son in the following words:

"O my son! A man intending to marry is actually going to plant a Sapling. He should, therefore, see where he is planting it. A woman of base origin seldom gives birth to noble offsprings. For this reason you should try to seek the hand of the best consort even if it takes you a little longer to find one."

In view of the significance of choosing a good wife Hazrat Umar (R.A.A.) observed in reply to the question of his son relating to the right of the son to his father:

"He (the father) should choose a virtuous woman to be his (the Son's) mother, speak to him in a decent manner and teach him the Holy Quran."

Choice of good wife to be the mother of one's offsprings

as emphasized by the Holy Prophet (S.A.W.) constitutes the best principle of training and upbringing of children in the world today.

It has been borne out by the results of scientific enquiry into heredity that the child begins to inherit and develop the moral, physical and mental qualities of its parents right from the very moment of its coming into the world. Hence if a good consort (wife or husband) is chosen for one's self on the basis of nobility and good disposition the offsprings born of the union of such a couple would grow up with the virtues of chastity, modesty and consistency. A child who inherits such family traits, gets sound moral training, it will develop ideal character which will serve as a model of righteousness, moral excellence, nobility and kindness.

In short it is incumbent upon one wishing to marry to choose for himself a virtuous consort if he wants to have children of noble origin with moral virtues and unshakable faith.

3. Exogamy

Islam emphasizes the importnace of exogamy i.e.; the choice of unrelated woman for matrimony in preference to a kinswoman. This preference of unrelated woman is designed to ensure nobility of descent, safety of children against the potential danger of heriditary diseases, expansion of the family circle as well as to strengthen collective bonds.

Children born of unrelated couples are physically strong with marked bonds of mutual affection and attachment. The Prophet was averse to conjugal union between closely related people. The wisdom of his discouragement of such union is that couple of the same flesh and blood often give birth to weaklings who inherit diseases of their parents and paternal and maternal grandfathers.

Says the Holy Prophet (S.A.W.):

"Marry not with your close relations, because
your offsprings will be infirm and weak."

In another tradition he urges upon us to marry in unrelated family so that we may not be weak.

According to scientific enquiry into heredity, children born of union between close relations are physically weak with intelligence below the average. They also inherit bad habits that are harmful to the society.

This is the scientific truth revealed by the Holy Prophet (S.A.W.) fourteen hundred years before at a time when the scholars and scientists were absolutely a stranger to it. It actually constitutes one of the miracles of the Holy Prophet (S.A.W.).

4. Choice of a Virgin

Islam also emphasizes the choice of maiden in preference to a widow or divorced woman. There are innumerable advantages of choosing a maiden for wife. Firstly, the family remains immune from financial problems and all sorts of conflicts. The home atmosphere is free from animosities and tensions. The reason for this is that the maiden who is married for the first time is naturally fond of her husband to the highest degree. On the contrary, a widow or a divorced woman does not love her second husband half so much as she does her firtst man; nor does the second husband return the same amount of affection as she bestows upon him. The striking difference between the behaviour of the first and second husbands is expressive of their respective affections.

Hazrat Aisha (R.A.A.) is reported to have talked to the Prophet (S.A.W.) about the matter under discussion.
Said she:

O Messenger of Allah! suppose you go into a valley where there is a tree, some of whose leaves are browsed upon by an animal and another tree untouched by any animal.

Then which tree, you would like to be browsed by your camel? The Holy Prophet (S.A.W.) replied: I would like the tree unbrowsed by any other animal. Hazrat Aisha (R.A.A.) said: I am that very tree. In this way she wanted to show her superiority on other wives of the Holy Prophet (S.A.W.).

The Holy Prophet (S.A.W.) has himself described the advantages of marrying virgin women. He said:

Marry virgin women. They are sweet hearted, give birth to many children. Rarely they deceive and conspire and are delighted with petty things.

This was told by the Holy Prophet (S.A.W.) to Hazrat Jabir (R.A.A.), when he returned from the Battle of Zat-ir-Riqa. He enquired from him if he had married.

Hazrat Jabir said: Yes, O Prophet (S.A.W.) of Allah. He said: Is she a virgin or previously married? Hazrat Jabir (R.A.A.) said: she was previously married (widow or divorced).

The Holy Prophet (S.A.W.) said: why did you not marry a virgin girl with whom you would play and enjoy. She would reciprocate the same feelings.

I said, "O Messenger of Allah! My father fell a martyr in the battle of Uhud leaving seven daughters behind. So I have married an experienced woman who cares the girls' hair well and looks after them properly."

"You did well provided Allah willed it to be so," remarked the Prophet (S.A.W.).

It is clear from the above tradition that under certain circumstances a woman with previous experience of wedlock is to be preferred to a maiden so that she might be helpful in bringing up the orphans and looking after them properly. Such a woman would fulfil the needs of orphans and help in carrying out the following divine command:

"Cooperate with one another in doing good" (5:2)

5. Preference for Prolific Woman

Islam also enjoins that one should choose a fertile woman for wedlock. There are two ways of identifying such a woman.

(a) Her body is free from the effects of contraceptives. This could be ascertained with the help of a doctor.
(b) The case history of the woman's mother and sisters may also serve as a guide in this respect. If they are all found to be prolific, it may be concluded that the women in question is most likely to be fertile.

It has been medically established that a healthy and physically strong woman is generally prolific. Such a woman is at the same time capable of shouldering domestic responsibilities. She has the capacity to discharge the duties of breeding children and conjugal obligations in an excellent manner.

It is necessary to point out here that a person who marries a fertile woman is desirous of multiplying his progeny and also craves that his children should grow up to be good men and women. He will, therefore, have to fulfil his obligations in the best possible manner and given equal importance to the provision of necessary means for meeting domestic expenses and to his duties towards the education and training of his children. He will otherwise be accountable to Allah for any lapse in the fulfilment of his obligations. Says the Holy Prophet (S.A.W.):

> "Allah will enquire of every guardian as to whether he has fulfilled his duties towards his charge or not so much so that the guardian will be questioned about his family."

To sum up, any one who is keen to discharge his obligations towards his progeny in accordance with the principles of Islam should marry a fertile woman so that the Muslim Ummah may multiply numerically for it is an Ummah which Allah has described as a good people brought forth to serve as a guide to other peoples.

Once a man came to the Holy Prophet (S.A.W.) and said, "O Messenger of Allah! I have chosen a woman for myself who is rich and comes of a noble family but she is incapable of bearing children. Shall I marry her?" The Prophet (S.A.W.) forbade him to marry such a woman. The man came again with the same question and was forbidden again. When he came third time to press his request, the Prophet (S.A.W). observed: "You should marry a fertile woman, for I want you to outnumber other peoples."

(Abu Dawood, Nisai and Hakim).

These then are the basic principles of matrimony as they are related to the breeding of children.

As the family owes itself to man and wife, Islam emphasises the importance of choosing the right consort in view of children's education and training. It attaches primary importance to matrimony because it gratifies the demands of human nature. It is matrimony which enables the male members of the family to trace their lineage to their ancestots and ensures the safety of a society from dangerous diseases.

Moreover, matrimony provides impetus for the full co-operation of parents in the upbringing of children as well as engenders in the couple the fondess and parental affection for their offspring.

The main reason for the advantages accruing from conjugal union is that the choice of the consort on either side is made on sound grounds and in accordance with practical rules.

When a Muslim knows where to start building his family in order to have offspring with good moral conduct and unshakable faith in Allah he will experience little difficulty in the fulfilment of his responsibilities in regard to matrimony and breeding of children. This is because a Muslim lays the foundation of th proper training of his children and the betterment of the society as a whole by the choice of a virtuous wife.

Thus according to the teachings of Islam the task of training the children begins the very day when a good man and good woman are united by the bonds of matrimony.

Ideal union is the solid foundation of te sound training of children as it gives rise to a generation of virtuous people.

CHAPTER II

PARENT'S ATTITUDE TOWARDS CHILDREN

By the attitude of parents towards children is meant the way the former express their sentiments of compassion, love, kindness and sympathy for their children. Allah has instilled such sentiments in parent's hearts which demand that children should not be treated with contempt, as they were treated during the days of pagan ignorance. Children's separation or death should be endured with patience and fortitude with the hope that Allah would reward them in the Hereafter.

It is these feelings and sentiments that we now proceed to discuss.

1. Parent's Inherent Love for the Son.

It is common knowledge that parents have instinctive love for their sons. Their hearts are filled with compassion and noble feelings for their offspring. It is but natural for the father to keep an eye on his son, treat him with compassion and kindness and to focus his attention on each and every affair of the son.

If the parent's hearts are devoid of such noble sentiments for their offspring, the human race will vanish from the face of the earth. The parents will cease to discharge their obligations towards their children. They will ignore their responsibility for the maintenance, education and training and welfare of their offspring.

The Paternal compassion and love for the children has been beautifully described in the Holy Quran. At one place they have been referred as the ornament of terristrial life:

"Wealth and children are an adornment of life of the World." (18:47)

At another place children have been called a great gift for which we should thank Allah:

"We aided you with wealth and children and increased your number in soldiery" (17:6)

At yet another place they have been described as the delight of the eyes:

"A good people are those who pray 'Our Lord! Vouchsafe us comfort of our wives and of our offspring." (25:74)

These and other similar verses of the Holy Quran are expressive of the sentiments of love and compassion for children with which the parents are enlivened. They tell us that the parents have instinctive love for their offsprings; that the parents hold them dearer than their own lives and that the children are the inseparable parts of their lives. The purpose, for which Allah has ingrained the love of children in the hearts of the parents, is that the latter should give the children proper training and eduation, take care of them, realize their needs and importance of their well-being and fulfil their responsibilities in this regard.

"The nature (framed) of Allah in which He hath created man. There is no alteration in Allah's creation" (30:30)

2. Parents' Compassion for Children is Divine Blessing

One of the sentimetns with which Allah has imbued the hearts of parents is the feeling of compassion for children and the realization of the need to treat them with kindness and affection. The realization of this need proves good results in the training and character-building of the children.

A heart without divine mercy is always irritable and callous. Such a sinister disposition of the parents would result in the ill-breeding of the offsprings and their fate will be sealed. The progeny of such parents will be thrown into the abyss of ignorance.

That is the reason why the Shariah inculcates compassion and mercy in the hearts of the people. The parents, the elders, the teachers and guardians of children have been exhorted to develop the habit of having compassion and mercy as well as enrich their personalities with moral excellence in conformity with the Islamic Shariah.

In view of the importance of compassion, the Prophet (S.A.W.) has urged upon the people to be polite and have the sense of respect and fine feelings for others. Says the Holy Prophet (S.A.W.):

"He who has no compassion for our younger people and does not respect the elders, does not belong to us."

(*Abu Dawood and Tirmizi*)

Imam Bukhari narrates the following tradition, with reference to Hazrat Abu Hurairah:

"Once a man came to the Prophet (S.A.W.). He had a child with him whom he was hugging frequently. The Prophet (S.A.W.) asked him if he was filled with compassion for the child. The man replied in the affirmative. The Holy Prophet (S.A.W.) observed, "Allah has more compassion for the child than you and He is far more merciful than all the merciful people."

Whenever the Prophet (S.A.W.) found any of his companions to be hard upon his children, he would tell him that he was doing something wrong and that if he wished his family and children well, he should behave towards them in an agreeable manner.

Imam Bukhari quotes Hazrat Aisha (R.A.A.) to have narrated that once an Arab came to the Prophet (S.A.W.) and asked him: If he kissed his children with affection and added that his people never caressed, the children like that. The Prophet (S.A.W.) replied, "If Allah has deprived your heart of compassion, what can I do."

(*Al-Adabul Mufrad*)

Abu Huraira (R.A.A.) reports that the Prophet (S.A.W.) once kissed Hazrat Hasan (R.A.A.) in the presence of Iftra bin Habis Tamimi. Iftra observed that he had as many as ten children but he had never kissed any one of them. The Prophet (S.A.W.) turned to him and said, "Nobody has compassion for the man who has no compassion." (*Bukhari*)

A woman came to Hazrat Aisha (R.A.A.) who gave her three dates. The woman gave away two of the dates to her two children and kept one for herself. The children having finished the two dates looked at their mother expectantly. The mother cut the third date into two equal pieces and gave the children one piece each. When the Prophet (S.A.W.)

returned, Hazrat Aisha (R.A.A.) told him the whole story. The Prophet (S.A.W.) observed Allah has become kind to her because of her compassion for the children"

When the Holy Prophet (S.A.W.) saw any kid on the verge of death he was moved by the sight and his eyes were filled with tears. The Prophet's (S.A.W.) expression of mercy and affection for the child would teach the individuals of the ummah to have compassion for children.

Hazrat Asma bint Zaid (R.A.A.) narrates that the Prophet (S.A.W.) received a message from one of his daughters requesting him to come to her as her son was about to die. The Prophet (S.A.W.) sent her a message in reply telling her that all that Allah gives and takes away belong to Him only and that He has predetermined the time of every event. The Prophet (S.A.W.) exhorted her to have patience and pray for the child.

But the daughter insisted that the Prophet (S.A.W.) should come to her. On receiving this message the Holy Prophet (S.A.W.) rose and set out for his daughter's place. He was accompanied by a number of his companions including Sa'd bin 'Ubada, Mu'az bin Jabal, Ubaiy bin Ka'b, and Zaid bin Sabit. When the child looked at the Prophet (S.A.W.), he took him and laid him in his lap. The child was at that time breathing his last. The Prophet's eyes were filled with tears at that tragic sight. Hazrat Sa'd bin Ubada said, "O Messenger of Allah, it is strange that you are weeping." The Prophet (S.A.W.) replied "This is just an expression of compassion with which Allah has imbued the hearts of His servants." According to another version, the Holy Prophet (S.A.W.) said, "This is compassion with which Allah has imbued the hearts of those He chose. The truth of the matter is that Allah has mercy for those who are merciful."

(*Bukhari and Muslim*).

The above Tradition bears it out that when the hearts of parents are saturated with compassion they realize their obligations towards children and are ever ready to discharge those obligations. Consequently they try to carry out the commands in respect of their offsprings. That is but natural.

3. Hatred for Daughters is the Worst form of Savagery.

According to the Islamic doctrine of equality and social justice men and women deserve equal parental affection. This is what the following verse of the Holy Quran means:

"Deal justly, that is nearer to piety." (5:8)

Noman bin Bashir quotes the Holy Prophet (S.A.W.) as having said:

"Deal justly with your children, deal justly with your children, deal justly with your children."

(*Sunan Ibn-Maja, Sunan Tirmizi, Musnad Ahmad, Ibn Hibban*)

Putting these commands of Allah and the Prophet (S.A.W). into practice the Muslims have always dealt fairly with their children, have always loved them and treated them well. They have never discriminated between sons and daughters, having more affection for th sons than the latter. The long centuries of Islamic History provide unequivocal proof of this fair treatment of children.

If the parents in any Muslim society bestow more affection on their sons than duaghters, the reason for this is milieu wherein they have been brought up. Allah has not justified such a discrimination anywhere in the Holy Qur'an. Such a discriminate treatment is absolutely un-Islamic, and only the social customs are responsible for it. These customs are vestiges of pagan ignorance. Suh s sordid state of affairs has been described in the Holy Quran in the following words:

"When one of them receives the tidings of the birth of a female his face remains darkened and he is angry inwardly. He hideth himself from folk because of the evil of that whereof he has had tidings, asking himself: Shall he keep her (the daughter) in contempt or bury it beneath the dust. Verily, evil is their judgement."

(16:58-59)

One of the reasons of such attitude is also the weakness of faith; for the people in the days of pagan ignorance did not acquiesce in the distribution of the Providence. They were displeased when Allah bestowed a daughter upon them; whereas giving birth or curbing the birth of a daught r is in the power of neither man nor woman. Nor is it in the power of anyone on earth to alter Allah's creation. Consider what an irrevocable verdict has been given in the followng verse of the Holy Quran:

> "Unto Allah belongeth the sovereignty of the heavens and the earth. He createth what He will. He bestoweth female offspring upon male offspring upon whom He will. Or he mingleth them, males and females and He maketh barren whom he will. Lo! He is Knower, Powerful." (42:49-50)

There is an interesting story of a rich Arab noble man and his daughter which runs as follows:

The Arab's surname was Abu Hamza. He contracted a woman into marriage, hoping that she would bear him a son. But the woman gave birth to a daughter. The Arab noble left his home and went to reside in another house. Perchance he passed one day by the house of the woman who happened to be playing with her daughter at the moment and singing a few verses, which are translated as under:

> O Abu Hamza, what is the matter with you. You do'nt come to us and live in another house. He does not come to us probably because we do not give birth to sons. By God this is something beyond our power.
>
> We women receive only what is given to us i.e. when Allah bestows a son upon us, we accept him. When He bestows a daughter upon us we gladly accept her too, and hold her dear to our hearts.

Abu Hamza was moved by her song and returned to his wife. The song which expressed the woman's firm belief in Allah and her submission to Him changed the man's mode of thinking. He kissed his daughter and acquiesced in what Allah gave him.

The Holy Prophet (S.A.W.) lays special emphasis on the importance of dealing justly with female offsprings along with male offsprings in order to erase the imprints of the pagan customs from weaker minds. He urges upon the parents and the guardians of their daughters, to look after them properly and meet their needs so that the parents and the guardians may on the one hand be entitled to enter Paradise and earn Divine pleasure and on the other hand the daughters may be brought up in accordance with the Divine

Will and thus the Islamic principles of bringing up children are translated into action.

Some of the Prophet's sayings relating to the need for special attention to daughters and meeting their requirements are as follows:

Anas bin Malik reports the Holy Prophet (S.A.W.) to have said, "The man who met the needs of his two daughters till the age of puberty, will appear along with me on the Day of Judgement like this pair of fingers (He showed a pair of his two fingers holding them tight together). (*Muslim*)

Aqba bin 'Amir Aljuhani narrates this tradition:

The Prophet (S.A.W.) said, "Whoever has three daughters and brings them up properly with patience and restraint, provides for them and arranges for their clothing out of his best means, he will be saved from the flames of Hell by those three daughters."

Abu Saeed (R.A.A.) quotes the following words of the Holy Prophet (S.A.W.).

"Whoever has three daughters or three sisters and he treats them well, meets their requirements and fears Allah in respect of his obligations towards them, he is sure to enter Paradise."

It is incumbent upon the guardians to act on the above edicts of the Prophet (S.A.W.) and the Islamic principles relating to the upbringing of daughters which stress the need to focuss equal attention on the care of sons and daughters and give them equal rights so that they may qualify for entering paradise whose breadth alone is equal to the heavens and earth. In this way they will be able to earn the pleasure of Allah and attain the lofty position which Allah describes as the seat of truth.

4. Reward for Bearing the Shock of Son's Death.

When a person attains to the acme faith and firmly believes that all the decisions regarding good and evil are made by Allah, the mishaps cease to have any significance for him. No calamity is too great for him. He surrenders himself to Allah in event of disaster or in face of a danger. His conscience thereafter is gratified and his heart is blessed with contentment. He submits to the divine will and the decision of the Providence.

What faith requires in the event of a son's death, has been described by the Holy Prophet (S.A.W.) in one of his traditions:

"If the son of any one dies, he should bear the shock patiently and say: We all belong to Allah and to him do we return'. Allah will build a house for such a man in Paradise which will be called 'The House of Gratitude'.

Abu Musa Ash'ari quotes the Prophet (S.A.W.) to have said:

"When the son of any one dies Allah says to the angels: Have you taken the life of my servant? The angels reply in the affirmative. Allah says again: Have you deprived him of his darling? The angels reply in the affirmative. What did my servant say then? asks Allah. The angels reply: The man praised Thee and thanked Thee and said that all belongs to Allah and to Him have all of us to return. Then Allah orders the angels to build a house for the man in Paradise which shall be called. 'The House of Gratitude.'

The fruit of such endurance is reaped by the man who endures the loss in all sincerity and hopes for a reward from Allah. The fruit of endurance will be bestowed upon the enduring person on the Day when neither wealth nor sons will yield him any benefit.

"Endurance paves the way for entrance into Paradise and saves a man from the flames of Hell."

Abu Saeed reports the Prophet (S.A.W.) to have once said to the women:

If three children of any one of you die, they will serve as a means of her salvation. One of the women asked if two children die, instead of three? The Prophet said: Even then the bereaved woman will be saved.

Hazrat Jabir narrates yet another tradition:

The Prophet (S.A.W.) said: If three sons (Children) of any one die and the bereaved person endures the loss with patience, he will enter Paradise. We, the Companions of the Prophet (S.A.W.) asked him if two children died, what would be the reward? The Prophet replied "Yes even if two children died, the man will enter Paradise." *(Bukhari)*

The narrator says that if he had asked the Prophet (S.A.W.) about the death of only one child, he would have given you the tiding of entering Paradise. Hazrat Jabir said that he also thought so.

A result of enduring the death of a child patiently would be that the child would intercede on behalf of his parents on the Day of Judgement.

One day it so happened that as Hazrat Aisha was sitting with a friend of her, the Prophet came in and observed directly "If three children of a Muslim died before reaching the age of puberty, those children would be brought to the door of Paradise on the Day of Judgment. They would be asked to get into Paradise. The Children would say that they would go into it only when their parents enter first. They would then be told that they and their parents should all get into Paradise. (*Tabarani*)

Abu Hussain says that his two children died. He asked his father Abu Huraira (R.A.A.) to narrate the Prophet's traditions so that the sorrow he was suffering on account of their loss may be alleviated. Hazrat Abu Huraira (R.A.A.) accordingly narrated the following tradition:

> "The Holy Prophet (S.A.W.) has said that small children will not be any different when they are in Paradise. They will hold the fringes of the garments worn by their parents in exactly the same manner as I am doing at this moment and will not part with them so much so that Allah will send the father or the parents of each child also into paradise." (*Muslim*)

In this connection the patience, strength of faith and acquiscence of Allah's will shown by Hazrat Umme Saleem (R.A.A.) over the loss of her child is worthy of mention: The whole incident has been related in Sahih Muslim and Sahih Bukhari in the following words:

"Hazrat Anas relates that the son of Abu Talha was ill. When Abu Talha was out on business, the child expired. On his return Abu Talha asked after the health of the child. Umm Sulaim the mother of the child told him, "The child is in more peace now than before (this was ambiguous statement meaning two things at the same time. It meant that the child was much better and also that he is no more and therefore, no longer sick). The lady then brought the meal for her busband and he took the meal. Umm Sulaim then dressed and bedecked herself and thus got ready for husband. Abu Talha had sexual intercourse with her. When she found him fully gratified, she said to him, Well Abu Talha, do you think that a man who borrows money from some people should refuse to pay it back on demand? Talha replied in th negative. Then she told him to surrender to the Will of Allah in the case of his son and bear his loss with patience. Abu Talha was enraged and said, "Why did you not tell me this before? You have coveyed the news of my child's demise when I am polluted." He then went straight to the Holy Prophet (S.A.W.) and told him the whole story. The Prophet (S.A.W.) praised the behaviour of Umm Sulaim and prayed, "May Allah bless your night." According to another Tradition, the Prophet (S.A.W.) prayed, "May Allah bless you both (with another child)."

Umm Sulaim later bore a son to Abu Talha who was named Abdullah. A man belonging to an Ansari family reported that he had seen six children of Abdullah and all of them learnt the Holy Quran by heart. "This was the blessing of the Holy Prophet's prayer" added the narrator.

It is a fact that when faith takes root in a believer's heart, it manifests itself by producing striking results. The weak is made strong by faith, the coward is made bold, the miser generous and the restless and worried person patient and eduring.

The parent should have complete trust and firm faith in Allah so that they may remain calm in the face of any disaster. If their son dies, they should not sit hrooding over the loss, but should repeat the following verse of the Holy Quran:

'Inna lillahe wa inna ilaihe raje'oon.

We all belong to Allah and to Him have all of us
to reutrn.

For whatever Allah gives and takes back belongs to Him only and He has pre-determined the Span of everything. Man should, therefore, bear his loss patiently and pray for His reward for the deceased. He should continuously pray to Allah, "O God! Make for us the mishaps of this life easier to suffer, enable us to submit to Thy Will, take us under tutelage in this world as well as in the Hereafter. O My Lord! Thou art a better Guardian than all the common guardians."

5. The Interest of Islam Is to Be Preferred to the Love of offsprings.

The hearts of parents are naturally imbued with affection and compassion for their children. But this does not mean that they should be carried off by emotions and completely ignore their obligations in regard to Jihad in the way of Allah and propagation of Islam in the world. The interest of Islam claims priority to all other interests and considerations. The ultimate goal of a Muslim is the establishment of Islamic society.

It is the real aim of his life. The reason for this is that to a Muslim guiding mankind to the right path is the noblest of all tasks.

The Companions of the Holy Prophet (S.A.W.) and their successors fully realized the significance of this task. They knew no philosophy or action other than Jihad. Their main concern was to propagate Islam and the glorification of Islam.

The Islamic history can boast of the feats performed by the companions of the Prophet (S.A.W.) and their successors in the dissemination of the message of Islam and the glorification of Allah's name on earth. They considered no sacrifice too great for the sake of Allah's religion. What they wished in their heart of hearts, to fall martyr in the way of Allah.

When we read in history of the great sacrifices those people made for the sake of Islam, we are wonder struck. But this is not something to wonder at. When faith takes root in the hearts of believers, it manifests itself in such great events.

We reproduce below the reply of Hazrat Ibada bin Samit to the king of Egypt Maqooqas when he warned him of the concentration of the Romans in great strength after having failed in his attempt to lure the Muslims with an offer of money. Said Ibada (R.A.A.):

"Do'nt you be proud of your wealth and allies. You have

warned us of the Roman army and its numerical superiority saying that we will not be able to face it. By God, if what you say is true then we can't be browbeaten by the Roman army nor can it deliver us from the predicament which you suppose us to have been placed in. Our position vis-a-vis yours is that we have to choose either of the two alternatives: if we emerge victorious over you, we will have th whole booty of war or should you be triumphant then we will reap the fruits of life in the Hereafter. Allah, Almighty said in the last of his books:

Many a small army has overcome big armies by the will ofAllah and Allah is with those who endure patiently."
(2: 249)

Everyone of us prays each morning and each evening that he may fall a martyr in the battlefield and is determined never to return to his home town or country and never to meet his family. We are not at all anxious about our wives and children. Every one of us has come hither bidding his family adieu for good. We intend to figh in the way of Allah in order to uphold His world.

And you have spoken of our poverty and lack of supplies. But you are mistaken. We are happy and contented in every sense of the expression. Even if the entire wealth of the world is bestowed upon us, we will never ask for more than what we have.

This was the position taken by Hazrat Ibada bin Samit during his negotiation with the Egyption ruler which is one of the examples of courage and valour of our ancestors with whch the history of Islam is replete.

They always preferred to make sacrifices in the way of Allah and Jihad and the propagation of Islam above the interest of their families and affection for their kith and kin, because they never for once forget Allah's command which runs as follows:-

"O Prophet (S.A.W.) say: If your fathers and your sons and your brethren and your wives and your tribe and the wealth you have acquired and merchandise for which ye fear that there will be no sale and dwellings you desire are dearer to you than Allah and His Messenger and striving in His way: then wait till Allah bringeth his command to pass. Allah guideth not wrong doing folk." (9: 26)

We have been told many incidents relating to Imam Hasan-ul-Banna Shaheed. One of them is cited here. It has been reported that Imam Hasan-ul-Banna used to go to nearby villages on the occasion of Eid in search of young men who invited the people to the path of Allah. On one such occasion as he was making ready to go out, his son Saiful Islam fell seriously ill and there was no hope of his survival. His end was close at hand. His wife asked him to celebrate the Eid at home and remain with his ailing son sothat the family may be relieved of the worry caused by the boy's illness. The Imam getting hold of his bag replied, "If Allah cures my son, we would be greatly indebted to Him. But if He has pre-determined the time of his death, then his grandfather knows, where the graveyard is. Having said these words, the Imam set out, reciting the verse of the Holy Quran cited above.

This story serves as an example of the spirit of sacrifice to uphold the faith in Allah. We have a model in it of the character of the man who takes it upon himself to call the people to the path of Allah. Had our ancestors the same spirit of sacrifice and had the contemporary Islamic missionaries been imbued with such spirit, would ensure their success both in this world and in the Hereafter.

A father having firm faith in Allah should be imbued with the love of Islam, the spirit of Jihad and missionary work. In fact, he should become the zeal for jihad and the missionary spirit personified. It is quite possible that such a man comes recokoned as one of those who consolidate the glory of Islam, add to its prestige and by virtue of their will power succeed in establishing the Quranic social order. If every father approximates to this type, then the task of the glorification of Muslim Ummah will be on smooth railing.

People having perfect faith in Allah are spiritually exhilerated and have the intuition of the bliss resulting from their faith. The Holy Prophet (S.A.W.) has spoken of such people in these words:

Whoever has three virtues tastes the sweetness of faith: (a) Allah and His Messenger are dearer to him than all the things in the world

(b) His likes are governed by the likes of Allah and

(c) He feels that to be an infidel is like being thrown into the fire. (Narrated by *Anas*, *Sahih Bukhari*)

According to a tradition quoted in Sahih Bukhari, "Hazrat Umar said to the Holy Prophet (S.A.W.): O Messenger of Allah! You are dearer to me than every thing except my heart. The Holy Prophet (S.A.W.) replied: None of you can be a perfect Muslim until he holds me dearer than everything.

Hazrat Umar said, "I swear by the Being Who has revealed the Holy Book, from now onward you will be dearer to me than my heart."

The Prophet observed, "Well Umar! Your faith is complete now".

There is another relevant tradition in the Sahih Bukhari: The Prophet (S.A.W.) said, "None of you can be a true believer unless every desire of his is governed by what I have brought (that is the Holy Quran).

The Prophet (S.A.W.) is also reported to have said: "None of you can be a believer unless he or she holds me dearer than wealth, children and all the human-beings".

6. Chastizement of Children in Course of Training

A child in its early years is brought up under the care of his parents. As long as it is receiving education and training, it is necessary that its parents, guardians and teachers should try each and every method of correction, edification and refinement so that the child may have learnt all the morals taught by Islam when he attains the age of puberty and his social behaviour may be of the highest order.

Islam has a method of its own which to adopt in the breeding and disciplining of children. If a child positively responds to the instructions given in a nice and kind manner, it will be imporper for the guardian or parent to boycott him. If boycott does not produce the desired effect and the child responds to admonition, then he should not be subjected to corporal punishment. But if he turns a deaf ear to mild exhortation and admonition, there is no harm in beating him or her. But it should be borne in mind that he should be beaten in such a way that no visible injury is caused to his body. He is expected to respond to the process of correction by mild chastisement, he will give up bad habits, and behave in a normal way.

We have derived all these methods of training and disciplining children from the practice of the Holy Prophet (S.A.W.) and his companions so that the teachers and parents of children should carry out the task of breeding, disciplining and training their students and offsprings on purely Islamic lines.

We cite a tradition included in both Sahih *Bukhari and Sahih Muslim* relating to the exhortation of children benignantly. The tradition has been narrated by Hazrat Umar bin Abi Salma:

Hazrat Umar bin Abi Salma says that he had been under the training of the Holy Prophet (S.A.W.) in his early childhood. During supper his hand was moving round in the dish containing curry. The Holy Prophet saw it and said: "O child! Begin with the name of Allah, the Beneficent and Merciful. Use your right hand in eating and take whatever is nearer to you (that is refrain from moving your hand hither and thither).

We also find a tradition with regard to separation from children:

"Abu Saeed relates this incident: The Holy Prophet (S.A.W.) has forbidden to throw a pebble with the help of one's forefinger and thumb and has observed that such an act would help neither in hunting an animal nor inflicting a wound on the enemy. It may nevertheless hurt the victim's eye or break his tooth.

In yet another tradition it has been told that a relative of Ibn Mughaffil threw a pebble in the manner prohibited by the Prophet. The fellow was a bit frivolous. Ibn Mughaffil asked him to refrain from doing so and told him that throwing a stone like that was forbidden by the Prophet (S.A.W.) because it was ineffective in hunting. But the fellow threw pebbles again in the forbidden manner, turning a deaf ear to Ibn Mughaffil. The latter said to him: You have done the same thing in spite of the fact that I have informed you of the Prophet's injunction. I will never talk to you any more.

As regards chastisement of children we find a tradition in the Sunan Abu Dawood and Musnad Hakim. It was narrated by Amr bin Shoaib:

"The Prophet (S.A.W.) has said that we should call upon our children to offer prayers when they are seven years old and when they are ten years they should be punished for missing prayer and should have separate beds."

The above stages of training and discipline relate to early childhood. If a child does not respond positively to exhortation and soft words of admonition, and continues to indulge in inequitous activity, then he should be boycotted for good.

The following traditions may be cited to this effect: Ibn Abbas reports the Holy Prophet (S.A.W.) to have observed that the strongest links of faith are as under:

(a) Develop friendship and harbour animosity for the sake of Allah only (This is international concept of friendship and enmity)

(b) Foster love and nourish hatred in one's heart for the sake of Allah. (This is the basis of Islamic social order).

In *Sahih Bukhari* a separate section has been devoted to the subject of the boycott of disobedient children. We find the following tradition in this section.

Hazrat Ka'b narrates that he was one of those who could not participate in the battle of Tabook. The Prophet (S.A.W.) asked the believers not to talk us for as many as eighty five nights. This boycott put those in an extremely difficult situation who did not take part in the battle referred to and they found life miserable. There was not a single believer who talked to them and sat together with them. At long last Allah accepted their repentance and revealed the following verse of the Holy Quran:

And to the three also (did He turn in Mercy) who were left behind when in earth, vast as it is, was straitened for them, and their own souls were straitened for them till they bethought them that there is no refuge from Allah save toward Him. Then turned He unto them in mercy that they (too) might turn (repentant unto Him). Lo! Allah! He is the Relenting, the Merciful. (9:118).

We learn from the life of the Prophet (S.A.W.) that he

put one of his wives away from him in order to bring about a change for the better among his wives.

Hazrat Imam Suyoti says that Hazrat Abdullah bin Umar (R.A.A.) abandoned one of his sons and had nothing to do with him until his death. The reason for this boycott was that the boy refused to acknowledge a tradition narrated by Hazrat Umar (R.A.A.), the father of Hazrat Abdullah. According to that Tradition the Prophet (S.A.W.) had permitted women to go out to the mosques for offering prayers.

Such was the punishment given to a man who deviated from and refused to obey a single command of the Holy Prophet (S.A.W.) although he had strong faith in Allah and his Prophet and adhered to all the other teachings of Islam.

But if some one turns an apostate, he should be totally cast out. Faith in Islam demands that all kinds of relations with such a person should be severed. Such a course of action is clearly enjoined by the Holy Quran. Some of the verses to this effect are as follows:

> "Thou wilt not find folk who believe in Allah and the Last Day loving those who oppose Allah and His messenger even though they be their fathers or their sons or their brethren or their clan." (58:22).

Says Allah alluding to the Prophet Nooh (A.S.):

> "And Noah cried unto His Lord and said: My Lord! My son is of my house-hold. Surely Thy promise is the truth and Thou are the most just of judges. Allah said: O Nooh! He is not of Thy household; he is of evil conduct, so ask not of Me that whereof thou hast no knowledge. I admonish thee lest thou be among the ignorant."
>
> (11:45-46)

And with reference to Abraham (A.S.) it has been said:

> "And when his Lord tried Abraham with His commands, which he fulfilled and He said: I have appointed thee a leader for mankind. Abraham said: Of my offspring (will there be leaders)? Allah said: My covenant includeth not wrong doers." (2:124).

The way Hadrat Ibrahim dealt with his father has been

described by Allah in these words:

> "The prayer of Ibrahim for the forgiveness of his father was only because of a promise he had made to him, but when it became clear unto him that his father was an enemy to Allah, he disowned him. Verily, Ibrahim was soft of heart, long suffering." (9:114).

These and similar verses of the Holy Quran make it crystal clear that if one's offspring and close relatives obdurately stick to infidelity then faith demands that they should be disowned and all kinds of relationship with them should be cut off. For from the Islamic standpoint the fraternity based on Islam claims preference to the ethnic, territorial and linguistic relationship and the bonds of civic and economic well-being. The Quranic injunction to this effect is as follows:

> "Say: If your fathers and your sons, and your brethren, and wealth you have acquired, and merchandise for which ye fear that there will be no sale and dwellings you desire are dearer to you than Allah and His messenger and striving in His way, then wait till Allah bringeth His command to pass. Allah guideth not wrong-doing folk."(9:24)

And this is the immutable tenet of Islam:

"The believers are brethren of each other."

The following tenet of Islam, too, is not amenable to change:

"The more righteous is the more honourable among you."

No principle other than this lucid doctrine is left for us to believe in.

What we have discussed in this chapter are the psychic states and the elemental passions of the parents that are absolutely essential in the upbringing of children. These passions such as love, affection, benignance, and compassion are rooted deep in the parents hearts. In the absence of such sacred passions the cosmic law of the survival of human race would cease to operate and the parents would attach no importance to the breeding of children and their obligations in regard to the safeguards of children's rights. If there are no elemental passions referred to above, the edifice of family could not be raised on a strong base.

We have also mentioned certain attitudes which are reminescent of the days of pagan ignorance as for example treating daughters with contempt. In the course of discussion we have pointed out that Islam tries to do away with this sinister attitude by inculcating true faith and firm belief in Allah. It lays dawn certain principles for the parents to treat their male and female offspring at par, to refrain from discriminating between them and keep in view the demands of justice and the principle of equality.

Some sentiments and feelings are exceedingly important from the utilitarian stand point. For instance the urge to strive in the way of Allah and to propagate Islam is given priority to one's passion for the family. As we have emphasized that the interests of Islam should get preference to self-interest. The Muslim cannot succeed and establish his prestige in the world unless the love of Allah and His messenger and the urge to strive in the way of Allah does not get the better for one's affection for the family, kith and kin and household.

Some of the attitudes towards children are of a disciplinary nature for instance, exhortation, rebuke chastisement etc. Thus according to Islam there are four stages of breeding and training of children:

(1) Exhortation,
(2) Rebuke and admonition,
(3) Boycott and
(4) Chastisement that does leave no mark on the child's body.

It will be improper to be too hard upon the child. If he or she responds to a corrective method, then a harsher method should not be resorted to. That is what Islam teaches us in respect of training disciplining, correction and reform the people as well as those who are entrusted with the task of training and educating the children should be well conversant with the Islamic rules of correction so that they may adopt only such methods to reform the society and to discipline and educate the new generation as are reasonable and discreet in every respect.

It is Islam alone which lays down those basic principles whereby we can deliver the new generation from corruption and aberrations and enrich it with moral excellence, purity and civility.

CHAPTER III

OBLIGATIONS OF GUARDIAN AT THE BIRTH OF CHILD

The Muslim Ummah is indebted to the Shariah for injunctions pertaining to a new born child as well as for such principles as bear on the physical condition of the baby. It is incumbent upon the guardian or the nurse to be well acquainted with those injunctions and principles and try to fulfil the requirements of baby according to them. In any case it is necessary for the person responsible for bringing up a child to discharge his or her function in this respect on the lines laid down by the Holy Prophet (S.A.W.) who was our first guardian.

Some of the injunctions in this context are as under:

1. To Give the Good Tiding of the Birth of a Child and Express Good Wishes.

It is extremely commendable that a Muslim conveys the tiding of his child's birth to his brother in faith. The latter will certainly be delighted to hear it (feeling that he is being invited to share the pleasure of parents). This strengthens the mutual bonds of fraternity and relationship. Giving the good tiding of a child's birth and the expression of best wishes over it in itself is a sign of the extension of love and friendship among the Muslim families. If the parents for some reason or other do not receive the news of their child's birth, they should pray for the welfare of the baby as soon as they learn of it. Allah is expected to grant their prayer.

Conveying the tiding of a child's birth has been mentioned at several places in the Quran. The reason for this is that such a practice strengthens the social bonds of the Muslims.

Allah says with reference to Hazrat Ibrahim (A.S.): "And our meassengers came unto Abraham with good

news. They said: Peace! He answered: Peace!
and immediately brought a roasted Calf. And when he saw their hands reached not to the Calf, he mistrusted them and conceived a fear of them. They said: Fear not. We are sent unto the folk of Lot. And his wife, standing by, laughed when We gave her good tidings of the birth of Isaac and after Isaac, of Jacob." (*11:69-71*).

Alluding to Hadrat Zakarya (A.S.) it has been said: "And the angels called to him as he stood praying in the sanctuary: Allah giveth thee the glad tidings of a son whose name is John. (3:39).

At another place the same good tiding is given in the following words:

"O Zakarya! We give thee good tiding of the birth of a child. His name will be John. We have never before created anyone with the same name." (19:7).

We are told in the Holy Prophet's biographies that when he was born, Sowaiba, a slave girl of Abu Lahab conveyed the news of that happy event to his master. She said to him, "A son has been born to Abdullah tonight." Abu Lahab's joy knew no bounds when he heard the good tiding of his nephew's birth. He set the girl free then and there. Allah did not leave him unrewarded for this good deed and according to *Sahih Bukhari* even after his death he is given sweet water to drink from the hollow under his thumb.

Soheli quotes Hazrat Abbas to have said that he saw Abu Lahab about a year after his death in an extremely miserable condition. He said to Hazrat Abbas: "Ever since I have come away from your people I have known no happiness and peace. On Monday, however, the severity of torment is reduced.

And Monday was the very day when the Holy Prophet (S.A.W.) came into this world and *Saubia* conveyed the good tiding of his nativity to her master, Abu Lahab who was extremely glad to hear it.

Imam Hafiz Ibn-Qayyim quotes in his book 'Tuhfat-ul-Wadood' the following statement of Abu Bakr Al Munzir as to extending congratulation on the birth of a baby:

"Hazrat Hasan Basri is reported to have narrated that one

day a man came to him while another was sitting beside him who was blessed with a son. The new comer said to him: "Accept my congratulation on the birth of this horseman."

"How do you know that the child would be a horseman?", asked Hazrat Hasan Basri, "Who knows if he grows to be a donkey man rather than a horseman?"

"What else is one to say, then on such occasion?" enquired the man.

"Well, you should say: May Allah bless the child bestowed by him! Thank God for His gift! May the child always be a source of goodness to you and may he live to grow into full bloom," said Hazrat Hasan Basri.

The tiding of the birth of both the son and the daughter should be conveyed without discrimination and congratulations should be extended on both the occasions alike. This is not only becoming of Muslims but also the social bonds among them are strengthened by it. Such felicitations result in the establishment of durable relations. In fact the relations so established grow stronger with the passage of time. In families that equally rejoice on the nativity of females no less than males, love and affection reign supreme. All the Muslims should follow the example of such families and foster the bonds of love and atmosphere of unity among themselves so that they may all live like brethren and members of the same family.

2. Saying the Call to Prayer and Iqamat into Ears of New-born Baby.

One of the injunctions of the Shariah relating to the new-born child is to say the call to prayer (Azaan) and *iqamat* into the right and left ears of the baby respectively. The following traditions may be cited to this effect:

Abu Rafi' reports that when Hasan bin Ali (R.A.A.) was born, he saw the Holy Prophet (S.A.W.) recited the call to prayer into the child's ear. (*Abu Dawood, Tirmizi*)

Hazrat Hasan bin Ali (R.A.A.) quotes the Holy Prophet (S.A.W.) to have said: "If a child is born to someone and he says call of prayer and *iqamat* into the right and left ears of the baby, it will be immune from epilepsy."

Ibn-Abbas (R.A.A.) also relates a tradition to the same

effect which runs as follows :

"On the day Hasan bin Ali was born the Holy Prophet said the Call of Prayer into the left ear of the baby."

The wisdom of saying the call of prayer and *iqamat* in this way has been explained by *Hafiz ibn Qayyim Jauzi* in his book *"Tuhfat-ul-Wadood"*.

"The wisdom of this is that the first voice falling on the ears of the baby conveys words describing the Greatness and Glory of Allah. They also bear witness to His Unitary existence whereby a person enters into the fold of Islam. It is actually a sort of preaching designed to make known the way of Islam to one coming into the world just as a dying believer is called upon to repeat the confession of faith. It is true to say that although a new-born baby is unable to understand the words of the call to prayer, yet those words produce the desired effect on its head and heart."

An advantage of saying the call to prayer thus is that Satan, who lies in wait right from the time of the child's birth, is driven away. The moment Satan draws close to the baby, he hears the call whereby he grows weaker and runs off in despair.

Another advantage of the call to prayer is that the child is called to Islam before it hears the misguiding call of Satan. Thus the child remains close to the nature with which Allah has created man. This process precedes the influence exerted by the Devil.

Besides there are numerous other advantages of this practice.

It may be judged from its advantages enumerated by Hafiz Ibn Qayyim the reason for the great importance attached by the Holy Prophet (S.A.W.) to the belief in the Unity of Allah and the Faith in Islam. He considered it necessary to drive away Satan from the baby and purge its heart of evil desires before it is brought up and has experience of the ways of the world.

3. Administration of *Tahnik* (giving of dates to the Newborn baby).

Administration of *tahnik* to a child at the time of birth is also a commendable act as it constituted the Prophet's practice. The act and its utility are explained as follows:

The Arabic word Tahnik means to chew a date and rub the new-born baby's palate with it. This is done by gently applying with one's finger a masticated date to the roof of the baby's mouth so much so that its mouth is filled with the date and is mixed up with the baby's saliva.

If a date is not available then *tahnik* may be done with something else tasting sweet so that the requirement of the Prophet's practice is fulfilled.

The process of *tahnik* is possibly designed to strengthen the baby's tongue, mouth, palate and jaws so that it may be able to suck milk from the nipples of its mother's breast in a natural way. It is desiraable that the person performing *tahnik* is righteous. This has its own blessing as it holds the prospects of the baby's growing to be a righteous person.

The jurists have commended the administration of *tahnik* in the light of the following traditions of the Holy Prophet (S.A.W.):

"Hazrat Abu Huraira quotes Hazrat Abu Moosa to have narrated that Abu Moosa was blessed with a son. He took the new-born baby to the Holy Prophet (S.A.W.) who named the child Ibrahim and administered *Tahnik* to it. He then returned the baby to its father."

Hazrat Anas narrates that a son of Talha (R.A.A.) was ill. He died while Talha was out. On his return Talha asked after the child. Umme Sulaim the mother of deceased child replied:

He is in greater peace than before.

She then brought supper which Hazrat Talha ate and thereafter had sexual intercourse with his wife. When this was over, Umm Sulaim asked him to prepare for the burial of the child. The next morning Hazrat Talha called on the Holy Prophet (S.A.W.) and reported to him the whole incident. The Prophet (S.A.W.) asked him if he had had sexual intercourse with his wife the previous night. Hazrat Talha replied in the affirmative. The Prophet (S.A.W.) then prayed to Allah to bless the couple. Subsequently they had another son. Abu Talha gave the child to Abu Moosa along with seven dates for bringing it to the Prophet. The Prophet (S.A.W.) grasped the child and enquired if anything had also been sent with the child. The companion of the Prophet (S.A.W.) informed him that there were seven dates also. The Prophet (S.A.W.) took the dates, chewd them and put them into the baby's mouth, performed *tahnik* and gave it the name of Abdullah.

Khalal reports that he was told by Muhammad bin Ali that he had heard the mother of Imam Ahmed bin Hanbal narrate the following incident:

When she began to have pangs of child-birth, her husband was asleep. She told him that the pangs were unbearable. He said, "Allah will give you relief." No sooner had he uttered those benedictory words than the auspicious child was born. The husband ordered the dates to be brought which had been sent to them from Makkah. He then asked the child's mother to perform *Tahnik* on the child which she did accordingly.

4. Shaving the Head of the New-born Baby

It is commendable to shave the head of a child on the seventh day of its birth and distribute silver equal in weight to its hair among the poor and the deserving. There are two advantages of this practice:

(a) **Medical Advantage.** Shavinr the head of a newborn child gives it strength, opens the pores of its head and sharpens its senses of sight, smell and hearing. (*Tuhfat-ul-Wadood*).

(b) **Collective Good.** Giving in alms silver equal in weight to the child's hair is a way of providing social security. It helps in fulfilling the needs of the destitutes and furthering the spirit of cooperation, compassion and mutual help.

The jurists prove the shaving of a new-born child's head and the distribution of silver among the needy as a practice commended by the Prophet in the light of the following Traditions:

Imam Malik cites in his Al Moatta the tradition narrated by Ja'far bin Muhammad which was conveyed to him by his father. According to this tradition Hazrat Fatima (R.A.A.) weighed the hair shaven from the heads of Hazrat Hasan, Husain, Zainab and Umme Kulsoom and gave away in charity an amount of silver equal the weight thereof.

Hazrat Abdullah bin Abu Bakr narrates with reference to Hazrat Muhammad bin Ali Bin Husain (R.A.A.) that the Holy Prophet (S.A.W.) sacrificed a goat on the occasion of shaving the head of Hazrat Hasan (R.A.A.) and asked Hazrat Fatima (R.A.A.) to shave the baby's head, weigh the hair and distribute an amount of silver equal to the weight thereof. Hazrat Fatima accordingly weighed the hair which turned out to be equal to a dirham or a little less.Yahya bin Bukair quotes Hazrat Anas bin Malik to have narrated that the Prophet (S.A.W.) ordered the heads of Hazrat Hasan and Husain to be shaven on the seventh day of their nativity. They were accordingly shaven and an amount of silver equivalent to the weight of their hair was distributed among the needy.

Some people regard partial shaving of a baby's head as permissible. But such practice is forbidden by the Shariah.

There is unequivocal edict of the Holy Prophet (S.A.W.) to this effect. Hazrat Abdullah bin 'Umar narrates that the Holy Prophet (S.A.W.) forbade partial shaving of a new-born baby's head. (*Sahih Bukhari and Sahih Muslim*)

The forbidden practice of partial shaving includes its following forms also:

(1) Shaving the head at some places and the rest thereof.
(2) Shaving it in the middle and leaving the hair around.
(3) Shaving it around and leaving the hair in the head and middle.
(4) Shaving the hair from the frontal portion of the head and leaving them intact at the back.

According to Hafiz Ibn-Qayyim Jauzi, Allah and His Messenger love justice to such a degree that they disallow injustice in all forms and forbid man to do injustice to his ownself. Therefore, they regard shaving of the head in part and leaving its hair intact in part as transgression. The Prophet (S.A.W.) has disallowed to sit in a manner that a part of one's body is exposed to the sun while the other part thereof remains in shadow. The reason for this is to sit like that would be tantamount to doing injustice to a part of the body. Another example of such unjust act is to walk with one foot bare and the other with a shoe on. The Prophet (S.A.W.) has forbidden it and has enjoined that one should walk with either both the feet bare or with shoes on both.

The wisdom of this injunction is that the Holy Prophet (S.A.W.) wanted to see the Muslims live in the Society in a befitting, manner. Thus moving with half of one's head shaven is not in consonance with the dignity and comeliness of a Muslim's personality. It is incompatible with his Islamic characteristic which distinguishes him from other peoples of the world and by virtue whereof he stands out as distinct from the wicked, weak and decadent nations.

It pains us to notice that a large number of our elders and teachers are absolutely a stranger to such injunctions. As a matter of fact most of them are astonished when they are told of these Islamic rules, for they appear to them as unfamiliar with nobody to act on them with the exception of a few, of course, who are blessed by Allah.

I would like to tell all such people that the Shariah does not admit of ignorance as a rule. The person who fails in adhering to the Islamic principles and the rules regarding the upbringing of children cannot escape accountability on the Day of Judgment as it is incumbent upon every Muslim to be acquainted with all such injunctions of Islam.

Athough injunctions discussed above fall under the category of injunctions commended by the Prophet (S.A.W.) (i.e. are not mandatory) yet it is necessary for the Muslims to act on them. They must be applied to all our families, progeny and relatives. If we are indolent in putting the commendable into practice, we are bound to shirk duties and mandatory commands as well. This would in the long run lead us to practical renunciation of Islam. Consequently one who appears to be a Muslim would be caught in the snare of infidelity which will in its turn lead him astray to the point of no return and thus he will stand totally excommunicated.

I call upon the teachers and the guardians of children to give a careful thought to the above injunctions pertaining to practices commended by the Holy Prophet (S.A.W.) and try to make their children accustomed to acting upon them so that they may please Allah and demonstrate their faith in Islam both in word and deed. It may then be hoped that Allah would enable the Muslims to be victorious over the enemies of Islam and their past glory is revived. This is not a difficult task for Almighty Allah at all.

CHAPTER IV

NAMING THE CHILDREN AND INJUNCTIONS PERTAINING THERETO

In every society it is customary that the parents select a name for their new-born child by which it is identified. The people know and recognize the child by the name so chosen. In the Islamic system this practice is attached great importance. Islam provides for certain injunctions in which Islam sets great store for the choice of suitable names for the new-born children. It furnishes a wealth of information in this connection and provides ample guidance for the training of children and building their character.

We give below necessary injunctions with regard to naming children.

(a) When is the child to be named?

Hazrat Samura quotes the Holy Prophet (S.A.W.) to have observed: "The *aqiqa* (shaving the head) of every child is necessary. On this occasion an animal is to be sacrificed on the seventh day of its birth. On that very day it should be named and its head shaven.

(Sunan Sihah).

The above tradition bears out the necessity of naming the new-born baby on the seventh day of its turn.

Sahl bin Said Al Sa'idee narrates that Munzir bin Abi Usaid was taken to the Holy Prophet (S.A.W) soon after his birth. The Prophet (S.A.W.) seated the baby on his thigh. Abu Usaid was also sitting nearby. The Prophet (S.A.W.) began to play with the hands of the baby. Abu Usaid asked someone to take the child back and he was accordingly lifted from the Prophet's thigh. Thereupon the Prophet (S.A.W.)

enquired where the baby had gone. Abu Usaid replied that it had been taken back. "What name has been chosen for it?" enquired the Prophet (S.A.W.). Abu Usaid told him the name selected for it. The Prophet (S.A.W.) said, "No. He will be called Munzir." (*Bukhari and Muslim*)

Hazrat Sulaiman bin Al-Mughira narrates the following tradition with reference to Hazrat Anas:

"The Prophet (S.A.W.) said that a son had been born to him that night who had been named Ibrahim."

From the traditions cited above it may be inferred that some liberty has been allowed in choosing the name for the new-born child. It is permissible to name it on the day of its birth or to delay naming it by three days or it must be given a name on the occasion of *aqiqa.*

(b) Decent or Indecent Name

The parent or the guardian should take care to choose a fine name for the baby. Holy Prophet's sayings should be taken into consideration in this connection.

Hazrat Abu Darda narrates that the Prophet (S.A.W.) observed:

"You will be called on the Day of Judgment by the names of you fathers. You should, therefore choose beautiful names for your children." (*Sunan Abu Dawood*)

Ibn 'Umar quotes the Holy Prophet (S.A.W.) to have said: "The names most liked by Allah are Abdullah and Abdul Rahman."

Coversely, the parents and the guardian should avoid such ugly or indecent names to call their children by as may militate aginast her or his pride or self-respect and make a laughing stock of her or him. The Prophet's practice in this respect has been described by Hazrat Aisha (R.A.A.) in these words: He used to replace an indecent name. (*Tirmizi*)

Ibn 'Umar narrates that Hazrat 'Umar had a daughter who was called 'Asia (meaning a sinning woman). The Holy Prophet (S.A.W.) substituted the name Jameela (Beautiful) for it." (*Tirmizi and Ibn Majah*)

Hazrat Abu Dawood narrates that the Holy Prophet (S.A.W.) replaced the names like 'Aasi, 'Azeez, 'Utulla (meaning hardness) Satan, Hakam, Ghurab and Habab (a kind of snake and according to some a fiend). He substituted the name of Aslam for Harb and Munba'th for Mudhtaje'. Bani-ul-zania was renamed Baniul-Rashda and Bani Mughwia was renamed Bani Rishda. (Abu Dawood adds that he avoided to mention the links of narrators for the sake of brevity).

Saeed bin Al Musayeeb relates that his grandfather called on the Holy Prophet (S.A.W.). The Prophet (S.A.W.) asked his name. He said "Huzn" (meaning hard stony ground. The Prophet (S.A.W.) wanted to rename him Sahl (Meaning green and soft ground). But Huzn refused to abandon the name given to him by his father. Saeed says that since that time his family has acquired the trait of hardness like stony ground.

Imam Malik states in Moatta that Yahya bin Saeed narrated the following incident:

Hazrat 'Umar bin Khattab (R.A.A.) asked a man what his name was. The man said that he was called Jamra (meaning a firebrand). The Caliph enquired who was his father. He said that he was the son of Shihab (meaning meteor). "Which family do you come of?" asked the Caliph next. "I belong to Hirqa" (meaning burning sensation). Hazrat 'Umar then asked the man where he lived. The man replied that he resided at a place known as Harratunnar (meaning the burn and heat of fire). "Which part of the area do you live?" he was asked. The man informed the Caliph that he lived in the part of the place called *Zat Laza* (meaning the area of flames). Hazrat Umar said, "Run up to your homestead. The People there are being burnt to death."

When the man returned home he found the place just as what Hazrat Umar had told him.

The guardian or parents are also urged not to call their child by the names of Allah such as *Ahad*, *Samad*, *Khaliq*, *Razzaq* etc. However these names may be used by prefixing the word *Abd*, as Abdullah, Abdus Samad, Abdul Khaliq, Abdur Razzaq etc.

When Hani visited Madina with a delegation, he was generally called Abul Hakam. The Prophet (S.A.W.) summoned him and said, "Hakam (One who issues commands) is only Allah and He alone is the Ruler. Why do the people then, call you Abul Hakam?" He replied that whenever there arose any dispute among his people they called upon him for arbitration and the verdict he gave was accepted by either party. The Prophet (S.A.W.) said, "What an explanation! Don't you have a son?" The man said that he had three sons by the names of Shuraih, Muslim and Abdullah. The Prophet (S.A.W.) said, "Who of them is the eldest?" The man said Shuraih was the eldest. "Well then," observed the Prophet (S.A.W.), "You are Abu Shuraih (father of Shuraih).

(*Sunan Abu Dawood*)

Abu Hurairah (R.A.A.) narrates that the Prophet (S.A.W.) once observed that the most abominable person to Allah is one who calls himself Malik (the king or monarch) for Allah alone is the Sovereign."

The guardian is also forbidden to choose such names as imply good omens and beatitude to an excessive degree. The reason is that if men bearing those names are called in their absence, the negative reply would be unpleasant. Such names are Aflah, Nafe', Ribah and Yasaar. All these names are beatific but they are undesirable in the light of above explanation.

Samura bin Jundab quotes the Prophet (S.A.W.) to have said, "The expressions that Allah likes most are *Subhanallah*, *Alhamd-o-Lillah*, *La Ilah Illallah*, and *Allaho Akbar*. Do not name your son Yasaar, Ribah, Najeeh, and Aflah, for you ask if he is there and he would reply in the negative, this would cause gloom over you. Don't you tell me more such names lest I should forbid them too."

(*Muslim, Abu Dawood and Tirmizi*)

Ibn-e-Majah epitomizes a lengthy tradition in the following words:

"The Prophet (S.A.W.) has forbidden us to call our slaves by four names: Aflah, Nafe', Ribah and Yasaar".

The guardians are also prohibited to choose such names for their children which imply servitude of false gods, as for example Abdul Uzza (the bondsman of a false god), Abdul Kaba, Abdun Nabi. These names are not only forbidden but the jurists are unanimous that they are also unlawful.

But the Prophet (S.A.W.) said of himself during the battle of Hunain:—

I am a Prophet and do not tell lies. I am son of Abdul Muttalib (the word Abd means bondsman and implies servitude of a being other than Allah. What the Prophet nevertherless meant was that he was the son or rather the grandson of Abdul Muttalib)."

The above observation of the Holy Prophet does not warrant the use of names implying hondsmanship to beings other than Allah. Hafiz Ibn-Qayyim aptly remarks that in this case the name is used by way of information and that particularly an occasion like the battle of Hunain using a name in the above manner for information or as a war slogan as was done by the Prophet (S.A.W.) was not unlawful. The Companions of the Prophet (S.A.W.) mentioned the names of their tribes in the presence of the Holy Prophet such as Bani Abd Munaf, Bani Abd Shams, Bani Abdul Dar etc. but the Prophet (S.A.W.) was not annoyed by those names.

To sum up, to inform by name and formally choose it for one to be called by are not the same thing. Thus the use of a name implying bondsmanship to anyone other than Allah designed for information is premissible. But the use of such a name for christening one is unlawful.

Besides, the guardian should abstain to choose a name for the new-born child which has kernel of the signification of personal decline, anthropomorphism or romance. The Arabic names mentioned below are, therefore, generally disliked: Nihad, Sosan, Miadah Nareman, Ghaadah, Ahlam etc.

Ban on such names is designed to safeguard the Islamic identity of the Muslim Ummah and ensure the perpetuity of its distinguishing characteristics and prestige. The names given above are regarded as undesirable also because they imply depravity, lack of identity and aimless life. The moment the ummah stoops to depravity and indignity, it will split up into small parts, tempting every aggressor to subjugate it and each individual of the ummah would be debased. The present condition of the ummah holds up a mirror to the situation we have depicted. Allah can deliver it from this state of decline.

The Prophet (S.A.W.) induces the ummah to call its individuals after the prophets. He stresses the desirability of preferring the excellent names of Abdullah and Abdur Rahman. Similar names signifying bondage to Allah alone should be chosen so that the Muslim Ummah may stand out among the nations of the world in every field and may come up to the standard determined by the Quran: "ye are a nation disciplined to serve as the model for the whole of mankind." Such a nation would illuminate the world with the light of truth and enrich it with the fundamental laws of Islam.

Abu Wahab, al Jushmi reports the Prophet (S.A.W.) to have observed, "Name your children after the Prophets of Allah. With Allah the most favourite names are Abdullah and Abdur Rahman. The most veracious names are Haris and Humam, whilst the most odious ones are Harb and Murra (meaning force and severity).

(c) Desirability of giving Kunniyat or Arabian Surname to a New Child.

From the Islamic viewpoint *kunniyat* or Arabian surname also produces salutary effects on the breeding of children.

(i) It inculcates respect for the child.

An Arab poet says:

"When I call him I call him with his *kunniyat.* Thus I esteem and honour him. I do not call him with derogatory names, as this is a nefarious act."

(ii) Generation of collective consciousness and building of character.

A good surname generates the consciousness in the child that he or she is being treated at par with the grown-ups and that he or she has entered the age wherein a person is respected.

(iii) The children are pleased with being called by their *kunniyat*. They feel that their finer sensibilities are respected.

(iv) A good surname also makes the child realise how elders as well as younger people are to be called. It was in view of these noble ends that the Holy Prophet (S.A.W.) used to call the children by surnames. The Prophet's practice contains instruction and guidance for the guardians and teachers.

Hazrat Anas says that Prophet (S.A.W.) excelled all human-beings in morals. He narrates: "I had a brother whom the Prophet (S.A.W.) called Abu Umair. Whenever the Prophet (S.A.W.) came to see me, he would say to the boy: "Abu Umair! Where is your *nughair* (singing bird)?". The narrator says that the name of the boy was probably Khateem."

The Prophet (S.A.W.) permitted Hazrat Aisha to have the surname of Umm Abdullah on account of her sister Asma bint Abu Bakr's son Abdullah.

Hazrat Anas was commonly known as Abu Hamza long before a son was born to him. Similarly, Abu Huraira, whose real name was Abdur Rahman bin Sakhr, had been called by his surname before he had any issue.

Traditions also bear it our that one is allowed to have a surname with reference to a person other than his offspring. A striking example of this is the surname of Hazrat Abu Bakr. He had no son by the name of Bakr, but he was nevertheless surnamed as Abu Bakr. Similarly although Hazrat Umar had no son named Hafs, yet he had the surname of Abu Hafs. Again Abu Zar (R.A.A.) did not have any son called 'Zar'. The same was the case with Khalid bin Walid who was commonly called Abu Sulaiman, although he had no son named Sulaiman. The examples may be multiplied. One more example is worthy of mention. Hazrat Bilal's *Kunniyat* was Abu Aeqzan because he used to wake the faithful for the morning prayer by his call.

(a) It is commendable according to the Prophet's practice to give a surname or *Kunniyat* to a newborn baby,
(b) Grown up people may also adopt or be called by surnames,
(c) It is not necessary that one must be the father of a son or daughter to have a surname,
(d) It is also not necessary to have a surname with reference to one's own son.

If parents do not concur on the choice of a name for thier son, then the father enjoys the right to choose it. This is indicated by the traditions cited above.

"Call them by the names of their fathers; this is

more equitable with Allah." (33:5)

We have already cited the Prophet's tradition narrated by Hazrat Anas: "A son has been born to me tonight. I have named him Ibrahim."

(iii) It is not permissible for anybody to call his son by nicknames. Neither the father nor anyone else is allowed to call the child by such derogatory names as the pigmy, the blind, the dumb, the cowdung insect or the like. Names like these are inconsistent with the teachings of Islam. Says Allah:

"Call not one another by nicknames." (48:11)

A child's psychological deviation and abnormality of social behaviour may partly be attributed to the nicknames or the derogatory names given to him or her. This is a subject we have reserved for a detailed discussion in the sequel.

(iv) Is it permissible to have the surname of Abul Qasim?

The Ulama are unanimous that to call a child after the Holy Prophet is permissible. They produce the authority of the following tradition in support of their position cited by Imam Muslim. Hazrat Jabir (R.A.A.) narrates that a boy was born to one of the members of his tribe. He called him after the Prophet Muhammad (S.A.W.) Some of the tribesman would not allow him to have for the boy the Holy name. The father of the boy put him on the back and went off to call on the Prophet (S.A.W.) He said to him, " O Messenger of Allah! I am blessed with a son whom I have named Muhammad. But my people would not allow me to call him after you. The Prophet (S.A.W.) replied that there was nothing wrong to call the children after his name, but you should avoid to have my surname. "I am" continued the Prophet (S.A.W.) "undoubtedly Qasim (distributor) and distribute among you the share of wealth or booty due to each."

The Ulama, however, differ on the question adopting or choosing the *Kunniyat* of the Holy Prophet (S.A.W.). Numerous sayings are to be found to this effect. We cite some of them here and then indicate the one that must be preferred:

1. **It is undesirable to have the surname 'Abul Qasim'.** This position is supported by the Tradition quoted above.

There is another tradition to the same effect narrated by Hazart Abu Huraira: "The Holy Prophet (S.A.W.) said that his name may be given to children but they should not be called by his surname." This is also the view held by Imam Shafi'ee.

2. There is nothing wrong at all to have the Prophet's surname.

A tradition narrated by Hazrat Aisha (R.A.A.) is produced in support of this view. Says Hazrat Aisha (R.A.A.).

"Once a woman visited the Holy Prophet (S.A.W.) and said: O Messenger! I have given birth to a son and have named him Muhammad. I have also chosen the *Kunniyat* of Abul Qasim for him. Please tell me if you like it or not? The Prophet (S.A.W.) replied: Who has declared the choice of my name for children lawful and the choice of surname unlawful?"

Ibn Abu Shaiba quotes Ibrahim to have said, "The son of Hazrat Aisha's sister, Muhammed bin Ash'as was surnamed Abul Qasim.

Ibn Abu Khethma reports Hazrat Imam Zahri to have said:

> "I have seen four sons of the Prophet's companions who were named Muhammed with surnames "Abul Qasim". The names of those boys were: (1) Muhammed bin Talha bin Abdullah (2) Muhammed bin Abu Bakr (3) Muhammad bin Ali Ibn Abi Talib and (4) Muhammed bin Sa'd bin Abi Waqqas.

Imam Malik was asked if a person may have the name Muhammed coupled with the surname Abul Qasim. Imam Malik replied, "This has not been prohibited, nor is there any harm in having both."

3. It is not permissible to name a boy Muhammad coupled with the surname Abul Qasim.

It is disallowed to name a child Muhammed and give him the surname Abul Qasim at the same time.

Either he may have the name or the surname. The Ulama who take this position cite the following tradition in its support as narrated by Hazrat Jabir:

"Said the Holy Prophet: Whoever chooses my name for his son, should avoid my surname for the same child and the other may sound." (*Sunan Abu Dawood*)

According to Abdur Rahman, Abu Musa reported his uncle to have narrated that the Prophet (S.A.W.) had observed: "Do not give both my name and surname to the same child". (*Ibn Abu Shaiba*)

Again Ibn Abu Khaithema narrates that when Muhammad bin Talha was born, Talha called on the Prophet (S.A.W.) and said: "My son's name is Muhammed. Can I combine the surname Abul Qasim with it?" The Prophet (S.A.W.) forbade him to couple his name with the surname and added that the boy's *Kunniyat* was Abu Sulaiman.

4. Having a surname after the surname of the Prophet is not wrong. The following tradition is cited to substantiate this position:

Munzir cites a tradition with reference to Muhammed bin Al Hanafiah which runs as follows:

"Hazrat Ali (R.A.A.) asked the Holy Prophet (S.A.W.) if a son was born to him after the demise of th latter, whether it was permissible to call him after the Prophet. The reply was in the affirmative. Hazrat Ali (R.A.A.) then enquired, "Can I give him your surname, too?" The Prophet (S.A.W.) again replied in the affirmative.

Hameed bin Zanjawiya writes in his book *Kitab-ul-Adab:*

"I asked Ibn Abi Owais what the position of Imam Malik was, regarding the person who was named after the Prophet (S.A.W.) and given his surname also Ibn Owais pointed to an old man who was sitting with us and said: "This Muhammad bin Malik whose father gave him the name Muhammad coupled with the *kunniyat* Abul Qasim. Imam Malik said that the ban on combining the name Muhammad with the surname Abul Qasim was valid only for the life time of the Holy Prophet (S.A.W.). The reason was that if anyone was called by the prophet's name as well as surname, the Prophet (S.A.W.) would have to take the trouble of responding or paying attention unnecessarily. But now after his demise there is no harm in his name with the surname.

The position taken by Imam Malik seems to be the most reasonable in the light of the above tradition. We, therefore, prefer it to other views. Thus there is no harm in coupling the name Muhammad with the surname Abul Qasim.

It may, therefore, be said that the traditions which prohibited combining the Holy Prophet's name with his surname were complied with only during the Prophet's life time. The point in avoiding this practice was that such a combination would cause confusion when calling the person having both the name and surname of the Prophet (S.A.W.); for one could not know whether the Prophet (S.A.W.) himself is being addressed or someone else. But since after the demise of the Holy Prophet (S.A.W.) the combination could not give rise to any cofusion, the name Muhammad could legitimately be coupled with the surname Abul Qasim. The legitimacy of such a combination is borne out by the tradition narrated by Imam Zahri, wherein he said that he had seen four such sons of the Prophet's companions whose name was Muhammed coupled with the surname Abul Qasim.

Since we are acquainted with the matter in such great details, there is no harm to name one's offspring after the Prophet (S.A.W.) as well as calling him by his surname. At the same time one should refrain from choosing a name for one's child which does not befit his or her personality and the purpose of life and militates against the child's sense of self respect. It is incumbent on the parents to call their offspring by beautiful names and surnames, which may be agreeable to them as well as the people around. This would generate a sense of self-respect among the children as well as affection and sense of honour for their relatives, so that they may address those with whom they brush shoulders and the people of the same age group in a decent and dignified manner. The children will thus learn at an early stage commendable manners and morals.

If we really want to revive the glory of our past and emerge once more as the best ummah in the world, then we should harmonize every aspect of our life with Islam and seek guidance from it. We should accordingly choose such names for our sons and daughters as are suited to their Islamic identity and are in accord with the Prophet's edicts and divine injunctions.

INJUNCTIONS PERTAINING TO AQIQA

1. Meaning of AQIQA

. The literal meaning of the word *'aqiqa'* is to cut off. It is derived from the same root as the world "aq' signifying cutting off relations with one's offspring and abandoning him or her for good. The root of both the words is 'aq' which also means to cut. An Arab poet, in one his couplets uses 'aq' to mean cutting off an amulet:

"In the city where I grew up and came of age; Where
youth cut off the amulet hung round my neck;
It is the first place whose soil touched my body."

As a term used in the Shariah *'aqiqa'* signifies slaughtering a goat on the seventh day of a child's birth.

2. The Significance of Aqiqa According to the Shariah.

There are innumerable traditions that may be cited to prove that the ceremony of *aqiqa* was commended and practiced by the Holy Prophet (S.A.W.). Some of them are as follows:

Salaman bin Ammar quotes the Prophet (S.A.W.) to have observed: It is necessary to perform the *aqiqa* of every boy. Salughter an animal for his sake and relieve him from suffering."

Hazrat Samura narrates this tradition:

"The Prophet (S.A.W.) said: The *aqiqa* of every male offspring is necessary. It should be performed on the seventh day of his birth. He should be named the same day and also his head shaven.

Hazrat Aisha (R.A.A.) quotes the Prophet to have stated: Two goats of the same age resembling each other sholuld be slaughtered for a boy and one would suffice for a girl.

Umm Karzul Ka'bia asked the Holy Prophet (S.A.W.) about *aqiqa* and the Holy Prphet is said to have replied, "*Aqiqa* of every boy is necessary. It should be performed on the seventh day of his birth. His head should be shaven and a name should be chosen for him the same day."

3. The Position of the Jurists as to the Proof of Aqiqa in the Shariah.

Aqiqa is treated as sunnah and as a practice commended by the Holy Prophet (S.A.W.) by a host of jurists including Imam Malik, the Madina jurists, Imam Shafi'ee and his school, Imam Ahmed, Ishaq, Abu Saur and a number of other jurists, ulama and mujtahids. They produce the above traditions in support of their position. They, however, advance th following arguments to repudiate the view of those who regard *aqiqa* as a duty:

(a) That if *aqiqa* were a duty, it would have been included in the fundamental mandates of the faith. Had it been so important, the Holy Prophet (S.A.W.) would have stated it in unequivocal terms so that no body might have any excuse for omitting it.
(b) That the Prophet (S.A.W.) treated *aqiqa* as a way of the parent's expression of affection for the child. Says the Prophet: (S.A.W.) If a child is born and it is considered desirable to offer sacrifice on its hehalf then it must be offered.

This tradition shows that the Prophet (S.A.W.) regarded *aqiqa* as commendable. This is a proof of its being a desirable practice and not an imperative duty.

2. Those who declare *aqiqa* an imperative duty include Imam Hasan Basri, Lais bin Sa'd etc. They produce the following tradition narrated by Bareeda and Ibn Ishaq:

The people will be questioned about *aqiqa* on the Day of Judgement just as they would be questioned about offering prayers five times a day.

They also refer to a tradition narrated by Hazrat Samura in support of their argument:

The Prophet (S.A.W.) said: The *aqiqa* of every boy is necessary."

They explain that the boy whose *aqiqa* is omitted will be withheld on the Day of Judgement at the time of intercession of his parents. In other words, *aqiqa* is an imperative duty.

4. Refusal to Acknowledge the Legitimacy of Aqiqa.

The jurists of the Hanafite School do not acknowledge the validity of *aqiqa* under the Shariah. They substantiate their position with reference to a tradition narrated by Hazrat 'Amr bin Shoaib:

When asked about *aqiqa*, the Prophet (S.A.W.) replied: I don't like *aqiqa.*

The Hanafites also cite another tradition in support of their view. This tradition as narrated by Abu Rafe' has been quoted by Imam Ahmed. It runs as follows:

Hazrat Fatima (R.A.A.), the mother of Hazrat Hasan bin Ali (R.A.A.) wanted to slaughter two sheep to perform the ceremony of Hazrat Hasan's *aqiqa* But the Prophet (S.A.W.) forbade her to perform *aqiqa*. He, however, asked her to get the boy's head shaven and distribute an amount of silver equal in weight to his hair. Again, when Hazrat Husain was born, Hazrat Fatima did the same as the Prophet (S.A.W.) had bidden her.

But all the earlier traditions support the commendability of *aqiqa* as a Prophet's practice. Most of the jurists take the same position. Besides, it has the support of innumrable ulama and scholars, who repudiate the Hanafite view refusing the legitimacy of aqiqa under the Shariah. They argue that the traditions which the Hanafites quote to substantiate their position has no validity whatsoever and it is, therefore, wrong to deny the lawful status of *aqiqa*. Look at in its context, the observation of the Prophet (S.A.W.) that he did not like *aqiqa* implies something quite different. The wording of the tradition as a whole is as follows:

"When asked about aqiqa, the Prophet (S.A.W.) expressing his dislike observed: I don't like aqiqa.

In other words, he considered it undesirable to give the name aqiqa to the slaughter of an animal in sacrifice. His companions said, they had enquired about aqiqa because a boy was born to one of them. The Prophet (S.A.W.) then said: Well, if any one of you wants to offer sacrifice on behalf of his son, he may do so. Two goats resembling each other for a boy should be sacrificed and only one for a girl.

Let us now consider the tradition wherein we find the following words:

"Do not perform *aqiqa* (offer a goat in sacrifice) but shave the child's head."

It is wrong to seek justification on the basis of this tradition for the refusal to acknowledge the lawful status of the *aqiqa* ceremony; for according to th tradition in question Hazrat Fatima (R.A.A.) sought permission to perform *aqiqa* for her sons Hazrat Hasan and Husain, but the Prophet (S.A.W.) asked her not to perform it as he had himself already performed it for both of them and considered unnecessary for Hazrat Fatima to do it. The fact that the Prophet (S.A.W.) himself performed the *aqiqa* ceremony of Hazrat Hasan and Husain (R.A.A.) is borne out by a number of traditions. Some of them are cited below:

Hazrat Ibn Abbas narrates with reference to Hazrat Ayub Ikrama that the Prophet (S.A.W.) performed the *aqiqa* of Hasan and Husain (R.A.A.) by sacrificing a sheep for each. (*Abu Dawood*)

Jareer bin Hazim quotes with reference to Qatada the following tradition narrated by Hazrat Anas:

"The Holy Prophet (S.A.W.) performed the *aqiqa* ceremonies of Hasan and Husain (R.A.A.) on the seventh day of their birth.

Recapitulation

According to all the imams and ulama the *aqiqa* ceremony of a new-born child is a practice commended by the Holy Prophet (S.A.W.) If the father of the baby could afford to offer the requisite sacrifice, it is incumbent upon him to do so in order to keep alive the Holy Prophet 's practice and earn the reward for it in the Hereafter. This would strengthen his bonds of affection with his kith and kin, the people with whom he brushes his shoulders, the neighbours and friends. Keeping this in view, the people rejoice over the birth of a child and express their pleasure by attending the *aqiqa* ceremony. Thus the individuals of the society cooperate with each other in translating the concept of social security into practice. The idea of social security manifests itself when the feast held on the occasion of *aqiqa* is attended by some poor and indigent people also. How lofty are principles laid down by Islam for sowing the seeds of mutual affection in the human society and to establish social justice for the benefit of the less fortunate members of the community. These principles bear testimony to the greatness of Islamic faith.

5. Appropriate Time for the Performnce of the Aqiqa Ceremony.

We have already cited the trdadition narrated by Hazrat Samura wherein the Holy Prophet (S.A.W.) is quoted to have said that the *aqiqa* of every newborn baby is essential, that an animal should be slaughtered on his behalf on the seventh day of his birth and that he should be named the same day.

This tradition is corroborated by another tradition which is as follows:

Abdullah bin Wahab quotes Hazrat Aisha (R.A.A.) to have reported:

The Holy Prophet (S.A.W.) performed the *aqiqa* of Hasan and Husain (R.A.A.) on the seventh day of their birth and also named them. At the same time he ordered their heads to be shaven which would drive away the evil from them.

Nonetheless we have the evidence of some other traditions according to which it is not asbolutely essential to perform the sacrificial rite of *aqiqa* on the seventh day of the child's nativity. Although it is commendable to observe it on that day. But one can legitimately perform the rite on the fourth, eighth or tenth day. The following remarks of some authorities relating to *aqiqa* are too clear to need any explanation:

Maimooni says he asked Abu Abdullah how the *aqiqa* rite of a new-bron child is to be observed. He quoted Hazrat Aisha (R.A.A.) to have said: It should be done on the seventh, fourteenth or twenty first day of the child's nativity.

Saleh bin Ahmad says that his father Ahmad told him to slaughter the sacrificial animal of *aqiqa* on the seventh day. If this is not possible on the 14th day and should this too be not practicable then it should be slaughtered on the 21st day of its birth.

Imam Malik remarks that although it appears that the

observance of *aqiqa* ceremony on the 7th day of the child's nativity is commendable, yet it would be suficient to perform it on the fourth, eigth or tenth day.

To sum up, if the father of the new-born child can afford to observe the *aqiqa* on the seventh day of nativity, it will be well and good, as the Prophet (S.A.W.) observed it on that day. But if he does not have the means to do it on the seventh day, then he may legitimately do it on any day, as has been remarked by Imam Malik.

In other words the injunction relating to aqiqa is flexible, just every other Islamic injuction provides for some latitude for the convenience of the believers.

6. Is the Aqiqa of Male and Female Babies As of Equal Consequence?

We have already stated that all the scholars and ulama are unanimous on the importance of *aqiqa* as a practice commended by the Prophet (S.A.W.).It is equally important for boys and girls.

As Umm Kurzi narrates in a tradition attributed to her, when she asked the Prophet (S.A.W) about aqiqa, he replied that two goats were to be sacrificed for a boy and one for a girl. (*Imam Ahmad, Tirmizi*)

Besides, Abi Shaiba quotes a tradition narrated by Hazrat Aisha (R.A.A.) wherein the Prophet (S.A.W.) is reported to have said that we should sacrifice two goats for the aqiqa of a boy and one for that of a girl.

The following points are established in the light of the foregoing traditions:

(a) The position of a boy and girl in the Shariah in respect of a male and a female child is alike i.e., the aqiqa ceremony of a girl must be observed just as that of a boy is required to be performed.

(b) But the position of the male is superior to that of a female in that the number of goats to be sacrificed for the former is double the number fixed for a girl.

According to Imam Malik one goat is sacrificed for each boy or girl. He was asked how many goats were to be slaughtered for the aqiqa of boy and girl respectively. He replied one goat for a boy and also one for a girl. He substantiates his position with reference to the following traditions:

(a) According to Hazrat Ibn Abbas, on the occasion of the aqiqa ceremonies of Hazrat Hasan and Hazrat Husain, the Holy Prophet (S.A.W.) slaughtered one sheep for each.
(b) Jafar bin Muhammad quotes his father to have reported that Hazrat Fatim'a (R.A.A.) slaughtered one sheep each for the aqiqa of Hazrat Hasan and Husain (R.A.A.).
(c) Imam Malik reports that Hazrat Abdullah bin Umar used to slaughter one goat each in the aqiqa ceremony of boys and girls.

The sum and substance of the discussion is that the man on whom Allah has opened the doors of his bounty or who is well-to-do should slaugheter two goats for his son's *aqiqa* and one for his daughter's. It is also horne out by the record of the Holy Prophet's practice who ordered to slaughter two goats to be slaughtered for a boy and one for a girl. Middle or lower middle class people may slaughter one goat for a boy or a girl. This would enable to earn them the reward of keeping the Prophet's practice alive.

An Objection Answered

Some people object to the discrimination in favour of male or boys vis-a-vis girls in respect of aqiqa.

Many answers may be given to this objection:

(a) A Muslim is bound to obey any order given to him by Islam and abstain from every thing it forbids. This is what the following verse requires:

"But no, by thy Lord! They believe not until they make Thee a judge of what is in dispute between them, then find not any straitness in their hearts as to that which thou decidest and submit with full submission." (4:65)

Since the preference to boys in the matter of aqiqa is proved by the practice of the Holy Prophet, we remain committed to submission and following his example.

(b) The wisdom of this preference is to show that right of the male deserves superiority over the right of the female; for Allah has bestowed more physcial power on man than on woman. He is also entrusted with the responsibility of controlling domestic affairs and meeting the needs of the household. Moreover, man has greater balance of mind than woman and is more capable of controlling his emotions:

Says Allah :

Men are incharge of women, because Allah has made the one of them to excel the other and because they spend of their property for the support of women. (4:34)

(c) The reason for sacrificing two goats in the boy's *aqiqa* ceremony is that it is attended by a greater number of people. The greater the number of people assembling on such occasion the stronger will be the bonds of love and affection among them. This would also allow a greater scope for catering to the needs of the indigent.

7. Breaking the Sacrificed Animal's Bones Is Loathsome.

In performing the *aqiqa* ceremony of a new-born baby it should always be borne in mind that the bones of the animal slaughtered is not to be broken. This should be avoided at the time of slaughtering the animal as well as eating of its meat. Each bone should be cut at its root and not broken at any place.

Hazrat Jafar bin Muhammed quotes his father to have reported that the Prophet (S.A.W.) told Hazrat Fatima (R.A.A.) about the animal she sacrificed for the *aqiqa* of Hazrat Hasan and Husain that she should send one of its legs to the boys' nurse and also eat of its flesh herself and distribute it among others.

Ibn Jureej refers to Hazrat 'Ata who used to say that each part of the animal sacrificed in the *aqiqa* ceremony should be cut as a whole. Hazrat Ibn Munzir quotes Hazrat Aisha (R.A.A.) with reference to Hazrat 'Ata to have made similar remarks about the parts of the sacrificial animal.

There are two advantages of cutting animals parts as indicated above :

(a) Distribution of the meat of the animal sacrificed in *aqiqa* would impress its value and sanctity upon the minds of the needy and others who share it. This is possible only when the entire part thereof is presented to each without breaking the bones and without chopping off any organ. The people who receive the meat would naturally feel that the person sacrificing the animal is generous. In fact the ceremony under discussion provides one the opportunity to demonstrate one's munificence.

(b) Another idea behind presenting each part of the sacrificial animal in its entirety to seek beatitude hoping that each part of the new-born child would be perfect and strong and he or she will be hale and hearty. *Aqiqa* as a matter of fact is the sacrifice offered for each and every part of the child's body.

8. Injunctions Pertaining to Aqiqa.

(a) The following injunctions must be kept in view when performing aqiqa.:

The general rule is that whatever can be legitimately offered in sacrifice in general may also be offered in the case of *aqiqa*. All the ulama are unanimous on this fundamental principle. The injunctions as to *aqiqa* are as under :

(i) The sacrificial animal should be a little more than one year old. This applies to sheep and goat also. In the case of a sheep or ram if the animal is fleshy and corpulent then a six months old lamb would suffice, provided that when such a lamb is mixed up among one year old goats and lambs, it could not be recognized. But the goat to be sacrificed should at all events be a little more than one year old.

(ii) The sacrificial animal should have no physical flaw. Sacrifice of a blind, one-eyed, lame or lean animal is, therefore, disallowed. It is also not permissible to slaughter in the aqiqa ceremony any animal whose teeth have fallen, which is born without ears or is mad and, therefore, incapable of grazing; or whose ears, tail or hip is cut off provided that the portion so cut off is more than two thirds of the part in question.

Apart from the flaws referred to above any animal with minor defects may legitimately be slaughtered in aqiqa; for instance, an animal with ears torn in between or with a broken horn or with a little limp hut capable of moving in a normal manner such as one which can walk with three feet using the fourth feet as a prop to move on. Examples of other animals with minor faults include an animal that is mad but not to such a degree that it is incapable of grazing or browsing or one with greater number of teeth intact or one with a part of ear, tail or hip cut off but the portion so cut off is less than two thirds of the part in question.

(iii) If a cow or buffalo is intended for sacrifice in *aqiqa*, it must be a little more than two years old. If a camel is to be slaughtered it must be a little over five years.

(b) The difference between *aqiqa* and sacrifice in general is the animal meant for the latter may be shared a maximum number of seven persons, whereas the animal slaughtered for aqiqa is exclusively meant for a single child. *Aqiqa* does not admit of sacrificing one camel for seven children at one and the same time. If the same animal could be shared by more than one child, then the very purpose of shedding the blood of an animal for the sake of a new-born baby would be defeated; for every part of the animal slaughtered for the purpose constitutes a sacrifice offered for each part of the baby's body.

(c) A camel or a cow may be slaughtered instead of a goat, but it must be slaughtered for the *aqiqa* of a single child. For example, Hafiz Ibn Qayyim Aljauzi says of Hazrat Anas (R.A.A.) that he used to slaughter camels on the occasion of his sons' *aqiqa*.

It has been narrated about Hazrat Abu Bakr (R.A.A.) that he slaughtered a camel for his son Abdur Rahman and invited the people of Basra to partake of it.

Some Ulama are of the opinion that according to the Prophet's tradition the purpose of *aqiqa* is served by slaughtering only a goat. But the people who think it permissible to slaughter a camel or a cow substantiate their position by the following tradition:

> "The *aqiqa* of a boy is necessary. You should, therefore, shed blood on his behalf."

But the Prophet (S.A.W.) did not specify any particular

species of the animals to be slaughtered. From the literal sense of the tradition it may be inferred that it is permissible to sacrifice any animal in aqiqa, whether it is a goat, a cow or a camel.

(d) What holds good in the case of sacrifice in general also holds good in the case of aqiqa. For instance, it is permissible to eat the meat of the animal slaughtered in sacrifice in general or in aqiqa or distribute it among the needy, send it as a present or give to the nurse for the sake of her pleasure. This is clear from a tradition quoted by Behaqi as narrated by Hazrat Ali (R.A.A.).

"The Prophet (S.A.W.) asked Hazrat Fatima (R.A.A.) to weigh the hair of Hazrat Husain's head, distribute in alms an amount of silver equal in weight to those hair and give the leg of the sacrificial animal to the nurse."

If any one wants to arrange a party on the occasion of aqiqa and invite his friends and relatives to it, he may do so. Most of the jurists have allowed it because it fosters the spirit of benevolence in the Islamic society and encourages its members to do good to each other, to be charitable and to give to nurse a little more than what she has already got. Islam stresses the importance of the aqiqa ceremony inasmuch as it strengthens the unity of the Ummah and welds it into an impregnable whole.

(e) While slaughtering for the aqiqa, one should say that it is for the aqiqa of such and such boy or girl. As Ibn-al-Munzir quotes Hazrat Aisha (R.A.A.) to have narrated:

"The Holy Prophet (S.A.W.) has said: Slaughter the animal mentioning the name of the child; begin with the name of Allah and say these words:

This is the aqiqa of the child (boy or girl) named so and so."

If the person slaughtering the animal has the intention of performing aqiqa but does not mention the name of the child concerned, the aqiqa serves its purpose.

9. The Philosophy of Aqiqa.

(a) It is a kind of sacrifice through which the new-born baby draws closer to Allah right from its earliest days.

(b) Aqiqa is a *fidya* (escape goat) whereby the child is protected from calamities and shocks. It is similar to the sacrifice accepted by Allah in the form of the slaughter of a ram on behalf of Hazrat Ismaeel. (A.S.).
(c) Aqiqa gives to the child the right of intercession on behalf of its parents on the Day of Judgement.
(d) It is the expression of pleasure through abiding by Islamic injunctions as it also consists of a function to rejoice over the birth of a child according to the Islamic custom; for the Holy Prophet (S.A.W.) longed to see his Ummah outnumber other nations.

(e) Aqiqa strengthens the bonds of affection between the individuals of the Islamic society; for it provides the people the opportunity of getting together to express pleasure over the birth of the child and partake of whatever is served on the table.

(f) It is a unique mode of collective security that fulfils the requirements of social justice and eradicates poverty, want and sense of frustration and deprivation from the society.

This then is the utility and wisdom of *aqiqa*.

The following is a list of feasts allowed by Islam on specific occasions:

(1) Feast arranged for guests.
(2) Meal offered to a visitor.
(3) Feast on the occasion of the birth of a child.
(4) Dinner to which people are invited.
(5) Wedding feast.
(6) Feast on the occasion of aqiqa.
(7) Feast on the occasion of a boy's circumcision.
(8) Mourning feast.
(9) Feast on return from a Journey.
(10) Feast arranged on completion of the construction of a house.

CHAPTER V

CIRCUMCISION

The Meaning of Circumcision.

By circumcision is literally meant cutting off the extra foreskin covering the glans penis. But according to the Shariah circumcision is the removal by surgery of the lower portion of the glans penis which forms its fringe in a circular shape. It is this portion of the human sexual organ which the Shariah injunctions pertain to. That is exactly what the Prophet (S.A.W.) speaks of in the following Hadith as quoted by Imam *Ahmed*, *Tirmizi* and *Nasai*:

"Bath is obligatory when two fringes meet."

We come across these words in (*Tabarani*)

"When two organs meet and the glans penis disappears, it is obligatory to take bath whether semen is discharged or not."

The Significance of Circumcision according to Shariah.

We find numerous traditions to this effect, whose authenticity has been unanimously endorsed by the jurists; as for example the following sayings of the Holy Prophet (S.A.W.).

"Full mouth-wash, cleaning the nose, getting the moustaches trimmed, brushing the teeth, cutting the nails and shaving the hair growing below the navel over the (pubes) and in the armpits are the demands of nature.

(*Musnad Imam Hambal*)

Again Hazrat Abu Huraira quotes the Prophet (S.A.W.) to have said:

"Nature consists of four things:

Circumcision, shaving the hair growing the navel (over the pubes or the region above the sexual organ), getting the moustaches trimmed, cutting the nails and shaving the hair growing in the armpits."

Is Circumcision Obligatory or Just a Sunnat (Prophet's example to be followed)?.

The jurists who regard circumcision as *sunnat* include Imam Hasan of Basra, Imam Abu Hanifa and others. The argument advanced by them in favour of their position is based on the following words of the Prophet (S.A.W.).

"Circumcision is a *sunnat* to be followed by the males and a mark of honour for a female."

These jurists further argue that it is a *sunnat* because the Prophet (S.A.W.) mentions it along with some of his own customs like cutting the nails, and shaving the hair growing in the armpits. Thus circumcision is only a *sunnat* and not an obligatory practice.

Yet another proof is produced in favour of its being a *sunnat* and that consists of the following remarks of Hazrat Hasan Basri:

> "A large number of people were Muslims including the Holy Prophet (S.A.W.). There were black people as well as white, Romans as well as Iranians and Negroes. None of them was questioned (as to circumcision). Had circumcision been obligatory, their profession of Islam would not have been regarded as acceptable."

Those who treat circumcision as obligatory include Imam Sha'bi, Imam Rabia, Auza'ee, Yahya bin Saeed-al-Ansari, Imam Malik, Imam Shafi'ee and Imam Ahmed. Imam Malik goes to the length of declaring cirucmcision mandatory. He says that an uncircumcised person is not allowed to lead prayer; nor is his evidence acceptable.

The foregoing Imams have declared circumcision obligatory on the following grounds:

'Osaim bin Kuleb narrates that his grandfather called on the Prophet (S.A.W.) and told him that he had embraced Islam. The Prophet (S.A.W.) said: Remove the hair grown in the state of disbelief (shave your head) and get yourself circumcised." (*Imam Ahmed and Abu Dawood*).

Harb cited the following saying of the Holy Prophet (S.A.W.) from Imam *Zahri's* book *'Masail'*.

"Whoever embraces Islam should get himself

circumcised, however old he may be."

The authenticity of this tradition is not tenable. But corroborated by other traditions, it becomes authentic.

Ibn Abbas observes, "The prayer of an uncircumcised person in not accepted, nor the animal slaughtered by him is to be eaten." (*Narrated by Waki*)

Musa bin Ismaeel quotes Hazrat Ali (R.A.A.) to have narrated:

"We saw these words inscribed on the leaf placed in the handle of the Holy Prophet's sword: An uncircumcised person cannot be left free after embracing Islam until he gets himself circumcised.

Khattabi observes that although circumcision is mentioned with acts practiced by the Holy Prophet (S.A.W.) yet a majority of Ulama believes in its being obligatory. The grounds of their conviction is that circumcision is an Islamic custom constituting a mark of distinction between a Muslim and infidel. If the corpse of a circumcised person is found among those of numerous uncircumcised persons, it is necessary to offer the funeral prayer for the former and his body should be buried in the graveyard of the Muslims.

The jurists stressing the obligatory character of circumcision give the following reasons in support of their standpoint:

It cannot be said of an uncircumcised sexual organ for certain that extra foreskin is absolutely clean and thus the fulfilment of the requirements of ablution and prayer remain doubtful. The foreskin covers the glans penis and it is possible that drops of urine infiltrate into it. Obviously it does not lend itself to proper cleansing. Unmistaken cleanliness and saying of prayer is, therefore, dependent on circumcision. That is the reason why numerous jurists of old and some jurists of the later days as well prohibit the leading of prayer by an uncircumcised person. In respect of individual prayer, however, uncircumcised state may, of course, be excusable to a certain extent. It may be likened to the state of such a person, who urinates in drops. This state is regarded as an excuse in the case of prayer.

Again the above viewpoint is also supported by divine injunction. Says Allah:

"Then We made you this revelation enjoining that ye should follow Abraham's example apart from all other people."

It is clear from the above verse that the Prophet (S.A.W.) and his ummah is bound to tread in the footsteps of Abraham (A.S.).

The practice of circumcision is a legacy of Hazrat Ibrahim (Abraham A.S.), which is alluded to in the following tradition narrated by Abu Huraira:

"The circumcision of Hazrat Ibrahim (A.S.) was performed at the age of eighty years".

There is yet another tradition to the same effect:

"Hazrat I rahim (A.S.) was the first man to host a feast, to wear Shalwar (Pyjama) and circumcise himself. Subsequently the practice of circumcision was continued by all the Prophets till the (last of the) Prophets appeared."

Again, Hazrat Abu Ayub narrates this Tradition:

The Prophet (S.A.W.) said that there were four practices which constitute the legacy of Prophets.

(i) circumcision (ii) use of perfume (iii) brushing the teeth and (iv) wedlock.

The above traditions clearly testify to the obligatory character of cicumcision.

Refutation of arguments advanced in favour of declaring circumcision a mere sunnat:

The wording of the tradition which forms the basis of the status of *sunnat* give o circumcision is as follows:

"Circumcision is a sunnat in relation to males and a mark of honour in realtion to females."

The scholars of *Hadith* hold that the authenticity of this tradition is untenable and that such faulty traditions do not warrant the deductions of *Shariat* injunctions. The jurists have laid it down as a rule that if the tradition in question is conceded to be true it would mean that the Prophet (S.A.W.) adopted the practice of circumcision and enjoined upon the Muslims to follow it. Thus it has come to assume obligatory character; whereas *sunnat* is just a custom. The Prophet's saying that circumcision is a *sunnat* in relation to males implies that it is necessary under the *'Shariat*.

The Jurists opposed to regarding circumcision as a mere *sunnat* inasmuch as the Prophet (S.A.W.) mentioned alongwith other *sunnats* like cutting the nails further argue that the same tradition refers to some obligatory acts like taking bath, full-mouthwash and cleaning the nose as well as some commendable acts such as cutting the nails and brushing the teeth. Cutting the nails is just a custom but in certain cases it is obligatory to cut them in order to fulfil the requirements of ablution. For instance when the uncut nails are very long filled with dirt, it becomes obligatory to cut them off. The above jurists therefore, maintain that the tradition which forms the basis of the status of *sunnat* as given to circumcision contains reference to both commendable and obligatory acts.

As for Hazrat Hasan Basri's argument that the Holy Prophet (S.A.W.) initiated a lot of people into Islam but he never interrogated any one of them regarding circumcision, the only answer to it is that they were already circumcised and it was unnecessary to question them about it. Circumcision was customary with the Arab's right from the very beginning and it was a practice prevalent among the Jews, too. Besides, one of the two sects of Christians used to get themselves circumcised.

Those who embraced Islām or remained heathens know that circumcision was an Islamic custom. Hence the people who entered the fold of Islam got themselves circumcised immediatley thereafter as they hastened to take bath before doing so.

This is what has been stated by Hafiz Ibn Qayyim, which is corroborated by the above tradition quoted by 'Osaim bin Kuleb, wherein the Prophet (S.A.W.) is reported to have asked the people embracing Islam to remove from their heads the hair grown in the state of heathenism and get themselves circumcised. Similarly another tradition to the same effect as cited by Imam Zahri corroborates the statement of Hafiz Ibn Qayyim. The tradition is as follows:

> "Whoever embraces Islam should get himself circumcised even if he is a grown up man."

The Prophet (S.A.W.) simply used to exhort the people to do good and also indicate what was good and what was wrong. It was not his job to probe into each and every matter. He accepted whatever was told to him by those joining the fold of Islam on the face of it or whatever was overtly manifest in them leaving their concealed affairs to Allah.

To sum up, circumcision is an essential and distinguishing mark of Islam. The Shariah attaches great importance to it and is as such obligatory for males. Whoever does not get himself circumcised after embracing Islam or before coming of age would violate the Islamic injunction and would be guilty of sin. For circumcision is not only a mark of Mulsim and an Islamic practice, but is also good for the males health and prevents many a dangerous diseases.

We shall discuss the advantages of circumcision in the sequel.

Is Circumcision of Girls also Obligatory?

The consensus of all the jurists and ulama is that the circumcision of girls is commendable and not obligatory. However, according to a tradition quoted by Imam Ahmad bin Hanbal circumcision is necessary for males and females alike. But there is another tradition quoted also by him that circumcision is necessary for the males and not for the females. This supports the position of all those scholars and Ulama who regard circumcision as commendable instead of its being mandatory. The custom prevalent among the Muslims also shows that it is commendable rather than obligatory for women. It is, moreover, argued that the Prophet (S.A.W.) declared circumcision necessary for males only and not for females. There is no proof of his enjoining upon the girls to get themselves cicumcised. However, Shaddad narrates that circumcision is delcared obligatory in relation to males and a mark of honour for women. This tradition to a certain extent implies the desirability of circumcision in the case of women and it just hints at it. If we concede that the above traditiion is authentic, even then it does not prove that circumcision is obligatory for women. What may be inferred from the tradition in question at best is that circumcision is commendable or desirable for, women for the words 'a mark of honour for females' are a clear testimony of its being commendable.

Circumcision has not been declared obligatory for women probably because the shapes of male and female organs are different.

Proper Age for Circumcision

Most of the Ulama are of the opinion that when a boy is nearing the age of pubescence he should be circumcised. The reason for this is that no sooner he comes of age then he becomes an obligated person and is bound to act on the injunction of shariah. Therefore, when he is of age, he should already be circumcised so that his services to Allah may be regular in accordance with Islam and acceptable to Him.

The guardian or the parents are advised to get their male offspring circumcised at the earliest after his birth. The boy will thus find himself circumcised when he reaches the age of pubescence and discretion and has no anxiety on that score. They are, therefore, best advised to get the boy circumcised on the seventh day after his birth. Hazrat Jabir narrates that th Holy Prophet (S.A.W.) performed the *aqiqa* of Hazrat Hasan and Husain on the seventh day of their birth and also got them circumcised on the same day.

The Good That Circumcision Does

There are various advantages of circumcision from both the religious and medical viewpoints. This is borne out by the observations made by ulama and physicians.

The Religious Advantages.

(a) Circumcision is one of the basic demands of a human nature as it is also an Islamic practice of much consequence according to the Shariah.

(b) It is a symbol of the right and natural way which was given the status of law for us through the sacred message brought by Abraham (A.S.). This right path of Abraham (A.S.) has instilled deep into our hearts the belief in the

Unity of Allah and has beautified our bodies with natural charms. Circumcision, cutting of moustaches and nails, shaving the hair growing in the armpits are all natural charms that beautify our physical appearance. According to Abraham's way they consist of the process of embellishing our bodies. Says Allah:

"And afterward we inspired thee (Muhammad S.A.W. saying:) Follow the religion of Abraham, as one by nature upright" (16: 23)

"(We take our) colour from Allah and who is better than Allah at colouring. We are His worshippers." (2: 138)

(c) Circumcision is a mark of distinction between the Muslims and the followers of other religions.

(d) Circumcision is an acknowledgement of being God's servant, a demonstration of obedience to Him and a sign of bowing before His sovereignty and rule.

Medical Advantages of Circumcision

(i) Circumcision does not only ensure cleanliness and shapeliness of the sexual organ but also restrains concupiscence.

(ii) Medically speaking, circumcision comprises a rule of hygiene. It also protects man against disease. Dr. Sabri Al Qabani enumerates the following advantages of circumcision in his book on sexual life:

(a) Amputation of foreskin saves a male from the oily substance that accumulates beneath the skin and causes foul smell.

(b) A circumcised person is generally immune from cancer. The cancer of penis is developed by the male whose skin is narrow. Circumcised people seldom develop such cancer regardless of the religion they follow.

(c) The earlier a boy is circumcised the less will be in the habit of urinating in bed.

(d) The penis of an uncircumcised person remains beneath the foreskin at the time of erection and this is harmful to health.

(e) A circumcised individual is less addicted to masturbation than an uncircumcised one.

These are the advantages that have necessitated treating of circumcision as obligatory by the Shariah. Any sensible person can realize the virtues and wisdom inherent in the Shariah.

The injunctions dealt with in the previous three chapters in respect of matters from birth to circumcision pertain to the upbringing of children. The parents of every child ought to comply with those injunctions and start bringing up their children in conformity with them right from the day of their birth.

What would be the good of such upbringing? The answer to this question would not be far to seek when the child grows up. When he reaches the age of discretion and comes to know of the events of his birth, *Aqiqa* and circumcision, he would realize that his parents have duly fulfilled their responsibilities as to his rearing and that they started lavishing their love and affection upon him right from the day he opened his eyes upon the world.

Adherence to the above injunctions makes the child healthy and strong. When he grows up and begins to understand the affairs of life and the reality of things, he realizes at the same time that he belongs to a Muslim family in which the injunctions of Islam are followed, the requirements of the Shariah are given due consideration and the teachings of the Prophet (S.A.W.) are translated into practice. He would also think that the parents who have brought him up are really good father and mother, who fulfil their obligations duly. The realization of all these things firmly implants Islam in his heart and his character is consequently built on the Islamic base. In the final analysis, a child so brought up demonstrates cardinal virtues by conducting himself in a manner as if those virtues are essential ingredients of his nature.

Islam does not content itself with providing guidance for the rearing of the child in the infancy. It also serves as the beacon light when he grows up and comes of age.

In the following chapters we propose to discuss the kind of obligations Islam imposes on the parents and guardians with regard to the breeding and training of children so that the child brought up in a Muslim family may feel proud of the fact that Islam provides the best principles of life and generates in an excellent way the sense of duty in the Muslims and persuades them to fulfil it.

We deal at length, then, on the subject of rearing and training of children.

CHAPTER VI

CAUSES OF CHILDREN'S DEVIATION

There may be many causes of children's deviation and aberration from the moral and social norms; for the mileau in which one lives, is wicked and full of temptations.

The parents and guardians ought to realize the vital importance of their responsibilities in this regard and guard the children against evil influences as a sacred trust. If they have no sense of duty with respect of children and do not know even so much as what spoils them and what steps must be taken to remove the causes of their deviation, then a tragic generation of criminals and hooligans would inevitably emerge.

In this chapter we propose to discuss the factors leading to the deviant behaviour of children and suggest its remedy so that the people seeking to prevent children from going astray may be provided guidance and acquainted with the immutable and everlasting principles bestowed upon us by Islam.

The following are some of the more important causes of children's aberration.

I. Want.

It is quite obvious that when a child does not get adequate food and clothing at home and is thus deprived of the basic necessities of life, finding nobody to support him, he will be compelled to bid adieu to his home and seek to gratify his want elsewhere. Consequently he will be drifted into *bosom* of criminals and wicked people and will finally sink into the abyss of depravity and inequity, and will thus grow up as a hardened criminal posing a constant threat to the life and property of the law-abiding citizens.

The Islamic system of social justice provides certain basic principles for solving the problem of want and hunger. By acting on those principles man will not just be relieved of want but will be able to live with honour and dignity. Islam also provides certain laws that give complete guarantee of food, clothing and shelter. It prescribes for us certain practical rules, whose enforcement would do away with want and hunger. For instance, the Islamic laws provide to every individual of the society to earn his living by legitimate means. Those of us who are handicapped and incapable of earning their livelihood are provided for by the payment of monthly allowance out of the government treasury. Nor is this all. The Islamic government bears the expenses of an indigent person's family besides providing him a job. Under the Islamic system of social security orphans, widows and old people too, are taken care of in a way that he does not feel indignity and disrespect. If all the relevant laws of Islam are properly enforced crime, hooliganism and inequity will be totally eliminated from the society and hunger, want and indigence will for ever be eradicated tooth and nail.

II. Discord Between Parents

In a society wherein the families lack harmony and are in a sad disarray and the continued discord between parents often erupts into wrangling, the minds of children are adversely affected. Such wranglings and quarrels are one of the causes of their aberration. When the child witnesses the parents quarreling all the time, he decides to quit the dismal atmosphere of his home and finally turns his back upon it. He spends most of his time with his friends. If these happen to be wicked people, as they are likely to be, it is needless to say that he will be spoilt in their company and acquire all sorts of bad habits. In other words he will be completely off the rails and will come to presume that he has the licence of doing anything he has a fancy to. He will finally turn a criminal and a ruffian posing a constant threat to the society at large.

It is for this reason that Islam urges upon us to choose an accomplished consort for ourselves coming of a noble family.

This should be done in all sincerity and good faith so that a permanent atmosphere of love and understanding might prevail between husband and wife. This would forestall any possibility of family feuds and discord between them.

In the first chapter of the present book we have dwelt on the basic rules and conditions of making a good choice of husband or wife for one's self, which constitute the cardinal principles of forming an ideal family with mutual love and affection among the members thereof.

III. Divorce and Consequent Destitution

Divorce between parents and the resultant evils also make the children go astray.

There can be no two opinions as to the fact that a child opening his eyes on the world finds himself deprived of mother's love and the care of a guarding father is drawn by the lure of criminal life and finally he turns a corrupt man, a vagrant and a bad character.

When the divorced mother marries someone else, things take a still worse turn for her children. In such a case they will turn vagabonds and be good for nothing. They will be swayed by caprices.

As the result of divorce a woman having children is reduced to a destitute and is forced to leave her home in quest of livelihood, abandoning the children to the perils of the world and the world does with them whatever it likes. Nothing can be expected from a generation that knows no parental love, compassion and care. Children who suffer from want with no food, clothing and shelter would prove to be of little service to the society. It is but natural that such children become vagabonds and delinquents, having the licence to do what they please.

It is exactly for this reason that Islam urges upon husbands and wives to respect their mutual rights so that their married life may not produce a tragic generation.

RIGHTS AND DUTIES OF HUSBAND AND WIFE

Obedience of husband doing anything good and useful is necessary for the wife. *Bazzaz* and *Tabarani* narrate the following incident that occurred during the Holy Prophet's lifetime.

"Some women deputed one of them as a representative and sent her to the Prophet (S.A.W.) with the message that Allah has declared *Jehad* obligatory for the males who, when victorious, get the booty or remain alive with the Creator getting their sustenance from Him. Should they fall martyrs, women look after their husbands. Would they not be rewarded for that? The Prophet (S.A.W.) replied: Tell whichever woman you meet with that obedience of husband and respect for his rights is equivalent to Jihad (striving in the way of Allah), but that only a few of you women do that."

Keeping Guard on One's Chastity and Husband's Property

"Shall I tell you what the best treasure a man can acquire? It is a good wife. When he looks at her she delights him, when he orders her to do something, she obeys him and when questions her about his property, she should have it in her safe custody and guard her chastity.

Respect of Husband's Wish

When the husband calls the wife to bed, she should not refuse to go to him. There is a tradition to this effect:

> The husband calls his wife to bed but she refuses to go and the husband remains displeased with her to whole night. The angels curse such wife till the day-break.

Hitherto we have discussed the husband's rights and wife's duties. We now proceed to discuss wife's rights and husband's duties.

(a) It is incumbent upon the husband to meet the expenses of his wife and children. Says Allah:

> "The duty of feeding and clothing of nursing mothers in a seemly manner is upon the father of the child." (2:233)

The Prophet (S.A.W.) has said, "Fear Allah in respect of women. You have accepted as a divine trust and have made their private parts lawful for yourselves. You are, therefore, under the obligation to feed and clothe them in a legitimate manner."

(b) It is the right of the wife to be consulted in domestic matters and the husband's duty to consult her. There is a saying of the Prophet (S.A.W.) to this effect which is cited below:

"Consult wives on their daughter's affair" (This means that husbands should seek the advice or rather permission of their wives before accepting marriage proposals for their daughters).

(c) The husband is under the obligation to ignore some blemishes of his wife because she may be having numerous traits that would conceal her faults. The Holy Prophet (S.A.W.) has said, "No believing man would bear ill-will against a believing woman. If any of her habits is unpalatable to him, some other habits may be agreeable." (*Sahih Muslim*)

(d) It is the duty of husband to consort with his wife kindly, as it is the right of the wife to receive kind treatment from her husband. He should be jovial with her and talk to her delightfully. Says Allah:

"Consort with them in kindness for if ye hate them, it may happen that ye hate a thing wherein Allah has placed much good." (4:19)

And the Prophet (S.A.W.) has observed: The best of you are those who are best in their treatment of wives, and I am the best of you all in this respect.

The following tradition is quoted in *Sahih Bukhari* and *Sahih Muslim:*

"The Prophet's wife Hazrat Aisha (R.A.A.) used to witness sports from the open space in the Prophet's mosque. When she did it the Prophet (S.A.W.) put his palm on the door and held out his arm. Hazrat Aisha (R.A.A.) placed her chin on the Prophet's shoulder."

Again, we have the following saying of the Holy Prophet (S.A.W.):

"The man with perfect faith is one who is the most polite and who behaves with his wife in a delightful manner. (*Bukhari and Muslim*)

There is yet another tradition that we find in *Sunan Abu Dawood* and *Sunan Nasai.* It runs as follows:

The Prophet (S.A.W.) used to race with Hazrat Aisha (R.A.A.). First the latter outpaced the Prophet (S.A.W.) and then the Prophet (S.A.W.) outran her. Having equalled the score, the Prophet (S.A.W.) said: "First you outpaced me and now I have outrun you. The score therefore, is equal."

Hazrat 'Umar, whose justice and fairplay is proverbial, has observed:

A man should be like a child when amidst his family, and when once out of door he should be manly like a rock.

(e) Lending a helping hand to wife in household work.

But consort with them in kindness (4: 19).

The way to implement the contents of this verse is as follows:

(i) Those under the obligation to rear children and look after them should duly fulfil their obligation and live up to the Prophet's Tradition :

"Man is the caretaker of his house and will be called to account for it." (*Bukhari and Muslim*)

(ii) Children should be guarded against factors leading to aberration from the moral norm. The Prophet commands:

"Do not harm others, nor be harmed by them."

(*Imam Malik, Ibn Majah*)

This principle requires that the parents and guardians should prevent children from reading books on sex and crime, detective and romantic fiction as well as literature that would lead them away from religion.

It is the duty of the husband to lend a helping hand to the wife in the household work and the wife has the right to get such help from him. In helping his wife, the husband will be following the example of the Holy Prophet (S.A.W.).

According to *Tabarani*, when asked what the Prophet (S.A.W.) did at home, Hazrat Aisha replied, "Just as what you normally do. He removes one thing and puts another thing in its place. He equally shares domestic work with his wives. He cuts the lumps of meat and sweeps the house also. Besides, he helps the servant in his work."

These then are the rights and duties of man and wife as

determined by Islam. They are not only completely in harmony with conjugal life but also fulfil the demands of justice. Conformity to the above rights and duties creates an atmosphere of harmony rather than of discord between husband and wife, love takes the place of hatred between them and the whole family consequently leads a happy and harmonious life. In such an atmosphere relations are seldom strained and nobody is the source of trouble to his or her partner.

Divorce:

Maltreatment and misbehaviour on the part of husband or wife results in discord and strained relations between them. If things come to divorce, the husband should take all precautions before resorting to it; for it may be possible to avoid such a drastic course of action and good sense between the couple may prevail.

Precautions to be taken in this connection are as follows:

(a) *Homily and Exhortation:*

The relevant verse of the Holy Quran should be translated with action.

"Keep on exhorting. Verily, exhortation benefits the believers." (51:55)

(b) *Separation of Bed:*

This is a psychological punishment. It is possible that this step brings the wife to reason.

(c) *Light Corporal Punishment That Does Not Cause Visible Injury:*

When the husband is sure that beating is the last resort to correct his wife, he should give her light beating in a manner that it does not result in any visible injury on her body. Care should be taken not to strike at the sensitive parts of her body such as the chest, face or stomach. If, the husband inflicts grievous injury, it would mean that he torments his wife for the sake of torment. On the contrary light beating would be taken to mean that the husband means no torture to her and that his chastisament is solely designed to correct and warn her.

The husband ought to know that the Holy Prophet

(S.A.W.) never struck a woman in his lifetime.

Ibn Sa'd quotes Hazrat Aishah (R.A.A.) to have said, "The Prophet (S.A.W.) never struck any woman with his hand. It is another thing, of course, that he may have done so during a holy war."

Ibn Sa'd again reports that whenever a woman complained to the Prophet (S.A.W.) of the physical punishment she got at the hands of her husband, the Prophet (S.A.W.) said to the man, "One of you strikes a woman as if he strikes a slave and a little later he embraces her unabashed."

(d) *Recourse to Mediation:*

This means an attempt at reconciliation or making peace between man and wife by providing an opportunity of mediation to the sensible and influential people representing both the parties. According to this method, the representatives of either party consider the complaints of man and wife against each other and try to make peace between them by furthering mutual understanding. This usually conduces to making amends by the parties for their respective faults and thus divorce is averted. This method of mediation between man and wife has been mentioned in the Holy Quran in the following words:

> As for those women from whom ye fear rebellion, admonish them and banish them to beds apart, and scourge them. Then if they obey you, seek not a way against them. Lo! Allah is Ever High, Exalted, Great.
>
> And if ye fear a breach between them twain (man and wife) appoint an arbiter from his folk and an arbiter from her folk. If they desire amendment Allah will make them of one mind. Allah is Ever Knower, Aware. (4:34-35)

If all these measures do not produce the desired effect and if it appears difficult to restore harmony between husband and wife then the husband should pronounce *Talaq* once during a period of cleanliness when he does not go to his wife for sexual purpose. Pronouncing '*Talaq*' only once initially is a precautionary measure allowing the couple one more chance for reunion and starting their normal conjugal life. Says Allah:

"If he divorces her, there is no blame on them both if

they return to each other if they think that they can keep within the limits of Allah. And these are the limits of Allah which He makes clear for people who know."
(2:230)

It is clear from the Quranic verses as well as the Prophet's traditions that all the measures mentioned above are to be taken before the marriage is actually dissolved; for divorce is pregnant with horrible consequences for the offspring of the separating couple. That is why the Prophet (S.A.W.) has said:

"With Allah the worst and yet lawful act is divorce,"

When divorce actually goes into effect i.e. after the dissolution of marriage (consequent three times), it is incumbent upon the husband to provide for the woman during her period of waiting as well as for the children so that the divorced woman and the children do not suffer. Says Allah:

"And provide for them, the wealthy according to his means and the strained according to his means, a provision according to usage. This is a duty on the doers of good." (2:236)

If the husband is poor and lacks the means to provide the necessities of life to the divorcee and his children, the Islamic Government is bound to provide those necessities to the children, arrange for their education and meet their other expenses till they grow up. This is the only effective way to save the children from the afflictions resulting from the dissolution of marriage between their parents and to prevent them from deviation. But apart from this responsibility of the Government, Islam urges upon the philanthropists among the Muslims to support such children whenever they come to know of their plight and earn the reward reserved for those who act on the following advice of the Holy Prophet (S.A.W.):

"Whoever has extra animal for riding should give it to the fellow traveller who does not have it; and whoever has extra provision for journey should give it to the fellow traveller who does not have it."

There are other sayings of the Holy Prophet (S.A.W.) to the same effect:

"Others too are entitled to a share in one's wealth, apart from the poor-due." (*Tabarani* and *Ibn Majah*)

Tabarani quotes the Prophet (S.A.W.) to have said: "Allah has made it obligatory for the well-to-do people to give to the destitutes so much out of their wealth as would suffice their needs. Destitutes without food and clothing are unable to work unless the wealthy help them. Doubtless, Allah will call to account (those who do not help) and give painful punishment."

Bazzaz and *Tabarani* quote also the following Tradition: "Whoever sleeps at night having eaten to his heart's content while knowing that his neighbour has gone to sleep without meal, has no faith."

How to Spend Leisure Time

The reason why children and boys in particular, go astray is that they spend their leisure time in aimless activities. As the child grows, he tends to take more and more interest in sports and nourishes increasing desire for being at leisure and enjoying the beauty of nature. We have observed that children are ever active, always doing this thing or that. Sometimes they are found playing, sometimes rubbing their heels on the ground, sometimes moving their legs in sleeping. At one time they are seen taking exercise and at another playing football. In view of this natural tendency among the children, it is necessary that the tutors and guardians provide guidance to them so that they may spend their leisure time in such activities as are profitable for their health,, strengthen their muscles and keep them physically fit.

Play and Exercises

If children are not provided with playing grounds to play freely, clubs to take exercise and build their bodies, facilities to get themselves educated and trained and opportunity to be active in a profitable manner, they gradually drift into bad company and associate with spoilt children, finally deviating from social norms and indulging in immoral activities.

Islam teaches us to inculcate in our children and youngsters the habit of doing acts that ensure their physical fitness and keep them hale and hearty.

The Vital Importance of Prayer

The best of all these acts is the habit of worship, particularly offering one's prayer five times a day, which according to Islam is the essence and pillar of faith.

Effects of Prayer on Health

(a) Prayer is a compulsory exercise wherein a Muslim moves his limbs and joints. It quickens the muscles, accelerates circulation of blood and stimulates the limbs.

(b) Prayer is the means of being cleanly. This is because a Muslim has to perform ablution in a prescribed manner before saying his prayer. Ablution is designed to cleanse the exposed parts of the body including the hair, mouth, nose and teeth. This procedure of cleansing the body is besides bath. When this becomes obligatory, the whole body is rubbed and washed. In addition, one has to keep one's body, clothes and place clean in order to be able to offer prayer.

What has been mentioned above comprises essential conditions of the validity of prayer.

By saying prayers regularly one gets into habit of keeping one's self mobile. One goes to the mosque five times a day and thus remains active the whole day long. This prevents one from being lethargic.

That revered man (S.A.W.) who never said anything to express his personal desires urges upon the parents to exhort the children to offer prayers when they are seven years old and get accustomed to offer it regularly and learn the rules prescribed for it. Says the Prophet (S.A.W.):

> "Instruct the children to offer prayer at the age of seven and force them to offer it by beating at the age of ten and separate their beds."

One must learn all the aspects of prayer including the state of mind, the different acts done in it, the surahs to be recited, the number of *rakats* both *Fard* (obligatory) and *sunnat* (additional prayer according to the Holy Prophet's practice). Training of all these things may be received from the parents at home or from the religious instructors at the mosque.

Arts of War, Sports Etc.

Besides, children should be trained in the arts of war, riding, swimming, jumping and wrestling when they are free.

If is necessary that the parents should get the children accustomed during their leisure hours to purposeful reading, decent entertainments and taking part in various games. For this purpose extensive playing grounds, big clubs, libraries, public centres, and swimming pools are required in the cities. Care, however, should be taken that Islamic decorum is maintained at all such places.

We cite here some of the Islamic injunctions in this regard. Says Allah:

"And make ready for them whatever force you can and horses tied at the frontier to frighten thereby the enemy of Allah and your enemy." (8:60)

There is yet another verse noteworthy in this context:

"Say: Are those who know and those who know not alike?" (39:9).

Hazrat Umar (R.A.A.) advises us: "Teach your children archery and swimming and call upon them to get the training of riding on horseback with a high jump."

The Prophet (S.A.W.) says, "Value five things before five things occur, viz;

(a) Life before death,
(b) Health before indisposition,
(c) Work before unemployment,
(d) Youth before old-age and
(e) Affluence before starvation. (*Hakim*, *Behaqi*)

The Prophet (S.A.W.) also calls upon us to practice archery (this would apply to shooting and the use of all the manual weapons) and do riding but says that he prefers archery to horsemanship. (*Nasai*, *Tirmizi*)

Again, the Holy Prophet (S.A.W.) has observed:

"Anything that does not remind of Allah is either a trifling, play or inadvertency with the exception of four things:-

(a) Walking between four marks (made by the archers (b) Taming the horse (c) Playing with one's wife and (d) Learning to swim. (*Tabarani and Hakim*)

Other relevant traditions of the Holy Prophet (S.A.W.) are as under:

"May the man be blessed who demonstrates his force before the enemy this day." (*Ibn Ishaq* and *Ibn Hisham*)

Once a few Abyssinians playing in the courtyard of the mosque with weapons used in war. The Prophet (S.A.W.) said to them:

"O ye people of *Irfida* do play as you do so that the jews may know that our faith is very *broad.*"

There is yet another tradition of Holy Prophet (S.A.W.) worthy of mention in this context:

'With Allah a strong believer is better and dearer than a weaker one. Evertything has an advantage. You should like the thing that benefits you. Seek help from Allah and do not lose heart. When you are distressed by the results of anything you do, say not: Had I done such and such thing, such and such would have been the outcome. You should rather say: What has happened to me is that which Allah had predetermined. The conditional conjunction 'if' is expressive of Satan's doing.

If parents, guardians and tutors translate the teachings of Islam into practice, their children would be healthy, educated and strong. They will not move in bad company and consequently deteriorate morally or go astray. On the contrary they would do something good in their leisure hours and thus ameliorate their life in this world as well as in the Hereafter. They will grow up to be the proud soldiers and missionaries of Islam.

Bad Company

Bad company corrodes the innate capacities of children. Boys who fall a prey to bad company lack intelligence and strength of character and belief. They turn wicked by associating with vagabonds and bad characters and turn out to be the worst criminals. Deviation and vagrancy predominate their character and finally they become completely incorrigible and are irredeemably ruined.

Islam urges upon the parents and guardians to keep an eye on the children. It calls for circumspective vigilance on their activities from morning till evening when they reach the age of discretion and for ascertaining the sort of company they keep.

Islam approves of making friends with good boys so that the children may acquire commendable habits and get accustomed to decorum. On the other hand it lays stress on shunning bad company in order to prevent the children from going astray:

The Holy Quran enjoins avoidance of wicked people's company in the following words:

On the day when the wrong-doer gnaweth his hand, he will say, "Ah, would that I had chosen a way together with the Messenger of Allah!

Alas for me! Ah, would that I had never taken such a one for friend!

He verily led me astray from the Reminder after it had reached me. Satan was ever man's deserter in the hour of need." (25:27-29).

His comrade will say! Our Lord! I did not cause him to rebel; but he was himself far gone in error. (50:27)

"Friends on that day will be foes one to another, save who kept their duty to Allah." (43:67)

Says the Holy Prophet (S.A.W.):

"A man acquires the habits of his intimate friends. See who of you has made friends with whom."

Sahih Bukhari and *Muslim* contain the following tradition:

A good companion and a bad one are to be compared to the *musk* dealer and the man who blows in the furnace respectively. The former will either sell his *musk* or give it to you as a present. In either case, the fragrance of the *musk* will delight you. As for the man who blows in the furnace will either burn your clothes or will emit offensive smell.

Tirmizi gives another tradition to the same effect:

"Shun the company of a bad man becuase you will be

known by his company."

It is incumbent upon the parents to act on the divine injunctions and Prophet's teachings and thus enrich them with moral excellence and make them praiseworthy so that their character may serve as symbol of goodness and a source of inspiration for the Islamic *Ummah*. Their accomplishments will lead to the uplift of the entire society and entire *Ummah* will be proud of them.

Maltreatment of Children by Parents

All the authorities on child psychology are unanimous that if parents and guardians maltreat their children by chastizing them severely, rebuking them all the time, heaping insults upon them, calumniating and mocking them, the children will react strongly and behave in a revengeful manner. Constant fear and frustration would result in the release of pent-up emotions in their behaviour. Things will finally come to such a pass that they would either commit suicide or kill their parents or run away from home for good in order to escape oppressive treatment at the hands of their parents.

The parents should not be surprised if such children emerge as the most dangerous criminals and deviate from the social norms with unconstrained freedom; nor is their lack of manners and incomplaisance something unexpected.

The eternal and correct teachings of Islam require every responsible guardian and dutiful parent to set an example of moral excellence. Mete out to children affectionate and compassionate treatment so that they may be cultivated on the right lines, imbued with courage and strength of character and realize that the parents have great affection with them and hold them in high esteem.

The teachings of Islam provide us the following guidance in this respect:

Says Allah:

"Allah enjoineth justice and kindness and giving to kinsfolk (according to the right)." (16:90)

Besides:

"(Believers are those) who control their wrath and are

forgiving toward mankind; Allah loveth the benevolent." (3:134)

Another relevant verse is:

"Be soft spoken to the people" (2:83)

Again,

"Had you been of bad temper and callous, these people would have gone away from you." (3:159)

Imam Bukhari quotes the following saying of the Holy Prophet (S.A.W.):

"Allah likes mildness in all matters."

According to another tradition the Prophet (S.A.W.) said:

Allah engenders mildness among the members of a family to which He intends to do good. Had mild disposition been a creature it would have been the best of all creatures and had bad temper been a creature, it would have been the worst of all creatures.

Abu Shaikh cites the following tradition of the Holy Prophet (S.A.W.) in his book *'Thawab'*:

"Allah blesses the father who helps his son in doing good."

According to another tradition the Prophet (S.A.W.) is reported to have observed:

"Allah the Merciful has mercy on those who are compassionate. Have compassion for the people of the earth and the One Who is in heaven shall have mercy on you."

These are the principles bestowed by Islam with regard to the kind treatment of children and dealing with their affairs in the best possible manner. If the parents desire that their children should live with honour and be enriched with moral excellence and decent social behaviour, it is incumbent upon them to translate the principles of Islam and fulfill all the Islamic requirements.

Oppressive parents commit a great sin by maltreating their children. They would be breeding them on wrong lines by setting an example with their nefarious behaviour. In fact they lead their children astray themselves and persuade them to disobey by their own behav ur, for them house is the first school where children receive their initial training and education. It should, therefore, be taken for granted that it is the parents who sow the seeds of rebellion in their offspring.

Once a man came to Hazrat Umar (R.A.A.) and complained of his son's disobedience. Hazrat Umar summoned the boy and rebuked him for his insolence and negligence of his duty toward his parents.

The boy enquired, "O ruler of believers! Does a son has no rights to his father?"

Hazrat 'Umar replied that the sor did have his rights.

"May I ask what those rights are", said the boy.

"Well, the choice of a mother with sterling qualities (i.e. marrying a virtuous woman who could breed his children well), giving him a good name and teaching him the Holy Quran"

The boy said, "My father did nothing of the sort. As for my mother, she is a negro. She was formerly a *Zoroastrian.* My father calls me a *gabrela* (young one of a magian) and he has not taught me a single verse of the Holy Quran."

Hazrat Umar, then, turned to the boy's father and said to him, "You have come to me to complain of your son's disobedience in spite of the fact that you maltreated him and did him the harm which inevitably resulted in his rebellion."

Thus Hazrat 'Umar (R.A.A.) held the man responsible for his son's disobedience as he did not fulfil his obligations with regard to the boy's training.

It has been mentioned in some of the books of biographies that once *Hazrat Moaviya bin Abu Sufyan* was displeased with his son Yazeed. He sent a messenger to *Ahnaf bin Qais* to seek his advice in the matter. Ahnaf's reply was as follows:

"Children are our hope and our sheet anchor. We are to them like soft soil and the canopy of sky. If children want to have anything, give it to them; if they are displeased try to appease them. This would make them love you and would work for you hard. Don't be a burden upon them; otherwise they will be fed up with you and wish you dead."

The moral we may draw from the observation made by *Hazrat Umar* and *Hazrat Ahnaf bin Qais* is that we should be kind to our children and adopt suitable methods to correct and cultivate them.

The Harm Lascivious and Detective Films Do

Films consisting of sex and detective stories and scenes have a share in the subversion of children. Such films cause their moral deterioration and make them wicked. The feats of police and the obscene scenes shown in the cinema halls and on the TV screens can never produce salutary effects on their mind. Moreover, subversive literature and lustful fiction also cause irreparable damage to them. Their lust-inciting and immoral contents would subvert even the grown up people not to speak of youngsters.

It is evident that when the boy sees obscene, lascivious and detective films and reads fiction of similar nature at the age of discretion, all the scenes shown in such films or the events related in such fiction are indelibly imprinted on their minds. They are recollected again and again and consequently the boys start doing all that they may have seen or read. There can be nothing more harmful to them than the kind of films or fiction mentioned above.

it goes without saying that children who enjoy unrestrained freedom and are not looked after properly are bound to go astray.

It is an undeniable fact that the scenes of subversive films exercise such a harmful influence on boys in their teens that no efforts of parents or tutors can set them right.

In view of the fact mentioned above it is more incumbent upon the parents to bring up their children on the right lines and refrain from denying them their rights.

Saving children from the subversive films and literature is a part of the parents' duty. They are also under the obligation to prevent them from any deed that may incur Allah's wrath and their perpetual chastisement.

Says Allah:

"O ye who believe! save yourselves and your families from the Fire." (66:6)

The way to implement the contents of this verse is as follows :

(i) Those under the obligation to rear children and look after them should duly fulfil their obligation and live up to the Prophet's tradition:

"Man is the caretaker of his house and will be called to account for it." (*Bukhari* and *Muslim*).

(ii) Children should be guarded against factors leading to aberration from the moral norm. The Prophet (S.A.W.) commands: "Do not harm others, nor be harmed by them." (*Imam Malik — Ibn Majah*)

This principle requires that the parents and guardians should prevent children from reading books on sex and crime, detective and romantic fiction as well as literature that would lead them away from religion. In short, children should be disallowed aught subversive and irreligious.

We will discuss in greater details the question of breeding and upbringing children in the Second Volume of this work wherein the relevant basic principles of Islam would be dwelt on for the benefit of those interested in Islam which is the religion of nature and reformation as well as a way of life. A knowledge of the above principles would enable them to bring up their offspring on the right lines:

"Who is better than Allah for judgment to a people who have certainty in their belief?" (5:50)

Unemployment

General lack of job opportunities in the society also causes juvenile delinquency. If the head of a family is jobless and has no means to earn his livelihood otherwise, nor any money to feed his children and wife and meet their various needs then all the members of the family would desert him and try to find ways and means to satisfy their wants on their own. The father himself, overburdened with heavy responsibilities would try to earn his living by unlawful means in league with other miscreants. Such means include felonies like larceny, robbery, extortion and bribery. This would mean that the entire comunity would sink into the abyss of corruption and consequently head fast towards a catastrophe.

As Islam bestows the principles of social justice and

enjoins the protection of collective rights, it also provides for the remedy of unemployment. The cause of unemployment may be either non-availability of a job or idleness.

Unemployment resulting from paucity of jobs or something else means that the man wants to do something but is unable to do it although he does have the potentiality of doing it. In such a case the government would either provide a suitable job to him or the members of the society would be under the obligation to extend him financial help.

The responsibility resting with the government in this respect is proved by a tradition narrated by Hazrat Anas:

He relates that an *Ansari* (a local inhabitant of Madina) came to the Prophet (S.A.W.) and asked for alms. The Prophet (S.A.W.) asked him if he had any belongings. The man replied, "Yes, I have a thick sheet of cloth which serves partly as a bedding and partly as something to cover us. We also have a bowl with which we drink water."

The Prophet (S.A.W.) commanded him to fetch both the things and the man obeyed. The Holy Prophet then took them from the man and said to the people present at the moment. "Who of you will buy these things?"

There was a prompt response from one of them, "I am willing to buy them for two *dirhams.*".

The Prophet (S.A.W.) exchanged the two things for the price offered and handing the two *dirhams* to the owner said, "Spend one *dirham* on feeding yourself."

The man did accordingly and returned to the Prophet (S.A.W.) with an axe. The Prophet (S.A.W.) fixed a handle to the axe with his own hand and said to the man, "Go and cut the wood and sell it." "And listen," added the Prophet (S.A.W.), "I do not want to see your face for fifteen days."

The man took the Prophet's advice and when he turned he had accumulated ten *dirhams.* He bought clothing for some of those dirhams and food for the remainder. The Prophet (S.A.W.) then said to him, "This is much better for you than the stain of begging on your face with which you would have arisen on the Day of Judgment and presented yourself to Allah."

The following tradition bears it out that it is the responsibility of the society to meet the needs of a jobless person till he secures employment. The narrator of the tradition is *Abu Saeed Khudri* (R.A.) The Prophet (S.A.W.) said:

"The man who has extra conveyance should give it to one who has none and the traveller who has extra provision should give it to the fellow-traveller who has none."

In another tradition the Prophet (S.A.W.) is quoted to have said:

"The man having had meal to his heart's content goes to sleep knowing that his next door neighbour is hungry, has no faith in me at all."

Also says the Prophet (S.A.W.):

"Allah and His Prophet (S.A.W.) are absolved from tutelage of the affluent amidst whom a poor man dies unhelped."

The words of another tradition in the same context are as under:

"If anyone feeds him (the destitute alluded to in the above tradition) and gives him something by way of help, others are absolved from blame."

(*Kitab Ikhtiar-ul-Taleel-ul-Mukhtar*)

Unemployment Due to Idleness

Some people who are lethargic, like to remain idle although they can work and secure a job. It is the responsibility of the Government to keep strict vigil on such individuals. If it comes to the notice of the authorities that someone evades or shirks work, he should be urged to work and should be told of the dignity of labour. If he does not pay heed to such advice, then he should be forced to work.

Ibn Jauzi (a biographer of Hazrat Umar R.A.A.) writes that Hazrat Umar (R.A.A.) met some persons who did no work. He said to them, "What sort of guys are you?"

"We are fatalists resigned to the Will of Allah," they replied.

"No, you are, liars", retorted Hazrat 'Umar (R.A.A.), "A person who is resigned to the Will of Allah is one who sows the seed and leaves the crop to Allah to make it grow and bear fruit." The Caliph further added, "None of you should give up work and pray to God to provide for him, though he knows that silver and gold do not fall from the blue."

It was Hazrat 'Umar (R.A.A.) who exhorted paupers depending on charity not to sit idle in their closets. He reminded them of the Prophet's saying, "O You indolents! excel in doing good acts and don't be a burden on the Muslims!"

The above statement of Hazrat 'Umar (R.A.A.) seems to imply that in Islam the poor-tax is paid to meet the needs of the indigent and to provide them means of livelihood so that the people may not become idlers and parasites like drones thriving on the output of bees. However, the government is under the obligation to meet the needs of the old, the sick and the handicapped who cannot work to earn their livelihood. The government should see to it that such people lead better life and that the believers and non-believers alike are ensured the benefits of social security. Hazrat *Imam Abu Yousuf* recites an incident in his book "*Kitab-ul-Kharaj*":

"Hazrat 'Umar (R.A.A.) saw a pauper begging alms at the door of a house as he passed by it. He was both old and blind. Hazrat Umar (R.A.A.) caught him by the hand from behind and asked, "Which of the People of Books do you belong to?" He replied that he was a Jew. "Who was it that drove you to this extremity?", the Caliph asked: He replied, "I am just asking something for the amount of *Jizia.* I grew old and infirm and have to meet my needs." Hazrat 'Umar (R.A.A.) took the needy Jew home and gave him something. He then summoned the government Treasurer and said to him, "Look at this destitute. There may be many others like him. By God! we shall be doing injustice if we leave him without support in old age after having used up the earnings of his youth (i.e. the amount of *Jizya* paid by him). Chartitable contributions are meant for the paupers and the destitutes. People of Books like him are destitutes."

There is another incident related about Hazrat 'Umar (R.A.A.). Once he passed through the habitation of a Christian clan. All the people belonging to it were suffering from white leprosy. Hazrat 'Umar (R.A.A.) issued orders that they should be paid from the public exchequer so much amount as would suffice to meet their needs and expenses of medical treatment in a manner that their sense of self-respect is not injured."

This is the remedy of unemployment that Islam provides for. It is not only based on the principle of justice but is also full of wisdom and compassion. The incidents related above also bear it out that Islam is a religion of love and mercy, of humanitarianism and justice. Allah has revealed Islam as a beacon-light for the guidance of mankind, which illuminates the dark alleys of life. The person who is insensible to these facts cannot know what Islam is like and that the Holy Prophet (S.A.W.) was sent as a luminary for the guidance of humanity.

Parent's Apathy towards Children's Upbringing

One of the causes of children's misconduct, moral degeneration and underdeveloped personality is parent's indifference to their training refinement and education.

So far as the mother is concerned she is the very embodiment of love for her children. She bears the child in her body for months together and finally gives birth to it. When it comes into the world she meets all its needs and looks after it in every possible way. The verse of a poet may aptly be quoted in this context:

"Mother's bosom is a school. Prepare it properly and you will have produced a whole nation of well-bred and noble people."

Both the parents have to share equal responsibilities with regard to children; or to be more correct, mother's responsibilities are greater and much more important. For it is she who takes care of the child right from its birth and continues to do so till it grows up. She leaves no stone unturned to fulfil its needs during that period. It is exactly for this reason that the Holy Prophet (S.A.W.) has referred to mother's specific responsibilities apart from those of others.

"And the mother is caretaker of her husband's household and is responsible for looking after it (i.e. she will be questioned about it."

The Prophet's remark is designed to make the mother realize that her responsibilities with regard to her children are equal to those of her husband. She must, therefore, fully co-operate with her husband in the task of breeding and cultivating the children. If both the parents fail in this task with mother devoting all her time to other activities like entertaining guests at home or having good time as a host of her friends or remains out of doors absolutely oblivious of her children, and the father similarly spends most of his time enjoying the company of the friends complacently, their children would consequently grow like orphans. Their personalities would remain disintegrated with complexes and phobias. Such children would corrupt the society and would, in the ultimate analysis, mar the entire Muslim Ummah.

The plight of such children has been aptly depicted by a poet who says:

"An orphan is not one who has been left behind in the world by his parents miserable without any support but one whose mother has abandoned him whilst she is alive and whose father is egocentric and self-indulgent."

Nothing can indeed be expected from parents who thus wash their hands off their offsprings. And the children deprived of mother's watchful eye and training and of the process of disciplining and cultivation by the father would naturally tend to be delinquents and criminals.

Should the parents themselves happen to be deprived indulging in debauchery regardless of what is lawful and unlawful, their offspring would turn incorrigibly immoral and criminal: for such offspring cannot but tread in the footsteps of their parents. Says a poet:

"Plants and vegetation growing in the garden is dissimilar to that grown in the jungle."

This is true of the way the children are brought up. Children who have sucked milk from the breasts of faulty women cannot be expected to attain perfection. Islam imposes heavy responsibilities on the parents with regard to the breeding and training of children. According to the teachings of Islam it is incumbent upon the parents to bring up their children in a manner that they are enabled to shoulder the responsibilities of life. It should be impressed upon the children's mind that if they fail in the due discharge of their responsibilities they will have to suffer a painful chastisement. Says Allah:

"O ye who believe! Save your family from the fire whose fuel consists of human-beings. This fire is guarded by stern and powerful angels, who never disobey Allah and do only what they are commanded to. (66:6)

The Prophet (S.A.W.) also repeatedly stressed the need to look after the children with great care and called upon the parents to fulfil their requirements and train them properly. The following traditions may be cited in this context:

(a) "Every man is the guardian in his house and shall be questioned about his duty of guardianship. And every woman is the caretaker of her husband's household and shall be questioned about her obligations in respect of house-keeping." (*Bukhari and Muslim*)

(b) "Teach your children manners, teach them excellent manners." (*Ibn Majah*)

(c) "Teach your children goodness and teach them how best to behave in life." (*Abdur Razzaq and Saeed bin Mansoor*)

(d) "Command your children to act on the injunctions of Islam and refrain from doing acts forbidden by it. This is one of the ways to save them from the fire." (*Ibn Jareer*)

(e) Teach your children three things:
   (i) To love their Prophet (S.A.W.)
   (ii) To love the Prophet's family
   (iii) "To recite the Holy Quran. This is necessary because those who carry the Quran in their hearts (and act thereon) would be under the shadow of God's Throne and there will be a day on which there will be no other shadow."

Responsibilities imposed upon the guardians in respect of training the children will be dealt with in the second volume of this book.

Orphanhood

Children are spoilt also because of orphanhood. Such children, as are deprived of the care of their parents in their early years, develop a sense of frustration.

An orphan is one whose father is dead in his or her early childhood. Such child finds no one who has compassion for him. If the guardian treats him badly instead of loving him and pays no heed to his training and education in order to enable him to lead a life befitting a human being nor is he given sufficient food to eat then such an orphan will inevitably deviate from the moral norm. He will gradually drift towards criminal life and will finally tear the texture of the Muslim Ummah, causing disorder in the society and vitiate the morals of the whole young generation.

It is for this reason that Islam calls on the guardians and close relations of the orphan to treat him well, meet his requirements and look after him properly. Islam enjoins the guardians of the orphan to train and educate him and teach him manners and morals so that he may grow to be an accomplished and thorough gentleman. The guardians should have affection and compassion for him and mete out kind treatment to him in all sincerity.

Some of the Islamic injunctions enjoining kind and compassionate treatment of the orphans are as follows:

"And they question thee (O Muhammed) concerning the orphans: Say to improve their lot is best. And if ye mingle their affairs with theirs then (they are) your brothers." (2:220)

"Oppress not the orphan" (93:9)

"Have you observed him who calls the judgment a lie? That is the one who treats the orphan with harshness." (107:1-2)

"Those who devour the wealth of orphans wrongfully, they do but swallow fire into their bellies and they will be exposed to burning flames." (4:10)

These were the Quranic injunctions. We cite here some of the Prophet's sayings also to the same effect:

"He who puts his hand on the head of an orphan (receives him compassionately), will be rewarded by Allah by recording as many good acts to his credit as the number of hair on his head." (*Ahmed and Ibn Hibban*)

"Whoever takes an orphan amidst the Muslims and shares food with him till the orphan is able to stand on his own feet, Allah would ensure for such a person a place in Paradise, provided that he is not guilty of any major sin."
(*Tirmizi*)

"I and the person providing for an orphan would be in Paradise like these two fingers (the Prophet (S.A.W.) pointed his middle finger and the finger next to the thumb)."

In the light of these divine injunctions and the Prophet's edicts, the maintenance of an orphan is incumbent on his or her close relatives. And if these relatives are indigent themselves, it is the responsibility of the Government to look after the orphan and meet his needs. This would exclude the possibility of the orphan's deviation and he would have no sense of frustration of being forlorn.

These, then, were the causes of juvenile delinquency that force a serious threat to the society as a whole. If the parents, guardians and teachers do not take steps to remove those causes and seek guidance from Islam in the task of upbringing children, they will sink deep into depravity and turn criminals and would not only jeopardize the security of the Muslim Ummah but would finally imperil the tranquillity of the entire humanity. They would proceed on the path of sin and crime too far to bring them back to the moral and social norms.

The parents and guardians would be best advised to follow the dictates of Islam in the training and disciplining of children and prevent them from going astray. They should translate the principles of Islam into action and make righteous individuals of them and implant in their hearts the belief in Islam firmly. They should inculcate in them cardinal virtues and teach them how to conduct themselves in a decent and polite manner so that they may appear to be as good as angels both in respect of spiritual purification and adherence to the divine injunctions. It is such progeny as this that serves as a model of uprightness, moral excellence and sacrifice to other nations.

In the end I pray to Allah in all humility to enable the

sons of Islam to come up to the expectations of Islam, to bless them with the firmness of faith, to turn them into individuals whose deeds are in tune with their words and make such an Ummah out of them that would lay the foundation of an immaculate civilization to spread the light of knowledge and such an Ummah that would be strong enough to triumph over the forces of evil and turn the course of history. I pray to Allah to restore the former glory of Islam and that is not difficult for Him. All praise be to the Lord of the universe!

CHAPTER VII

RESPONSIBILITIES OF GUARDIANS

Various responsibilities are imposed upon the guardians in connection with the upbringing of children. They are enumerated as follows:

(1) Religious Training
(2) Moral Training
(3) Physical Training
(4) Intellectual Training
(5) Training of Personality
(6) Social Training and
(7) Sexual Training.

Islam imposed heavy responsibility upon guardians who are entrusted by the community with the task of educating and schooling the children. This is an onerous task indeed. It is difficult in proportion as it is important. It begins after a few years of the child's birth and continues up to the age of pubescence, when the grown up child comes under the obligation of adhering to Islamic injunctions and abiding by social conventions.

Whoever the guardian may be, the teacher, the father, the mother or some other caretaker appointed by the community, if he honestly discharges his responsibility in this regard and fulfils the obligations imposed upon him with determination and in conformity to the Islamic requirements, he may be said to have mobilized all his energies, talents and abilities to build the character of an individual and succeeded in the due discharge of his duties. He can then be expected to raise the edifice of a virtuous family. If he achieves this much he undoubtedly paves the way for the creation of an ideal society. The procedure prescribed by Islam is to begin with the individual then proceed to the improvement of the family and finally of the society at large.

The responsibilities of guardians whose importance has been stressed in the Holy Quran and the Prophet's (S.A.W.) traditions constitute the mandatory obligations imposed upon them and that proved the vitality of the responsibilities in question. In other words, they are not to be neglected as such on any account.

We cite here some of the verses of the Holy Quran to this effect:

"And enjoin prayer on thy people (members of family) and strictly adhere to it (thyself)." (20:132)

"O Ye who believe! Ward off from yourselves and your families a fire." (67:6).

"And certainly you will be questioned what you did." (16:93)

"Allah chargeth you concerning your children." (4:11)

"And mothers should suck the offspring for a period of two years." (2:223)

"They are not to kill their children." (60:12).

"And stop them, for they must be questioned." (37:24).

Some relevant traditions of the Holy Prophet (S.A.W.) are as follows:

(1) "Man is the caretaker of his family and he will be questioned about his charge. Woman is also the keeper of her husband's house, she will be questioned about her task."

(2) It is much better for a man to discipline his children and teach them manners than to give a measure (consisting of about 7 lbs.) of grains in charity. (*Tirmizi*)

(3) No father can bestow on his offspring anything better than propriety." (*Tirmizi*)

(4) Acquaint your family with goodness and teach them discipline." (*Abdur Razzaq, Saeed bin Mansoor*)

(5) Imbibe in your children three things:

(i) Love of the Prophet (ii) Love of the Holy Prophet's family (iii) Recitation of the Holy Quran."

(6) *Abu Sulaiman Malik bin Huwairith* narrates that a few young men including myself went on a visit to the Holy Prophet (S.A.W.) and stayed with him for twenty nights. The Prophet (S.A.W.) felt that we were badly missing the members of our family. He was an extremely compassionate person. He asked us whom we had left behind. We told him about our families whereupon he said to us, "Go to your families, educate them and ask them to do all that I am doing; say prayers as you see me say, and when the

time for prayer comes one of you should recite the call to prayer and the oldest of your should lead the prayer. (*Al-Adab-Al-Mufrad lil Bukhari*)

(7) "As long as the following five questions are not replied by an individual on the Doomsday, his or her feet will not shake:

(i) In what activities did he waste his life?

(ii) How did he make use of his youthful years?

(iii) How did he spend

(iv) How did he earn?

(v) How far did he translate his knowledge into practice?

The foregoing verses of the *Holy Quran* and sayings of the Holy Prophet (S.A.W.) create awareness in parents and guardians with regard to the breeding and training of children.

Our ancestors never lost sight of the Quranic verses and the Prophet's traditions in bringing up their children. They attached great importance to their upbringing on the right lines and this practice continued from generation to generation. They entrusted their kids to the best available scholars and teachers for education and training. It is these people who are best qualified for imparting Islamic education and the giving right kind of training to youngsters and for imbibing in them the Islamic beliefs.

We quote here some facts from history bearing testimony to the great importance attached by our forefathers to the schooling and education of their offspring.

Jahiz narrates that when *Afia bin Abi Sufian* entrusted his sons to the care of a teacher, he said to him, "Before correcting and disciplining you should have an eye on your faults and get rid of them; for their accomplishment would be linked with your outlook. Whatever you regard as good and whatever you treat as bad, they too would treat it to be so. Relate to my sons the events of lives of the wise and acquaint them with the morals and manners of the men-of-letters. Admonish them on my behalf and teach them morals. Play the role of a physician in schooling them; for a physician gives medicine to his patient after careful thought and does not make haste in prescribing it. Please do not act on any possible excuse from me. I repose trust in you, taking it for granted that your tutelage is sufficient guarantee to educate and train them."

Ibn Khaldoon writes in his *Muqaddima:*

The Caliph *Haroon-al-Rashid* entrusted his son Ameen to a tutor and while doing so he said to the tutor; "Listen. O Ahmer! The Caliph assigns his dear son to your tutelage. Take him into your care. He will be under the obligation to obey you. You will treat him in the manner as the Caliph expects you to treat him (i.e. since you have been appointed tutor, you should act like a tutor). Teach him the *Holy Quran.* Acquaint him with the news and events. Make him learn poetry by heart. Teach him how to behave in life. Create in him the sense of propriety so that he may known what to say suiting the occasion and how to say it. Prevent him from laughing out of place and provide him the opportunity to benefit from every moment of your guardianship without giving him a cause to feel dejected. Dejection would thwart his mental capacities. You should not be too lenient with him; for this would make him an idler. Make him honest and upright with rapport and benignant attitude. But if these methods fail, then be hard upon him and rebuke him severely."

One of the methods adopted by our ancestors in the education of their offspring was the establishment of strong relations (close rapport) between the tutors and the children. If the tutors were not close with them for some reason or the other they felt distressed thinking that their children were not being educated satisfactorily. *Imam Raghib-al-Asfahani* writes:

"The Abbaside Caliph *Mansoor* asked his *Omayyad* captives: What troubled you most in captivity? They replied: We were distressed because we were unable to look after the education of our children."

Abdu Malik bin Marwan had the following advice to offer to his son's tutor:

"Teach them truth just as you teach Quran. Persuade them to develop good habits. Teach them poetry so that they may be courageous and brave. Let them accompany you when you meet scholars and noble people. Prevent them from associating with the churls and inferior people for such people are ill-mannered and immoral as compared to others. Respect them in the presence of others but admonish them in private. Chastize them for telling lies, for lies lead to calumniation and calumniation in its turn leads to the fire."

A philosopher said to his son's teacher, "Do not take them from one field of knowledge into another field until they attain proficiency in the first field because thinking goes wrong when intellect is overtaxed".

Hazrat 'Umar bin Khattab (R.A.A.) wrote the people of Syria in one of his letters:

"Train your offspring in swimming, archery and horsemanship."

Avicenna's advice with regard to the training and schooling of children is as follows:

"The classfellows of a child in his class should be well-bred children having good manners and habits, because a child quickly acquires the habits of another child and befriends
him in a very short span of time."

Hisham bin Abdul Malik had this advice to offer to the tutor of his son. "Here is my son who has been fostered and reared under my care. I now entrust him to your tutelage for training and teaching him discipline. I advise you to teach him the Divine Book first of all. After that teach him poetry; take him round the Arab tribes; make him learn by heart selected verses of the poets from each tribe; make him learn by heart selected verses of the poets from each tribe; create in him the sense of the legitimate and the illegitimate, as well as the taste for good poetry and distaste for worthless poetry and also relate to him the stories of war and tribulations."

There were a few allusions to the selection of the tutors of the highest order for the schooling and education of children designed to make the teachers and tutors of today realize the vital importance of schooling and teaching the kids which constitutes their basic responsibility. Children are entrusted to them to play the role of custodians. If they neglect their responsibility, they will be taken to task and called to account on the Doomsday.

As the parents and teachers are under the obligation to train and educate the children enabling them to live judiciously, they should fully understand the extent of their responsibility, the various aspects of their task as well as the manner in which that responsibility is to be fulfilled.

There are seven phases or aspects of the training and education of children which are as under:—

(1) Religious training or Inculcation of Belief.
(2) Moral training,
(3) Physical training,
(4) Intellectual training
(5) Psychological training or the Development of Personality
(6) Social or Collective training and
(7) Sexual Training.

In this books we propose to deal with these seven phases of training.

INCULCATION OF BELIEF

What is meant by inculcation of belief is that as soon as the child attains the age of discretion he should be acquainted with the tenets of faith and the essential elements of Islam and should be taught the basic principles of the Shariah.

The Tenets of Faith

The tenents of faith mean to believe sincerely in the unknown and the invisible realities which are proven beyond a shadow of doubt. Faith in such realities includes the following beliefs:—

(1) Belief in Allah (His Existence and Unity).
(2) Belief in the Angels.
(3) Belief in all the revealed Books.
(4) Belief in all the messengers of Allah.
(5) Belief in the fact that two angels are appointed to question a man or woman after his or her death as well as the fact that the wicked are tormented in the graves; that resurrection, accountability in the Hereafter, the blissful life of Heaven and the torments of Hell are inevitable.

The Elements of Faith

The elements of faith include all the forms of worship both physical and performing such as prayer, fasting Zakat and performance of Hajj provided that one can afford to perform it.

The Basic Principles of Shariat

They cover anything relating to the order of life designed by Allah and the teachings of Islam; for instance, beliefs, the forms of worship, morals, law-making, decorum of life, rules etc.

Hence it is incumbent upon parents and guardians to bring up children in accordance with the fundamental teachings of Islam so that they may steeped in the Islamic faith with all its beliefs, forms of worship and way of life. When thus cultivated, they would be welded to Islam heart and soul with no guide other than the Holy Quran and with no leader other than the Holy Prophet (S.A.W.) to follow.

We regard inculcation of faith as all-inclusive in the light of the Prophet's edicts in which he calls for acquainting children with the tenets of faith, the elements of Islam and the injunctions of Shariah. Some of his edicts and traditions to this effect are cited below:-

> "Teaching how to recite the Kalima expressive of Allah's Unity."

When the child learns to speak he should first of all be taught how to say the *kalima* whereby faith in Islam is confessed. This *kalima* is expressive of the absolute Unity of Allah and belief in the prophethood of Muhammed (S.A.W.). As we have the evidence of Hakim who quotes in his Musnad Ibn Abbas to have narrated that the Prophet (S.A.W.) has enjoined to teach our children as soon as they learn to speak the *kalima*:"

"There is no god other than Allah."

The Advantage of Teaching Kalima

By learning *Kalima* at impressionable age, the first words the child understands are those that constitute the proof of his embracing Islam.

In this context we have explained at the outset under the head of the injunctions relating to birth of a child that saying *'Azan'* in the baby's right ear and *Iqamat* in its left ear is an approbatory and commendable act. This is the best and most effective method of inculcating faith.

The child is to be acquainted with injunctions relating to the lawful and the unlawful as soon as he attains the age of discretion.

Ibn Juraij and Ibn Mansoor both quote the following tradition with reference to Ibn Abbas:

> "Act in obedience to Allah and refrain from disobeying him. Command your offspring to comply with injunctions and abstain from whatever is forbidden. This will ensure yours as well as your offsprings safety from the fire."

The wisdom of all this is that as soon as the child is capable of perception, he should be familiarized with the divine commands and it should be seen that he or she acts on those commands. The child should also be accustomed to abstinence from the acts forbidden by Islam. And no sooner the child reaches the age of discretion, he should be acquainted with what is lawful and unlawful. If his link is established with Islam in early childhood he will find that there is no law and no way of life other than Islam.

The child is to be Ordered to Observe the Norms of Worship.

According to Abu Dawood Hazrat Abdullah bin Amr bin 'Aas reported the Prophet (S.A.W.) to have said, "When your sons are seven years old ask them to offer prayers and if they do not offer prayer at the age of ten, then beat them and let them have separate beds."

On the analogy of this edict regarding prayer the children should be made to observe fast at a certain age provided that they have the strength to do so. If the father of a child can bear the expenses of his Hajj he should also be habituated to perform it.

The advantage of such training is that the child learns all the forms of worship in his early childhood and is accustomed to observing them at an early state. It is also designed to breed children on the basis of obedience to Allah to inbue them with a sense of gratitude to Him and habituate them to seek His protection, trust in Him and to bow to Him in all humility. By adhering to the forms of worship the child's soul would be purified, his body would be healthy, his conduct would be set right and he would be edified.

Love of the Prophet and his family and recitation of the Holy Quran.

Hazrat Ali (R.A.A.) reports the Holy Prophet (S.A.W.) to have said," Inculcate in your children three virtues: (a) to love the Prophet (b) to love the Prophet's family and (c) to learn how to recite the Holy Quran, for those who recite it would find themselves on the Day of Judgment in the Company of prophets and God, favourites under the shadow of His throne, when there would be no other shadow."

It may be inferred from this tradition that the children should be fully informed about the Propnet's wars, the events of his companions' lives, great figures of history, battles of the Islamic history.

Advantages of Such Training and Teaching History of Islam

There are various advantages of teaching the children Islamic history.

(a) The first advantage is that the sons of Islam would be inspired by the great feats and the fighting spirit of their ancestors and would strive to emulate them.

(b) They would develop a sense of Islamic history, take pride in it and consider it a source of honour and prestige. By inculcating the habit of reciting the Holy Quran in children and relating to them the accounts of the wars waged by the Holy Prophet (S.A.W.) and the feats performed by our ancestors, we would produce salutary effects on their minds. How the children are inspired by such accounts may well be judged by the comments made by some of the prominent figures associated with the training of the kids.

i) Sa'ad bin Abi Waqqas (R.A.A.) has this to say on the subject: "We related the accounts of the Prophet's wars to our children in the same way as we teach them surah of the Holy Quran.

ii) Imam Ghazzali recommends in his book *Ahya-ul-Uloom* that the boy should be taught the Holy Quran, historical events, the stories of great historical figures and the injunctions of Islam.

iii) Similarly, Ibn Khaldoon emphasises the importance of teaching the Holy Quran to the boys and making them memorize it. He explains that the teaching of Quran was given primary importance in the schools of Muslim cities and countries, for it constitutes one of the distinguishing characteristics of Islam and strengthens the faith.

iv) Avicenna recommends in his book 'Alsyasat' that the education of children is to commence with the teaching of the Holy Quran in accordance with their intellectual and physical capacities so that they may suck the edifying milk of chaste language and the faith may be imprinted on their hearts indelibly.

v) An incident is quoted in the books of history regarding the various phases of training imparted to a child. Once Fazl bin Zaid came across the son of a bedouin woman and was deeply impressed by his accomplishments. So he questioned the woman about the boy. She told him that when the boy was five years of age, she entrusted him to a tutor who made him learn the Quran by heart and thus the boy recited the Holy Book; the tutor taught him verses of the poets and the boy quoted those verses which inspired him to learn all about the great deeds of his people. He was acquainted with those deeds accordingly; when the boy attained the age of discretion, the tutor taught him how to mount a horse and he became adept in horsemanship and could differentiate between the kinds of horses, he armed himself and as he passed by the doors of the tribe's houses his attention was drawn to the call of some one shouting . . . . ."

As has been mentioned at the outset, when our forebear entrusted their children to the tutors the latter were instructed to begin their education with the teaching of the Holy Quran and make them learn it by heart so that their tongues may be seasoned, souls purified and hearts thrilled and eyes tearful, with belief rooted deep in their hearts

Recapituation

The sum and substance of the above discussion is that the Holy Prophet (S.A.W.) has stressed the importance of acquainting children with the tenets of faith and the injunctions of the *Shariah* right from the very beginning. He also called for imbibing in the minds of the children the love of himself, his family and the Muslim conquerers. The purpose of such training is to implant faith in their hearts in its entirety and make them adore their chivalrous forebear and the warriors of Islam. When the children grow up having received training on these lines they will not be taken in by atheism and will remain impervious to the slogans of the disbelievers and the renegades.

The parents would be well-advised if they bring up their children on the lines indicated above and thus save their beliefs from misguiding and atheistic influences.

It has been acknowledged by the educationists and the moralists that a child is born pure and cleanly with an instinctive tendency towards belief in the Existence and Unity of the God. If the child with such predelictions is imparted purposeful training and is also fortunate enough the have good company and an environment saturated with faith, he will grow up to be a staunch Muslim with excellent morals and manners.

This is the natural aspect of faith as pointed out by the Holy Quran, endorsed by the Holy Prophet (S.A.W.) and testified by the scholars.

The Holy Quran identifies this instinctive nature of faith in the following words:

> "The nature framed of Allah in which He has created men. There is no altering the laws of Allah's creation." (30: 30)

The tradition of the Holy Prophet (S.A.W.) to this effect is as under:

> "Abu Huraira quotes the Holy Prophet (S.A.W.) to have said: every baby is born in the nature of Allah. His parents later turn him into a jew, a christian or a magian." (*Bukhari*)

This inborn tendency of a child has been acknowledged by the modern educationalists an moralists as well. The observations of both the Eastern and Western Scholars testify to this aspect of human nature. They also serve to prove that nature plays a vital role in the improvement and correction of human behaviour as well as in the moral development of tribes and nations. We give below the opinion of Hazrat Imam Ghazzali in relation to the moulding of children's conduct, which bears it out that the goodness and delinquency of a child is to a large extent traceable to its innate capacity and natural prediliction. Says Imam Ghazzali:

"The child is a trust with its parents. Its pure mind is an essence. If trained to be good and acquainted with goodness, it will grow up to be virtuous with its well-being guaranteed both in this life and the life to come. If it is trained to be wicked and is given the licence to do whatever it chooses, it will grow to be deprave and will finally be ruined. The only way to protect the child is that the parents should teach it manners and morals and refine it."

How aptly does a poet describe the importance of breeding children on the right lines:—

"Our youths grow according as they are trained by their parents."

"No youth becomes decorous by dint of reason. He owes his morals and manners to the training of his parents."

From the importance of the role played by nature in the growth of children we are led to draw the conclusion that a child brought in an inequitous family, educated in a misguiding environment and moving in the company of wicked associates, would naturally tend to corruption and be immoral. He would acquire heathnish and un-Islamic manners and would before long break the bonds of discipline and fall into abyss of delinquency. He would gradually abandon Islam and would join the ranks of the infidels. At this stage he will be incorrigible and it will be extremely difficult to restore his faith and guide him back to the path of Islam.

I identify here some of the causes of children's deviation for the guidance of parents and guardians and indicate the social and environmental factors that vitiate their healthy and normal growth. I emphasize once again that if the parents and guardians neglect the education and training of their children they are bound to go astray, drift into the bosom of infidelity and embrace atheism.

1. If boys are sent to foreign and missionary schools they will be prone to the influences exerted by the environment of those institutions and will receive their education and training from missionanries or mission-oriented teachers. In such an environment their minds will develop deviant tendencies and they will slowly be drawn towards atheism and infidelity. In other words, he will develop aversion for Islam.

2. If the father entrusts his child to misguided and atheist tutors they will teach him only the philosophy of atheism, which take roots deep in his mind. The child will

naturally grow up to be ungodly with unbridled freedom.

3. If the father permits his son to read the books written by the agents of atheism and the materialists and allows him the licence to go through the criticism levelled against Islam by the missionaries, the fascists and other anti-Islamic elements, then the kid is sure to fall a prey to scepticism and nourish doubts against the Islamic faith. The history of his own people and forebears would appear to him ridiculous. He would begin to mock them and this derisive attitude would culminate in a total war against Islam.

4. If the father allows his son unrestricted freedom and leaves him to do whatever he likes and befriends misguided and wrong thinking people, adopts misleading ideas and fallacious ideologies imported from abroad, then the son will scoff at all the religious values and moral principles taught by the revealed religions and divine laws of the world.

5. If the father allows his son the freedom to associate with people belonging to the atheist groups and leaves him alone in the darkness of disbelief and permits him to move freely in a mileau that has no link whatseover with Islam in any respect, the son will receive education in accordance with misguiding and atheistic philosophy and will grow up to be an atheist and disbeliever posing a threat to all the religious and moral values and he will be on war path against all the sacred standards. Says a poet·

The verdure growing in a garden cannot be similar to that growing in a jungle. Boys who have sucked the milk of defective women cannot be expected to attain perfection. As Islam imposes heavy responsibility on parents and guardians with regard to the education and training of children on the basis of Islamic beliefs and above all to teach them the essentials of Islam the parents and guardians should realize the importance and the extent of that great responsibility.

The various aspects of the responsibility in question are as follows:

Instruction to have firm faith in Allah's being, His miraculous power and His wonderful creation.

Such instruction may be given by calling upon the children to ponder over the creation of the heaven and earth. But this could be effectively done when the child attain the age of discretion. The best way is to proceed from the observation tangible things to ideatational process, from the known to the unknown; from the particular to the general; from the extensive to the complex, so that they may be fully acquainted with the problem of belief through reasoning and argumentation.

If the child receives religious education in his early years and enlightened with the solid proofs of Allah's Unity, then his heart so illuminated cannot be darkened by any subversive philosophy and the forces of evil cannot wean away his enlightened mind; nor can his religious consciousness and beleiving soul can be enervated; for he would be blessed with firm faith and perfect satisfaction.

From the low to the high and from the concrete to the abstract is a mode of approach to truth. This is exactly the method adopted in the Holy Quran. We cite a few verses to illustrate this method:

> He it is who sendeth down water from the sky, whence you have drinks and whence are trees on which ye send your beasts to pasture.
>
> Therewith He causes crops to grow for you, and the olive and the date palm and grapes and all kinds of fruit. Herein is indeed a portent for the people who reflect. And He has constrained the night and the day and sun and the moon to be of service unto you and the stars are made subservient by His command. Herein indeed are portents for the people who have sense.
>
> And whatsoever He has created for you in the earth of diverse hues therein indeed is a portent for people who take heed.
>
> And He it is Who has constrained the sea to be of service that ye eat fresh meat from thence, and bring forth from thence ornaments which ye wear. And thou seest the ships ploughing it that mankind may seek of his bounty, and that haply may give thanks.

And he hath cast unto the earth firm hills that it quake not with you and streams and roads that ye may find a way.
And landmarks too and by the star they find a way. Is He then Who creates as him who createth not? Will ye then not remember?" (16: 10-17)
"Lo! In the creation of the heavens and the earth and the difference of night and day and the ships which run upon the sea with which is of use to man and the water which Allah sendeth down from the sky thereby reviving the earth after its death, and dispersing all kinds of beasts therein and (in) the ordinance of the winds, and the clouds obedient between heaven and earth: are signs for people who have sense. (2: 164)
"So let man consider from what he is created. He is created from a gushing fluid. That issued forth from loins and ribs. He is verily able to return him unto life. On the day when hidden thoughts shall be searched out then will he have no might nor any helper." (86: 5-10)
Hast thou not seen that Allah causeth water to fall from the sky and We produce therewith fruit of diverse hues; and among the hills are streaks white and red, of diverse hues, and other raven-black.
And of men and beasts and cattle in the like manner diverse hues? The erudite among His bondsmen fear Allah alone. Allah is Mighty, Forgiving" (35: 27-28)

Let man consider his food:
How We pour water in showers, then split the earth in clefts, And cause the grain to grow therein, And grapes and green fodder, And olive-trees and palm trees, And garden-closes of thick foilage, And fruits and grasses: Provision for you and your cattle (80: 24-32)

Have they not then observed the sky above them, how we have constructed it and beautified it, and how there are no rifts therein?
And the earth have We spread out and have flung firm hills therein, and have caused of every lovely kind to grow thereon.

A vision and reminder from every penitent slave."

(50: 6-8)

These and numerous other Quranic verses make the reason proceed from the sensible to the rational, from the particular to the general and from the simple to the complex.

To engender in children the sense of humility before Allah, the fear of Allah and spirit of devotion to Him.

In order to do this their inward eye should be opened enabling them to see the humiliating and awe-inspiring omnipotence of Allah. His sovereignty over everything in the universe, the wonders wrought by His omnipotence in all the phenomena ranging from the smallest to the biggest; from the lifeless to the living; from the grass to the growing tree; in the form of beautiful flowers with various hues and fragrance and in the wonderful forms of innumerable created beings.

An insight into the wonders of divine creation will inevitably impress the human mind and will imbue it with a sense of humility, the presence of manifestations of Allah's greatness. The mind will thus be awestricken and filled with the fear of Allah and will take pleasure in His worship and service.

One way of creating the sense of humility, and fear of God in the child is that as soon as he attains the age of discretion, he should be habituated to offer prayer in all humility and sincerity and to listen to the Holy Quran with rapt attention.

The Holy Quran describes the venerability of the God earing and the humble in the following words:

"Successful indeed are the believers who are humble in their prayers."

(23:1-2)

Allah has revealed the best announcement a book conformable in its various parts, repeating, whereat do shudder the skins of those who fear their Lord, then their ranks and their hearts become plaints to the remembrance of Allah; this is Allah's guidance, He guides with it whom He pleases".

(39:23)

"And give good tidings O Muhammad (S.A.W.) to the

humble, whose hearts fear when Allah is mentioned."

(22: 34-35)

"When the revelation of the Beneficent are recited unto them, they fall down, adoring and weeping." (19: 58)

"Is not the time ripe for the hearts of those who believe to submit to Allah's reminder and to the truth which is revealed." (57: 16)

The state characterized by humility, thrill, and sadness was a trait shared in common by the Prophet (S.A.W.) his companions, the righteous forbears of Muslims and the sages enlightened with truth.

Hazrat Abdullah bin Masood narrates that the Holy Prophêt (S.A.W.) once asked him to recite the Quran before him. Hazrat Abdullah said, "Am I to recite the Quran to you who are the medium of the revelation of the Quran?" The Prophet (S.A.W.) said, "I like to hear it from others." Hazrat Abdullah then started reciting the *surah An-Nisa* and when he came to the following verse the Prophet asked him to stop:

"But how (will it be with them) when We bring of every people a witness, and We bring thee (O Muhammad) a witness against these? (4: 41)

"When I looked at him," says Hazrat Abdullah, tears were triekling down his eyes." (*Bukhari and Muslim*)

Hazrat Abu Saleh reports that some people from Yemen came to visit Hazrat Abu Bakr (R.A.A.). They started reciting the Quran and were weeping while reciting it. Hazrat Abu Bakr (R.A.A.) said, "We too were like you, but our hearts were hardened with the passage of time."

Innumerable examples of being overwhelmed by the sense of humility and weeping during the recitation of the Quran and offering prayers are found in the accounts of our righteous forebears. There are numerous books containing astonishing incidents showing their moral excellence, edification and education.

At the initial stage the exercise of being overstrung by sorrow and the sense of humility may prove to be tedious and troublesome. By admonition, repetition and demonstration the child may be helped to develop the habit of being overstrung. This would add to his natural qualities and virtues. A couplet of an instructive poet may well be cited in this context.

Discipline is beneficial in childhood and not at a later stage.

When you twist the branch of a tree, it will become twofold but when you try to soften wood, it will not soften. The exercise of being overstrung by the sense of submission and of weeping is the fundamental trait of a saint. The Prophet (S.A.W.) has pointed out this trait in the following tradition:

"Recite the Holy Quran and weep and if you do not feel like weeping, then try to be overstrung in order to weep. (*Tabarani*)

Creation of the Consciousness of God's Omniscience and Omnipresence.

To make the child wide awake to the Master's Eye constantly watching him in all circumstances and whatever he does and to kindle in him the consciousness of the fact that He is fully aware of his secrets and everything he whispers to others, of whatever he thinks, feels and does and the secrets hidden in the people's hearts and the sins they commit with their eyes. To engender such a state of mind in the child should be the most important and the primary responsibility of the parents or guardians.

(a) To make the child conscious of Allah's presence when he acts or to make him contemplate His omnipresence, it is necessary that the child learns to be sincere in all that he says and does for the sake of Allah so that whenever he intends to do something he always keeps in view Allah's presence. In this way the child will develop in his heart a craving for the service of Allah and he will be reckoned as one of the people who are alluded to in the following verse of the Holy Quran:—

"And they are ordered naught else than to serve Allah, keeping religion pure for Him, as men by nature upright, and to establish worship and to pay the poor-due. This is true religion." (98: 5).

Similarly the parents and guardians should impress the fact upon the child's mind that Allah will accept only that act of his which he does to seek His pleasure. Says the Holy Prophet (S.A.W.):

"An act is acceptable to Allah in proportion as it is sincere and as it is done to seek Allah's pleasure."

There is another tradition to the same effect:

"Good acts conform to intentions and everyone would be rewarded according to his or her intention."

(b) The concept that Allah watches a man and knows his mind when he is thinking should firmly be implanted in the child's mind. To inculcate this state of mind in the child such ideas should be imparted to him which awaken him a sense of proximity to Allah which are beneficial not only to him but also to the society as a whole. As a matter of fact the child is to be taught that he should subject his reason, heart and wishes to the message brought by the Prophet Muhammad (S.A.W.). It is also necessary for the guardians to invite the child to account to himself for all the misguiding ideas and foul thoughts that may occur to him. The child should be made to learn by heart the last verses of the Surah Al-Baqarah from verse 284 to verse 286. The meaning of these verses and the purpose thereof should be explained to the child. In this way he will learn to contemplate the presence of Allah, do heart searching, turn to the creator of the universe and pray to Him in all sincerity for whatever he wants.

In order to train the child in the contemplation of the presence of Allah while feeling anything, he should be taught to purge his mind of evil thoughts and sentiments. He will thus he purged of the feelings of jealousy and animosity, will refrain from backbiting and taking advantage of foul means and cease to gratify sinister desires. In other words, the bliss of contemplation is infused into the consciousness and feelings of the child. The Holy Prophet (S.A.W.) refers to this method of spiritual training in the context of benevolence:

"Worship Allah in a way as if you see Him. If you do not see Him, He does see you at any rate." (*Shaih Bukhari*)

The following verse of the Qur'an refers to the same thing:-

"If a slander from the devil wound thee then seek refuge

in Allah. He is Hearer and knower. Those who ward off evil, when a glamour from the evil troubleth them, they do but remember Allah's guidance and see wisely." (7: 200-201)

Our righteous forebears adopted the method mentioned above for the spiritual training of their offspring. To illustrate how they applied this method we cite here an incident mentioned by Hazrat Imam Ghazzali in his book *Ahya-ul-Uloom:*

> "Sahl bin Abdullah narrates that when he was three years old he used to rise at night and observe his maternal uncle Muhammed bin Sawar offering prayer. One day his uncle asked him, Why do'nt you remember Allah?" The boy replied, "How am I to remember Him?"

The uncle said, "When you lie down on your bed repeat in your heart the following words thrice without using you tongue.

Allah is with me Allah is looking at me. Allah is my witness."

He did accordingly for several nights. Then the uncle asked him repeat the same words seven times. The boy having acted on this advice for a few mights informed the uncle that he had done as he bade him. The uncle instructed him to repeat the words eleven times each night. In this way the boy's heart was imbued with the sweetness of faith. After the lapse of a year the uncle told Sahl to remember what he had taught till he breathed his last as it would benefit him both in this life and the life to come. Sahl accordingly repeated the sacred formula for several years which filled his heart with the bliss of faith.

Then one day his uncle said to him, "Well Sahl, can the person who is blessed with Allah's company and feels that He is seeing and guarding him, disobey Allah? So you should ever defy Allah's command."

This, then, was the method of spiritual training and of strengthening faith by which Sahl bin Abdullah was elevated to the ranks of a great saint. He awed all his spiritual eminence to the training of his maternal uncle who impressed the meaning of faith and contemplation on his mind in his early childhood.

If the parents or guardians seek guidance from the above principles they will be able to make of their children such

Muslims as will take pride in their religion, history and the great feats performed by their ancestors. They would produce a generation free from atheism, crimes jealousy and animosity.

The western educationalists and scholars set great store by the kind of inner training or the training of faith we have discussed. They strictly adhere to the principles of such training and thereby safeguard the new generation against ungodliness infamy, delinquency and bad company.

We quote here the opinions of some of the Western thinkers and writers.

(1) The great novelist Dostoevsky writes that when he gave up God, he was taken in by Satan.

(2) The great French Philosopher and dramatist Voltaire speaking derisively of the agnostics, materialists and sceptics observes, "Why have these people fallen a prey to scepticism? Had there been no God, my wife would have made cuckold of me and my servants would have taken to stealing my things."

(3) The renowned American psychologist Henery Long writes in his book "*Return to Faith*" that the parents today are at the horns of dilemma as to the moral training and correction of their children inasmuch as they are themselves devoid of the religious and spiritual efficacy possessed by the people in the past. According to Long these parents are at a loss to find a solution to the problem confronting them because they have not been able to find a substitute for religious influence which is the great force generated by the faith in the Creator of the universe and a firm belief in the sanctity of His Creation.

We come across the following account of Stalin's daughter in the Magazine Alhajj (No. 3, Vol. 23) published from Makka.

What caused Stalin's daughter Swetlana to abandon her homeland and children was religion. She was born and bred in an ungodly family whose members were absolutely a stranger to the concept of God and never mentioned his name even un-wittingly. When she entered the age of discretion she strongly felt without coming under the influence of any extraneous influence, without any extraneous cause that just as no justice can be administered between human-beings without believing in Allah, life is worthless without belief in Him. She felt in her heart of hearts that man needs belief in God as much as he needs water and air to live."

(4) The great German philosopher Kant maintains that morality presupposes three fundamental beliefs:-

i) Belief in the existence of God

ii) Belief in the immortality of soul.

iii) Belief in accountability after death.

The sum and substance of the foregoing discussion is that beleif in God is the very basis of the child's psychological and moral training and improvement. The expert opinions quoted above bear out the subsistence of strong relationship between faith and morality as well as between belief and action. Under the head of responsibility for moral training we will throw light on the role played by belief in the correction of child's behaviour and moral uplift.

In short, the religious training of children is the vital responsibility of parents and guardians as it is the fountain-head of morality. The springs of all accomplishment lie in this inner training and as such it is absolutely essential for breeding a child well so that he may grow to be a true believer. Without such training the child would lack the courage to bear the burden of any responsibility and cannot be trust-worthy. He would be unable to understand the purpose of life or the human significance of life nor can he be capable of performing any noble task. Without spiritual training, his life will be a little better than that of a beast and will consist of no more than eating food when hungry and gratify sensual desires. A child who has not received any religious training drifts into the company of criminal and finally associates with disbeleivers and immoral elements who do not know the lawful from the unlawful. This is the plight of the delin-quents to which the Quran refers in the following words:

> "Those who disbelieve take their comfort in this life and eat even as the cattle eat, and the Fire is their habitation." (47:12)

It is, therefore, necessary for the father and the guardian to lose no time in proving to the child the existence of God by cogent arguments and strengthen his belief in Him by giving examples. Preaching faith in an instructive style was the method adopted by the Holy Prophet (S.A.W.), our first patron. He used to preach the children in a manner which dignified them and the belief in Allah took root deep in their hearts. We cite here some of the Prophet's sayings as examples.

(a) Ibn Abbas narrates: One day I was following the Holy Prophet (S.A.W.) on his way. He said: Listen boy! I want to teach you something. Remember Allah and He will protect you. Remember Him and you will find Him present If you want anything, beg it of Him. Whenever you need help, seek it from Him. Know that if all the people are agreed to benefit you, they can do so only as much as Allah has determined for you. If all the people unite to harm you they can do so only as much as Allah has already ordained. Every thing has been decreed immutably.

In another tradition the Holy Prophet (S.A.W.) is reported to have said: Remember Allah and you will find Him present. Remember Him in happiness and He will provide you succour in adversity. Know that you will never get what has not been ordained for you while you are bound to get what has been ordained. Suffering is associated with happiness and adversity with comfort.

At the end I would suggest that the guardians and parents should teach the children the best books to inclucate in them the belief in the unity of Allah as they reach the age of discretion. I am of the view that education is to be imparted in phases. At every stage the child's age and degree of discretion and understanding is to be taken into consideration.

The Stages of Education

First Stage: Ten to fifteen years. Books recommended:
(1) *Al Ma'rifat* by Shaikh Abdul Kareem Rifa'ee.
(2) *Al 'Aqaid* by Imam Hasan Al Banna
(3) *Al Jawahir-al-Kalamiah* by Professor Tahir-ul-Jazairi.
Second Stage: From the puberty to twenty years.
Books recommended:
(1) Usolui 'Aqaid by Professor Abdullah 'Arwani

(2) Alwujoodul Haq by Dr. Hasan Huwedi
(3) Shubhat Wardood by the present author Abdullah Nasih Ulwan

Third Stage: Above twenty years.
(1) Kubr-al-Yaqiniat-al-Kawnya, by Dr. Muhmmad Saeed Ramazan-al-Boti.
(2) Allah Jalla Jalalahoo, by Professor Syed Hawi.
(3) Qissat-ul-Eman by Professor Nadeem Hibr.

At the first and second stage more books on beliefs and ideas may be selected. (In other countries every guardian, teacher or parent may select books in their language in keeping with the age and mental capacity of the child.)

It is exceedingly necessary for every young Muslim to read good books for the inculcation of faith, mental refinement and correction of outlook. Merely going through the books, however, is not enough. They should be intensively studied and their contents must be assimilated so that belief may be set right and reinforced.

In Arabic the most important books on the subject are listed below:

1) Waheeduddin Khan — *Al Deen Fi Mawajehat-il-Ilm.*
2) Waheeduddin Khan — *Al Islam Yatahaddi.*
3) Various Western Authors: *Allaho Yatajalli Fi 'As-ril 'Aalam.*
4) Kareesee Mauriseon — *Al Ilm Yad'oo Ilal Eman.*
5) Abdul Razzak Naufil — *Allah Wal Ilmul Hadees*
6) Dr. Khalis Kanjoo — *Al Tibae Fi Mihrib-al-Eman.*

(If translations of these books are available well and good. But in case if they have not been translated as yet, books on the subject available in local languages should be carefully selected by the Parents).

This was the method adopted by our forebears in the moral and practical training and education of their children. The spiritual leaders and guides in the past also trained their disciples on the same lines.

We have mentioned in the prvious pages the manner in which Sahl bin Abdullah Tustri was trained by his maternal uncle Muhammad bin Sawar. He did not only inculcate faith in his nephew by this method but also purified and refined his mind. Having been subjected to such inner training, Sahl's heart was incured to the contemplation of God and was imbued with the fear of Allah and trust in Him. In order to engender this state of mind in himself, Sahl used to repeat the following formula in private and public and in seclusion and in meetings:

"Allah is with me. He looks at me. He is my witness."

Allaho ma'e, Allaho nazirun ilaiya, Allaho Shahidi.

The Harm Done by Irreligious Training

The training of a child is isolated from Islamic belief religious instructions and inner relation with God Almighty would be grounded in inequity and decadence. He would, in other words, be bred in an ungodly atmosphere and would consequently become a slave of sensual desires.

If the child so trained happens to be of peaceful disposition, he will grow up to be stupid and apathetic and would lead the life of an indolent person. He would be seemingly active but actually inert. Other people hardly feel that he really exists. The following words of a poet — aptly depict such a torpid figure:

"He is such a person that when alive would no do good to anybody and when dead his kith and kin would not mourn him."

If the animal instinct is predominant in the child he would grow to be a debauchee and would try to gratify his sexual appetite at all cost. He would seek carnal pleasure in total disregard of the sanctity of legitimacy. He would have no qualms of conscience and would never feel ashamed of himself. He would be impervious to the dictates of reason and would sing of epicurian cult in unison with Abu Nawwas:

What is this world? Eat and drink and he merry.

If you don't do all this, then the world is not worth anyting.

If the child is prejudiced he will cause disruption in the world, perpetrate atrocities and treat the people with contempt. He will try to browbeat the people, will boast of his language and take pleasure in his acts. He will have no scruple to raise an edifice with human skulls and to shed the blood of innocent people. He will be a model of brutality as described by a poet:-

> "The world and its people are meant for us. When we take hold of them, we do it like tyrants and aggressors. We turn into rebels and brutes and nobody can dare be cruel to us. In fact, we act like brutes from the very start. When our infant gives up sucking milk even the greatest tyrants prostrate before him."

If the child is under the influence of the demon, he will weave the web of machinations, cause rift befween friends, lay mines for devastation, throw poison to massacre the people, contaminate clean water for sport, present sins in an attractive form, be guilty of debauchery and cause hatred and ill-will among the people. He will, in short, act in a manner as described by a poet:

> "If you cannot do good to the people, then do harm to them, for only good or harm can be expected from young men."

Such children grow up to slaves of their desires. They follow their sensual appetite blindfold and all their activities are governed by beast by beastly propensities. They are impervious to reason to such a degree that they look upon themselves as gods to be worshipped. Says Allah:

> "And who goeth further astray than he who followeth his lusts instead of guidance from Allah." (28:50)

From the foregoing discussion it may be inferred that inculcation faith in Allah alone can set right and temper the disposition of a deviant child. Such inner training would guide him to right path and reform his mind. Without inculcation of faith, it is impossible to reform the child, tame his wild passions and improve his morals.

Correlation between Faith and Morality

The educationists and thinkers of the West and other nations have therefore, chalked out the lines of training and education on the assumption that there is strong correlation between faith and morality and between belief and action. They have made it crystal clear that there can be no peace of mind without religion and no improvement of children without inculcation of faith in Allah.

The following are the observations of some of the eminent thinkers and reformers to this effect:-

(1) The German Philosopher Fichte says, "Morality is inconceivable without religion."

(2) Mr Gandhi observes:

"Relgion and morality are inseparably linked. They constitute an indivisible unit. Relgion is the essence of morality while morality is like atmosphere for religion. In other words, religion fosters morality just as water makes the crop grow."

(3) A British Judge Danning remarks in course of his denunciation of the scandalous behaviour of a former minister:

The very existence of morality is imposible without religion. There can be no law without morality. It is religion alone by which good and evil are judged. It is religion alone which conduces man to the building of ideal character, which is the aim of every man, and which he strives to achieve. Religion cuts at the very roots of egoism and protects man against the upsurge of wild desires. Religion induces him to pursue good ends and do the best acts. Religion fosters in man living conscience and by dint of living conscience man is able to attain to the extreme heights of morality."

We have already cited Kant's remark in this context: Morality is impossible without three fundamental beliefs:

(a) Belief in the existence of God,

(b) belief in the immortality of soul and

(c) belief in the accountability after death."

No wonder if Islamic Shariah lays special emphasis on the moral aspect of children's training and enjoins upon the parents and guardians to focus their attention on imbibing cardinal virtues in them.

We cite here some of the Prophet's sayings with regard to the moral training of children:

"No father has ever given a better gift to his son than good morals." (*Tirmizi*)

"Esteem your children and improve their morals and manners." (*Ibn Maja*)

"Teach morals and manners to your children and

members of Family."

(*Musnad Abdul Razzaq, Musnad Saeed bin Mansoor*).

It is the right of the son upon his father that latter should teach him manners and *call* him by a good name."

(*Al Baihaqi*)

"A boy's aqiqa should be performed on the seventh day of his birth and he should be simultaneously named and the hair of his head shaven. When he is six years old he should be taught morals and manners. When he is nine yeras old, he should be given a separate bed. When he is thirteen years old he should be punished if he does not offer prayer and keep fast. When he is sixteen years old, his father should arrange for his marriage and should, at the time of marriage, make it clear to him that he has taught him morals and manners, trained and educated him and finally married him and that he sought Allah's protection from the son's trial in the world and from torments in the Hereafter." This means that the father wishes his son to escape the sufferings of the worldly life and the torments in the life to come. It may also mean that the father seeks Allah's protection from the trial he has to undergo here and hereafter because of his failure in the proper training of the son.

The conclusion which may be drawn from the sayings of the Holy Prophet (S.A.W.) is that the guardians in general and the parents in particular have to bear heavy responsibility in respect of correct of breeding and training of the children. It is incumbent upon the parents to correct their children, refine their habits, teach them morals, keep them away from the company of the urchins and exhort them to be nice and kind to other people. The parents are moreover, under the obligation to accustom the children in their early years to be truthful, honest, consistent, to be ever ready to suffer for others, to do justice to the aggrieved, respect the elderly people, to be hospitable and respectful towards the guests, love the neighbour and be kind to him.

Again, it is incumbent upon the parents to see that the children do not call names and use foul language and prevent them from such acts as may suggest that they have not been bred well and that their morals and manners are extremely objectionable.

it is also the duty of the parents to prevent the children from acts that do not come up to the standard of nobility and righteousness.

The parents, again, are under the obligation to imbibe in their children humanitarian consciousness, purify their feelings and emotions and teach them to be kind to the orphans, do good to the destitute and help the widows. In short, the due discharge of all the obligations relating to the teaching of manners and morals to the children and engendering in them humane attitudes should be of paramount importance with the parents, guardians and teachers.

Evil to be Guarded Against

Since according to Islam the first phase of children's training is to imbue the children with the of spirit of contemplation of God, it is therefore essential for parents, teachers and guardians interested in the moral uplift of children to keep in view four bad habits in particular, for they comprise meanest and most immoral acts:

1) Lying
2) Stealing
3) Abuse and
4) the habit of being easily impressed by others.

According to Islam the habit of lying is the worst. Islam, therefore, particularly enjoins upon the paretns to create in children hatred for lies and strive to save them from the consequences of hypocrisy. That lying is the worst habit is adequately proved by the fact that Islam describes it as the sign of disruption. The Prophet (S.A.W.) says, "anyone who has four qualties is a hypocrite and he is a hypocrite in proportion to the degree of each quality he possesses. (Those four qualities are)

(a) Whenever anything is entrusted to him, he commits breach of trust,
(b) Whenever he speaks he tells a lie,
(c) Whenever he makes a pledge, he goes back upon it. and
(d) Whenver he quarrels, he reviles.

"Hazrat Abu Huraira quotes the Prophet (S.A.W.) to have

said that there are three sorts of people with whom Allah will not talk on the Day of Judgement, nor will He absolve them of blame, nor look at them. Theirs is a painful doom. Those three sorts of people are: (a) Aged adulterer, (b) Ruler who lies and (c) a proud pauper or destitute (*Muslim*)

One who lies is included in Allah's list of liars.

Hazrat Abdullah bin Masood narrates the following tradition of the Prophet (S.A.W.):

"The Prophet (S.A.W.) said, "abstain from telling a lie because it leads to inequity and inequity in its turn leads to the Fire. A man goes on telling lies and thinks of lies so much so that his name is included in the list of liars."

(*Bukhari and Muslim*)

Lying is also breach of trust.

Hazrat Sufyan bin Usaid Al Hadhrami tells us that he heard the Prophet (S.A.W.) say, "The bigest breach of trust is that you tell something to your brother-in-faith who believes what you say although what you tell him is actually falsehood."

This in short, is the Islamic point of view about those who utter lies or flasehood. They are hypocrites deserving Allah's chastisement. They are also guilty of breach of trust. It is, therefore, imcumbent upon parents to warn their children of the consequences of lying. Create hatred in them for falsehood and prohibit them telling lies so that he may not be incorrigibly accustomed to telling lies.

As the guardian or parent should be a model for the purpose of imparting good training, he should abstain from telling lies in order to stop the children, say, from crying or pacifying them. If they are not scrupulous enough to avoid telling lies it would mean that they are committing the meanest and worst act of encouraging the children to lie by thier example. The children would cease to believe the untruthful guardian or parent and would, therefore, turn a deaf ear to their exhortations.

It is for this reason that our first patron and ideal guide the Holy Prophet (S.A.W.) urges upon parents and guardians to abstain from telling lies for the purpose of amusing or luring the children or from doing so by way of jest so that no lie is recorded in the heaven in their account.

Hazrat Abdullah bin 'Aamir narrates that one day his mother called him while the Prophet (S.A.W.) was present in our house. She said to me, "Come son, I will give you something." He asked her what she wanted to given him. She replied that she wanted to give him dates. The Prophet (S.A.W.) observed: Had you not given him dates, your lie would have been recorded. *(Abu Dawood, Al Baihaqi)*

Hazrat Abu Huraira quotes the Prophet (S.A.W.) to have said, "If any one calls a child to come and take something but does not give him anything, this would be tantamount to a lie."

Our forebears used to exhort their children to be truthful and strictly abide by their promises. They attached so much importance to this aspect of training that the children were imbued with the spirit of candour and commitment. In this connection the incident narrated by the great saint Hazrat Abdul Qadir Jilani is specially worthy of mention.

Hazrat Abdul Qadir says, "Veracity and candour was imbibed in me when I was still a small child. Once I set out from Mecca on my way to Baghdad for the purpose of prosecuting my studies. My mother gave me forty dinars to meet my expenses during the jousuey, making me promise at the same time that I would never tell a lie. When we entered the area of Hamadan, a gang of dacoits fell upon us. One of them came to me and asked if I had anything with me. I replied that I had forty dinars. The dacoits thought that I was joking and passed on. Then another member of the gang was upon me. He repeated the same question. I told him what I had. He took me to the ring leader of the gang. On his enquiry also I told him of what I possessed. The chief asked me why I was telling the truth. I said that I had made a pledge to my mother that I would always tell the truth and that I feared that I might be guilty of breaking it. No sooner did the leader of the dacoits neared me than he was frightened and started screaming and tearing his clothes. He said to me: 'You fear that you my break the promise you gave to your mother, whlile I have never been afraid of breaking the pledge I made to Allah.' Having said so, he ordered the dacoits to return to the respective owners all the things they had grabbed. He then said to me: I repent of my sins in your presence. On hearing him his accomplices declared that just as they followed him in robbery so also would they follow his example in repentance. Thus, impressed as they were by veracity, all of them repented of their crimes.

Stealing is as dangerous an habit as lying. It is prevalent in the society whose members are unfamiliar with Islamic morals and who have not been moulded in accordance with the principles of faith and morality.

It is clear that if the habit of contemplation, fear of Allah and the sense of duty and trustworthiness is not inculcated in the child, he would commit crimes like fraud, adulteration breach of trust and usurp other people's belongings when he grows up. He would turn out to be a damned criminal posing a serious threat to the individuals and the society at large.

It is, therefore, incumbent upon the parents to sow the seeds of Allah's fear and contemplation in the hearts of the children, and acquaint them with the serious consequences of the habit of stealing which is actually the advanced stage of fraud and breach of trust. Besides the children should be told that moral aberration entails painful doom on the Day of Judgement.

It is most unfortunate that innumerable parents today do not care to keep an eye on their valuables lest the children should steal them. If a child tells them that he found a valuable thing on the way or a friend gave it to him as a present, the parents would readily believe him without a question. It is but natural that the child would resort to fabrication to get himself absolved from blame. It is also natural that he is more emboldened to commit crimes when his habits and activities are left unprobed by the parents. And if the parents themselves encourage and support the child in dong criminal acts he would become an incorrigble offender and a habitual thief. Says a poet:

> When the children have sucked milk from the breasts of faulty women (brought up by bad women) they can't be expected to attain perfection.

It will not be out of place to quote a judicial case in this connection. A shariat court passed the verdict to amputate a thief's hand. When the time came for carrying out the sentence, the thief shouted, "Cut off my mother's tongue before you cut off my hand for when I committed theft for the first time in my life by stealing an egg from the neighbour, she did not care to check me nor did she ask me to return the egg to the owner, On the contrary she laughed heartily and said: 'What a manly man has my son grown to be! Had my mother not expressed pleasure over my criminal act, I would never have become a thief."

(*Akhlaqul Ijtimaia by Saba'ee,*)

Importance of Contemplation

We now quote some incidents about our righteous ancestors as to the importance of contemplation in the inner and outward improvement of children including inculcation of the sense of obligation and trustworthiness as well as avert activity.

Hazrat Umar (R.A.A.) promulgated the law that nobody shall mix water in milk. But the question is if the law has the eye to see an unlawful act being committed so that the offender may be apprehended. The law does not have the eye to do it. What really serves the purpose of law in this connection is the contemplation of Allah's presence. This is borne out by an incident involving a woman and her daughter. The greedy mother intended to add water to milk in order to earn more profit. But the daughter who was a Muslim in the real sense of the word prevented her from such an act as it was forbidden by the head of the Muslim Ummah. She said to the mother, "If the caliph does not see your act, the Lord of the Caliph does."

Abdullah bin Dinar narrates that once as Hazrat Umar accompanied by him, was on his way to Makka a shepherd headed towards him. Hazrat Umar said to him by way of putting him to test, "Would you sell to me one of your goats? The shepherd replied that he was a slave.

"You can tell your master that the goat was eaten by a wolf " suggested the Caliph.

"Well, where has Allah gone?" was the shepherd's reply.

Children brought up in an un-Islamic environment are generally foulmouthed and accustomed to abusing. There are two basic causes of this vulgarity: (a) bad example and (b) bad company.

(a) Bad Example.

When the child hears his parents abuse and use foul language, he will follow their example and will get into the habit of abusing in reason and out of reason.

(b) Bad company

If the child is left to roam about in the street and mix up with the urchins he will naturally learn abusive language. It is also possible that he becomes even more foul-tongued than the urchins themselves, acquire worse habits and develop the worst possible character.

These then are the causes of children's deviation that call for talking politely to the children, using beautiful and excellent expressions and thus teach them to speak in a courteous manner by their example. It is also incumbent upon the parents and guardians to exhort children to shun the company of the street urchins so that the latter's aberrations may not influence them. The parents should also warn the children against the serious consequences of a foul-tongue. They should, for instance be told that due to railing man's personality is debased.They go down in the people's esteem and the people around would dislike them.

The parents should teach the children such traditions of the Holy Prophet (S.A.W.) wherein railing and abusive language is forbidden and which tell us that cursing and abuse entail painful doom in the Hereafter. It is possible that by learning such traditions the children give up railing. Some of the traditions to this effect are as follows:

(1) Abusing a Muslim is inequity and killing him is infidelity." (*Bukhari and Mulsim*)

(2) The greatest sin is railing at one's parents."

The Prophet (S.A.W.) was asked how a man could rail at his parents. The Prophet (S.A.W.) replied, "A man may abuse the father of another man who in his turn may vilify his father. Similarly he may use abusive language for another

man's mother, who in his turn may vilify his mother.
(Sahih Bukhari and Musnad Imam Ahmed)

(3) A man says something that displeases Allah but the man does not care for His displeasure in spite of the fact that he shall be hurled into Hell because of what he said. *(Bukhari)*

(4) Men shall fall headlong into Hell on account of what they may have uttered with their tongues.
(Sunan Nisai, Sunan Ibn Maja, Sunan Abu Dawood, Musnad Imam Ahmed)

(5) A believer is one who neither taunts nor curses, nor vilifies, nor rails." *(Tirmizi)*

How nice the boy who uses polite words in his conversation, who is soft spoken! How nice is the boy whose polite conversation delights the person who hears him! How great is the boy who listens to abusive language and obscene talk and abhors it! Such a child is like a lovely rose in his family and has a good reputation among the people around him.

We relate a few incidents showing the great importance attached by our forebears to polite speech and good conversation. The parents and guardians should train their children on the same pattern.

During the reign of Hisham bin Abdul Ma   the country was on the throes of famine. The people belonging to various tribes came to Hisham. One of them was a fourteen year old boy named Durdas bin Habib. They were all over awed by the Caliph, and none of them had the courage to speak to him. Hisham surveyed them and caught a glance of Durdas whom he found to be the youngest of the tribesmen. He said to the guard, "Whoever, wants to see me does see me, even if he be a boy." Durdas apprehended that by the boy the Caliph meant him only. So he broke the ice saying, "O ruler of the believers, My coming to you is not intrusion into your business but to me it is an honour. All these people have to apprise you of their problem, but none of them has the courage to speak. What is meant by speech is to clearly express one's self while silence means that the very purpose in view is defeated. Unless one talks how can you know what has one to say. Hisham was astonished by the way the boy spoke. He asked him, "Tell me, what is the matter?"

Durdas replied, "O ruler of believers! We have been in the grip of famine for the last three years. During the first year our fat was melted, during the second our flesh was wasted and now during the third the marrow of our bones has been eaten up. You possess a lot of surplus wealth. If it is reserved for the sake of Allah, then distribute it among his deserving bondsmen."

"If the surplus wealth belongs to Allah, continued the boy, "Why have you withheld it? And if it belongs to you, distribute it as alms amongst His bondsmen. Allah rewards those who are charitable and who do good."

"O ruler of the believers!" added Durdas, "The ruler is to the ruled like the soul to the body. A body devoid of soul is dead."

The Caliph said, "This boy has said three things, admitting of no excuse in any one of them." The Caliph then ordered distribution of one hundred thousand *dirhams* in the whole township where Durdas lived. He also ordered one hundred thousand *dirhams* to be given to Durdas besides.

"O ruler of believers! interposed Durdas, "Please distribute my share also among the people of my township. I don't want that the amount earmarked for them falls short of their needs."

Hisham asked the boy, "Tell me if you need anything for yourslef."

"My only requirement", answered Durdas, "is the common wale of the Muslims".

Unstability and the deterioration of personality is the most outstanding blemish of the twentieth century Muslim youth, both male and female. Everywhere one finds the Muslim boys, girls, young women and young men aping the west blind fold. They are all being washed off by the flux of depravity and inequity. They care little for the faith and their conscience is dead. Life for them is but the acquisition of ephemeral wealth, gratification of sensual desires and enjoying unlawful things unabashed. If the world does not give them all these things, then the world to them is worthless.

Some people with a shallow outlook on life think obscene dance, shameful mixing of sexes and blind fold imitation indicative of progress, evolutionary and modernity. All such people suffer from defeatist mentality. They are ready to surrender before actually suffering a defeat in the crusade of life.

Those who describe obscene dance, shameful promiscuity and blindfold imitation as progress, renaissance and modernity are like black-beetles. Their very demeanour and gait smack of immodesty. The way they talk indicate that their personalities consist of molten metal that could be moulded to suit any mileau. These black-beetles are always on the lookout for immodest females who are salacious like themselves. Whenever they find such a woman they ran after her, woo her and thus commit character assassination of themselves. These black-beetless are guilty of one immoral act after another, go on changing ceaselessly until they fall into the abyss of death and nothingness. Says a poet:—

(1) A man who does not develop his personality deserves to be destroyed in a short span of time.

(2) The man who apes alien way of life is deprived of his own personality (i.e. his identity would be blurred in his own eyes).

The Prophet's (S.A.W.) edicts for parents and guardians in this respect are cited below:·

(1) Aping alien's bearing and blindfold imitation are to be avoided.

Says the Prophet (S.A.W.), "Do just the opposite to what the heathens do. Get your moustaches shaven and grow beards." In another tradition the Prophet (S.A.W.) is reported to have said "Get your whiskers trimmed, grow beards and look different from the Zorastrians." *(Bukhari and Muslim)*

(2) "The man who fashions himself after the aliens is not of us. Do not fashion yourselves either after the Christians or the Jews."

The wordings of another tradition are as follows: "Whoever fashions himself after another nation belongs to that nation." *(Tirmizi)*

(3) Tirmizi quotes the traditions: "None of you should

be unscrupulously flexible and say that he is with all the other people. If they do good acts he too would do good acts and if they do bad acts he would follow suit. You should rather learn to follow the people if they do good and to save yourself from their harm if they do evil."

In the light of the above traditions you may decide for yourself what is to be accepted from the aliens and what is to be rejected.

(a) *Legitimacy:* This includes learning of useful sciences and beneficial aspects of civilization; for example learning of the sciences of medicine, engineering, physics, chemistry, the use of military equipment and weapons, the realities of matter, the mysteries of atom etc etc. for all these sciences come under the following edicts of the Holy Prophet:—

"It is the duty of every Muslim to acquire knowledge."

(Ibn Majah)

The following tradition means the same thing:—

"Wisdom is the lost property of every wise man. When he finds, he is exclusively the rightful owner of it."

The divine injunction quoted below conveys the same sense:

"And make ready for the enemy whatever force you can muster." (8:60)

(b) *Prohibition:* Under this head falls all the things that are not in harmony with the characteristics of the Muslim Ummah and its moral genius. They include morals, customs conventions, transactions and every thing that does not belong to the Islamic social set-up and smacks of an alien social system. For these things impair the identity of the individual, reduce his personality to naught and generate in him defeatist mentality. They subvert the standards of morality.

(c) *Indulgence in comforts and luxury is forbidden.*

Hazrat Umar sent the following directive to the Muslims living in Iran.

"Abstain from comforts and the costume of heathens."

(Sahih Bukhari and Muslim)

Imam Ahmed expresses the substance of the directive in the following words:

"Give up indulgence in comforts and the custume of the Persians."

There is also a Prophet's (S.A.W.) tradition to the same effect:

"Refrain from indulging in comforts, for this is unbecoming in Allah's bondsmen."

By luxury and comforts is meant to undulge in worldly pleasures and he engrossed too much in what is legitimate. In material well being man feels so contented and gratified that he neglects the duty of inviting the people to the path of Allah and fighting for His sake. He goes down on the scale of morality and sinks into the abyss of decadence. Besides, he gets into the habit of seeking pleasures and develops various kinds of weaknesses and diseases.

Prohibition of Music

Imam Ahmed bin Hanbal, Ahmed bin Munee' and Ahmed bin Abu Usama quote the Holy Prophet to have said:—

"Allah has sent me as a blessing and guidance for all the worlds and has commanded me to break the flute, musical instruments, the jars of wine and the idols which were worshipped in the age of ignorance."

The Prophet (S.A.W.) has, moreover, said:

"There will be people among my Ummah who will treat adultery, silken costumes, wine and musical instruments as legitimate for themselves."

(*Bukhari*, *Ahmed*, *Ibn Majah etc.*)

Ibn Asakar in his History and *Sabsari* in his work *Amali* quote Hazrat Anas bin Malik to have narrated the following tradition:

"Any one who goes to the singing girl and listens to her song, Allah will put into his ears molten lead on the Doomsday."

Imam Tirmizi quotes the following tradition as narrated by Hazrat Abu Moosa (R.T.A.):

"Whoever has heard the singing of a song will not be allowed to hear the voice of the heavenly creatures."

Every sensible man is aware of the harmful influence of forbidden voices on the morals of children. They make the children pleasure seekers and fond of inequity and immoral acts. Consequently they are addicted to indulgence in the gratification of sensual desires and sexual appetite.

It will not be out of place to mention here Islamic injunctions as to the use of radio and television so that the parents and guardians may know in what way it is legitimate to use these media and the other ways of sound.

Doubtless, devices like television and tape recorder are the great inventions of modern age. In fact, these media of information are the high water mark of the material civilization of today. What makes or mars them is the use they are put to. They can be used either for good or for evil. If we make use of these media for fostering good, inculcation of Islamic beliefs, dissemination of knowledge, promotion of moral values, establishment of the present generation's link with its history and forebears, furtherance of religious ends and legitimate worldly interests, then there can be no two opinions about the justification of their use. But when these very devices are applied to cause moral aberrations, corruption, degeneration and promotion of a system of life other than Islam. then every believer will regard their use as unlawful.

An assessment of programmes shown on the Syrian T.V. would reveal that a majority of them show such activities as degrade humanity and incite the young generation to debauchery and wickedness. They induce women to throw off their veils, encourage men and women to mix freely, underline the doctrine of licentiousness and engender new forms of corruption in the society. Number of programmes designed to foster moral values and propagate religion is negligible. If this situation persists, then viewing the T.V. programmes would be a great sin.

Following arguments may be advanced in support of our position:

The scholars of Islam are unanimous that there are five purposes of the Shariah:

(a) Protection of religion
(b) Protection of reason
(c) Protection of descent
(d) Protection of self, and

(e) Protection of wealth and property.

They are also agreed that the entire contents of the Holy Quran and the Prophet's (S.A.W.) traditions aim at the above five things.

As the television programmes consists of obscene music, subversive plays and sex-inciting films designed to degrade human dignity and encourage debauchery, viewing such programmes is totally unlawful under the Shariah. This prohibition aims at the preservation of honour as well as the legitimacy of descent. Hence the use of television under the circumstances is totally forbidden on grounds of Shariah.

Hazrat Abu Saeed Khudri quotes the Holy Prophet (S.A.W.) to have said:

"Do not harm and do not be harmed."

(Ibn Majah, Malik, Dar Qutni)

In the light of the above tradition of the Holy Prophet (S.A.W.) we declare that buying a television set and bringing it into home by a Muslim is unlawful because television uses human-beings in programmes which cause inconsistency and disintegration of personality and which incite sensual desires and latent wishes.

This prohibition is designed to safeguard the Muslim family against corruption and to deter the potential harm done by T.V. That is exactly what the Prophet's (S.A.W.) tradition signifies.

'Do not harm and do not be harmed.'

Because of the unlawful character of the obscene, subversive and immoral entertainment provided in the programmes shown on T.V., the cogency of arguments advanced in favour of the prohibition of the use of TV is evident. Therefore, it goes without saying that viewing television programmes is unlawful. This, however, does not apply to documentaries and informative programmes.

Having resemblance of woman is forbidden.

Hazrat Saeed bin Al Musayab narrates that once Hazrat Moawia (R.A.A.) came to Madina and addressed us. At the end of his speech he took out something similar to a lock of hair (a wig) and said that it had been in vogue among the

Jews. The Holy Prophet (S.A.W) came to know about it and described it as deception.

Ibn Abbas quotes the Prophet to have observed, "Imitation of women by men and of men by women incurs Allah's curse." (*Bukhari, Abu Dawood, Tirmizi*)

The wording of the same tradition as contained in Musnad Imam Hanbal, Sunan Abu Dawood and Ibn Majah is as follows:—

"Allah curses men appearing like women and women appearing like men."

Hazrat Ali (R.A.A.) tells us, "I saw the Prophet (S.A.W.) with silk in his right hand and gold in his left and say: These two things are forbidden for my Ummah:"(*Abu Dawood*)

Hazrat Abu Musa Ash'ari reports the Prophet (S.A.W.) to have observed:

"The use of gold by the menfolk of my Ummah is unlawful while it is lawful for the womenfolk." (*Tirmizi*)

The use of wig and gold and imitation of women by men, and similarly the imitation of men by women and their appearing in men's costume wherein their bodies remain exposed would be like playing the eunuch and tantamount to one's depersonalization and inconsistency of character. All such manifestations cut at the very root of masculinity, constitute an affront to human personality and a disgrace to morality. In fact, the nefarious vogues and practices referred to above lead the entire nation to psychological disintegration and are the most ominous forms of subversion. They are the cause of our youths' corruption, negation of personality and immorality.

Prohibition of giving up purdah, show of beauty, mixing of men and women freely and looking at women other than one's wives.

Says Allah:

"O Prophet tell thy wives, daughters and the women believers to let down upon them their over-garments. This is more proper, so that they may be known and not be given trouble. And Allah is Ever Forgiving Merciful."

(33: 59)

Again, in *Surah Al-Noor* it has been said:

"Tell the believing men to lower their gaze and be modest. That is purer for Them. Surely Allah is aware of what they do."

And tell the believing women to lower their gaze and be modest and to display their adornment only that which appears thereof. And let them wear their head covering over their hosoms. And they should not display their adornment except to their husbands and to their fathers." (24: 30-31)

The question arises here whether according to Shariah the woman is under the obligation to cover her face also?

We give the first answer to this question in the light of the interpretation put by the companions of the Holy Prophet (S.A.W.) on the first of the verses quoted above. We will also refer to the authority of the commentators of the Holy Book.

The relevant portion of the verse is:—

"O Prophet (S.A.W.) tell thy wives, daughters and the women believers to let down upon them their over-garments."

Commentary

(a) "Ibn Jarrer quotes Hazrat Ibn Abbas (R.A.A.) to have said, "Allah has commanded the believing women that when they go out of doors on any business they should cover their faces with over-garment and keep one eye open."

(b) "I, Ibn Sereen asked 'Obeda bin Haris to comment on the following words of the Holy Quran:-

"to let down upon their over-garments."

In reply to my question he said 'like this and then he covered his head and face with the piece of cloth he had, taking care to leave one of the eyes uncovered."

(c) Allama Ibn Jareer Tabari's commentary of the same relevant portion of the Quranic verse is as follows:

"When women have to go out of doors, they should not appear like slave-girls, i.e. they should not keep their hair and face exposed. On the contrary they are required to fully cover themselves with over-garments so that a wicked person seeing them may not take them for slave-girls and know them to be free women and refrain from passing indecent remarks."

(d) Allama Abu Bakr Al Jassas says:

"This verse implies that young women have been placed under the obligation to hide their faces and observe purdah while going out of doors so that no wicked person may nourish any wish for them."

wicked person may nourish any wish for them."

(e) Allama Qazi Baizawi offers the following comments on the words "to let down their over-garments upon them'—

"This means that when they go out of doors they should cover their faces and bodies with thick over-garments."

The same verse is interpreted by Allama Naishapuri in the following words:

Like the women of the days of ignorance, the Muslim women at the initial stage of Islam used to go out of doors just as they were clad at home and having only dupattas to cover their heads. Thus there was no difference between a free woman and a slave-girl. For this reason the women have been commended to cover their heads and faces."

From the commentaries cited above it is clear that the companions of the Holy Prophet (S.A.W.) all of whom were scholars and commentators of the Holy Quran are unanimous in the light of the verse in question on placing the believing women under the obligation of wearing cover-garments and hiding their faces from male strangers.

Second answer to the same question is provided in the light of the proven traditions of the Holy Prophet (S.A.W.) and the practice of the women of his companions.

In the authentic collections of traditions *Sunan Abu Dawood, Tirmizi and Imam Malik's Moatta* we read that the Holy Prophet (S.A.W.) commanded women wearing *Ahram* during pilgrimage not to put on veils and gloves.

The words of *Sunan Abu Dawood* are as follows:--

"The Holy Prophet (S.A.W.) has forbidden the women wearing *Ahram*, to put on veil and gloves."

It is evident from this tradition that in the days of the Holy Prophet (S.A.W.) that veil and gloves were in vogue among the women, but as intending pilgrims wearing *ahram* they were asked not to wear them. But the Holy Prophet's (S.A.W.) command in this respect was not unqualified.

In *Sunan Abu Dawood* we find this tradition narrated by Hazrat Aisha (R.A.A.):—

> "As we were accompaying the Prophet (S.A.W.) wearing *ahram*, horsemen passed by us. As they went past us every one of us (women) covered our heads and faces with overgarments (cloth sheets) and when the horsemen had bypassed us we removed our over-garments."

Again in Imam Malik's Moatta the following tradition narrated by Fatima bint Munzir (R.A.A.) is given:

> "We covered our faces even wearing *ahram*. Hazrat Asma bint Abu Bakr was with us but she took no objection to our act."

In *Fathul Bari* the following advice of Hazrat Aisha (R.A.A.) is cited:

> "Woman should cover her head and face with her over-garment (Sheet of Cloth).

The authenticity of an incident about a woman of Banu Qenqa is established by *Sehah Sitta*. A woman used to go the market for shopping covered with her overgarment. A jew came in front of her and started making fun of the woman. He then tried to force her to remove her veil. As he got hold of her veil to put it off, the woman called for help. A Muslim rushed to her rescue and beheaded the jew.

It is borne by the authentic traditions that the Holy Prophet's (S.A.W.) wives and daughters and the womenfolk of his companions used to hide their faces whenever they went out of their homes, even if they happened to wear *ahram*. They believed that *purdah* is an obligation and they must observe it.

We now give a third answer to the question relating to purdah with reference to the observation of the Imams who are acknowledged authorities on religious problem.

All the well known Imams among whom Imam Shafi'ee, Imam Ahmed bin Hanbal and Imam Malik are the most prominent, hold that woman's face is included in the parts of her body essential to be covered. It is therefore unlawful to keep it exposed. They advocate in the light of the observation made by the Prophet's (S.A.W.) companions and other preceding authorities that the women should wrap up their heads and faces with chadars and cite the following verse of the Holy Quran in support of their position:

And to draw their veils over their bosoms (24: 31)

As the womenfolk of the Prophet's Companions used to cover their faces and wore veils as they went out of their homes, their action serves us a practical proof of the above verse. The meaning of the verse in question is further subs-tantiated by the observations made by the Prophet's companions and their successors. We have already quoted their observations in course of alluding to commentaries of the above verse, wherein the problem of *purdah* has been dealt with at length.

But the position of the Hanafi School is that *Purdah* does not include woman's face. It may be kept exposed, provided that there is no potential danger of any untoward incident in doing so. If such a danger is feared, then according to the Hanafites, keeping the face exposed is unlawful.

The Hanafites advance the following arguments in support of their position:

The First tradition which alludes to Fazl bin Abbas.

"Once Hazrat Fazl bin Abbas was travelling along with the Holy Prophet (S.A.W.) on camel's back. As women wearing *Ahram* went past them, Hazrat Fazl looked at them. The Holy Prophet (S.A.W.) covered the eyes of Hazrat Fazl with his hand whereupon Hazrat Fazl turned his face the other way."

This is an authentic tradition and has been quoted by *Muslim, Abu Dawood and Ibn Majah.*

On the basis of this tradition the Hanafites argue that had the face of woman been included in those private parts of women which have to be covered under the Islamic injunctions, Hazrat Fazl would not have looked at them. In other words the women would have put on veils and Hazrat Fazl would not have looked at them.

Second tradition relating to the problem under discussion is narrated by Hazrat Aishȧ (R.A.A.). She says that once Hazrat Asma bint Abu Bakr (R.A.A.) called on the Prophet. She was wearing thin clothes at that time. When the Prophet (S.A.W.) saw her he turned his face the other way and said to her "O Asma, when a woman comes of age, it is necessary that no part of her body should remain exposed except this and this (pointed to both his palms).

All the jurists other than the Hanafites draw the following conclusion from both the traditions mentioned above:

The Fazl bin Abbas tradition is no justification for keeping women's face exposed before a male stranger, for the women at whom Hazrat Fazl looked were intending pilgrims appearing in *ahram* and in such a condition woman can legitimately keep her face unveiled, provided that this involves no possibility of causing an untoward incident. The reason for this is that the woman's condition of *ahram* requires the exposition of her hand and face. A tradition to this effect has already been cited.

The tradition, involving Hazrat Asma (R.A.A.) is mursil i.e. a tradition whose narrators sequence is broken.

According to Ibn Kaseer (see his commentary, Vol. III, Page 283) the above tradition is *Mursil* because its narrative sequence is as under:

It was narrated to Al Waleed by Saeed bin Basheer, to Saeed by Qatadah, to Qatadah by Khalid bin Darek and to Khalid by Hazrat Aisha (R.A.A.) but Khalid did not hear it from Hazrat Aisha (R.A.A.) himself.

The verdict of the majority of Ulama about a *mursil* tradition is that it is weak and as such it cannot serve as a basis of argument and the conclusion therefrom cannot be reliable.

The foregoing juristic argumentation bears it out that the woman's face is included in the parts of her body whose covering is obligatory and exposition is unlawful. Even the Hanafi jurists who justify the exposition qualify their injunction by the absence of any potential danger of an untoward incident. In other words, if any such danger looms large, then exposition of woman's face is unlawful.

In modern society which is already degenerated no sane person would like to cause corruption. It is therefore, incumbent upon every person with a sense of honour would call upon their wives and daughters to follow the example of the pure womenfolk of the Prophet (S.A.W.) and companions (R.A.A.) and keep their faces covered when they appear in public and thus pay tribute to those woman's purity, modesty and respect in our society by their right interpretation of the Quranic injunctions and the Prophet's (S.A.W.) traditions. Every parent and guardian should act on these injunction of his own honour and safety and should always try to conduct himself in a righteous and cautious manner. He should follow this course if he wants to be in the company of the Prophet (S.A.W.), martyrs and the rewarded servants of Allah in the Hereafter. What a good company it will indeed be!

Prohibition of showing off one's beauty and ostentation of adornments is borne out by the following tradition:-

Abu Huraira (R.A.A.) quotes the Holy Prophet (S.A.W.) to have observed, "Two kinds of people belong to Hell:

(a) Those who keep the whips like cow's tale and

(b) Women who are naked in spite of being clad and who walk with conquetish gait and bewiteh the hearts and whose heads are like the humps of the grown up Camels. Such women can never enter Paradise. In fact they will not be able even to smell the fragrance of Paradise although it reaches a distance of five hundred miles."

"Says Allah:—

"And stay in your houses. Bedizen not yourselves with the bedizenment of the Time of Ignorance." (33:33)

Says Allah in another verse:

As for women past child-bearing who have no hope of marriage, it is no sin for them if they discard their outer clothing in such a way as not to show adornment. But to refrain is better for them. Allah is Hearer, Knowner. (24: 60)

Prohibition of the free mixing of sexes is inferred from the following verse:

Tell the believing men to lower their gaze and be modest. And tell the believing women to lower their gaze and be modest. (24: 30)

But the question arises that when men and women assemble at the same place, how can it be possible to the members of either sex to keep their gazes downcast. If one

reads between the lines of the above verse, one may come to the conclusion that mixing of sexes is forbidden. This is clear from the following verse:—

And when ye ask of them (the wives of the Prophet (S.A.W.) anything, ask it of them behind a curtain. That is purer for your hearts and for their hearts.

(33: 53)

Says the Holy Prophet (S.A.W.):

"When a man and woman are together in private, there is a third fellow present and he is Satan." (*Tirmizi*)

There is another tradition of the Prophet (S.A.W.):

"Do not go among women" said he. A man asked what he thought about the husband's brother, the Prophet (S.A.W.) replied "It is death."

Ibn Abbas quotes the Prophet (S.A.W.) to have remarked, "None of you should remain alone with woman unless some close relation of hers (one before whom the woman can appear without *purdah*) is present. (*Bukhari*)

Prohibition of looking at female strangers is evident from the following verses of the Holy Quran;

In Surah Al Noor (No. 24) Allah enjoins upon the Prophet (S.A,W.) :

"Tell the believing men to lower their gaze and be modest."

In Surah Bani Israel Allah says:

"Ears, eyes and heart all will be questioned about."

(17:36)

Hazrat Jareer narrates that he asked the Holy Prophet (S.A.W.) about glancing a woman incidentally. The Prophet (S.A.W.) replied, "Turn your gaze."

Hazrat Umm Salma (R.A.A.) says that one day she was with the Holy Prophet (S.A.W.). Hazrat Maimoona (R.A.A.) was also present at the moment. Suddenly Ibn Umm Maktoom arrived. This incident took place after revelation of the Quranic verse enjoining upon women to observe *purdah.* The Prophet (S.A.W.) asked both the ladies to hide themselves. The ladies pointed out that he was blind. "Are both of you blind too?" asked the Prophet (S.A.W.).

Hazrat Abu Saeed Khudri quotes the Holy Prophet (S.A.W.) to have said to his companions, "Refrain from sitting on the way side."

The Companions asked, "Is this absolutely essential for us? We just sit and talk with one another."

The Prophet (S.A.W.) replied, "If you like to sit on the way you may then you should fulfil your obligation with regard to thoroughfare.

"Could you tell us what that obligation is?" enquired the companions.

The Prophet (S.A.W.) replied, "To keep your Gaze to low, remove the nuisance, if any, reciprocate people's greetings, enjoin good and forbid evil."

It is too obvious to need any explanation that if all the nations and communities, if all the people including the young and the old, the males and females as well as the rulers and the ruled act on these eternal principles and keep in view the values embodied by them, refrain from being immodest by showing off their beauty, from mixing up of the sexes freely and looking at men from whom purdah is obligatory, they will all be pure virtuous, stable and will enjoy the blessings of peaceful life. In short, they will reach the acme of glory, for they will be treading the path of Allah and adopting the way of life prescribed by Allah for the Muslims. Says Allah:

> This is my straight path so follow it. Follow not other ways let ye be parted from His way. This has been ordained for you, that ye may ward off evil." (6: 153)

The process of translating these Islamic injunctions has been going on in our society for centuries together. It is the impact of the Quranic teachings that have been revealed to give good tidings for the entire world and to provide guidance for posterity.

Says Allah in the Holy Quran:

"Doubtless, this Quran giveth unto that which is straightest and giveth tidings unto the believers who do good." (17:9)

By following the principles and methods of training as laid down by Islam, the parents and guardians can effect the moral uplift of their children, develop their Islamic identity and enable them to seriously face the harsh realities of life in a manly manner. The Muslim parents and guardians are under the obligation to bring up their sons on the right lines and in conformity with the principles prescribed by Allah and given by the Holy Prophet (S.A.W.), thereby enriching them with cardinal virtues and propriety. At the end of this discussion I want to ask a question and that is:

Is there any other system of life embodying principles of training children and making them realize their responsibilities and realities of life comparable to those laid by Islam?

Can anybody deny that indulgence in a life of pleasures and comforts does not harm the personality of a child; that pornography and gratification of sensual desires does not mar a youngster's identity; that pleasures of obscene music and shameful dance does not exert sinister influence on him and that exposition of woman's face, exhibition of her adornments and unrestrained living together of man and woman does no harm the child.

It will be absolutely wrong to think that a boy's personality would remain intact when he imitates the fair sex and talks with affected pathos.

The specialists of child psychology and the scholars of education and training will all have to agree that seeking comforts and indulgence in pleasures, gratification of sensual desires and enjoying obscene dance and music are maladies fraught with multifarious evils and afflictions. For instance, the above maladies would result in loss of memory, impairment of personality, infirmity of character and impotency. Man develops numerous other diseases because of them and is irretrievably depried of purity.

In his book "Man The Forgotten" Dr. AlexiCarlyle writes that when man's sexual appetite is incited certain excretions are infused into his blood and affect the brain causing drowsiness with the result that man is incapable of thinking clearly.

George Paloshi has recorded in his book "Sexual Revolution" the remarks of U:S. President Kennedy made in 1965 to the effect that the future of U.S was bleak becuase its youths are extremely lecherous and have no sense of responsibility whatsoever. Six out of seven young men who are sent up for recruitment in the army, observes Kennedy, are of loose character and are rendered both psychologically and physically unfit for military service by sexual corruption.

In Lebanes newspaper a lady named Margaret Smith writes that the girl students of schools and collges think of nothing but of the ways to gratify their desires with the result that 60% of them fail in the exams and that the main cause of their failure is their obsession with sex that inhibits their concern for their studies.

The entire responsibility for preventing the moral deterioration of their children rests with the parents and guardians. They ought to make every possible effort to impress upon the child's mind the significance of human sanctity and build his or her character so as to enrich it with moral excellence.

We are all under the obligation to improve the morals of our children and keep a strict eye upon them.

If we enquire into the causes of a child's moral deterioration, we shall find that the main cause is the parents' negligence of their proper training and abandoning them to their fate.

Some of the causes of children's moral deterioration are as follows:

(1) The father gives his children a free hand to do whatever they like. As there is nobody to keep an eye upon them, they associate with bad characters without any fear of being called to account. Thus they acquire various vices and get accustomed to committing misdeeds.

(2) The father allows his children to see erotic films which deprave the children and cause split personality in them. The detective films displaying the feats of police result in their moral deterioration and induce them to commit crimes. Such films cause moral degeneration of even grown up people, not to speak of children. Such a father willingly throws his offspring into the abyss of depravity from which they can never be rescued.

(3) If the father does not prevent the children from watching such films and plays shown on television as incite sex and induce aberration from moral and social norms they are bound to develop split per-

sonality and morally deteriorate. Children so depraved will never know the meaning of manliness, nor will have that masculine pride which is the very essence of the male personality. Besides such children will be absolutely devoid of the dignity by which Islamic decorum is characterized.

(4) The man who pays no heed to the proper observance of purdah by his wife and daughters and ignores the exposition of their adornment allows his womenfolk to wear such constumes as are designed for ostentation rather than for meeting the requirements of purdah, consequently such womenfolk would go astray and become lewd. They would lose their honour, virtue and chastity. When things come to such a pass, it will be of no consequence to feel distressed and ashamed of one's self.

Says a poet:

Do you lament for Lubna, whereas you have dishonoured her yourself?
Lubna is past all remedy. What will you do now?

(5) If the father does not keep an eye on his sons and daughters while they leave home for going to the school and return therefrom, his children will take undue advantage of his negligence and go to places other than the schools, where they could have every thing to their hearts' desire. We have learnt of a number of cases involving seduction of girls by debauchees. Such girls are disgraced in the society and by the time the parents learn of their infamy they are already lewd and notorious whores.

(6) Most of the children whose father does not care so much as to have a look at their schools or places of work become corrupt and perverted. They are fond of collecting nude pictures to enjoy the voluptuous spectacles presented in them, read pornographic magazines, write love letters to their beloved, giving vent to their sensual passions. They do all such things unabashed, with impunity and without a twinge of conscience. If they persist in this course of perversion and immorality, they lose their personality

and never face the call of their conscience. When this stage is reached nothing can avail to redeem them.

The parents and guardians are under the obligation to attach primary importance to morals in the training and education of their children and rear them in a manner that they get into the habit of treating the people they brush their shoulders in a decent and polite manner of their own accord.

We quote here some traditions of the Holy Prophet (S.A.W.) in relation to morals and honest dealings.

(1) Said the Prophet (S.A.W.) "I have been sent for the perfection of high morals."

(*Imam Ahmed, Hakim, Baihaqi*)

Ibn Mardwaih narrates that a man asked the Holy Prophet (S.A.W.) about morality. The Prophet quoted the following verse of the Holy Quran:

Keep to forgiveness (O Muhammad), and enjoin kindness and turn away from the ignorant (7: 199)

"The meaning of this is that you should try to establish relation with him who cuts it off and whoever deprives you of anything give it to him and whoever does wrong to you forgive him.

(2) Hazrat Abu Darda quotes the Prophet (S.A.W.) to have observed:

"On the Day of judgement piety and moral excellence will weightier on the scale of actions than any thing else."

(3) Hazrat Abu Dhar narrates that a man came to seek Holy Prophet's (S.A.W.) advice. The Prophet (S.A.W.) said to him. "Fear Allah wherever you are". The man requested the Prophet (S.A.W.) to bless him with a little more teaching. The Prophet (S.A.W.) said, "If you have done a misdeed then do something good for a good deed does away with a misdeed." The man asked for some more instruction. The Prophet (S.A.W.) said, "Treat the people kindly."

(4) Hazrat Abu Huraira quotes the Holy Prophet (S.A.W.) to have said, "The more staunch a believer, the more will he be uplifted morally."

(5) Muhammed bin Nasrul Muroozi writes that a man came to the Holy Prophet (S.A.W.) from ahead and said, "O Messenger of Allah! What is faith?" The Prophet (S.A.W.) replied, "Moral excellence." The man came to him from the right side and repeated his question. The Prophet (S.A.W.) replied "Moral excellence." He appeared again from the left and put the same question. "Moral excellence" was the Prophet's (S.A.W.) reply. The man then drew near the Prophet (S.A.W.) from beind and put the same question. Holy Prophet (S.A.W.) said, "Don't you understand? Do not be provoked."

The foregoing traditions constitute the teachings of the Holy Prophet (S.A.W.) with regard to morality, honest dealings and decency in collective behaviours.

It is now up to the parents and guardians to translate those teachings into practice. They should strictly follow them and thus provide guidance to the children by their example.

They should give moral training to their children in the best possible manner inclucating in them moral attitudes so that theymay forgive those who do them wrong, reconcile with those who cut off relation with them, bestow things upon those who deprive them and of do good to those who afflict them. The children will thus earn a good name, the parents will be proud of them and any one who comes across them may have the feeling that they are angels in the form of humans. All this is possible only when we act on the following divine injunctions:

"Keep to forgiveness, and enjoin kindness and turn away from the ignorant." (7: 199)

The good deed and the evil deed are not alike. Repel the evil deed with one which is better then lo! he, between whom and thee there was enmity (will become) as though he was a bosom friend." (41: 34)

"And those who, when they do an evil thing or wrong themselves, remember Allah and implore forgiveness for their sins." (3: 135)

In the ensuing pages we propose to discuss the psychological and social training of children.

At the end, however, I want to impress upon the parents the great importance attached by the Holy Prophet (S.A.W.) to the training and education of children.

In the foregoing pages we made an attempt to show how the children are to be improved morally and how to guard them against evils. We also cited a number of Prophet's (S.A.W.) traditions in this context.

It is hoped that the parents will resolve to train and educate their children according to the Islamic principles as their primary obligation. If they fail in their duty they will have to bear the entire responsibility of children's deviation from the moral principles.

If children's moral uplift is not cared for, their personality will disintegrate and their character will have no consistency. Consequently they will become immoral and pose a threat to the whole society and will finally lead it to a catastrophe. At this stage of degeneration, every child of the society will turn a habitual offender.

Hence the parents and the guardians are under the obligation to duly fulfil their responsibility for the moral improvement of their children. If they fulfil their responsibility, their children will be like the lamps illuminating their homes or like the fragrant flowers blooming on the plants in their courtyards. They will turn out to be the darlings of the society and angels moving about on earth.

"Act! Allah will behold your actions, and (so will) His messenger and the believers (9: 105).

CHAPTER VIII

RESPONSIBILITY FOR PHYSICAL TRAINING

Islam imposes upon the parents, guardians and tutors the great responsibility of imparting physical training to the children so that they may be able to live a full life. The obligations of the parents in this respect are as follows:

(a) Spending money on parents and children.

Says Allah:

The duty of feeding and clothing nursing mothers in a seemly manner is upon the father of the child (2: 233)

According to another tradition the Prophet (S.A.W.) is reported to have said:

"A dinar spent by you on your dependants carries a greater reward than one spent in the way of Allah, for the release of a captive or for the help of a destitute."

The father on the one hand deserves a great reward in the Hereafter by providing amenities to the members of his family and by spending money on his children, while on the other hand he is guilty of a great sin by keeping his family members hard upon in spite of being in possession of financial resources. The Holy Prophet (S.A.W.) has this to say who do not give what is due to their dependants:

"It is sin enough for a man to deny the rights of his dependants."

The wording of the same tradition as given in the Sahih Muslim are as follows:

"It is sin enough to cease feeding the person whom one is responsible to provide for."

By spending money on one's dependants is meant to provide them proper food, proper shelter and proper dress so that they may not be taken ill and consequently weakened or be attackd by epidemics."

(b) The Hygienic Principles of Eating, Drinking and Sleeping.

It was customary with the Holy Prophet (S.A.W.) to refrain from eating so much that it results in indigestion. He forbids excessive eating:

"Stomach is the worst utensil that a human-being can fill. For him only so many morsels are sufficient as can keep his back straight. If eating is absolutely essential, then one should fill only one third of the stomach and only one third quantity of water. The remaining one third should be left for taking breath." (*Imam Ahmed, Tirmizi*)

In drinking water the Prophet's (S.A.W.) practice was to drink it draughts alternated by a little pause two or three times. He forbade to exhale in the drinking pot or drink while standing.

Hazrat Ibn Abbas quotes the Holy Prophet to have said:

"Do not gulp water like the camel. Drink in two or three draughts. When you start drinking something say: *Bismillah* and you finish say *Al Hamdu lillah.*" (*Tirmizi*)

According to Abu Qatadah, the Holy Prophet (S.A.W.) forbade to exhale in the drinking pot. (*Bukhari and Muslim*)

And in the words of *Sahih Tirmizi* the Prophet (S.A.W.) forbade to exhale and puff inside the pot.

Hazrat Abu Huraira quotes the Holy Prophet (S.A.W.) to have said, "None of you should drink water (or anything lawful) while standing. If any one does it unwittingly he should vomit."

(c) Sleeping

As regards sleeping the Prophet's (S.A.W.) practice was to sleep on the right side, for sleeping on the left side would exert pressure on the heart and may cause difficulty in breathing.

Bara bin 'Aazib quotes the Holy Prophet (S.A.W.) to have said, "When you go to bed, perform ablution as you do before offering prayer and then sleep on your right side saying the following prayer:

"O God! I have resigned myself to Thee. I have turned my face towards Thee and have entrusted my affair to Thee and have made Thee my sheet anchor with fondness and respect in Thy presence. There is no refuge other than Thee. I have placed my faith in the Book Thou hast revealed and the Prophet (S.A.W.) Thou hast sent as Thy messenger." (*Bukhari and Muslim*)

Immunity Measures Against infectious Diseases

Some relevant traditions of the Holy Prophet (S.A.W.) are cited here:

(a) A tradition narrated by Ibn Jabir has been quoted by Imam Muslim, Ibn Maja and others. According to this tradition a delegation of Banu Saqeef came to the Holy Prophet (S.A.W.) which included a leper. The Prophet (S.A.W.) sent him the word that he should go back as the Prophet (S.A.W.) had accepted his bai'at (oath of Allegiance).

(b) The Prophet (S.A.W.) said, "You should run away from a leper as you take to heels at the sight of a tiger."

(c) According to Hazrat Abu Huraira the Holy Prophet (S.A.W.) observed, "A sick person should not be brought near a healthy person."

In the light of the above tradition it is necessary that the parents and guardians should isolate a child who contracts an infectious disease from other children, in order to prevent the spread of disease in the form of an epidemic.

The Holy Prophet's (S.A.W.) practice for the protection of the health and maintenance of physical fitness is an example to be followed by all the Muslims.

Treatment Diseases

Medicine is the effective means of treating ailments. There are various traditions relating to treatment by medication. Some of them are cited below:

Jabir bin Abdullah cites the Holy Prophet (S.A.W.) to have said, "There is a medicine for every disease. If a medicine is suited to the disease, the patient will be cured by the Will of Allah."

Usama bin Shareek narrates that he was with the Holy Prophet (S.A.W.) when some bedouins came to him and asked if they could take medicines for the treatment of diseases. The Prophet (S.A.W.) replied, "O bondsmen of Allah! Do take medicines. Doubtless Allah has created no disease for which there is no cure except one disease. They asked him what that disease was. The Prophet (S.A.W.) said: "Old Age." (*Musnad Imam Ahmed, Sunan Nisai*)

Hazrat Abu Huraira narrates that once he said to the Holy Prophet (S.A.W.), "We recite some formulas and blow to exorcise disease from the body, take medicine for treatment, take certain measures for the prevention of disease and do all sorts of things for keeping good health. Do you think that all these things would affect the destiny determined by Allah? The Prophet (S.A.W.) replied that all these things are also determined by Allah (that is, God has also made all these things effective. Their effect is Allah's power)."

All these traditions bear it out that parents and guardians are under the obligation to ask after the welfare of children when they fall sick and to provide them proper treatment; for the use of the effective means constitutes the demand of human nature as well as a proof of firm belief in Islam.

Application of the Principle: 'Do not Harm nor Get Harmed'

Abu Saeed Khudri quotes the Prophet (S.A.W.) to have observed, Do not harm nor get harmed."

The jurists and Ulama regard this tradition as a fundamental principle, from which they have derived corollaries for the safety of human existence and for their relief from troubles.

On the basis of the principle in question all the guardians, particularly mothers are under the obligation to instruct their children to follow the principles of hygiene and take all the possible measures to keep themsleves hale and hearty. It is also incumbent upon the guardians to consult specialists in order to keep their children immune from epidemics and other maladies.

Eating unripe fruits causes pain in the stomach and it may also result in the development of a disease. It is, therefore, incumbent upon the guardians to prevent children from eating unripe fruits and be advised to eat only ripe ones.

Eating vegetables and fruits without properly washing them may also cause different maladies. The children should therefore, be advised to wash them before eating.

Over eating sickens the stomach. It also produces harmful effects on repiration and digestive systems. This necessitates the development of habit among children to have their meals at fixed times.

Eating with dirty hands is also a cause of disease. It is therefore, necessary that Muslim children should be taught to wash their hands before and after taking meals and the rules laid down by Islam.

Some children are wont to blow into the spoons or the pots. This would make the food unwholesome. The guardians should, therefore, forbid the children to do such an unhygienic thing.

Such instructions would make children abide by the principles of hygiene and they would consequently enjoy perfect health, their bodies would be immune from diseases and make them physically strong, smart and active in life.

Sports, Exercise and Riding

Training the children in various sports and horse-riding is actually in compliance with this divine instruction:

"Make ready for them all thou canst of force......"

(8: 60)

This is also what the Prophet (S.A.W.) means by the following words:

"A stronger believer is better and dearer to Allah than a weaker one."

That is why Islam emphasises the importance of swimming, archery and riding. This is evident from the following tradition of the Holy Prophet (S.A.W.):

Tabarani cites a saying of the Holy Prophet (S.A.W.) with reference to authentic sources:

Whatever is not included in the service to Allah consists of play or oblivion and negligence with the exception of four things:

(a) 1) A man's walking between two marks (for shooting an arrow)

2) Taming one's horse.

3) Caressing one's wife.
4) Learning how to swim

(b) The Prophet (S.A.W.) recited the following verse of the Holy Quran:-
"Make ready for them all thou canst of force......"
He then, said, "Listen! By force is meant archery."
(c) Bazzaz and Tabarani narrate with reference to authentic sourses that the Prophet (S.A.W.) observed, "Learning archery is essential for you and it is also the best sport.

(d) When the Holy Prophet (S.A.W.) went through the circles of archers he encouraged them and urged upon them to practice archery saying that he was with them.
(e) It has been stated in *Sahih Bukhari and Sahih Muslim* that the Prophet allowed Abyssinians to play in his mosque with weapons of war and also permitted Hazrat Aisha to witness the game. He said to them. "O Banu Arfida, it is alright."

As this demonstration was in progress, Hazrat Omar made his appearance. He picked up a pebble from the ground and threw it at the players. The Prophet (S.A.W.) said, "O Umar, leave them."

It has been mentioned in a tradition of the Holy Prophet (S.A.W.) that competition is warrantable in three things:-
(a) In slaughtering sacrificial animals.
(b) In taming the horses and riding
(c) In archery and lancing.
The reason for this is that competition plays an importany part in the preparation for Jihad.

Preventing the Child from indulging in comforts and luxury.

This is necessary because when the child grows up he may be able to discharge his responsibilities for waging the war in the way of Allah and inviting the people to the path of Allah as well as develop the power and courage to do so in the best possible manner.

For this reason simplicity in life has been enjoined upon the Muslims in numerous traditions of the Holy Prophet (S.A.W.). It has been emphasized that they should be taught how to lead simple life. We cite here examples of two such traditions:

(1) A tradition was narrated to Moaz bin Jabal wherein it has been said, "Abstain from luxury and comforts. The bondsmen of Allah do not indulge in comforts and pleasures."

(2) Tabarani narrates the following tradition with reference to Ibn Shaheen, and Abu Noaim Qa'qa bin Abi Hadrad:- "You should try to follow the example of your ancestor ma'd bin 'Adnan in asperity and eloquence. Adopt simple way of life and practice lancing or archery."

The Holy Prophet's (S.A.W.) life provides the ideal pattern of the manner of eating, drinking, clothing and dwelling. The Muslim nations should try to tread in the path of Holy Prophet (S.A.W.) so that the Muslim peoples should always be in a state of readiness to march and be able to face aggression from any quarter with dauntless courage.

History bears it out that when Muslims indulged in a life of luxury, comforts and pleasures, slept on soft beds of silk and brocade and were taken in by the glamour of material civilization, their downfall ensued before long and they laid down arms before the enemy, and the Muslim youth lost the habit of consistency, bravery and the urge to be alert to wage war in the way of Allah.

Our debacle in Spain is still fresh in our minds.

To train the children how to live seriously and courageously in a manly manner as well as guarding them against lethargy, fickle mindedness and split personality.

The Holy Prophet (S.A.W.) has made this clear in the following traditions:

(1) Desire whatever is profitable for you, pray for God's help and do not be disheartened.

(2) Whatever makes one unmindful of Allah is either play or lapse with the exception of four things:

a. A man's walking between two marks for shooting an arrow.

b. Taming one's horse.

c. Caressing one's wife.
d. Learning how to swim.

(3) Abu Huraira (R.A.A.) quotes (*Tabarani*) the Prophet (S.A.W.) to have said:
"A debauchee cannot remain a believer while committing adultery. A thief cannot remain a believer while committing larceny, nor does he remain a believer while drinking liquor. (*Bukhari and Muslim*)

In *Sunan Nasai* the following words have been added: "If he did it he stood excommunicated."

Hazrat Abu Huraira quotes the Prophet (S:A.W.) to have observed, "I have not seen two kinds of men doomed to be committed to the Fire:

(a) Those who will have whips like the cow's tail with which they will beat the people and
(b) Women who will be dressed but will be naked and will walk with coquetish gait to attract the attention of the people and whose heads will be like the hump of the Khorasan's camels. They will not be able to smell even the fragrance of Paradise, not to speak of entering it, although its fragrance could be sensed from remote places (The narrator did not mention the length of the distance).

There are some of the typical traditions of the Holy Prophet (S.A.W.) which emphasize seriousness, firmness, diligence and manliness in life. He teaches to guard against ficklemindedness and deterioration of character.

It is clear that if the child develops ficklemindedness and inconsistency, he will become inequitous as he grows. He will be irresponsible and capricious. His personality will disintegrate, he will develop various complexes and he will fall a prey to dangerous diseases.

In view of the factors mentioned above, the parents and guardians are under the obligation to focus attention on their children in their early years, and acquaint them with what is meant by asperity, manliness, dignity and other virtues.

It is also necessary for the parents and guardians to prevent their children from such acts as may damage their personal integrity and manly character and result in their moral deterioration and weaken their mental and physical potentiality. This is absolutely necessary in order to imbibe in the children positive mode of thinking, foster their physical and mental growth and protect their character. They will thus be imbued with cosmopolitan spirit and will have a strong urge to fulfil their ambitions.

I have dealt in brief with the basic principles laid down by Islam for the upbringing of children.

If you realize their importance and put them into practice, you will be producing a healthy generation full of utility and vigour and ready to shoulder the responsibilities of truly Islamic way of life.

In this way you will not only fulfil the obligation imposed upon you for the training and education of children but will be able to present yourself before God on the Doomsday with a face brightened with a sense of success and would have the honour of moving in the enviable company of Prophets, martyrs and pious people.

SOME VICES

I would like to mention here a few vices that are to be found among the children as well as the adults, the youngmen as well as the grown up people. It is incumbent upon those responsible for the training and education of the new generation, particularly the fathers of children to keep an eye on such vices and not only realize their serious consequences themselves but also acquaint the youngsters with them so that they may be on guard against those vices.

According to my estimate there is a large number of children and young men who have fallen a prey to the following vices:

(1) Smoking,
(2) Masturbation
(3) Drug-addiction and
(4) Adultery and homosexuality.

I propose to discuss these vices at length in the ensuing pages.

1. Smoking

People in our society are getting increasingly addicted to

smoking. This is a vice more common than others. If we take stock of our milieu, we will find a very small number of youngsters and men and women both young and old who get rid of smoking once they are addicted to it. Only the people who possess extra-ordinary will-power and are sensible enough to prefer what is profitable to what is harmful and whose reason get better of their passion can rid themselves of this vice.

We must consider all these factors in an attempt to eradicate the vice of smoking:

(a) The harmful effects of smoking
(b) The relevant injunction of the Shariah.
(c) Remedy

(a) The Harmful Effects of Smoking

We dwell only on two of such effects:

(1) Physical and Psychological maladies.
(2) Loss of Money.

It has been established by medical research that smoking causes tuberculosis and lungs cancer. It also results in the loss of memory and appetite. The smokers face grows pale and his teeth take on yellowish colour. He experiences difficulty in breathing and develops general debility and nervousness. The smoker is also capricious and lethargic. We quote here the opinions of a few doctors in this regard.

In a German magazine a report was published to the effect that the medical research centre at Bethesda in the American state of Maryland ten specialists conducted research on the effects of smoking on human health. The findings of their investigation and experiments are as follows:

(i) The rate of mortality among the smokers is sixty percent higher than among non-smokers.
(ii) The smokers develop the diseases mentioned below as many times more than non-smokers as indicated against them respectively.
    (1) Lungs cancer — 10-8 times
    (2) Burning and inflammation of nasal and respiratory tracts — 6-10 times.
    (3) Throat cancer — 5-4 times.
    (4) Mouth cancer

(5) Cancer of alimentary canal (the tube through which food passes into the stomach) — 3-4 times.
(6) Abdominal ailments — 2-4 times
(7) Other Common diseases — 2-6 times
(8) Cardiac diseases — 1-7 times.

(iii) Smokers develop cardiac diseases 70% more than the non-smokers and the burning of the nasal membrane and respiratory tracts five hundred times more. They also suffer from lungs cancer more than anybody else. They get lungs cancer a thousand percent more than the non-smokers.

The Syrian Society has issued the following statements with regard to tuberculosis:

The facts stated below have been established after many years of academic debate and research.

Where a man smokes, his body is filled with 80 to 90 % smoke, apart from the sooty matter that sticks to his respiratory tract. This sooty matter consists of various chemical substances. Some of them cause cancer, while others irritate the lungs and serve as a breeding ground for tubercular germs. Hence smokers are more susceptible to cancerous growth and consumption. Besides, smoking causes other incurable and stubborn ailments of the lungs, for instance, burning and inflammation of lungs, gasping etc. Smoking paves the way for cardiac diseases. Nicotine quickens heart beat and produces adverse effects on blood pressure. The smokers shorten the span of their life at their own cost. In view of these findings of medical research, one should, of necessity, abstain from smoking and if one has already got addicted, should give it up.

There are other harmful effects of smoking as well.

It is known for certain that even people with limited income spend over one fourth of their earnings on smoking. This is waste of money responsible for the ruining of families. For a man addicted to smoking deprives his family of their requirements by spending money on smoking. Sometimes the smokers take bribe or commit larceny in order to gratify their habit.

It may well be judged how destructive is the habit of smoking and what harmful influence it exercises on morality, human health and social life. But unfortunately most people do not realize it.

The Shariat Injunction in respect of Smoking

(a) It is the unanimous verdict of all the jurists and scholars of Islam that one ought to refraim from doing whatever is harmful and dangerous to one's life and the commitment of such as act is unlawful. This is borne out by the following tradition of the Holy Prophet (S.A.W.):

"Do no harm and do not be harmed."

The following verses of the Holy Quran also mean the same things:

And be not cast by your own hands to ruin." (2 : 195)

Again,

"Do not kill yourselvers. Verily Allah is ever Merciful to you." (4:29)

Since it has been proved that smoke is injurious to human health and causes disease, one should abstain from it as its use is unlawful.

(b) It has been acknowledged by the intellectuals and people with a sense of decency that somking is an impure thing, injurious to health and causing dis-agreeable smell in the mouth. Allah has declared only the pure and cleanly things lawful while prohibiting uncleanly and foul things, the aim is to protect human body and prevent man from being immoral and from wrong thinking as well as to make him amiable in the society. Says Allah:—

" Exchange not good for the bad." (4 :2)

Again,

" Allah has made lawful for them all good things and prohibit for them only the foul" (7: 157)

Once again,

" Say the good and the evil are not alike even though the plenty of evil attract thee." (5 : 100)

Somking produces other harmful effects also. It makes the mind sluggish and the body weary. This is felt only by the man who takes to smoking and gets addicted to it gradually. The more he gets addicted to it the more sluggish will his mind be and the more fatigued his body.

The Holy Prophet (S.A.W.) has forbidden the use of

anything that makes the mind and nerves inactive, just as he has forbidden the intoxicants. We cite in this connection a tradition narrated by Hazrat Umm Salama as quoted by Imam Ahmed in his *Musnad* and *Abu Dawood* in his *Sunan*:—

Hazrat Umm Salama Says that the Prophet (S.A.W.) has forbidden the use of anything that produces infirmity and intoxicates."

These unequivocal edicts categorically declare smoking unlawful and make it obligatory to abstain from it; for smoking is highly injurious and undoubtedly uncleanly. Moreover, smoking is the waste of money, which causes worries to individual and the family and the society on the whole is deprived of many good things. The Prophet (S.A.W.) therefore, has forbidden the waste of money as has been reported in *Sahih Bukhari*.

The jurists who declared smoking legitimate or at the most abominable were not in a position to do otherwise. The medical research in those days was not advanced enough to make them aware of the harm done by smoking. Therefore their attitude towards smoking was determined by the principle of jurisprudence that the essence of everyting is legitimacy (that is its being legitimate). But now when the harmful effects of smoking have been established by medical research and it has been demonstrated what harm it does to respiration and the human body, there remains no justification to impede the prohibition of smoking. It is a vice beyond any shadow of doubt, that it is highly injurious to human health. It is also proved that addiction to smoking is a sin.

How to Cure Addiction to Smoking.

The Primary responsibility of the prevention of the habit of smoking rests with the government. The measures to be taken in this connection is to .acquaint the people with the harmful effects of smoking and to warn them to abstain from it. This may be done through the media of information such as radio and television as well as newspapers and periodicals. The government may also seek the cooperation of the doctors and the specialists in its campaign against smoking. The writers and intellectuals may also be called upon to extend their co-operation. Moreover, the Government should levy heavier tax on tobacco, increase the price of cigarettes and thus restrain the sale and purchase thereof.

Such measures will be the first step towards eradication on the menace of somking. In advanced countries like USA and Britian some such measures are being taken to control and put an end to the habit of somking.

Elderly people addicted to smoking should remember God and fear Him and abstain from unlawful things which include smoking. They should develop the will-power and must have the determination to thwart the urge to smoke. They should turn to account the divine gift—reason and wisdom to tread the straight path that has no turns and twists. As a matter of fact when a man's faith is firm and has the will-power, he can relinquish his sinister desire and rid himself of the vice of smoking. By dint of strong faith, determination and common sense man can attain perfection and can lead pure and happy life.

As for the youngsters who get addicted to smoking because of neglect of their parents and guardians, it will be dangerous to leave them to their fate. They would pose a threat to the society as a whole. It is, therefore, absolutely necessary to take effective steps to rid them of the habit of smoking.

The parents and guardians are under the obligation to keep their children under strict observation and set the deviant ones right so that they may be immune from the diseases caused by smoking.

2. Masturbation

The immoral habit of masturbation is common among lads and young men. It is generally caused by the spectacle of women moving about in public places in attractive costume with immodesty, coquettish gait, showing off their beauty. It is no wonder that the budding youth is deeply affected by their enchanting sight.

Apart from these factors at work in the actual social life, the scenes shown in the stage plays and films are far more voluptuous. What do the boys see in them? Every thing that incites sex, degrades human dignity and depreciate chastity; everything that cuts at the very root of human pride, modesty and honour. Romantic novels, erotic fiction and other sex-inciting literature also ruins the physical and psychological health, the reason and morality of the youths.

All these stimulants and incitements are enough to spur a boy or girl to the path of debauchery and sexual corruption.

If the heart of a young boy is devoid of God's fear nothing on earth can stop him from dedauchery; nor can anything make him conscious of the consequences of sexual immorality. He will therefore, have to choose between two courses as there is no third alternative left for him:

(1) He will either have to gratify his sexual appetite by unlawful methods or

(2) overwhelmed by the intensity of sensual desire, he will have to resort to masturbation.

Both these courses lead to the impairment of human body, heredity and mental health. As this subject requires a detailed discussion, I consider it necessary to answer the following questions:—

1. What harm does masturbation do?
2. What is the position of Shariah with regard to masturbation?
3. How to rid one of the habit of msturbation?

I. The kinds of trouble caused by masturbation.

These fall under three heads.

(a) Physical Ailments.

Physical enervation and inactivity, thinning of the body due to loss of flesh, shaking of the sides, palpitation, weakening of vision and memory, disruption of the digestive system, burning of both the lungs resulting usually in consumption, anemia and the fluctuation of blood pressure.

(b) Sexual Maladies

The habit of masturbation causes impotency and man is consequently incapable of performing conjugal function i.e. of sexual intercourse. The wife of an impotent man will naturally be disgusted with him and separation between the couple would be inevitable.

Another trouble caused by habitual masturbation is that man cuts shy of the opposite sex. In other words, the woman he marries would not regard him as a guarantee of her purity. This often leads to divorce; or else, she befriends other males for the gratification of her sexual urge.

(c) Mental Ailments

The psychologists are of the opinion that a habitual masturbator developes dangerous mental and psychical maladies. Some of these are as under:

Loss of memory, weakening of will-power, tendency for seclusion, shyness, the feeling that life is an insoluble problem, phobia, lethargy and inertia, depression, thinking all the time to commit some crime or suicide. Habitual masturbation causes other abnormalities besides those just mentioned, which make the mind dull and incapable of thinking. They also cause irresoluteness and disintegration of personality. The experts have discussed in details the abnormalities resulting from this sinister habit.

2. The Position of Shariah with Regard to Masturbation

From the Shariat standpoint masturbation is a sin. Following arguments may be advanced in support of our contention.

(a) Says Allah:

> "And those who protect their private parts from others except their wives and the salve-girls purchased by them are not liable to censure. But those who want more than this are transgressors." (23: 5-7)

The second part of the above verse applies among other things to masturbation:

"Those who want more than this are transgressors."

The above verse extends to all the methods of gratifying sexual desires other than conjugal life; for instance adultery, homosexuality, masturbation etc.

'Ata, a companion of Hazrat Ibn Abbas says, "I have heard of people who will gather together on the Day of Judgment with their hands impregnated. I think they will be the masturbaters."

Saeed bin Jubair who is regarded as one of the successors of the Prophet's (S.A.W.) Companions has this to tell us: "Allah most painfully tormentad a people who used their sexual organs with their hands wrongfully."

It has also been mentioned in the Prophet's (S.A.W.) traditions that there will be seven kinds of people at whom Allah will not look. Among such people will be included those who enter into wedlock with their hands i.e. commit hand practice.

It is clear from the foregoing statements that masturbation is unlawful.

(b) We have already mentioned the following basic principle in the course of our discussion of the declaring smoking unlawful:

"Anything causing harm and poses a threat to life ought to be abstained from; and the doing of such a thing is unlawful."

This principle has been derived from a saying of the Holy Prophet (S.A.W.):

"Do no harm and do not be harmed."

The Principle also owes its origin to the following divine decree:

"Do not imperil your lives with your own hands." (2: 195)

As masturbation causes physical, psychological, mental and sexual abnormalities, it is unlawful within the meaning of the saying of the Holy Prophet (S.A.W.) cited above.

If masturbation is unlawful what position does the Shariah takes with regard to a man who is overwhelmed by the intensity of sexual appetite, which it is impossible for him to curb and which compels him to commit fornication?

The answer to this question is that when man finds at such a cross-road, he should prefer the alternative which is less harmful as well as less immoral.

It is obvious that masturbation is an evil act. But fornication and homosexual act is a greater sin, for both these evil acts directly produce harmful effects on the community. They also leave a blemish on a man's character and disgrace him. Moreover, both fornication and homosexuality tarnish the image of a man's family. Some times it leads to bloodshed and takes root in the hearts of both the parties. Under the circumstances, if a man overwhelmed by the intensity of sexual appetite, resorts to masturbation, he will adopt a course that is less harmful and evil than adultery and homosexual act.

For this reason the jurists have declared masturbation absolutely unlawful for the purpose of inciting the latent sexual instinct and to derive pleasure therefrom. But when sexual drive spontaneously overwhelms a man and he is on the verge of committing fornication, then he may legitimately resort to masturbation in order to assuage his sexual appetite. He may thus redeem himself by committing a lesser sin of individual character for the purpose of abstaining from committing a bigger sin of collective nature: In such a case he will neither deserve any reward nor punishment.

We suggest here some remedies for habitual masturbation:

(1) Early Marriage

This is the most effective and the sure way of gratifying sexual desire. There are additional moral, pychological and social advantages of getting married at the age of adolescence.

(2) Voluntary Fasting

If one lacks the means of marrying early in life, Islam prescribes an effective alternative and that is fasting voluntarily; for fasting assuages the sexual appetite. Besides, it intensifies the sense of Allah's presence and inculcates His fear in the heart. Fasting as a means of curbing sexual urge has been mentioned in a tradition of the Holy Prophet (S.A.W.) which runs as follows:

> "O ye young people! whoever of you is courageous enough to marry he should do so, because wedlock is the most effective means of keeping one's eyes downcast and the strongest guarantee against immodesty.
>
> Whoever does not have the courage to marry should keep fast because fasting is the antidote to lust."

This tradition has been narrated by numerous persons.

There are various voluntary fasts enjoined by the Shariah. I cite only a few examples.

(a) The David's Fast: The Prophet David (A.S.) used to

keep fast every other day. The Holy Prophet (S.A.W.) praises this way of fasting.

(b) Fasting on Mondays and Thursdays.

(c) Fasting during the first six days of the lunar month of Shawal (in wake of the Ramazan Eid). These fasts fetch greater reward if they are kept on alternate days.

(d) Fasting on the tenth day of every lunar month.

(e) A fast designed to curb lust which is referred in the saying of the Holy Prophet (S.A.W.):

"And whoever can not venture to marry early in life should keep fast."

(3) Precautions Against Sexual Impulses

It is an undeniable fact that the milieu around us abounds in multifarious evils and sinister attractions. Almost every individual is more or less inequitous. Under the circumstances, if a young man succumbs to sexual impulse and is led astray by corrupting diversions, he will obviously indulge in debauchery irretrievably, which will wreck his morals and he will turn a libertine licentiously gratifying his sexual appetite like an animal unabashed.

It is incumbent upon the guardians to exhort the children and if necessary, warn them against the serious consequences of sinister habits. If needs be, the children should be rebuked for their evil tendencies. In this way they should fulfil their responsibility for the disciplining, refining and training the youngsters. The children should be urged not to look at women improperly dressed and inviting them with their charms, abstain from reading erotic fiction and sex inciting literature, whose publication is the business of the people thriving at the expense of honour and morality. They should also be asked not to listen to sex inciting music, which has corrupted entire society.

Just imagine how ruinous would be the thing that blunts the sense of honour, tarnishes human dignity, creates moral inconsistency, stifles human personality and destroys the qualities of benevolence, respectability and moral excellence! May be that the exhortation of the guardians produces the desired effects and the youngmen keep in view the serious consequences of masturbation. They may consequently try to develop moral and psychological poise in their behaviour, pay heed to the maintenance of their mental and physical health and thus become righteous and true believers.

(4) Spending Leisure Time On Profitable Work

The consensus of the educationists and psychologists is that when a child has no work to do and finds himself alone, he indulges in wishful thinking, dreaming of delightful things and his mind is filled with fascinating ideas and sensual desires. When a young boy is engrossed in such indeas, his sex is incited and he is so overwhelmed by emotion that he finds no method for the release of his emotion other than hand practice. It is therefore necessary to devise healthy ways and means for ridding the boy of morbid thinking and sex inciting ideas and thus guarding him against any sinister habit pregnant with serious consequences: We suggest here some such methods:

First of all we should find out how the boy spends his leisure time. There are may useful ways of spending leisure time which are enumerated as under:

(1) Physical exercise which makes the body strong.
(2) Immaculate entertainment in the company of good friends whose association animates the soul.
(3) Reading of informative and enlightening books.
(4) Handicraft which creates interest in useful things.
(5) Delivering speeches on religious and educational subjects which are not only didactic but also informative.
(6) Cultural competitions that give lustre to the mind.
(7) Archery and other warlike exercises such as firing, shelling and other manoeuvres helpful in attacking the enemy.
(8) Reading of useful and informative magazines that provoke thought, refine the soul, inculcate the full sense of energy and are conducive to moral uplift.

(5) Good Company

The parents, teachers and guardians are advised to urge

upon their children to move in the company of good and peace loving friends — friends who remind him of anything good he may forget, exhort him to mend his ways if he goes astray, help him in doing good and console him if he is confronted with any difficult situation.

It is said that such friends are very small in number and in modern times true sincere and believing friends are conspicuous by absence.

We admit that there is a great dearth of such friends everywhere, but they can still be recognized by the marks of prostration on their foreheads. Such people stand out by their moral excellence and flawless conduct.

A young man should be on the lookout for such righteous people and whenever he finds them he should consider himself fortunate enough to associate with tnem so that they may he his friends in need, assist him in finding a way out of the predicaments he may be placed in life, repose confidence in them and count on their help in difficulties.

A man undoubtedly adopts the ways of his intimate friend and emulates his habits. Birds of the same feather fly together. The Holy Prophet (S.A.W.) has expressed this fact in he following words:

> "A man treads in the footsteps of his intimate friends. Any one of you should find out with whom he is intimate."

It goes without saying that a man who befriends depraved and immoral persons in the habit of disobeying Allah's command is misguided by the latter. They would take him along with them on the wrong path and cling to him to serve their own ends.

Young men should shun such company if they want to strengthen their faith, refine and edify themselves and keep their bodies strong and immune from diseases.

They, should, on the contrary associate with good people and true believers so that they may not only be happy in this world but also enjoy blissful life in the Hereafter. Says Allah:

"Friends on that day will be foes one to another except those who keep their duty." (43 : 67)

(6) Acting on Medical Advice

Experts on hygiene and doctors of medicine give the following instructions to assuage the intensity of sexual appetite and curb sensual desire.

1. Frequent cold baths during summer and repeatedly pouring cold water on penis.
2. Physical exercises and sports.
3. Avoid edibles seasoned with pungent spices, for such spices incite sex.
4. Minimum use of beverages such as tea and coffee.
5. Meat and eggs should not be taken abundantly.
6. Avoid lying on your back or stomach. One should rather sleep one one's right side as the Prophet (S.A.W.) used to do.
7. Always fear Allah.

It is a fact acknowledged by all that when a young man believes in his heart of hearts that Allah is constantly watching him and is aware of all his open and clandestine affairs and knows whenever he casts a lustful glance and the dark wishes and thoughts latent in his subconsicous; that if he commits excesses Allah shall call him to account and that if he deviates from the norms of Islam, Allah will torment him, he will undoubtedly abstain from acts incurring perdition, rid himself of bad habits and refrain from doing anything unlawful.

The fear of God takes root in a believer's heart and intensifies his sense of Allah's presence and greatness by attending academic symposia and religious meetings, offering prayers regularly including voluntary prayers, reciting the Holy Quran daily, offering the Tahajjud prayer (prayer said after midnight) when all the world is asleep, keeping the masnoon (practiced by the Prophet S.A.W.) and the voluntary fasts, associating with virtuous friends, moving in the company of true believers and being mindful of death and the life thereafter.

What befits believing young man is to adopt such a way of life as reinforces and intensifies his sense of Allah's presence so that he may not be taken in by the delusive things of the world, led astray by the glamour of the mundane life, commit unlawful acts, may pursue the ideal set in the following verse of the Holy Quran:

> "Then as for him who is inordinate, And prefers the life of this world, Hell is surely the abode. And as for him who fears to stand before his Lord and restrains himself from low desires, the garden is surely the abode."
>
> (79: 37-41)

Addiction to Intoxicants and Narcotics

This habit is also extremely dangerous and pernicious. We find that addiction to toxicants is common in a community which is insensitive to moral values and in which Islamic education and training is at a discount.

Children addicted to drugs and intoxicants are generally those who run away from homes because their parents pay no heed to their requirements and neglect their duty towards the training and guidance of children. Children also become intoxicant-addicts by taking undue advantage of their parents' negligence and the parents also do not take care of the children's behaviour and the need to correct it.

Such children join the company of inequitous people and acquire the latter's vices.

This topic calls for a detailed discussion. There are three questions which first of all crop up in our mind and we propose to answer them at length.

1. What are harmful effects of intoxication?
2. What is the position of Islam as to intoxication?
3. How to cure the addict?

HARMFUL EFFECTS OF INTOXICATION

(a) Diseases.

The doctors of medicine and the experts on hygiene

unanimously hold that the sedatives and intoxicants make the addict insane, weaken his memory, cause various intestinal and abdominal ailments, disturb the digestive system, cause mental torpor, distaste for food and mal-nutrition, makes him lean and thin as well as absent-minded and partially impotent. Besides, addiction to intoxicants causes tension in the veins and tissues of the patient's body. The degree to which the use of an intoxicant harms the addict may well be seen from the French census report. According to this report the number of people who die of the use of liquor is lesser than those who die of consumption. According to the census report for 1955 one hundred and seven deaths occurred as the result of drinking wine as against twelve thousand people who died of consumption during the last decade.

(b) Waste of Money.

People spend huge amounts on providing themselves with alcohol and other intoxicants, although they know that this is sheer waste of money which ruins the families concerned and reduce them to starvation. Besides, an alcohol addict does very little and therefore this output is below the average. In short, he is a burden on national economy. Culturally, too, he lags behind those who don't drink or use narcotics, for as the result of the use of an intoxicant he grows lean and thin, is absent-minded and suffers from various kinds of diseases.

The following news item appeared in the issue of the Cairo daily Al-Ahram dated 3rd May, 1965:-

Some seven million Americans are addicted to alcohol, of which about two millions are a drain on national economy because they do not turn up for work.

(c) Psychological, moral and social.

The personality of an intoxicant addict is the embodiment of many vices; for instance lying, cowardice, disregard of moral values etc. He commits crimes like larceny, adultery and violation of moral principles unscrupulously. He lacks moral poise and consistency. He is fickle minded and has no sense of responsibility.

Apart from these evils, he associates with wicked peple in their underground dens where he considers no evil act unlawful.

It is common knowledge that the imperialist powers try to further the use of intoxicants among the nations opposed to them, which serve them as a tool to undermine the glory, power and prestige of thôse nations. With the aid of this devil's tool nations are demorilized deprived of stability and are totally lost to the sense of duty towards jehad. Egypt has long been combatting the menace of intoxicants thrust upon it by the imperialist powers. It is now a quarter of a century since she has been striving to rid herself of the evil whose seeds were sown by the British imperialism. When England invaded China, the traffic of opium came to an end. For this reason England's war again China is known in history as the opium war.

According to the Islamic injunctions, use of narcotics and tranquillizers is unlawful. The ulema are unanimous on their prohibition.

As for the prohibition of liquor, the following verse of the Holy Qur'an contains unequivocal injunction:-

"O ye who believe, strong drinks and games of chance and idols and divining arrows are only an infamy of Satan's handiwork. Leave it aside in order that ye may succeed.

Satan seeketh only to cast among you enmity and hatred by means of strong drink and games of chance, and to turn you from remembrance of Allah and from His worship. Will you then keep back?"[1] (5: 90-91)

1. Wrong thinking people argue that the expression "keep back" or "abstain" occurring in this verse is no proof of prohibition. According to them had liquor been unlawful the Quran would not have enjoined upon the Muslims to asbtain from liquor but would have asked them to treat it as unlawful. However, the truth of the matter is that the verse contains seven evidences of declaring liquor unlawful: (1) Mentioning liquor alongwith games of chance and divining arrows; (2) treating it as a foul thing (3) Calling it Satan's handiwork; (4) The injunction calling upon the Muslims to abstain from it in itself being an injunction enjoining

The Prophet's interpretation of the above verse also signifies the prohibition of wine. Says he:—

"Curse be upon wine, upon one who drinks it, upon one who serves it, upon one who buys it, upon one who sells it, upon one who extracts it, upon one who fills it in the jars, upon one who carries it and upon one to whom it is taken."

There are numerous proofs of the prohibiton of the narcotics and tranquilizers. Some of them are as follows:-

(1) Narcotics and tranquillizers are governed by the following general injunction of the Quran:-

"He makes lawful for them all good things and prohibit for them only the foul." (7: 157)

(2) The Prophet's teaching not do harm and not to be harmed as reported by Imam Ahmed in His Masnad and Ibn Majja in his Sunan.

(3) The tradition narrated by Hazrat Umme Salma wherein she quoted the Prophet to have prohibited all intoxicating and deranging things. As narcotics cause disorder, they too are unlawful.

(4) Liquor is unlawful, because it gets the better of man's reason and overwhelms it. In such a state of mind, man is incapable of taking right decisions. Narcotics have also been prohibited for the same reason.

It is necessary to refer here Hazrat Omar's oft-quoted remark in this context which he made before the people from the Prophet's pulpit. He observed, "Wine is every thing that covers the reason."

This remark of Hazrat Omar bin Khattab (R.A.A.) bears it out that narcotics and tranquillizers are as unlawful as liquor, is undeniably unlawful. He was wise enough to make a general remark in order to dispel doubts and forestall

---

to give up use of liquor; (5) its being cause of enmity and hatred; (6) its being an impediment to the remembrance of Allah and prayer and (7) The question posed being in a negative style i.e., "will you abstain?" meaning will you not refrain from the use of liquor or "will you abstain from prayer?"

All these arguments prove the prohibition of liquor. The wrong thinking people only know how to repudiate the verses of the Holy Qur'an.

various kinds of questions that the people are likely to ask in this connection.

Thus everything which deceives reason, conceals and covers it and deprives of the capacity to distinguish between fair and foul is in reality nothing but a strong drink. As such it is unlawful and will always remain so.

It therefore follows that narcotics Hashish, Cocaine and opium whose increasing use in the world today constitutes a serious menace, are unlawful like wine, since they impair the potentialities of reason; for to the man who uses them, things near at hand appear distant and the other way round. His mind is haunted by illusions and he thinks of things that never exist in the world. His mind is saturated with illusions with the result that he forgets his religion as well as the mundane realities.

Hazrat Allama Qarafi and Allama Ibn Taimiah refer to the consensus of the religious authorities on the prohibition of Hashish. Ibn Taimiah even geos to the lengths of declaring the man a Kafir who treats Hashish as lawful.

How the question remains if liquor can be used as a medicine as the people often enquire. The answer to this question has been given by the Prophet himself. Once a man asked the Prophet about the use of liquor. He forbade him to use it. The man said that he had been using it as a medicine. The Holy Prophet replied that liquor in itself is a disease rather than a medicine. (*Sahih Mulsim*, *Masnad Imam Ahmed*)

We find this tradition in Sunan Abu Dawood:

"The Prophet (S.A.W.) said: "No doubt, Allah has created both disease and its cure. He has produced medicine for every malady. You should, therefore, seek cure but you should not use an unlawful thing as a medicine."

Ibn Masood quotes a saying of the Holy Prophet about intoxicants which is as follows:

"Allah has not created anyting with curing quality which he has forbidden for you." (*Sahih Bukhari*)

According all these injunctions, use of liquor is unlawful

even as a medicine. Therefore, any one who uses narcotics, intoxicants, tranquilizers or liquor as a medicine is guilty of a great sin.

But if alcohol is mixed with drugs for the purpose of keeping them fit for use, they can legitimately be taken only when their use is absolutely essential for the treatment of a disease. A doctor who is a good professional as well as a God-fearing Muslim can only apprise us of the utility and components of such drugs. The reasons for the qualified permission of the use of such drugs is that the basic principles of the Shariah take into account particularly the convenience of the people. Besides, a purpose of the Islamic rules and regulations is to remove bottlenecks and difficulties so that maximum requirements of the people are fulfilled. The basic tenet in this regared is contained in the following verse of the Holy Qur'an:

> "And the man who is constrained to do so and does it with no intention to swerve from the path of Islam, nor to overstep the limits laid down by the Shariah is no sinner."[1]

Three stages for the cure of an intoxicant addict may be suggested, viz:

(1) Good education.
(2) Removing the causes.
(3) Punishment for the use of intoxicants.

1. Good education can only be provided when the parents of children inculcate the fear of Allah in their hearts and when their minds are saturated both collectively and individually with a sense of Allah's presence. If such training is imparted in the early impressionable years, it takes root deep in their minds and is ingrained in their conscience resulting in the edification of the children.

History bears it out that when Arabs embraced Islam, with their hearts imbued with the sense of Allah's presence

---

1. in the context of the verse quoted above use of unlawful things is forbidden with the proviso that in case if one is compelled to use them as the last resort when no alternative is left then an unlawful thing may legitimately be used.

and His fear and when they began to trust in Allah and seek His help, they gave up all those habits which they acquired in the days of ignorance with gusto.

(a) We mention here the Arabs' fondness for liquor before the advent of Islam. They used to write poems in praise of wine and described its virtues in numerous ways. For example, we give here the translation of a couplet:·

When I die, bury me by the wine,
Its roots will moisten my skeleton after my death.

Besides, the Arabs invented various names, for wine; for instance, the water of life, the saliva excreted from the beloved's lips, delight, rosy, the daughter of grape, girl brought up in an earthen jar, the daughter of the tavern etc. etc. If a list is prepared it will comprise about a hundred such names.

In spite of all their fondness for wine, when the Arabs were told that wine was unlawful for them, from then onwards, all of them declared in unison: "Our Lord, we give it up." They did not simply pledge to give up drinking wine but spilled in the streets all the wine that they had. It is thus that faith exhibits itself when it takes root deep in the hearts and its seed is sown in the soul. Nor is this all. Faith works wonders in the edification and refinement of man. All the armies and navies put together are incapable of performing such feats. The human community will always be in need of such faith and such a powr of reformation and refinement.

(b) In order to rid the people of drinking and the use of intoxicants, it is necessary to remove the causes of its habits. The first and foremost task in this connection has to be done by the people in authority. The government should impose restrictions on the sale, purchase and use of wine, intoxicants an sedatives in the bazars and other places and thus put an end ot their traffic. Th drunkards as well as intoxicant and drug addicts will not be able to obtain them. The young people, therefore, cannot acquire the habit of drinking or the use of narcotics.

(c) As for the intoxicant addicts, they should be given severe punishments. The prescribed penalty for drinking wine is forty to eighty stripes. But this does not mean that they are not liable to penal punishments, such as imprisonment, fine and legal restrictions in addittion to the prescribed Hud. In fact, the seller and trafficker of wine should also be awarded the punishment they deserve.

If the government is serious about taking measures in the prevention and eradication of the use of liquor and other intoxicants, it can reform the society in the best possible manner by acting in all sincerity to investigate such criminal cases judiciously and persistently and forestall the dangerous consequences of drinking and the use of narcotics.

Evils of Fornication and Homosexuality

These deadly sins are common among the present day youths. We hear of innumerable cases of adolescent boys who indulge in debauchery and other forms of sexual corruption, and thus head fast towards a disastrous end.

How distressing would it be for the parents to find their offspring irretrievably depraved and debased! It will then be no use crying over split milk. Had they bred their children well, imparted them good education and training, kept them under strict observation and ascretained the kind of company they kept, they would not have seen such an evil day.

If the parents and guardians are not held responsible for the moral deviation and aberration from the social norms, who else then is to be regarded as responsible? It is indeed parents and guardians who look after the children and watch their activities. As such the parents and guardians are under the obligation to provide their children education and proper moral training and inform them of the consequences of evil deeds and debauchery.

Having drawn the attention of the readers to these vital points, we now proceed to discuss the various aspects of the evils of fornication and sodomy:

(1) What harm do fornication and sodomy do?

(2) What position does Islam take in this regard?

(3) What exactly is the cure of these maladies?

(1) Fornication and Sodomy do immense harm. Their harmful effects may be discussed in consideration of the damage done.
(a) to the health and body and (b) to the social, moral and personal aspects of a man's life.

(a) Harm done to health and body.

Fornication and homosexual acts cause the following diseases:

(i) Syphilis and gonorrhoea etc.

The penis is injured and inflammed; the lip, tongue or the eyelid is injured and inflamed; appearence of white specks on the centre of body. These are symptoms of the kind of disease under discussion. At the advanced stage of the disease the whole body may be numbed, the patient may lose eyesight and suffer from convulsion of arteries; the body may be disfigured; the patient may have the cancer of the tongue and sometimes he falls a prey to tuberculosis. In some cases the wife and children of the patient are affected by the disease, as it is contagious.

(ii) Sterility, difficulty in passing urine etc.

When the patient urinates, he feels that his urinary tract is bruised and also has burning sensation. The male urine sometimes contains pus: female patient discharges pus with urine; male patients suffer from the burning of bladder and testicles because of excessive discharge of semen, burning of urethra; burning of the ovary and uterus in the female patient. As the result of the difficulty in passing urine both male and female become sterile. Owing to excessive bruises in the urinary tracts of a male patient, he may be completely incapable of passing urine and if the cannot be rid of this condition, he may ultimately die.

(iii) The Abdominal disease.

Fornication and sodomy result in abdominal ailments which are infectious. Even a healthy person may fall a prey to such diseases because they are contracted from the female during sexual intercourse.

The incidence of dangerous diseases in a community will be proportional to the curse of fornication and sodomy.

The Prophet (S.A.W.) of Islam who was the most truth ful of men has said that when a community takes to debauchery, Allah causes various kinds of diseases in it with which its ancestors were unfamiliar. Ibn Majah, Baihaqi and Bazzaz quote the Prophet to have said:

> "O ye immigrants, you will be put on trial for five evils and I pray to God that you remain immune from them."
> The Prophet (S.A.W.) then enumerated those evils and added, "If a community falls a prey to debauchery and it commits this sin unabashed, it will suffer from plague and other various fatal and painful diseases unknown to its forebears."
> "Sensible people should learn a lesson from it."

(b) Harm done to collective, moral and personal life.

(i) The horrible consequence of fornication and sodomy are that identity of lineage is totally lost, and the seed of posterity is destroyed; that women lose their chastity and honour; that the human dignity is tarnished; that the community is ruined; that conjugal ties are severed; that the family is disintegrated; that the qualities of manliness and nobility are totally lost and that man gets deeper and deeper into the quagmire of ignominy and obscenity.

Fornication and sodomy are the two moral and sexual guilts pregnant with serious consequences for the society. Every individual of the community infested with these crimes should be presumed to have lost human dignity, sense of lineal respect and every boy and every girl to have grown licentious. Such a new generation cares little for moral values and does not know the very meaning of virtue and nobility.

Just imagine what will be the status of a community whose yonoung men are debauchees and whose women are lewd and which as a whole is sex-stricken and steeped in carnal pleasures.

Such a community is bound to be annihilated as is evident form the following verse of the Holy Quran:

"And when We would destroy a township, We send commandment to its folk who live at ease and afterwards they commit abomination in it and so the Word of doom has effect for it and We annihilate it with complete annihilation." (17:16)

The consensus of ulema is that adultery and sodomy are totally unlawful acts. Proofs of their unlawfulness are as follows:

Allah declares it unlawful in His decree contained in this verse of the Holy Quran:

"And come not near unto adultery. It is an abomination and an evil way." (17:31)

(ii) Following is the translation of verses No. 68 and 69 of Surah Al Furqan:

"And (believers are) those who cry not unto any other god along with Allah, nor take the life which Allah hath forbidden save in course of justice, nor commit adultery — and whoso doeth this shall pay the penalty. The doom will be doubled for him on the Dayof Resurrection and he will abide therein disdained forever."

(iii) The Prophet (S.A.W.) says:

"An adulterer ceases to be a believer while committing adultery."

(iv) In Mojam Al Tabrani the following tradition of the Holy Prophet (S.A.W.) has been cited:

"The faces of adulterers would be emitting flames like the fire."

(v) Again, in Musnad-e-Imam Hakim we come across the following tradition:

"The people of a township where adultery and usury are in vogue invite the wrath of Allah."

(vi) Ibn Abidyn and Kharashi quote the Prophet (S.A.W.) to have observed:

"On the Day of Judgement Allah will never look at the man who commits adultery with his neighbour's wife; nor will He absolve him of the guilt. He will rather say to him: Enter Hell with those who go to it."

As regards sodomy Allah says:

"What! Of all creatures do ye come unto the males and leave the wives Allah created for you? Nay, but you are transgressors." (26:165-66)

In another it has been said:

(vii) "And Lot (remember) when he said unto his folk: Lo! ye commit lewdness such as no creature did before you. For come ye not unto males and cut ye not the road (for travellers) and commit ye not abomination in your meetings? But the answer of his folk was only that they said: Bring Allah's doom upon us if thou art a truth-teller." (29:28-29)

(viii) The Prophet (S.A.W.) says about sodomy:

"Cursed is the man who commits the act the people of Lot used to commit. Cursed is the man who commits the act the people of Lot used to commit. Cursed is the man who commits the act the people of Lot use to Commit."

The Prophet (S.A.W.) repeated the above sentence thrice.
(*Musnad Hakim*)

(ix) There is yet another saying of the Prophet (S.A.W.) to the same effect:

"Of all the men I am most concerned about is one

who commits the act the people Lot used to commit" (*Ibn Majja*)

(x) *Mo'jam-al-Tabarani* and *Baihaqi* quote the Prophet (S.A.W.) to have remarked:

"There are four kinds of people with whom Allah is displeased and angrry from morning till evening." Hazrat Abu Hurairah asked who those people were:

The Prophet (S.A.W.) replied:

(a) Men who deliberately bear resemblance to women.

(b) Women who imitate men.

(c) The men who commits lewdness with beasts and

(d) The man who commits homosexual acts.

(C) Punishments for fornication and sodomy as laid down in the Shariah.

Shariah clearly lays down penalties for both fornication and sodomy, which are as follows:

(1) Penalty for fornication:

Two kinds of punishments have been prescribed for fornication:

(a) Flogging coupled with banishment.

(b) Stoning to death.

(a) The first kind of punishment is meant for an unmarried adulterer. One who is guilty of adultery, whether a man or woman, should be scourged with a hundred stipes each, as Allah commands:

"The adulterer and the adultererss, scourge each one of them with a hundred stripes. And let not pity for the twain withhold you from obedience to Allah, if ye believe in Allah and the Last Day. And let a party of believers witness their punishment (24:2)

According to the Hanafites banishment of an adulterer is a penal punishment. If the man in authority considers it expedient, he may banish the offender. But the other authorities on Islami jurisprudence (Shafiee, Hambli and Maliki) would have him exiled to place where a traveller cannot offer his shortened prayer during the journey. The penalty of banishment has been presented by the rightly guided caliphs.

(b) Stoning to death

Only a married adulterer is to be stoned to death, as is required by the following tradition of the Holy Prophet (S.A.W.). It is unlawful to kill any Muslim who bears witness that there is nothing worthy of worship but Allah and that I am His messenger, except in three cases:

1. A married adulterer.
2. Life for Life i.e. retaliation.
3. Deviation from the religion of Islam i.e. removing from the path trodden by the majority of the Ummah

(Sahih Bukhari & Sahih Muslim)

According to another authentic tradition, the Prophet (S.A.W.) ordered Maiz bin Malik and a woman from the Ghamidi tribe to be stoned to death; for they had confessed their guilt in the presence of the Prophet. Both of them were married persons.

(2) Sodomy

The consensus of all the Ulema is that sodomy is a heinous a crime as adultery, although they differ on the kind of punishment to be awarded to a homosexual. For stance Hazrat Imam Bukhari says, "The ulema have taken different positions on the determination of penalty for homosexuals. One group of them holds that one who commits sodomy is to be awarded the same punishment as is prescribed for one who commits fornication, that is, if the offender is married he whould be stoned to death and if unmarried, he should be scourged with a hundred stripes. This is more clear verdict of both the old and new Shafi'ites.

According to Imam Malik a homosexual is to be stoned to death, whether he is married or unmarried.

Another verdict of Hazrat Imam Shafiee is that the homosexual should be executed.

The Hanifites, however, hold that it is essential to award penal punishment for sodomy. But the form of this punishment would be determined by the person in authority. In case of homosexual offence committed for the the first time, the offender may be admonished and rebuked. But if he commits it a second time, he should be slain.

The basis of the arguments advanced by the jurists and scholars in favour of killing both the active and the passive partners involved in an act of sodomy is the following tradition of the Holy Prophet (S.A.W.).

"Whatever community you find indulging in sodomy, kill both the active and passive partners involved therein." (*Tirmizi, Abu Dawood and Ibn Majah*)

Mufazzil bin Fadala quotes Hazrat Ikrama with reference to Ibn Jareer to have narrated this tradition of the Holy Prophet (S.A.W.):

"Kill both the active and passive partners as well as him who commits a lewd act with beasts."

(3) Remedy

The remedy for this sinister habit is the same as has been stated in the context of masturbation. We need not, therefore, repeat it here.

However, we would like to add one thing to what has already been stated and that is the remark of the Holy Prophet (S.A.W.) which is of fundamental importance. He is reported to have said that what reforms the first generation of the Ummah will also reform the later generation. Hence if the reformation of the earliest generation of the Muslim Ummah was effected by enforcing Islam as the system of life, whereby the Ummah attained the height of glory and civilization, it can be reformed today by adopting the same system. It is through this system alone that it will regain its past glory and stability and become a power to reckon with. It will again become a model of virtues, benevolence and power to be emulated by the rest of humanity.

May God be pleased with Hazrat 'Umar (R.A.A.) who has observed:

"We are people whom Islam has made estimable. Whenever we renounce Islam by which Allah has honoured us and seek honour and respect otherwise, Allah will make us infamous." (*Musnad Imam Hakim*)

The same remark of Hazrat 'Umar (R.A.A.) has been versified by the poet philosopher Dr. Iqbal. The English translation is as under:

(1) When faith is gone, disorder follows and whoever does not revive religion, he will be lost to the world also.

(2) Whoever is happy in life without religion, he has so to say, adopted the course leading to a catastrophe.

We are under the obligations to carry out the Prophet's edict not to do harm and not to be harmed and the divine command to abstain from killing ourselves by doing with our own hands' pernicious acts. In order to fulfil this obligation it is incumbent upon the tutors and guardians and particularly the parents to take every possible measure for preventing the children from deviation and debauchery and to make them cautious putting them on their guard so that any emergent disaster may be forestalled. Such a disaster sometimes proves fatal, disfigures the body or causes incurable disease or wound.

Following precautionary measures are suggested to minimize emergencies. We summarize here the relevant portion of page 177 of Doctor *Nabih-al-Ghobra's* book "Al Mushkilat-us-Sulukia":

"For the physical safety of children an integrated, moderate and selfconsistent system is necessary as inculcation of a sense of security in them. In the first year of an infant's life, its protection is incumbent upon the members of the family, who will be held responsible for any negligence on their part. In the second year, it will be very useful to warn the baby against dangerous things. For instance it should be told such instructive stories which make him scared of a furnace, heater, fire and hot utensils and thus make him refrain from touching such things. It should be told that such and such thing is hot and causes pain and therefore it should not be touched and such and such thing is dangerous and should be avoided. Then touch his hand with a hot pot and quickly withdraw it so as to make the baby realize that it is hot, without burning its hand. In this way the child will learn to be cautious of its own accord, so that he may not be hurt. Again, if you find the child is about to fall from the chair and he does not have anything in his hand at the moment that is likely to injure him, then let it fall. However, it should be taught to be cautious by supporting it a little. Under normal circumstances we should try to strike a fair balance between the child's learning and protection. The members of the family should take necessary precaution against the danger of its receiving any injury during the play.

Dr. Nabih Ghorra and others have suggested the following practical measures for the safety of the child from any mishap:

(1) Poisonous medicines are to be kept under lock and key. The key to the lock of almirah etc., to be placed out of the children's reach. Besides, labels are to be pasted on the bottles of each medicine with its name written in capital letters. Care should be taken not to keep the bottle where edibles are lying. The poisonous medicines are used for different purposes; for instance pesticide or poisonous lotion.

(2) Medicines not needed are to be thrown away and should be kept out of children's reach. More over, it is advisible that medicine is not taken in the presence of children because children generally try to imitate grown up people. Innumberable cases of children come to light who are harmed by taking medicines. When any medicine is given to a child it should be told that what he is being given is not a drink but a medicine. If the child cannot be trusted, then the medicine should preferably be kept beyond its reach.

(3) Some heavy blockade is to be placed against every thing that burns such as a firepot, heater or similar devices, stoves or ovens etc, lest the child should rush towards such a dangerous thing and burn it-

self. Children often burn themselves by touching heaters and similar devices.

Children should not be allowed to play with things that emit flames. Matches and the like should therefore be kept beyond their reach.

Tea pots containing hot tea or utensils with hot food pose a big danger to the children. Uneducated mothers often inadvertently have the kettle on the edge of the table, ground or chair. The child falls upon it or kettle falls upon the child and thus the child's body is burnt and bruised.

During the days when fireworks are used, special precautions should be taken.

Similarly, the children are to be protected from electronics and electric wires.

(4) Sharp instruments like a pair of scissors, knife, blade, pins and glass wares are to be kept out of children's reach.

(5) Children should not be allowed to play such games as may prove fatal to them, as for example binding the rope round one's neck, putting one's head into a plastic bag etc., for in such cases the child may be stifled. When the child has a morsel in its mouth, it should not be kicked. It should not be allowed to catch with its mouth chips, pistachio nuts and the like. It is feared that such a thing may fall straight into the child's respiratory tract and cause its death.

(6) Mothers should refrain from laying the children along with them and cause them sleep, for in such a case the child may hiccup. The mother for instance falls asleep before the child and the sucking child later falls asleep with mother's nipple in its mouth. Thus the child is sometimes stifled to death because of hiccup.

(7) Windows of the upper storey of the house should not be kept open; or if it necessary to keep them open, care should be taken that children are not able to jump out of them. The outer walls of the balcony should be built in modern style, so as to allow the children to see the things outside but not to pass

over it. In many cases children have fallen through the windows or over the balcony of the upper portions of houses and lost their lives. Such is the result of negligence!

(8) While using machines and electric equipments, the parents should warn the children against the danger inherent in them. The children should particularly be sent away when machines like choppers, juicers are being used, for there has been many a case of children receiving grievous injuries by putting their hands into such machines. They may receive electric shock when the machine goes out of order all of a sudden.

(9) Children should be removed before closing a door, for they unwittingly put their fingers into it and thus get hurt.

These and similar precautionary measures may be taken by any sensible person.

Islam lays great stress on the physical training of the children and taking positive precautionary measures for their safety. If parents and guardians attach due importance to such training and precautionary measures the children will be strong and hale and hearty and they will be able to breathe in a pleasent atmosphere of security.

If the individuals of the Muslim Ummah have common sense as well as physical strength, strong will-power as well as unshakable resolution and imbued with national consciousness, their performance will be of a very high standard and consequently, the Ummah as a whole will be in possession of all the resources of conquest and superiority, ensuring the glory of Islam and the Muslims. When such a day of triumph comes, every Muslim of the world will rejoice. For Allah will bless them with His assistance. He honours whom He wants to honour. He alone is Great and Wise.

I want to impress upon the parents that this (Islam) alone is the right way of life, that this alone is the way to acquire power, that this alone is the highway of nobility and that there is no way of survival other than this.

The new generation is a sacred trust of Allah in our custody and it is absolutely essential to act on the eternal principles stated above for its physical training and spiritual and mental health, thereby enabling it to fulfil its responsibility in the future and hold aloft the honour of Islamic teachings like the companions of the Holy Prophet (S.A.W.), their followers and its great forebears.

The present generation which is wandering in the dark alleys of atheism, moral decadence and ignorance is sure to move forward one day in the light of religion, regain its moral excellence and champion the teachings of Islam, and this is not a difficult task for God Almighty.

* * * * *

MUSLIM CHILDREN

HOW TO BRING UP ?

Vol. II

Translated By
S. Zakir Aijaz

KITAB BHAVAN
New Delhi-110002

Kitab Bhavan
Publishers, Distributors, Exporters & Importers
1784, Kalan Mahal, Darya Ganj
New Delhi - 1100 02 (India)

Phone : (91-11) 23277392/93, 23274686, 30906494
website : www.kitabbhavan.com
Email : nasri@vsnl.com
Fax : (91-11) 23263383

First Edition 1991
IInd Reprinted 2006

ISBN : 81-7151-135-X (Set)
ISBN : 81-7151-137-6 (Vol. II)
Code No. : ZZZ054

Published in India by :
Nusrat Ali Nasri for Kitab Bhavan
1784, Kalan Mahal, Darya Ganj
New Delhi - 1100 02 [India]

Printed in India at :
Nice Printing Press
Khureji Khas, Delhi-110051

CONTENTS

بِسۡمِ اللّٰہِ الرَّحۡمٰنِ الرَّحِیۡمِ

CHAPTER IX

RESPONSIBILITY OF INTELLECTUAL TRAINING

The Intellectual training of Children.

What is meant by the intellectual training of the child is that the objects of his thinking should be useful and constructive such as the branches of religious knowledge, contemporary culture, knowledge of the development of human thought and civilization. Such objects of thought will be conducive to the maturity of his thinking and he will develop the habit of thinking in a refined and rational manner.

The responsibility of children's intellectual or rational training are far more important than other responsibilities pertaining to the training of children; which have already been discussed.

Religious training is the basis of the entire process of a child's breeding and education. His physical training is designed to make him active and smart, while his moral training aims at his edification. But the development of the faculty of reason consists in increasing its intelligence, refinement and education.

These, then, are the four responsibilities to be discharged by parents and guardians. There are other responsibilities besides. All of them are designed to help the child grow as an integrated and self-consistent personality, so that he or she may grow up as an upright person capable of discharging his or her obligations.

If the strength of faith is coupled with enlightenment and moral excellence with physical fitness, it will redouble the effectiveness of the child's personality. The child will make a great man indeed whose parents begin to discharge their obligations with regard to its breeding and care righ from the day he comes into the world and thus turn him i- an integrated personality.

As it is necessary to breed and train the child by stages, the following factors to my mind should especially be kept in view in the development of the child's intellectual capacities:

(1) Obligation with regard to education.

(2) Increase of intelligence and intellectual orientation.

(3) Mental Health.

We proceed to discuss these factors in detail.

The first and foremost responsibility that Islam imposes upon the parents and guardians is to educate their children and to enrich them with knowledge and culture, enable their minds to concentrate, acquaint them with the nature of things and inculcate in them the spirit of research and the power of taking decisions, so that they may have sound perception and understanding. This is how the growth of innate capacities of the child is fostered, how his intelligence manifests itself and how his reasoning faculty is developed. This is also the way to inculcate in him shrewdness.

A glance at the history of Islam would show that the very first verses of the Holy Quran revealed to our Prophet (S.A.W.) enjoin reading and learning:

"Read in the name of thy Lord Who createth; createth man from a clot. Read: and thy Lord is the most Bounteous, who teacheth by the pen; teacheth man that which he knew not. (96:5)

These verses emphasize reading and acquisition of knowledge and enjoin keeping aloft the banner of reason and rational thinking, opening up thereby the vistas of civilization.

There are innumerable Quranic verses and the Prophet's traditions about encouragement to acquire knowledge and the respect and esteem deserved by the Ulama. Every individual and every student should know such verses and traditions by heart. We cite here a few relevant verses:

"Are those who know equal with those who know not?" (39:9)

"My Lord, increase me in knowledge" (20:114)

"Allah will exalt those who believe among you and those

who have knowledge, to high ranks." (58:11)

"*Nun.* By the pen and that which they write with."(68:1)

And now some traditions to the same effect:
Says the Prophet (S.A.W.):

(1) "Whoever sets out in pursuit of knowledge, Allah makes for him the way to Paradise & smooth railing."
(Narrated by Abu Hurairn-Sahih Tirmizi)

(2) According to *Tirmizi* Abu Huraira (R.A.A.) quotes the Prophet (S.A.W.) to nave said:
"The world is devoid of blessing and whatever it contains is also devoid of blessing except remembrance of Allah and one who loves Him and knowledge and the seeker of knowledge."

(3) *Tirmizi* quotes Hazrat Anas to have narrated the following tradition:
"The Prophet (S.A.W.) said: Whoever sets out in pursuit of knowledge is in the way of Allah till he returns."

(4) According to *Tirmizi*, again, Abu Umama quotes the Prophet (S.A.W.) to have said: "A scholar is superior to him who worships just as I am superior to the lowest of you. In fact, Allah showers blessings on the person who teaches good. The angels and everything in the universe, even the ant in its hole and the fish prays for the welfare of such a person."

(5) Hazrat Abu Huraira quotes the Prophet to have said:
"When man dies, his activities come to an end except three activities:
   (a) Any Trust or anything he may have established for the benefit of the people,
   (b) Knowledge that benefits others and
   (c) Virtuous children who pray for him.

It was the effect of these verses and traditions that not only during the Prophet's life-time but also for ages thereafter the Muslims took pleasure in teaching of the various branches of the knowledge of the universe. It was a popular activity among them. They regarded the acquisition of the knowledge of every useful branch of learning as a duty. They profited by all the good things found in the civilization of other peoples and gave those peoples a new mode of thinking and living, harmonizing them with their own system and admitting everything to the spirit of Islam. The entire world enlightened its intellect with the various sciences taught by the Muslims and tried to derive the maximum benefit from the Islamic culture. The modern civilizations of both the West and the East are in reality the reflection of Islamic civilization, which reached them through Sicily, Spain and the Crusades. It was in reality the Islamic government of old which served as a guide, teacher and philosopher to the misguided and distressed peoples inhabiting the globe.

Dispassionate and just thinkers of the West have acknowledged the guiding role played by the Islamic civilization and have lauded the academic and cultural superiority of the Muslims.

Sarte, for instance, writes that Europe remained wonderstruck at the sight of Islamic art for nearly a millennium.

The Dutch orientalist *Dewsy* writes that while even the high priests in Christian Europe acquired average knowledge and all the other people were virtually illiterate, not a single illiterate was found in whole of Muslim Spain.

Lane Pool writes in his book on the Saracens in Spain that there was nothing but ignorance and sense of frustration in the illiterate Europe while Spain was the champion of learning and civilization.

Prevlet says that knowledge is the greatest contribution of the Arab civilization to the progress of the world. According to him it is hard to find any place in the world where impact of Islamic culture is not clearly manifest and that the most effective and invaluable is that aspect of knowledge that has engendered a force which would perform the great feats and which alone constitutes the fountianhead of the glory of modern times and that force is the physical science and the spirit of learning. The author concludes that the sum and substance of all these facts is that Islam is a creative force in the formation of civilization.

Abu Shubka has this to say in his book on the intellectual and spiritual relationship between the Arabs and the Europeans:

"The decline of the Arab civilization did not augur well for Spain and the rest of Europe. Spain owed its prosperity to the Arabs. When the Arabs departed, all its prosperity, power, beauty and fertility was replaced by ruins."

H.R. Gibb writes in his work on *New Trends in Islam* writes in course of his discussion of the impact on Islam of the sciences developed in Europe (whose basis is Islam itself) that it is his conviction and also the cosensus of authorities is that the findings of the researches conducted by the Muslim scholars and the conclusions drawn by them from their discussions have been helpful in every academic field and material progress. These findings and conclusions also pave the way for the initiation of experiments in Europe during the middle ages.

Victor Robinson observes after a lengthy comparison of the Islamic Civilization of Spain with Medieval Civilization of Europe that at a time when the great nobles of Europe did not know how to write even their names, the Muslim children at Cordova used to go to the schools; that Europeans could hardly read the old Testament available in their churches, while the Muslim teachers had established at Cordova a library whose stock of books was comparable with the great Library of Alexandria.

These and similar observations of the European orientalists bear clear testimony to the fact at a time in history when the scholars in medieval Europe were executed for bringing to light the findings of their research and the ideas inferred from their speculation, Islam was capable of promoting civilization and was rich with the light of knowledge.

What is the secret of this progressive force and furtherence of learning? The answer to this question lies in the basic principles of Islamic Shariah. Those principles, for example, are:

(1) Islam deals with both soul and matter and the world and religion together. Thus all the things required for the promotion of civilization are to be found in Islam; for instance, it has its own system of worship, rules and regulations of mutual transactions, collective laws and

injunctions relating to worldly life. Its motto is:

"But seek the abode of the Hereafter in that which Allah hath given thee and neglect not thy portion of the world." (28:77)

"And when the prayer is ended then disperse in the land and seek of Allah's bounty." (62:10)

(2) Islam gives the message of equality and humanity in order that every one who seeks refuge under the banner of Islam may participate in the task of building the society and the development of civilization and forget the distinctions of family, nationality, colour and language. The Islamic guideline is:

"The noblest of you in the sight of Allah is the best in conduct." (49:13)

(3) Islam enables all the tribes and nationalities to identify each other and opens the doors of establishing mutual relations. Says Allah:

"O mankind, we have created you male and female and have made you nations and tribes that ye may know one another." (49:13)

These were the basic teachings of Islam which the Muslim translated into action, widening thereby the mental horizons of other nations seeking guidance at the same time from the bright aspects of those nations' civilivations. Consequently vistas of progress in the fields of trade, industry, agriculture and other arts were opened up for the Muslims. In other words all the civilizations were heated in the crucible of Islam, giving birth to a new civilization that bore the stamp of Islam.

(4) Islam is an eternal and progressive religion, because it is superior to all the systems of life in the world. It is superior because it has been revealed by the Lord of the worlds and constitutes the legislation of the rules of rulers and because it fulfils the requirements of all times and places. It gives mankind such living perfect and vital laws that make him rightful owner of everything on earth. The basic message of Islam in this respect is:

"Who is better than Allah for judgement, to a people who have certainty (in their belief)?" (5:50)

An adequate proof of the eternity of Islam and the cause

for taking pride is that the western philosophers and scholars themselves bear testimony to its greatness and durability as a law.

Bernard Shaw says that the religion of Muhămmad (S.A.W.) is the noblest of all by virtue of its amazing dynamic quality and that it is the only religion in the world which has the capacity to face all the eventualities of life. According to Shaw the Prophet of Islam is the saviour of mankind and if a man possessing virtues similar to those of the Holy Prophet (S.A.W) takes over the control of modern age, all the problems can be successfully solved.

Dr. Izkuansa Bato is of the opinion that Islamic Shariah in most of its academic contents is superior to European laws. According to him it will be more true to say that Islam alone is the system of jurisprudence which provides more durable and stable laws than any other system, he adds.

The principal of the Vienna University Law College had this to say while addressing the Law Conference held in 1927:

> "The whole of mankind considers it an honour to be associated with a man like Muhammad (S.A.W.); for without receiving education from anybody, he gave to the world such a system of life fourteen hundred years ago that we should consider ourselves fortunate if we could attain level with it even two centuries hence."

The Egyptian poet Shauqi pays tribute to the Holy Prophet (S.A.W.) in the following words. (This is a translation of his Arabic couplets):

> The divine messages brought by the Prophets of old are extinct. But the new religion brought by him (the Prophet of Islam) will never die out.
>
> The teachings of this new religion freshen and freshen with the passage of time. In other words the beauty of its antiquity adds to the charm of those teachings i.e., the older they grow, the more fascinating they will be.

(5) Islam is the only religion which declares free education compulsory, regardless of religious education and the sciences. However, Islam takes into consideration in this connection the demands of necessity and speciality. The fact that Islam treats free education as mandatory

is borne out by the following traditions of the Holy Prophet (S.A.W.):

(a) Ibn Majah cites this tradition with reference to Hazrat Anas:
"Pursuit of knowledge is incumbent upon every Muslim. (Here the word Muslim applies to both men and women.)

(b) Tabarani quotes a tradition in his Al-Mo-jamul Kabeer as narrated by Hazrat 'Alqama. The tradition is as under:
"According to 'Alqama the Holy Prophet (S.A.W.) in a speech praised some groups of the Muslims and then said: What will become of the people who do not try to inculcate in their neighbours the consciousness of need to receive religious education, nor teach their neighbours themselves, nor exhort them, nor advise them to do good and refrain from evil. And what will be the fate of those who do not care to learn from their neighbours, nor acquire the consciousness of the need to learn religious principles, nor take the advice of their neighbours. By God every Muslim community will have to impart education to their neighbours and inculcate in them the craving for learning, exhort and advise them, enjoin upon them to do good and refrain from doing evil. And every community will have to acquire knowledge and religious consciousness from its neighbours and to take their advice. Otherwise I shall have to take punitive measures against those who fail in this."

(c) Ibn Majah quotes this tradition with reference to Hazrat Abu Saeed Khudri:
"Whoever conceals any profitable thing worthy of knowing with regard to religion, Allah will put the reins of fire in his mouth on the Day of Judgement."

If Islam treats acquisition of knowledge as obligatory, and threatens the man who feels shy of imparting knowledge with chastisement in this world as well as in the Hereafter, what more proof do we require of its being the only religion which regards acquisition and imparting knowledge as mandatory.

History of Islam bears clear testimony to the dissemination of knowldge free of charge as required by the traditions of the Holy Prophet (S.A.W.) and by his companion's categorical prohibition of receiving any remuneration for teaching. The practice of the Prophet (S.A.W.) himself was that he never asked for any wages in lieu of his missionary work and spreading the teachings of Islam among the people.

His position as well as that of the Messengers of Allah preceding him has been described in the following Verse of the Holy Quran:

"Tell them O Muhammad, I demand no wages for this teaching (Islam). My reward is due from Allah." (26:109)

The history of Islam also bears it out that the Holy Prophet (S.A.W.) sent Hazrat Mus'ab bin 'Umair to Madina (before the Prophet S.A.W. migrated himself thither) as a missionary and teacher. Similarly he sent Hazrat Moaz bin Jabal to Yemen and Hazrat Jafer bin Abi Talib to Abyssinia for teaching Islam. Apart from these three companions, numerous other companions were sent to various cities for the same purpose. But none of them received any wages for the task they performed.

We cite a tradition here regarding the undesirability of receiving any remuneration for teaching as narrated by Hazrat 'Ibada bin Samit. He says that he taught some people of the *Suffa* how to read and write (i.e. he taught them how to write and how to read the Holy Quran). One of them presented him a bow. Hazrat 'Ibada said to them, "Well, this bow is no money. I will shoot arrows with it in the way of Allah. However, I will ask the Prophet (S.A.W.) about it." So saying he called on the Prophet (S.A.W.) and enquired if he could accept it for the purpose of shooting arrows in the way of Allah. The Prophet (S.A.W.) said, "If you want to turn this bow into a yoke of fire for yourself, do accept it." Hazrat 'Ibada bin Samit could not but return the bow.

History of Islam bears it out that those who were assigned the task of teaching the Muslim children in the mosques received no wages. In fact for centuries the entire expenses of educating the children was borne by the government. Our forebears refused to accept the demand of those who claimed wages for imparting education. They used to tell such teachers that dealing in knowledge is inconsistent with the teachings of Islam. Hazrat Imam Ghazzali observes that the teacher is under the obligation to tread in footsteps of the Holy Prophet (S.A.W.) and should not demand any wages or compensation for imparting knowledge; nor should he crave for praise. According to Ghazzali, knowledge should be imparted for the sake of Allah and to seek His pleasure. Allah quotes the following words of one of his prophets:

> "O my people, I ask no price for this. My reward is due from Allah." (26:109)

From all these historical allusions we infer that Islam declares education free both at the official and individual levels; for the only purpose of education is Allah's pleasure, execution of his command and getting closer to Him. That is exactly why great contribution of the Muslims in imparting and disseminating knowledge has no parallel in the history of the world.

A thinker observes that Islamic State in its palmy days excelled the rest of the world in providing free education to all its citizens without any discrimination. The doors of the mosques, educational institutions and teaching centres were open to all. Any territory that came under the sway of the Islamic government presented the spectacle of free and universal education. Even to this date, education at the Al-Azhar University, the college and religious schools, is free. This is reminiscent of the early period of Islamic history.

In fact, the students themselves extend financial assistance to the schools so that they may be provided with adequate supply of food. Today the governments of other states are taking upon themselves the responsibility of bearing the expenses of education at the school level.

The question, however, remains that if the very function of the teacher is to impart education and he has no other means of incomes, can he not legitimately charge fee for his services?

The answer is that under such circumstances, fee may be charged especially when the government does not look after the interest of the teacher and the members of the society to pay no heed to his needs. By charging fee the teacher's pride and sense of honour will not be injured and he will at the same time be able to provide himself with the necessities of life. Hazrat Imam Ghazzali refers to this matter in his work" *Ahya-e-Uloomuddin*" and observes:

"Similarly it is permissible for him (the teacher) to charge fee for imparting knowledge in order to be able to be free of financial worries and continue spreading the light of knowledge. The aim of such a teacher is not only to earn his livelihood but also to promote education, ensuring thereby reward in the Hereafter. He should be allowed to charge so much fee as may facilitate the achievement of his objective."

According to Qalibi, Abul Hasan said that he knew an incident that happened to Ibn Wahb. It is as follows.

Ibn Wahb said, "Once as I was sitting with Imam Malik a teacher who taught writing came to him and said that he imparted knowledge to children but charged no fee as he came to know that it was undesirable to receive remuneration for teaching but the people no longer paid him as much as they used to do with the result that he was worreid about the needs of his family as he had no employment other than teaching."

Imam Malik asked him to go and teach, charging a fixed amount of fee. The teacher went away. Then one of the gentlemen sitting by Imam Malik said to him: "Abu Abdullah, how is it that you have advised him to charge fee for imparting education?"

Imam Malik replied, "Yes I have. If he stops to do his job, who will educate our children? Who is there to teach them discipline? If there is no teacher, what sort of men will our children grow up to be?"

The evil today is at its acme. The imperialist forces are at work to eradicate with their machinations the Islamic practices and vestiges of culture. Therefore, it is so much the more important that the parents and guardians pay greater attention to the education and training of their children and take special care to ingrain in their minds the knowledge of a belief in the Unity of Allah, to teach them the Holy Quran as well as all the branches of the Shariah; for it is obligatory to acquire anything that serves as means to do duty. If the parents and guardians do not choose proper teachers for their children, no matter if they have to pay for their services, then the new generation is bound to fall a prey to atheism, ignorance, moral degeneration and licentiousness.

As Ibn Sahnoon quotes Hazrat Ibn Masood with reference to Imam Sufian Sauri to have observed that three things were necessary for the people:

(1) A ruler to enforce his decisions among the people. If there is no ruler, the people will devour one another.

(2) The sale and purchase of the Holy Quran. If this transaction does not take place, then the Book of Allah would become unavailable.

(3) A teacher to impart education to children and receive fee for doing so. If there is no teacher, the people will remain illiterate.

We add one thing to these three in consideration of the situation obtaining in our own times and that is a teacher who could impart the knowledge of Islamic beliefs, teach the principles of good conduct, relate historical events and teach the Holy Quran. If the services of such a teacher are not availed of, the new generation will go astray and turn ungodly. Services of such a teacher are indispensable, whether they could be provided free of charge or by the payment of fee.

The question of receiving remuneration for furnishing information once threw doubt also into the minds of the Companions of the Holy Prophet (S.A.W.). Once during a journey, it so happened that companions in question arrived in an Arab village and asked the people of the village to provide them something to eat. But the villagers refused. Incidentally the chieftain of the village was bitten by a snake. They tried all the treatments known to them but in vain. One of them suggested that the travellers sojourning might perhaps be of some help and should therefore be approached. The villagers accordingly went to the travellers and sought their help in curing the chieftain. One of the companions of the Prophet (S.A.W.) said, "Well I know a cure. I will exorcise the effect of poison by reciting a verse of the Holy

Quran and blowing over the snake-bite. But remember that we asked for some food but you refused. So I will not cure your chieftain unless you agree to a compensation for the cure."

The chieftain agreed to give them a flock of goats in lieu of the cure. The companion of the Prophet (S.A.W.) then recited the first Surah of the Holy Quran and blew over the Snake-bite. As he repeated this, the chieftain was cured of the trouble. When he returned home, he had completely recovered. He ordered the agreed compensation to be given to the travellers.

One of the companions said, "Let us divide the goats among ourselves." But the companion who exorcised the poison by divine formula suggested instead that they should go to the Prophet (S.A.W.) first and seek his advice after relating the whole incident.

Accordingly the companions went back to the Prophet (S.A.W.) and told him the whole story. The Prophet (S.A.W.) turned to his companion who had cured snake-bite and said, "How did you know that the formula was used to exorcise by blowing?" and then he added "But you made the right suggestion. Divide the goats and let me have my share too." Having said this the Prophet (S.A.W.) laughed.

According to Imam Bukhari Hazrat Ibn Abbas added the following remarks to the above tradition:

"Well, the thing for which you received the most legitimate compensation is the Book of God."

The legitimacy of receiving the compensation was doubtful, but compensation was warranted by the following factors:

(1) The companions of the Prophet (S.A.W.) were travelling. They were hungry and needed the food badly. That was why they asked the villagers to feed them but the villagers refused.

(2) The context of the story suggests that the village or township where they sojourned during the journey was not Muslim. That was why they refused to provide food to the travellers. Obviously, the laws of Dar-ul-Harb (the place governed by the non-muslims) are different from those of Dar-ul-Islam (the place

governed by the Muslims).

(3) The compensation to which the companions of the Holy Prophet (S.A.W.) had agreed was the compensation for curing the snake-bite and not the compensation for teaching the Holy Quran.

There, then, were three reasons for which the Holy Prophet (S.A.W.) declared the compensation warrantable and remarked in a dignified manner, "Well, the thing for which you received compensation was the Book of Allah." This meant that by curing the divine formula, the companions had earned the best compensation.

To sum up, the Islamic Shariah does not permit at all to receive wages for teaching. However, if circumstances are such that justification is inevitable, there is no hitch in receiving compensation; for instance, a teacher's only function is to impart education and he has no sources of income whatsoever or the situation is such that the guardian has no alternative but to appoint a tutor in order to save the children from falling a prey to atheism, give them religious instruction and bring them up in conformity with the principles of Islam.

It is for these basic reasons that the Shariah treats receiving compensation for education as legitimate, whether it is religious instruction or temporal education.

(6) In Islam education occupies two positions:

(a) Essential Duty and

(b) Mandatory obligation.

These are explained as follows:

If receiving education means acquisition of knowledge that makes a Muslim perfect in all its aspects including the spiritual, intellectual, physical and moral aspects, then receiving education is an essential duty. This essential duty could only be fulfilled by acquisition of knowledge in proportion to necessity. It is an essential duty for men as well as women, for children as well as grown up people, for the masters as well as for servants. In short it is the essential duty for all the classes of the Ummah to acquire knowledge according to necessity.

On the basis of what has been stated above, we may say

that learning to read the Holy Quran and the acquisition of a knowledge of Injunctions relating to the forms of worship, the basic moral principles of Islam, the problems pertaining to what is lawful and unlawful, the rules of general health and knowledge of everything that may be required by a Muslim in both the spiritual and temporal spheres of life of a Muslim constitutes essential duty of every individual of the Ummah.

If by sciences are meant the science of agriculture, industry, trade, medicine, engineering, electricity, nuclear energy, defence and other useful branches of knowledge, then the acquisition thereof falls under the category of mandatory obligation. If there is nobody to fulfil this obligation, the entire Islamic society will be held guilty.

This, then, is the secret behind the force of Islam which engenders in men the consciousness of the need to promote civilization. It is the force by which the greatness of Islam can be judged and its dynamic quality can also be known, by virtue whereof Islam is capable of accommodating with the genius and revolutionary temper of modern age as well as it is in a position to claim to be everlasting, progressive and a ceaseless struggle.

The main reason for our lack of knowledge and lagging behind other nations on the path of civilization is that we have no idea of the dynamic force of Islam and have failed to enforce the Islamic system in all walks of life. Another reason for the degeneration of Muslims is the machinations of anti-Islamic forces by which they are busy erasing the imprints and vestiges of Islam from the face of the earth and have succeeded in divorcing the Muslims from their faith. Consequently the Islamic system has been confined to forms of worship and a code of conduct.

The day the Muslims acquaint themselves with the machinations of the anti-Islamic forces and enforce the Islamic system in every walk of life, they will regain their past glory under the sun and will assume the leadership of the world. They will hold up a mirror to the following verse of the Holy Quran:

"You are the best Ummah that has been raised up.

(3:110)

Again, says Allah:

"Verily, my path in straight. Tread ye on this path and not several paths. They will remove you far away from the path of Allah. This is what Allah bids you so that you may become righteous." (7: 154)

Another duty imposed on the parents and guardians is that at initial stage when the children enter the age of discretion, they should focus their attention exclusively on teaching them the recitation of the Holy Quran and the life of the Holy Prophet (S.A.W.) and the essential part of the Shariah. They should also be taught some poems and the Arabic proverbs and idioms. In this way they would be acting on the Prophet's edict:

"Teach your children three things:

(1) Love of your Prophet (S.A.W.).
(2) Love of the Prophet's family.
(3) Recitation of the Holy Quran, for those who recite the Holy Quran will be under the shadow of empyrean on the Day when there will be no other shadow."

(Al-Tabarani)

Acting on the Prophet's (S.A.W.) advice, the Muslims of the early period took keen interest in teaching their children the basic subjects and provided them with necessary information.

In this connection we cite here the observations of our forebears to show that they were keen on imparting to their children both religious instructions and temporal education and kept them under strict observation:

(1) Utba bin Abu Sufyan advised the tutor of his son to make him learn by heart beautiful and instructive verses and tell them stories of a high order.
(2) Hazrat 'Umar (R.A.A.) wrote to one of his governors; "Teach your children the arts of swimming and riding and make them learn by heart excellent couplets and proverbs.
(3) Once Mufazzal bin Zaid came across the son of a Muslim Arab woman and was deeply impressed by the boy. He enquired from the woman about the way the boy was brought up. The woman replied, "When the boy was five years old I entrusted him to a tutor, who

made him learn the Quran by heart which he recited excellently. He made the boy commit verse to memory and enabled him to quote the couplets of the poets. The tutor then created and fostered in him the interest in the great feats performed by his nation and thus imbibed in him the passion for a probe into the great deeds of his forebears. When he came of age, the tutor taught him riding and he achieved excellence in horsemanship and consequently developed the acumen of identifying the kinds of horses. He then armed himself and passed by the houses of the tribe listening attentively to the call made from any house."

(4) Whoever learnt the Holy Quran raised his value. Whoever studies the problems of jurisprudence intensively, was exalted. Whoever wrote the traditions of the Holy Prophet (S.A.W.) reinforced his arguments. Whoever acquires a deep knowledge of etymology and dictionary, developed leniency. Finally whoever focussed his attention on mathematics, lent weight to his opinion."

(5) Imam Ghazzali has recommended in his book *Ahya-e-Uloomuddin* that the child should be taught Holy Quran; instructive incidents should be told to him and events from the lives of righteous people should be related to him. According to Ghazzali, the child should subsequently be taught the religious injunctions and made to learn such poems by heart as are not erotic.

(6) Avicinna has offered invaluable advice in his book Al Siasa relating to the training of children. He recommends that a child's education should begin with the Holy Quran, keeping in view his physical and mental capacities. He will thus be able to easily identify the alphabets as well as to read and write. Subsequently he should be taught the principles of religion, goes on Avicinna, and then made to learn verses by heart and in the choice of verses that workable poetry should precede the eulogistic poems.

(7) Ibn Khaldoon also underlines the importance of

teaching the Holy Quran. He explains that the Quran occupies the basic position in all the courses of studies prescribed in the various cities of the world of Islam; for teaching of the Holy Quran is included in the Islamic customs, and it reinforces a Muslim's faith.

Ibn Qutaiba relates in his book 'Oyunul Akhyar' an interesting event. A man belonging to the Banoo Saqeef tribe came to the Caliph Waleed bin Abdul Malik. The Caliph asked him if he had learnt the Holy Quran.

The man replied, "No, I havn't. I was a bit too busy with sundry affairs to spare time for learning it."

Walid asked him, "do you know fiqh (Islamic law)?",

The man replied in the negative.

"Can you cite the couplet of any poet?"

The tribesman again replied in the negative.

Walid turned his face away from the man. One of the people named Abdullah bin Moawia who was present on the moment addressed the Caliph and then pointed towards the tribesman.

Walid said, "We have nobody else with us."

What Walid meant by this was that the presence and absence of a man is of little consequence, who has neither read the Holy Quran, nor is acquainted with the Islamic law, nor has learnt verses by heart nor is familiar with the principles of religion. Such a man hardly matters even if he is physically present.

The principle laid down by Islam with regard to children's education is that it should commence in the child's early years, when its mind is clear and memory is strong and when he learns everything quickly.

In a tradition quoted by Abu Dawood, the Holy Prophet (S.A.W.) refers to this fact. Says the Prophet (S.A.W.):

Learning in early years is like curving a line on the stone (i.e. making indelible impressions).

The truth of this remark has been acknowledged by educationists.

An Arab poet has expressed the same truth in his verses. The translation of his couplets are as follows:

(a) I find that I am forgetting what I learnt when I grew up but whatever I learnt in my childhood I clearly remember.
(b) Knowledge is acquired only in childhood. Calm and dignity developed after growing up is composure and selfpossession in real sense of the word.
(c) If anything is imprinted on the mind in the early years, it becomes indelible.
(d) Acquisition of knowledge in old age amounts to bearing hardship. At this state man's heart, audition, eye-sight and every thing are weary.
(e) What is man, but a combination of two things: reason and speech. Any one who lacks these capacities is dead.

Islamic Injunctions with regard to women's education

All the Ulama and ancient jurists and their successors are agreed that the principle of essential duty is extensible to women also There are two reasons for this:-

1. Women are under the obligation to abide by the injunctions of Shariah as men are.

2. Women are entitled to reward in the Hereafter like men.

In the first case men and women are equally under the obligation to offer prayers, keep fast, pay zakat, perform Hajj, to do good and justice. The woman can buy and sell, mortgage property or entrust it to some one. She can also appoint her legal counsel and is bound like man to call the people to do good and forbid them to refrain from evil.

It is of course another thing that the woman is physically different from man and, therefore, she is exempt from certain obligations. For instance, during the menstrual period or for forty days after the child birth the woman is exempted from offering prayer or keeping fast.

Similarly hard jobs like lifting weight is not keeping with the physique and the constitution of the fair sex. Jobs like fighting in the war with arms in normal conditions or the work of a mason or blacksmith are not suited to the delicate physique of the woman.

Similarly, the woman cannot be put on jobs that obstruct her natural functions like household work, rearing of children and looking after the homestead; for the woman has been created for these jobs and, therfore, she has to do only the jobs that do not affect or prejudice the very purpose of her creation. If there is cause of corruption in the society for any job she is made to do, then she should be removed from such a job. Examples: such jobs are employment of women in the same organization where men work. Offices and institutions for women should be separate from those meant for men.

Apart from the job referred to above, women can accomplish any work that men can.

Every right thinking man will, I think, agree with me that Islam enjoins upon women to refrain from doing certain jobs not because she is incapable of performing them but because they do not behove her and are incompatible with her respectable place in the Islamic society.

If this is not the case, then I can think of no man who will make the woman do jobs that cause her to forget her natural functions and neglect her duty towards her husband and children and household.

The poet Shauqi has aptly underlined the maternal function of the woman in the following verses:-

> "An orphan is not the child whose parents have left the world leaving it behind wretched and disdainful. An orphan is actually one who is totally neglected by his or her mother or one whose father is too busy to pay heed to him or her."

Who among us would like his wife to do hard jobs damaging her body, impairing her health and feminine delicacy and causing her different diseases.

Can there be anything more valuable for a woman in this life than the life of honour and human pride. If the woman falls a prey to corruption and debauchery, who else will rear the children.

There is a superb couplet which expresses the same idea. It is translated as follows:

> The grass that grows in the garden is not like that which grows in the desert.
>
> Children who have sucked the milk of lewd mothers can not be expected to be perfect.

We cite below the opinions of the Western thinkers about

the employment of woman out of the four walls of their homes:

Samuel Smiles writes in his book on Ethics that the system of life which calls upon the woman to work in factories and offices will undermine the family in the ultimate analysis, however rich she may grow, for it is the family which is the first to fall a prey to such a system and is consequently disintegrated by it. Smiles goes on to say that the real function of the woman is to perform duties relating to the household which comprises disposition of everything in an orderly manner, rear the children and meeting the domestic requirements by economy.

Smiles adds that the factories and offices have taken away from the woman her domestic functions with the result that the homes are no longer sweet homes, and the children come of age without proper care and upbringing, the conjugal has lost its warmth, the woman is no longer the loving wife but is only a worker devoted to the hard jobs of the office and as such inhibits all those things that foster affection and understanding between man and wife and safeguard the woman's virtue.

In the 6th issue of the *shajratuddur* magazine, an English lady has this to say:-

"If our daughters work in homes like maid servants, it would be much better for them than to work in offices and factories. For in offices and factories they are contaminated with all those iniquitous things that make life cheerless for ever. I wish that our cities were like those of the Muslim countries, where the virtue, chastity and respect of the woman is ensured and where the woman enjoys all the facilities and comforts with the security of her honour and virtue.

"The people of England should feel ashamed of themselves who allow their daughters to mix up freely with young men and thus turn them into models of iniquity. Why don't we adopt the system wherein the girls are made to do the work suited to the gunius of fair sex, as has been enjoined by divine revelations. For example, they should do the household work and leave to men the jobs meant for them. This is the only way to ensure the security of the woman's chastity and virtue."

In second case referred to above, i.e., the reward to be given in the Hereafter, the woman shares it equally with man. The verses of the Holy Quran bear clear testimony to the fact than man and woman equally deserve the reward to be had in the life Hereafter. Some of these verses are as under:

"Allah says: I suffer not the work of any worker, male or female, to be lost. Ye proceed one from another. So those who fled and were driven forth from their homes and suffered damage for My cause and fought and were slain, verily I shall remit their evil deeds from them and verily I shall bring them into Gardens underneath which rivers flow — A reward from Allah." (3:195)

"And whosoever does good deeds, whether male or female, and he or she is a believer these will enter the garden, and they will not be dealt with a whit unjustly."(4:124)

"Lo! Men who surrender unto Allah and women who surrender, and men who believe and women who believe, and men who obey and women who obey, and men who speak the truth and women who speak the truth, and men who persevere in righteousness and women who persevere, and men who are humble and women who are humble and men who give alms and women who give alms and men who fast and women who fast, and men who guard their modesty and women who guard their modesty and men who remember Allah and women who remember — Allah hath prepared for them forgiveness and a vast reward." (33:35)

That women are entitled to a reward in th Hereafter just as men are, is proved by a tradition of the Holy Prophet (S.A.W.) cited by Hafiz Abdul Barr in his work *Al Isteab* and Imam Muslim in his Sahih. The tradition runs as follows:

"Hadrat Asma bint Yazeed bin Al-Sakan called on the Holy Prophet (S.A.W.) and said, "I am an emissary from a group of Muslim women. They are all convinced of what I say. They say what I say. They act on my advice. Allah has sent you as His messenger to both men and women. We all have believed in you and started following you. We women observe purdah and remain within the four walls of our homes. But others (males) have been given privileges denied to us. They join the Friday congregation and funeral processions. They also fight in the way of Allah. When they are away waging war in the way of Allah, we rear their children. Do we deserve to share reward with them in the Hereafter?

The Holy Prophet (S.A.W.) turned his face towards his companions and said, "Have you ever heard any other woman put a better question about her religion?"

The companions replied in the negative.

The Prophet (S.A.W.) said to Asma, "Go back and tell your fellow womenfolk to maintain good conjugal relations, seek the pleasure of their husbands, say in support of whatever they have to say and lead a harmonious life with them. Doing all this is equal to all the services to Allah (on the part of men) you have mentioned."

When Hazrat Asma returned, she spontaneously repeated 'Allah-o-Akber! Allah-o-Akber! (God is great! God is great!) and expressed pleasure over what the Prophet (S.A.W.) observed.

It is clear from the above tradition that the woman is entitled as much reward for keeping the house, and managing its affairs, obeying her husband and rearing the children as man is entitled for waging the war in the way of Allah and observing other forms of worship.

We now cite some traditions in relation to imparting education to one's daughter.

1. Says the Prophet (S.A.W.) "If a man has three daughters, three sisters, two daughters or two sisters, whom he teaches discipline, treats them well and arranges for their marriage, he secures a place in Paradise."

(Tirmizi, Abu Dawood)

The wording of another tradition to the same effect is as follows:

"Whoever has a maid or a slave girl whom he educates well, teaches manner and decorum and then set her free, he will get double reward."

Sahih Bukhari and Sahih Muslim provide ample proof of the fact that the Holy Prophet (S.A.W.) imparted the knowledge of what Allah taught to him. For instance once a woman called on the Prophet (S.A.W.) and said to him that men had learnt all his edicts and that he should appoint a day for the women also so that they may come him and learn what Allah had imparted to him. The Prophet accordingly appointed a day for the women to assemble to receive religious instructions and the Prophet (S.A.W.) on that day taught them the injunctions he received from Allah.

Bulazari writes in his book *'Futooh-ul-Buldan'* hat one of the Prophet's (S.A.W.) wife Hazrat Hafsa bint 'Umar ibn-al-Khattab used to learn writing from a woman named Shifa Adavia during the days before Islam. When the Prophet (S.A.W.) contracted her into marriage he asked Shifa to teach her calligraphy as she used to do before.

From the above allusions it may be inferred that Islam enjoins upon women also to learn useful arts and academic subjects. If any one in past forbade to impart education to women, he meant to prohibit such education as may include obscene poetry, knowledge of harmful things and cheap manners. As a matter of fact the woman can learn anything which accrues both spiritual and worldly benefits. She can write instructive and edifying poetry and prose and no one can prevent her from doing so.

In the introduction to Ibn Sahnoon's book *Al-Mu'allimin* we come across this passage:

"God-fearing Qadi Ibn Esa used to teach his daughters and grand-daughters. According to Qadi Ayaz, he taught his daughters and nieces the Holy Quran and other academic subjects after the 'Asr prayer."

Before Qadi Ibn Esa, the conqueror of Sicily Asad Ibn-ul-Furat tought his daughter Asma who became a great scholar. Khushni narrates that there was a tutor who went into the palace of Muhammad bin Al Aghlab where he taught boys in the day time and girls at night.

The History of Islam bears it out that the woman rose to a very high academic cultural position during palmy days of Islam. Besides, during the earliest period of Islamic history the woman played an important role in sphere of education and training.

There were some poets and writers among women like Aliya bint-ul-Mehdi, Aisha bint Ahmed bin Qadim and the daughter of the Caliph Al Mustakfi Billah Walladah.

There were also physicians among them who included Karina Al Marozia, Syeda Nafisa bint Muhammad and according to Hafiz Ibn Asakir, who is also a narrator of the hadith that he had been the student of over eighty women teachers and guides.

Innumerable Muslim women attained a very high position of erudition and scholarship. Some of them taught even great jurists and renowned Ulama like Imam Shafiee, Ibn Khallakan, Imam Bukhari and Ibn Hibban. These examples bear a clear testimony to the importance attached in Islam to learning, development of intellectual potentialities and furtherance of culture.

Although Islam enjoins upon women to receive religious and mundane education, yet at the same time it imposes on the Muslims to make separate arrangement for women's education, so that the honour and virtue of the girls may be safeguarded. They may have a good reputation, may be held in high esteem in the Muslim society for both their education and moral excellence.

The first educationist who advocated segregation of women in the field of education was Allama Qabisi. He writes in his treatise entitled "*Al Taleem*":

"The best theory of education is that co-education should not be allowed. The two sexes should be imparted education separately."

When Ibn Sahnoon was asked about co-education he replied, "I do not like co-education because it spoils the girls."

The opinion offered by Ibn Sahnoon and Allama Qabisi aims its origin to the *Shariah* and the injunction of *Shariah* takes precedence of all others. Says Allah:

"And it becometh not a believing man or believing woman, when Allah and His messenger have decided an affair (for them) that they should (after that) claim any say in their affair, and whoso is rebellious to Allah and his messenger, he verily goes astray in error manifest." (33:36)

The source of the view advocated by Ibn Sahnoon and Qabisi is the verse of the Holy Qur'an cited below:

"And when ye ask of them (the Prophet's wives anything, ask it of them from behind a curtain." (33: 53)

If this has been ordained for the wives of the Holy

Prophet (S.A.W.), it will assume the status of a general ordinance and cease to be an exclusive injunction. The injunction relating to the obervance of purdah is general and applies to every woman and not confined to the mothers of believers (the wives of the Holy Prophet. (S.A.W.). This is the position taken by the scholars of jurisprudence.

The chastity and purity of the Holy Prophet's wives is unquestionable. But in spite of this they have been forbidden to appear before the strangers. Hence according to the general injunction contained in the verse cited above all the Msulim women are bound not to appear before the male strangers. The jurists and the scholars of principles have preferred this interpretation.

Says Allah :

Tell the believing men to lower their gaze and be modest. That is purer for them. Allah is aware of what they do.

And tell the believing women to lower their gaze and be modest, and to display of their adornment only that which is apparent, and to draw their veils over their bosoms and not to reveal their adornment save to their own husbands and fathers or husband's fathers, or their sons or their husbands' sons. (24:30-31)

In the above verse the following instruction have been given:

1. Gaze should be kept low.
2. The head and bosom should be covered with veils.
3. Adornments should be exposed to such men as are *mehrams.*

Are these three injunctions not a sufficient proof of the obligation imposed upon the woman to osbserve purdah, preserve their dignity, honour and virtue and refrain from freely mixing up with male strangers. Says Allah again:

"O Prophet! Tell thy wives and thy daughters and the women of believers to draw their cloaks round them. That will be better, that so they may be recognized and not annoyed. Allah is ever Forgiving, Merciful." (33:59)

How can we infer from this verse that the woman can lead a life freely mixing with men? It clearly enjoins upon women to observe purdah and put on cloaks.

Tirmizi quotes this saying of the Holy Prophet:

"Whenever a man is with a woman in private, the third person present is the Devil."

According to a tradition cited in Sahih Bukhari and Sahih Muslim, The Prophet (S.A.W.) said, "Avoid to thrust yourselves into the company of women." A man asked what the Prophet (S.A.W.) had to say about the close relations of the husband. (The word used in the text is equivalent to husbands brothers). He replied, "They are nothing short of death."

The above verses of the Holy Quran and the Prophet's traditions prove it beyond doubt that mixing up of men and women indiscriminately is totally unlawful.

The people who advocate mixing of men and women freely on the basis of conventions, psychological treatment or legal arguments actually misconstrue the injucntions of *Shariah*, intentionally express their ignorance of propensity of human nature, and blind themselves to the bitter experiences of promiscuous societies. Our contention that such people misconstrue the injucntions of the *Shariah* is substantiated by the foregoing verses of the Quran and the Prophet's traditions.

We have observed that the people deliberately blink the propensity of human nature because Allah has imbibed sex appeal in the male and female for each other. This appeal is but natural. "It is Allah's nature according to which He has created man and there can be no change in the principle of His creation."

Do the advocates of the mixing up men and women freely want to change the sacred universal principle. Do they intend to transform itself? Do they desire to tranform the ways of human life? If the indiscriminate mixing of men and women is allowed, the sexual appetite will be intensified and both the sexes will unscrupulously deviate from the moral norms. Such a situation leads to horrible corruption and debauchery will consequently rise to the highest degree.

It has also been assumed that if the two sexes are allowed to live together right from the early childhood, they will be accustomed to seeing each other and consequently the sexual instinct will not be incited. This is just an assumption. Even if it so happens, then the love of each couple will give in to hatred. Compassion between them will be replaced by oppression and sexual warmth will be damped. In such a situation no man and woman will be able to maintain conjugal relations. The assumption, therefore, is absolutely illusory.

We have also referred to the bitter experiences of the societies wherein men and women are allowed to mix up freely. Just cast a glance over those societies of the west and the east wherein women is depraved, and morally deterioriated and trapped in the quagmire of licentiousness. In such societies men and women are allowed to mix up freely at every level and in all walks of life. Promiscuity or the indiscriminate mixing of sexes is a quotidian phenomenon observed in the streets, schools, commercial centres, offices, universities and places of entertainment.

We mention here some of the experiences of promiscuous societies.

(1) Syed Qutb Shaheed writes in his book "*Islam and the world peace*":

"In the secondary schools of a single city in USA the number of pregnant girls students has risen to 48%."

(2) In the issue No. 650 of the Lebanese news paper "*Ahad*" the incidence of sex crimes in the American colleges and universities has been reported as follows:

(a) In American universities and colleges the incidence of sex crimes among boys and girls has been on the rise annually.

(b) The male students of American universities demonstrate and raise the slogan: "We want young girls. We want to please ourselves to our heart's content."

(c) The male students crowd at the windows of the girl student's room and steal their underwears.

(d) The Principal of the college concerned admonished both the male and female students of his college and said, "The boy and girl students are sex-stricken to an alarming extent. No doubt, the present way of life has a great deal to do with the student's aberrations."

(3) The Newspaper '*Ahad*' further reports:

"The results of the last year's census show that about one lac and twenty thousand children were illegitimately born of girls aged hardly twenty years and most of these girls are students of the universities and colleges."

According to a report of a police station in an American city that some sixty-six male and female students spent their last week-end in the month of May in Rhodes Island. But none returned to the university as all of them were put behind the bars; for they were found in a suspicious state. Some of those students were also found to be drug addicts."

(4) A social worker named Margret Smith says that girl students think of only their passion and seek the means to gratify them. Sixty percent of the girl students fail in the exams because they are more eager to gratify their sexual urge than to receive education. They prefer the carnal pleasure. Ten percent of such girls are lewd.

(5) George Baloshi quotes the Late American President Kennedy to have observed in 1962 that the behaviour of the American youths poses a serious threat to the future of the U.S.A. because they are sex-stricken and do not realize the responsibilities they have to shoulder. Mr. Kennedy is reported to have said further that six out of seven young men who offer themselves for recruitment in armed forces turn out to be medically and psychologically unfit for military service due to debauchery.

The President of U.S.S.R. Mr. Khrushchev also expressed his cocern over the bleak prospects of his country because the Russian youth was too obsessed with sex to fulfil responsibilities of the future.

(6) Will Durant writes that we are once again confronted with the same difficulty that upset Socrates, that is to say we are at our wit's end how to be guided by the moral principles of nature in removing the big obstacles responsible for the moral degneration of mankind. According to Durant, we are undermining our collective heritage by debauchery.

(7) The use of contraceptives on a mass scale is the direct cause of our moral deterioration. Formerly the moral imperative restricted sexual intercourse to wedlock and the matrimonial union resulted in the establishment of the paternal relationship that prevented the separation of man and wife. The father on his part considered himself committed to fulfil his responsibilities for the maintenance and breeding of children. But in the world today there is no link whatsoever

between sexual intercourse and procreation. The situation obtaining today is such that our fathers could not even imagine. The absence of conjugal bonds has transformed the pattern of relationship between males and females.

(8) It will be most shameful indeed that we allow some half a million American girls to enjoy themselves by being licentious. They are presented to the spectators in the roles of characters in obscene plays and stories. Such girls turn harlots and earn money through prostitution. Consequently those women also tread in their foot steps who are incapable of leading virtuous life by conjugal union. They are also sick.

(9) When a man (in America) fixed date for wedding, he moves with lewd girls who wander in the streets. Men also find the social mechanism in the form of educational institutions to gratify their sensual desires. It appears that man has discovered every possible method for the intensification of sexual appetite and its gratification.

(10) The new methods of gratifying the intense propensity for carnal pleasures have helped in strengthening Darwin's objections to religious beliefs. When the boys and girls came to know that religion denounces seeking carnal pleasures, they have started levelling criticism against religion on the basis of science and have thus cast aspersion on it.

(11) The body cannot escape the impact of sexual revolution. The spiritual energy genrerated by self-abnegation in ancient times is at the lowest ebb. Chastity and virtue which had once been the mark of distinction and honour is now the target of derision and cause of ill-repute. Modesty that used to enhance the beauty of human personality is absolutely lacking today. Men take pride in their sins and women raise slogans of equality with men and they demand the right to gratify their desires unrestrained. Sexual intercourse before marriage is not uncommon. Number of girls seeking carnal pleasures by offering themselves for fornication is greater than the prostitutes. The professional harlots are not under the control of the police but work behind lewd girls.

(12) The following news item appeared in the issue of the Cairo Newspaper, "*Al-yom*" dated April 1964:

"There were big demonstrations in Sweden when about a hundred and forty doctors called upon the government and the parliament to take necessary steps for the prevention of sex crimes which is undermining the public health. These doctors also demanded laws should be enacted and enforced to deter sexual corruption.

(13) Justice Bin Landey writes in his book the *'Revolt of the New Generation'* that the boys in America come of age prematurely and feel the sexual urge intensely in an early age.

The judge investigated the cases of three hundred and twelve girls and found that 255 of them were aged between eleven and thirteen and they were sexually self-conscious with clear signs of concupiscence and their bodies craving for sexual intercourse just as the bodies of eighteen years or older girls do.

(14) Dr. Edith Hawker says in his book on *the laws of sex'* that it is not uncommon even in the refined sections of the society that girls aged seven or eight years associate with boys to such an extent that they get involved in sexual relation with them. The author has cited several instances to substantiate his contention.

(15) Once a news item appeared in the British magazines that a 25 year old young lady teacher in a school taught a group of boys the methods of sexual intercourse. She was once seen stripping herself in the presence of students and demonstrating fornication licentiously.

In an issue of the London Magazine 'Middle East' dated 15th July 1979, it was reported that in Europe 75% husbands are guilty of the breach of their wives trust. Similarly 75% married women are unfaithful to their husbands. More often than not the husband knows of his wife's breach of trust and the wife also knows her husband's inequity. Nevertheless, their conjugal relations remain unaffected.

Some 80 to 85% unmarried adult males enter into illicit realtions with women. Almost every young has a keep. Those who have no keeps or mistresses tend to gratify their sexual desire with one woman after another.

(16) A Lebanon magazine *'Al Aman'* reports in its issue of the 30th Nov, 1979 that an Arab young man deserted his family and went to Denmark. He was witnessing a stage play when all of a sudden a woman appeared on the stage stark

naked. She then called her dog to copulate with her. When this act was over the whore invited everyone among the audience to do with her what the dog had done in the brilliance of the electric lamps and to the tune of music in its highest pitch. Then the Arab youth saw an African mount the stage in response to her invitation but he failed to witness the beastly act intended by the African.

(17) It is well-known that the head of the French National Party *'Lotsoke'* an old man of seventy four years was steeped in Debauchery. His special guard confessed that he had kept girls aged fourteen to eighteen years in an official residence. These girls were prepared to dance naked in the parties. They went to the villas of government officials for naked performances. This is a difficult problem which the French government is unable to solve.

(18) In Chicago a voluminous report of the CIA was published which spread over thirteen volumes. It has been recorded in this report that the most depraving licence and the life of libertines is not only undermining the family system of America but is also destroying the American culture. It is an evil for which neither the police nor the court knows any remedy.

(19) The American magazine *Herald Tribune* in its issue dated 29th June 1979 said that in the western countires in general and in the American society in particular fornication with sisters and daughters has spread like pestilence. A resume of the deliberations of the American thinkers and intellectuals has been published. These intellectuals have come to the conclusions that although such incidents are not rare, yet they have not yet assumed such proprotions that it would be easy to verify them. However, they hold that in one out of ten American families such horrible sins are committed.

This, then, is the case with forbidden women. In schools or offices where boys and girls will study or work together anyting may happen,particularly when there is no relationship between them. Such boys and girls are bound to be lewd.

This, in brief, is an account of debauchery rampant in the western society as the result of freely mixing up of women with men.

Despite of all these heinous crimes the system of co-education from the nursery to the college level is in force in the countries of both the West and the East. Nor is this all. In these countries unrestrained promiscuity remains uncurbed to this day.

After the foregoing lengthy discussion of the subject can any sane and right-thinking person support the position that the free mixing of man and woman restrains the sexual urge and that such a social pattern is commendable?

Shaikh Zahid Al Kausari has an interesting passage in one of his essays relevant to our discussion. The Ottoman ambassador accredited to England was once attending a high level meeting in England in which the top officials and leaders of the British empire were present. One of the dignitaries said to the Turkish ambassador, "Why do you cling to the position that the Muslim women of the east is backward, segregated from men and deprived of the modern enlightenment?" The Ottoman ambassador replied, "That is because our women do not like to give birth to the children of other women's husbands." On hearing this the British dignitary felt ashamed of himself and could not think of any answer.

As we have touched the question of commingling of the males and females, let me pause a little to tell the parents the real cause of this state of affairs.

The thing is that the primary purpose of Zionism and all th subversive materialsitic idoelogies is to annihilate the Mulsim society and to dismantle the entire edifice of the Islamic set-up. In order to achieve this end, the sytems referred to undermine the moral values, and attempt to transform the youths (both boys and girls) outlook on life and sow the seeds of depravity and moral deterioration in every section of the Muslim society. All these system use the woman to foster subversion and weave the web of machinations as the most effective tool. This is sentimental element which they exploit for imposing their imperialistic system and subversive ideologies.

The biggest champion of imperialism says that wine, music and women are the things that can destroy the Msulim Ummah to such an extent that a thousand cannons cannot do and,, therefore, it should be saturated with lust.

An eminent missionary of the masonic cult observes that it is necessary for them to get hold of the woman, for no sooner do we stretch our hands towards her, then whatever is unlawful would be within our reach and consequently the forces of religion would disperse.

Again, we cite here a passage from the documents of Zionist sages:

"It is our duty to try our level best to domolish the edifice of morality. This would facilitate our triumph. Freud was one of us. He will expose sexual relation in the broad day light so that nothing may be raised in the eyes of the youths belonging to any nation whatsoever and the main aim of their life may be the gratification of sexual appetite. When this happens he will sink into abyss of depravity."

Those in the Islamic countires who raise the slogan of mixing up of men and women freely and try to introduce it into the social life of Muslims are in reality atheists and are performing the function of propagating the programme of anti-Islamic forces like the cult of materialistic and a moral freedom and championing the cause of imperialism, zionism and masonic creed.

Under the circumstances it is incumbent upon the parents and guardians to keep their daughters and girls separate from the boys. This would provide an atmosphere of sanctity and chastity for their growth and Islamic society will be safeguarded against moral degeneration of the individuals and deviation from the moral norms. In such an atmosphere both the boys and girls would be physically and mentally healthy and the Muslims will be immune from the conspiracies hatched by the anti-Islamic forces to undermine the Muslim women.

A daughter of Islam named Aisha Taimuria speaks proudly of her virtue, chastity and modesty in the following verses:

(1) With the hand of chastity I safeguard the sanctity of purdah and I am superior to the girls of my age in respect of courage.

(2) My knowledge of letters and education have done me no harm. Harm will be done only when I grow attractive

for the intellectuals like venus.

(3) By covering my head and face with a veil and being modest I confront no difficulty in attaining a high position in the society.

Responsibility for Intellectual Growth

One of the main responsibilities imposed by Islam on parents and guardians is to impart intellectual training to the children in an early age. This training should continue up to the age of puberty. This intellectual and mental training is designed to establish the child's mental link with the following facts:

1. (a) Islam is both a religion and a form of government.
   (b) The Quran is a system of life and law.
   (c) The history of Islam is a treasure of our glory and honour.
   (d) The Islamic culture is the means of our spiritual and intellectual sustenance.
   (e) The essence of pride and valour is dedication to the missionary movement of Islam.

It so being the case, as the child enters the age of discretion and bearing things in mind, it is the duty of the parents to impress the following facts upon the minds of the children:

(i) Islam is an eternal religion whose principles are applicable at all times and at all places. It is all-embracive, consisting of everlasting principles. It admits of change while being eternal.

(ii) The glory, power, and the rise of our forbears' civilization owed itself to the fact that they moulded their mode of thinking and feeling according to the principles of Islam and sanctified them in their hearts.

(iii) Children should also be briefed about the plots hatched by the enemies of Islam. These plots include:

(a) the treacherous zionist plans.
(b) the plans prepared by the oppressive imperailist systems.
(c) the plans of Comunism and
(d) the plans of malicious christianity.

There are the plans and plots designed for the extermination of Islamic beliefs, sowing the seeds of deprvavity among the Msulim families and spreading evils in the Islamic society. The first and last prupose of these conspiracies is to damp the spirit of Jihad and resistance in the Muslim youth and to exploit the natural resources and material wealth of the Muslim countires and finally to erase the imprints of Islam from all the Muslim societies.

(iv) The children should also be told about the Islamic culture and civilization by which the Muslims were blessed with the highest degree of prosperity. This is a fact borne out by history.

(v) Finally the children should be told that we Msulims are a nation who have not followed the examples of depraved people like Abu jahI, Abu Lahab and Ubay bin Khalaf. On the contrary our history begins with the accounts of great people like the Holy Prophet Muhammad (S.A.W.), Hazrat Abu Bakr, Hazrat 'Umar, Hazrat 'Usman and Hazrat Ali.

Besides, our conquests did not begin with the battles of Laboos, Dahis and Ghabra. They rather began with the battles of Badr, Qadsia and Yarmook.

Again , we have not taught philosophy of wisdom to the world by contributing seven poems. We have rather illuminated the human mind with the Quranic teachings. We did not 'propagate the creed of Lat and 'Uzza, but rather conveyed to the world the Quranic teachings.

2. The basis of this kind of intellectual nourishment is a tradition narrated by Hazrat Ali as quoted by Imam Tabarani with reference to some narrator. The tradition is as under:

Inculcate in your children three qualities:

1. The love of your Prophet. (S.A.W.).
2. The love of your Prophet's family.
3. The art of reciting the Holy Quran.

Our forbears attached great importance to such mental nourishment. They considered it essential to teach their children the Holy Quran, the feats of the Holy Prophet (S.A.W.) in the various battles he fought against the enemies of Islam and the great achievements of our ancestors.

We quote here the observations of some of our forbears:

Hazrat Sa'd bin Waqqas (R.A.A.) says: We made our children learn by heart the accounts of the Holy Prophet's battles just as they committed a *surah* of Holy Quran to memory.

3. Hazrat Imam Ghazzali has this to say in his book-*Ahya-e-Uloom-uddin:*

The child's education should begin with the Holy Quran. They should also be taught historical and current events. They should then be imparted the knowledge of Islamic injunctions.

4. In his introduction to history, Ibn Khaldoon underlines the importance of teaching the Holy Quran and making the children learn it by heart, observes that the teaching of the Quran is the basis of education in every school of all the Muslim countries, in as much as the teaching of the Quran is an Islamic convention that reinforces the faith of a Muslim.

5. Hisham bin Abdul Malik asked the tutor of his son to teach him the Holy Book, make them commit excellent verses to memory, teach him rhetorics, acquaint him with the events of wars. What he meant by this was to imbibe in him moral virtues and to train him to be social and sociable (i.e. guard him against introversion).

These valuable views of our religious leaders and forbears truly depict the intellectual nourishment received by every individual of the Muslim society in the past. The rulers and the ruled, the scholars and the laymen, the teachers and pupils, all were subjected to intellectual training and the imprints of Islam were impressed upon their minds. Now, the question is how is this intellectual training to be imparted in the world today? This is to be carried out in four phases:

(1) Preaching and Insturction.
(2) Practical guidance.
(3) Purposeful study.
(4) Effective company.

1. **By preaching and instruction** is meant that the child should be taught the real nature, principles and injunctions of Islam. He should be made to bear in mind that the faith of Islam is the only religion that has the capacity to survive; that it is everlasting and progressive; that it aims at the imposition of the divine laws on the entire humanity. The guardians particularly the father is under the obligation

to impress upon the mind of the child that the honour and glory of the Muslims hinges on Islam alone and the Muslims can never succeed without the Quranic teachings. Power, civilization, progress and advancement is meaningless without the Holy Prophet's (S.A.W.) *Shariah.*

It is also the duty of the father to acquaint the child with the conspiracies formed against Islam by Zionism, imperialism, communism and Christinanity. All these creeds and ideologies are determined to exterminate Islam. They misconstrue the teachings of Islam and misrepresent the truth it preaches. They are out to erase the imprints of Islam. They have all resolved to eliminate the spirit of Jehad and determination from the hearts of the Muslims. What they actually aim at is that the pattern of the present generation's education and training should be based on atheism, deviation from the Islamic norms and moral principles.

Besides, the guardian and the father is also under the obligation to acquaint the child with Islamic culture and civilization that blessed mankind with civic life and the light of knowledge for centuries together. Europe drank at the fountain of their academic and cultural achievements for hundreds of years.

Continuous and persistent impression of these facts upon the minds of the children would ingrain their hearts the belief that Islam is a religion as well as an invaluable treasure of heritage, a system of life as well as an eternal law. Islamic history is a treasure of our greatness as a nation and that the secret of Muslims' progress is continuous activity and struggle.

In the modern times it is imperative to impart such edifying education to children and instruct them in an effective manner.

2. Practical Guidance

This means that the child should be under the guidance of a leader with certain qualifications. Such a guide should be sincere, wise with a full knowledge of Islam. He should also have the sterling quality of perseverance and constancy, and be capable of defending Islam and if needs be fighting in the way of Allah. He should be one strictly adhering to the principles of Islam and be bold enough to act on Allah's command without caring for strictures and censure from any quarter.

The trouble is that those who occupy the high position of spiritual and religious leadership today mispresent Islam to their followers with the exception of a few who are true guides.

Some of the leaders mentioned above concentrate mainly on the purification of the soul, but forget their duty of enjoining good and forbidding evils. They neither advise the people in authority nor do anything to counter transgression.

Some religious leaders attach importance only to such overt things as growing beard, wearing cloak, covering the head etc, but they do nothing whatsoever to give a fillip to enforce the divine commands on earth nor take any initiative to foster unity and cohesion in the society.

There are still others who focus their attention on specializing in the *Shariah* and Islamic jurisprudence. But they take no part in religious movements and jehad. They presume, notwithstanding, that they are doing a great service to Islam.

In other words there are various kinds of people performing the functions of religious and spiritual leadership. Thus they serve Islam only partially, although they are well-aware that Islam is an indivisible unit. As such no spiritual leader and religious scholar or any one whom the people appoint their leader is authorized to do away with the duties and obligations imposed by Allah and ignore anything enjoined by Him. This is clear from the following verse:

"Those who hide the proofs and guidance which We revealed after We had made it clear in the Scripture. Such are accursed of Allah and accursed of those who have the power to curse. Except such of them as repent and amend and make manifest (the truth). There it is toward whom I relent. I am the Relenting, Merciful." (2:159-160)

The Holy Prophet (S.A.W.) has also warned against the suppression of knowledge. Hazrat Abu Saeed Khudri has quoted the following saying of the Holy Prophet (S.A.W.):

"Whoever conceals profitable knowledge from the people,

will put into his mouth the reins of fire on the Day of Judgment."

(Ibn Majah)

A sign of those who assume the missionary office and religious leadership claim to be pure and pious in spite of their violation of the Prophet's edict and the divine injunction. Without paying the least heed to what the *Shariah* enjoins upon them, they try to demonstrate the link of their mortal personality with Allah arrogating to themselves the functions of representing Allah contending that they have attained to a position wherein they are infallible. Hence they think that nobody has the right to check them if they go wrong; nor is it permissible for any follower to object to any order given to him by his guide. For these spiritual leaders' claim to occupy a position of innocence and immunity. Innocence and immunity in reality, are exclusive virtues of the prophets. The attitude of Imam Malik is noteworthy in this context. Once he stood by the side of the Holy Prophet's (S.A.W.) grave and remarked, "There is none among us who has not defied any order or whose order has not been defied except the man lying in that grave." So saying the Imam pointed towards the Prophet's sacred grave.

The wise ulama and the sincere guides conduct themselves in a manner that serves as an everlasting example for posterity. Such is an example set by Allama Shaikh Saeed Al Nursi, who earned the name of Badee-uz-Zaman for his wisdon and piety. At one stage of his career as a spiritual guide he felt that his admirers and followers pay him undue respect and link his personality with God. So he advised his followers not to link his sinning and mortal personality with the Spring of Truth, to the path whereof he guides them. He exhorted them to establish relationship with the most sacred spring of God and that spring was the Book of Allah and the practice of the Holy Prophet (S.A.W.). He also made it clear to them that his position was no more than that one who deals in the divine goods and that he was far from being innocent as he also committed sins like others and erred in talking. Sin and error in preaching, added the sage, tarnished the manifestation of Truth with which his followers associated him. He warned them that he would thus misguide the people and take them awav from the path of Truth.

It is incumbent upon the tutors and the guardians to place their children under the guidance of a true and sincere scholar and sage who is competent to present Islam to them in its entirety and fully acquaint them with the Islamic beliefs, law, the political and spiritual aspects of the faith. He should also be able to explain them the significance of the purification of soul, jehad, worship and the affairs of the state from the Islamic viewpoint. The guide should keep in view what is actually necessary for the discipline and refinement of children and should teach them in a nice and effective manner. He should thus establish relationship between the thinking and conduct of the children and *Shariah* and the guidelines given by our forbears rather than link them with his own ephemeral and fallible personality.

If individuals are linked with an ideal and wise guide in the manner suggested above, they will grow up to be righteous and jihad oriented, imbued with a sense of God's presence, and humility. They will turn out to be outspoken, accustomed to offering prayer in the mosque and brave enough to face the anti-Islamic forces in the battlefield. Such individuals would accord with the concept of a poet expressed in the following words:

> Such youngmen who tread the high paths of glory and know no religion other than Islam.
>
> Islam took them into their bosom and bred them. Islam nurtured them in the same way as a plant grows and bears fruit. In this way they have grown under he tutelage of Islam and attained a prominent position.
>
> When they enter the battlefield, they become so chivalrous that they break impregnable citadels.
>
> At nightfall you will find them prostrate for fear of Allah.
>
> Islam has trained the youths of my nation in this way. Being so trained, they have become sincere, lovers of liberty, and honest.
>
> Islam taught them how greatness is achieved. That is why these youngmen have never suffered the ignominy of

captivity.

If the Muslim youth of today is also trained on similar pattern, Islam will regain its glory through them.

3. By purposeful study is meant that when the child reaches the age of discretion he should be provided a library with short books on the lives of heroes, the accounts of their great feats, the stories of righteous people etc.

The library should also be equipped with good volumes on beliefs, ethics economics, political science as well as books providing information about the conspiracies against Islam formed by materialistic ideologies, Christianity, Communism, the masonic cult and Zionism.

Such a library should also have edifying magazines containing useful material on Islam, the problems posed by the modern age and solutions thereto presented in an interesting and attractive style.

It is for the parents to choose books keeping in view the child's age and the level of intelligence so that the child may derive maximum benefit from them on the one hand and purpose mentioned in the Prophet's tradition is fulfilled on the other.

"Talk to the people in such a way that they understand what you mean."

(Hazrat Ali R.A.A. Narrated by Bukhari)

Hasan bin Sufyan narrates the following tradition to the same effect.

"I have been commanded to talk to the people keeping in view their level of intelligence. (*Dailami*)

If the guardians and tutors train their children on the pattern indicated above, they will undoubtedly meet the requirements of Islamic culture and would act on the message it embodies.

4. By beneficial company is meant that the parents should choose for the children good, peace-loving and educated friends well-acquainted with the basic elements of Islam and with full-awareness of their obligations and with personalities reflecting Islamic culture.

Obversely speaking the child should be kept away from dull boys as he enters the age of discretion so that he may not himself become dull. If he is allowed to move in the company of people who have no idea of Islam and who do not know the Islamic viewpoint about the universe, man and life, he too will become narrow-minded.

It is not enough for the child's friend to worship and offer prayers regularly, be refined and intelligent. He should also be reighteous to the highest degree, with his intellect mature and having full consciousness of collective problems so that he may prove to be the best and honest and righteous friend. There is an old saying, "Companion transforms his friend."

A wise man has observed, Don't ask say me what I am but ask me in whose company I move. You will thus know what I really am."

A poet expresses the same idea beautifully. Says he: "Do not ask about a man what he is. Rather ask about his companion; for everyone treads in the footsteps of his companion."

There is tradition of the Holy Prophet (S.A.W.) to the same effect

"A man treads in the footsteps of his friend. Some one of you should think whom he has made friends with."

It is, therefore, incumbent upon the parents and guardians that as soon as the child enters the age of discretion, they should find for him such associates as are virtuous, alive to their obligations and mileau wherein they live, and capable of acquainting their child with Islam and its comprehensive teachings as well as with the heroes who kept the banner of Islam aloft and who were prepared for the guidance of the whole of mankind.

At the end I would like to tell the parents that it is most deplorable that our children come of age but are not aware of the fact that Islam is a wealth valuable for both this world and the world in the Hereafter; that it gives us the Quran as well as the sword; that it consists of both worship and the affairs of the state; that it is the only religion characterized by enternal virtues; capable of surviving in every age and of surviving the revolutionary changes man's life is undergoing. Is it not a matter to regret for us that our children learn everything in their schools about the western thinkers and men of letters, about the thoughts expounded by the philosophers of the west and the east as well as the lives of those philosophers and thinkers but know nothing about the philosophers of Islam, Ulema, Jurists, thinkers and military leaders? If the task of teaching our children the achievements of our forbears is undertaken at all, it is negligible.

We should feel ashamed of the fact that when our children complete their education and come out of the schools, their personalities are impaired by alien culture. They are moulded by eastern and western thoughts to such an extent that most of the students born and bred in Muslim homes turn against their own religion, history and culture.

It is most shocking indeed that our children have to follow such guides as have no link with Islamic culture. They are rather out to sever that link. They paralyse the thinking of the children. The parents and guardians today deprive the children from such guides and teachers as are sincere and capable of acquainting the children with the real significance and all-inclusiveness of Islam.

It is also disgraceful that the new generation of Muslims is wasting its precious time in reading sacrilegious and obscene magazines and erotic novels, but sets no value on thought provoking books that provide detailed information about the Islamic way of life and dispel doubts about Islam created by the enemies of Islam, generating at the same time a sense of pride among Muslims in their glorious past.

It is the duty of the parents, guardians and tutors to do everything possible for the proper training of the children and the right orientation of their thinking and correction of their knowledge. When the parents and guardians feel that their children are being misguided by alien philosophies, they should judiciously try to set them right and shoud not tire of telling them how to counter the activities of the agents of atheism, anti-Islamic missionaries' conspiracies and the falsehood spread about Islam by the orientalists.

This is the only way we can nourish the thinking of our kids and guard their beliefs against conspiracies of anti Islamic forces and the misguiding alien ideologies.

If we adopt the method indicated above, our children will feel honoured for being Muslims, take pride in the history of Islam and the great achievements of their forbears. They will not consider acceptable any religion, law and system of government other than Islam. They will hold the Quran in the one hand and the sword in the other. They will once again treat Islam as a combination of religious service and system of Government. They will then be the true successors of the Muslims of the earliest times. A poet describes those Muslims in the following words:

(1) "O Prophet, You have left such companions behind you whose biographical accounts exhale fragrance in the universe.

(2) The basis of their conquests was virtue and compassion and whose politics was based on justice and benevolence.

(3) They did not confine religion to worship and prayers, and saying beads, but they worshipped at night in the mosque and in the day-time fought in the battlefield in the name of Allah.

5 . Mental Health

It is also incumbent upon the parents and tutors to maintain the mental health of their offspring and pupils. They are under he obligation to encourage every child and focus attention on his education keeping in view his level of intelligence so that he may grow up to be a right-thinking man with a strong memory and a pure mind and mature intellect.

To what extent are the parents responsible for their children's mental health? The answer to this is that the child's intellect, memory and body should be safeguarded against evil influences in the society.

We have dwelt at length in this book under the head of **'The Parent's Responsibility for the care of child's physical health'** what measures have to he taken in this respect. Here we propose to touch in brief on the same measures in order that the parents and guardians may fully grasp the nature and significance of their task.

The consensus of the physicians is that following evils are detrimental to man's thinking and memory. They make him absent minded and paralyse his intellect. They also harm his body. That is why the experts have advised to guard the children against various evils. These vices fall under four heads.

1. **Drinking and the use of intoxicants.**

Use of intoxicants in any form undermines man's health and makes him insane.

2. **Masturbation.**

Addiction to this causes tuberculosis, enervates memory, makes man absent minded and causes intellectual deviation.

3. **Smoking.**

It positively affects the mind and memory, weakens the capacity to think and causes nervousness.

4. **Sexual Inducements.**

These include obscene films, obscene dramas, nude pictures. They paralyse man's thinking and cause moral deviation enervate memory and diversion of attention. Apart from this, they are mere waste of time.

Dr. Alex Carlyle says that when man is sexually incited, his glands discharge a sort of fluid which goes into his brain through the blood causing the brain to slumber with the result that he is incapable of pure and healthy thinking.

There are other harmful effects of the evils in question besides those mentioned above.

What has been stated above may be epitomized as follows.

1. Obligation with regard to children's education.
2. Intellectual nourishment.
3. Measures for maintenance of mental health.

The parents and guardians will have to account before Allah for any neglect on their part for the discharge of the three responsibilities enumerated above and they will be pathetically ashamed of themselves for shirking the obligations imposed upon them. The predicament they will find themselves in is beyond words to describe. May Allah save us from such a plight! The following verse of the Holy Quran applies to such parents and guardians.

> "Our Lord! We obeyed our princes and great men and they misled us from the Way. Our Lord! Oh, give them double torment and curse them with a mighty curse." (33.67-68)

The Prophet (S.A.W.) expresses undeniable truth in the following Tradition.

"Allah will call to account every guardian for the protection of everything placed in his custody and ask him if he has protected it or destroyed it." *(Ibn Hibban)*

(633:67-68)

At the end I pray that May Allah reckon us among those who are obdedient to Him and to His Prophet and among those whose faces will be shining on the Day of Judgment and who may have duly discharged the obligations imposed upon with regard to their children and wives. O Lord! We have good hopes from You and You are the Most Honoured Being of Whom We beg!

CHAPTER – X

RESPONSIBILITY FOR PSYCHOLOGICAL TRAINING

By this responsibility is meant that when the child enters the age of discretion he should be trained in such a way that he is imbued with courage, contour boldness, full consciousness of things, benevolence, restraint and the psychological and moral virtues.

Psychological training of the child is designed for the effective performance of the task of building his character and formation of his balanced and self-consistent personality so that when he reaches the age of responsibility, he may be able to discharge his duties in the best possible manner.

The child is a trust right from its birth in the hands of those who bring him up. Islam, therefore, categorically enjoins upon the parents, guardians and tutors to lay the foundation of his mental health as soon as he opens his eyes upon the world and thus make him grow up to be a balanced personality with common sense and high ambitions.

It is also necessary for the parents and guardians to guard against such inducements that may lead to piquing his pride and shatter his confidence and impair his personality with the result that he develops a disdainful and pessimistic outlook on life.

I think that the parents and guardians should see to it that the children do not develop the following states of mind.

(1) Shyness (2) Phobia (3) Inferiority complex (4) Jealousy and (5) Anger.

We will deal in details the five states of mind mentioned above and suggest their remedy, which will atone for such states. But Allah alone is the Protector and all success is only due to Him.

(1) Shyness.

Shyness is a common trait of children. *Dr. Nabih Al Ghobra* writes in his book *"Al Mushkilat-ul-Sulukia"*.

"The early symptoms of shyness probably appear at the age of four months. When the baby is one year old these symptoms are quite clear. For intance, when it sees a stranger, it turns its face away or lowers its gaze or covers its face."

"When the child is three years old, it feels shy if it is taken to a stranger's house. It either sits in its mother's lap peacefully or sits silent by her."

Shyness is also hereditary. It is either diminished or increased because of the environment. Children who mix up with other people are less shy than those who do not mix up.

The most effective and complete treatment of shyness is to make the child accustomed to mixing up with other children. Either their friends should take them to their homes or the parents should take them along when they go to visit their relatives, or should kindly tell them to talk to other people, even if they are older or younger than they.

We now cite a few traditions and events of history to illustrate how the Holy Prophet (S.A.W.) and our forbears tried to rid the children of shyness and make them bold.

1. The Prophet (S.A.W.) once said to his companions, "There is a tree whose leaves do not fall. It is like a Muslim. Tell me what tree it is." Those present ransacked their brains to think of such a tree. Hazrat Abdullah bin 'Umar who had not yet come of age was also among them. He says that he thought of it to be the date, but he felt shy of saying. The companions asked the Prophet (S.A.W.) to let them know what the tree it was. The Prophet (S.A.W.) said, "It is the date tree."

(Narrated by Abdullah bin 'Umar as quoted by *Imam Bukhari*).

The wording of another tradition to the same effect is as follows: "I (Abdullah bin 'Umar) wanted to tell the Prophet (S.A.W.) that it was the date tree, but I was the youngest of his companions and therefore felt shy."

There is yet another tradition narrated by Hazrat Abdullah bin 'Umar pertaining to the same event: "I saw Hazrat Abu Bakr and Hazrat 'Umar talking. I did not want to speak. When we all left the place I told my father that I had thought of the date tree. If you had told it, it would have given me greater pleasure than getting a red camel would have given"

Hazrat Sahl bin Sa'id (R.A.A.) narrates that once a drink was presented to the Holy Prophet, (S A.W.). He drank some of it. A boy sitting by the right side of the Prophet (S.A.W.) at the moment, while grown up people were sitting on his left. The Prophet asked the boy, "Do you allow me to let those people share the drink?" The boy replied "Never, I would never prefer any body else to myself for what I am fortunate enough to get from you." *(Sahih Muslim)*

Ibn Abbas (R.A.A.) relates an incident which took place when he had not yet come of age. He says that Hazrat 'Umar used to include him in the Prophet's companions who took part in the battle of Badr and who formed his ('Umar's) advisory council. This enraged one of those companions. He said to the Caliph, "Our sons are not any different from him. Why don't you include them too, among your advisers?"

Hazrat 'Umar replied, "Are you aware of this boy's status?".

Hazrat 'Umar subsequently summoned Ibn Abbas to include him in his advisory council. Ibn Abbas says, "Hazrat 'Umar called me for the sole purpose of showing them the status I was entitled to."

Hazrat 'Umar then asked them how they interpreted the first verse of the *Surah Al Nasr.*

One of them said that the verse enjoined upon the Muslims to beg mercy of Allah whenever they were victorious. Other companions kept quiet.

Thereupon Hazrat 'Umar turned to Ibn Abbas and enquired what he thought of the interpretation. Ibn Abbas disagreed with the interpretation. Hazrat 'Umar asked him what interpretation he put of the verse.

Ibn Abbas replied, "The initial position of the first verse of the Surah contained the news of the Prophet's death, while last verse was revealed afterwards."

Hazrat 'Umar said, "My knowledge of the verse concurs with your interpretation."

Once Hazrat 'Umar was going through a street of Madina. Children happened to be playing there. One of them was Hazrat Abdullah bin Zubair. As soon as the children saw Hazrat 'Umar, they were overawed and ran away. But Abdullah bin Zubair stood silent and did not run along with his play mates.

Hazrat 'Umar drew near him and asked, "Why did you not run with other children? '

Abdullah bin Zubair said, "I have not committed any sin to be scared of you and run away. Besides, the street was not too narrow to make room for you to pass."

How bold and true was this answer!

Hazrat 'Umar bin Abdul Aziz saw his son wearing worn out dress on Eid day. Tears trickled down his eyes. When his son saw him with trearful eyes, he asked him, "O Ruler of believers, why are you weeping?"

The Caliph said, "I am afraid that when other children will see you in this torn and worn out dress, your heart will be broken."

The boy replied, "My heart would certainly have broken if I had been deprived of Allah's 'Pleasure or if I had disobeyed my parents. I hope that Allah will be satisfied if you are pleased with me.

When Hazrat 'Umar bin Abdul Aziz assumed the office of Caliphate, people poured in from all parts of the state to congratulate him. There was also a group of the people of Hijaz which included a lad who was hardly eleven years old. He moved forward to talk to the Caliph. Hazrat 'Umar asked the boy to go back so that some grown up person may come forward in his place. The boy said, "O Leader of the believers, Man is identified by two parts of his body; and they are his tongue and heart. If Allah bestows upon his bondsman a tongue that could speak and heart that remembers then he has the right to talk. Had age been a qualification for the office of Caliphate, then your high office would have been taken over by one older than you."

Hazrat 'Umar bin Abdul Aziz was amazed at the boy's speech and then recited the following couplets:

(a) Acquire knowledge because knowledge is not something innate and one who is enriched with the light of knowledge can never be like one who is ignorant.
(b) If an elderly person of a community does not possess knowledge, he is the youngest among his people.

In literary books the following incident has been related. There was a boy in the days of the Caliph Mamoon who talked to the Caliph in an excellent manner.

The caliph said to him, "Whose son are you?"

The boy replied, "I am the offspring of literature." Mamoon said, "This is the best lineage."

The Caliph then recited the following verses:

(a) You may be the offspring of any one you like, but do learn literature. By virtue of the civility resulting from the knowledge of literature you will need no lineage for your distinction.
(b) A manly youth is one who is proud of what he is and not of what his father was.

Once as the Caliph Mamoon entered his parlour, he saw a boy with a pen placed on his ear. He asked the boy, "Who are you?"

The boy replied, "I am the clerk of your government, nourished by your bounties and a candidate for your service. My name is Hasan Rija."

Mamoon was pleased by the excellent reply made by the boy. He issued the instruction, "Wise men have always been given preference because of the high standard of their performance. Therefore, promote this boy."

During the reign of Caliph Hisham bin Abdul Malik famine broke out in the country. People from Arabia came to seek his assistance. But they had no courage to speak to the Caliph. The group of Arabs included a minor boy named Durdas bin Habib. The Caliph caught the sight of the boy and said, "Whoever wants to come to me does have access, even if he is a child."

Thereupon the boy made so bold as to speak to the Caliph and said, "O ruler of believers, we have been a victim of famine for the last three years. During the first year our fat was melted, during the second we lost our flesh and during the third the very marrow of our bones has been taken out. You are in possession of huge amounts of surplus money. If it is meant for Allah, distribute it among His bondsmen. If it belongs to Allah s bondsmen, then why have you withheld it? If it belongs to you, then distribute it in charity among the famine-stricken people. Verily Allah rewards those who distribute alms and does not let the good done by the benevolent to go waste."

Hisham said that boy had advanced three such arguments as do not admit of any excuse. He then ordered one thousand dirhams to be distributed among all the Arabs, while one lac dirhams to be given to the boy alone.

But Durdas requested the Caliph that his share should also be distributed among his folk because he feared that amount given to them would not suffice to meet their needs.

Hisham asked the boy, "Don't you need any thing?"

The boy replied, "I have no aim other than the welfare of the common Muslims."

When the boy returned home, he was the most honoured person among his folk.

From the historical examples quoted above we may draw the conclusion that our forbears trained their children in such a manner that they were completely free from shyness. They had no sense of frustration either. The reason for this was that the children were trained to be bold and straight forward. Their fathers used to take them along with them to attend social functions and also had them present when they visited their intimate friends. The children were encouraged to talk to grown up people. The youngsters who were endowed with extraordinary qualities of the mind and intelligence above the average, and who could speak eloquently, were sent forward to talk to the Caliphs and the noblemen. Moreover, they were not only consulted on day to day problems but also were provided the opportunity to speak on academic problems in symposia which were held by great scholars and renowned ulama.

Boldness in academic matters is also an outstanding quality which enables children to understand every problem properly and to bear them in mind and goes a long way in their academic and literary attainments, building of character and maturity of thinking and social relationship.

It is incumbent upon the guardians, patrons and parents of contemporary age to train their children on the best lines so that they may develop distinct personalities characterized by boldness as well as respect for the grown up people. They should also be trained to take into consideration the feelings of others and have regard for every one according to his deservation. If boldness is not blended with the other qualities referred to, then frankness would amount to disrespect for others.

We would like at this stage, to draw a line of distinction between modesty and shyness.

In shyness the child suffers from extreme introversion and a sense of frustration. He avoids meeting the people. By modesty, on the contrary, is meant to be accustomed to Islamic decorum and cultivate Islamic virtues. For instance, we should train the child to feel ashamed of committing something unlawful or disliked. If children are taught to respect grown up people, to refrain from staring at ladies and from overhearing and prevent them from making mischief, it does not mean that they are made to develop shyness. It is no shyness if the child refrains from abusing, and talking nonsense and abstains from unlawful things and if he spends all his time in seeking Allah's pleasure. This would be modesty in the real sense of the word.

To drive home what modesty connotes in Islam we cite a tradition of the Holy Prophet (S.A.W.) as quoted by *Tirmizi:*

The Prophet (S.A.W.) said to his companions, "You should be duly modest in the presence of Allah."

The companions asked him: "O messenger of Allah, thank Allah, we are modest in His presence."

The Prophet (S.A.W.) observed, "That is no modesty. By being duly modest in the presence of Allah is meant to protect your head with all its parts and also to protect your stomach with everything included in it. Always be mindful of whatever is to come after death and the trial you have to undergo after it. Whoever is desirous of a reward in the Hereafter, renounces the glamour of this life and prefers the former to the latter. Whoever did this, he was shamefaced before Allah."

Hazrat Imam Ahmed who quotes this tradition also

includes the following words of prayer:

"Let Allah not see me the time when the observations of a learned man is not accepted and people are immodest before a man of serious disposition."

We come across this tradition in the writings of Imam Malik:

"Every religion has its morality, Modesty is the morality of Islam."

(2) Phobia.

This is a psychological condition found among children, grown up people both men and women. If phobia is found among children to a natural limit, it is somethig commendable and not a blemish; for it saves the child from accidents and other perils.

But if phobia exceeds the normal and natural limits, then the child is agitated. This is the real problem and there mustbe a sure cure for it.

A child psychiatrist says that when a child is in his first year he is overwhelmed by fear as for example when there is a sudden noise or some thing suddenly falls or a similar incident occurs. At age of six month the child is frightened by strangers. But a child who enters the age of three would be frightened by many a thing like animals, vehicles water and sewers.

Fear, according to the above psychiatrist, is manifest to a greater degree among girls as compared to boys. The intensity of fear in the child is proportional to the degree of its capacity to imagine. The greater this capacity the more intense is the fear.

The following factors lead to an increase in the child's fear.

(1) The mother frightens the child by grotesque figures, fiends and horrible creatures.

(2) Fostering the tendency to loneliness and introversion. If the child takes refuge behind the walls of the house, he is allowed to remain there.

(3) Mother's unjustified checks, exceeding fondness and agitation of mind.

(4) Telling the stories of supernatural beings such as genie, demons and ghosts.

In order to cure children of phobia, the following measures should be taken:

(i) Right from the early years the child should be imbued with faith in Allah. He should be taught to pray Him and resign to Him whenever it is frightened. When the child is trained on a pattern indicated above he will grasp the real meainings of faith and regular worship both physical and spiritual. This would effect a change in the child by virtue of which he will never be frightened in a crisis and will never be perturbed in the face of difficulty. Says Allah:

> "Lo! man was created anxious, fretful when evil befalleth him And when good befalleth him, grudging; save worshippers, who are constant at their worship."
>
> (70 : 19-23)

(ii) The child should be allowed freedom in his movements, made conscious of its responsibilities and trained to do various jobs in keeping with its age that his growth may accord with the following observation of the Holy Prophet (S.A.W.):

> "Every one of you is a shepherd and responsible for his charge."
>
> (*Bukhari and Muslim*)

(iii) The child should not be frightened particularly when it is crying. He should not be terrified by telling him that a genie, a demon or a thief has come. Being free from fear, the child's growth will be smooth and will develop the qualities of bravery and boldness. Grown thus, it will come up to the standard of the Holy Prophet (S.A.W.):

"A stronger believer is dearer to Allah than a weaker one and is better too." (*Sahih Muslim*)

(iv) As soon as the child attains the years of discretion, he should be made accustomed to mix up with other people, introduced to them and provided opportunities to visit them. This would make him feel in heart of hearts that he is being loved. This feeling should be present in every visit or social function. Brought up in this manner, he would hold up a mirror to the following tradition of the Holy Prophet (S.A.W.):

"The believer is both loving and loved. A man who does

not express affection for others nor do others express any affection for him has nothing good about him. The best of men is he who does maximum good to men."

(*Musnad Imam Hakim*, *Musnad Baihaqi*)

The psychologists suggest that the child should be provided maximum education about the thing he is scared of. If he is afraid of the dark, then the light should be put off to demonstrate to him what darkness actually is. If the child is scared of water, he should be provided an opportunity to play with water by putting it in a small pot. This will do him no harm either. If it is afraid of electronics, let him play with some electric apparatus. (*Al Mushkilat-ul-Sulukia P. 152*).

(v) Accounts of the wars waged by the Holy Prophet (S.A.W) and of the feats performed by our forbears should be related to the children. They should be urged to acquire the habits and sterling qualities of the Prophet's companions, their successors, the great Muslim leaders, conquerors, so that they may long for being as brave and bold as they were to spread the faith in Allah.

The remark of Sa'd bin Abi Waqqas should be borne in mind in this connection. He is reported to have said, "We used to teach our children the events of the battles fought by the Holy Prophet (S.A.W.) just as we used to teach them a Surah of the Holy Quran"

We have already mentioned the advice of Hażrat 'Umar bin Khattab to the parents to teach the children how to be brave and chivalrous and the methods of riding as well as to acquaint them with the techniques of war. The words of Hazrat 'Umar are as under:

"Teach your children archery and swimming. Tell them to mount a horse by jumping."

As regards religious training we have also quoted the following tradition as reproduced by Tabarani:

"Inculcate in your children three sterling qualities:
(a) Love of the Prophet,
(b) Love of his family and
(c) the way to recite the Holy Quran."

The sayings of the Holy Prophet (S.A.W.) and the observations made by his companions are unmistakable proof of the fact that Islam attaches great importance to audacity, chivalry and dauntless courage for the purpose of holding aloft the banner of Islam and demonstrate the glory of Islam throughout the world.

We describe here some aspects of the character of the sons of a companion of the Holy Prophet (S.A.W.) who are model for us to emulate. The Muslims would wonder at their dauntless courage as well as feel proud of them.

(1) When the Muslims marched to the battlefied of Uh'd to fight against the forces of the infidels, the Holy Prophet (S.A.W.) inspected the Muslim troops. He found among them some lads also who were hardly fourteen years of age. These boys were standing shoulder to shoulder with grown up men in order to wage a crusade to uphold Islam. When the Prophet (S.A.W.) saw them he was overwhelmed with compassion. He separated younger lads from them. They were Rafi' bin Khudej and Samura bin Jundub. The Prophet (S.A.W.), then included Rafi' in the Muslim army because he was adept in archery.

(2) When the Holy Prophet (S.A.W.) left Makkah for good and was on his way to Madina accompanied by his closest friend Hazrat Abu Bakr, he had to stay in the cave of Saur for three days. During his stay Hazrat Abu Bakr's daughters Hazrat Aisha and Hazrat Asmaa (R.A.A.) prepared meal for both the friends. Hazrat Asmaa (R.A.A.) tore asunder the cloth she wore round her waist. She then wrapped the meal she prepared for the Prophet (S.A.W.) and her father with one of the pieces of cloth. Thence forward she was surnamed, "the double girdled." Hazrat Abu Bakr's son busied himself with furnishing information to the Prophet. (S.A.W.). He brought the news of the people of Quraish in details every evening and sometimes stayed in the cave at night and left in the morning to be amidst the people of Makkah. In other words he remained a whole night with those people. This incident took place when Hazrat Aisha had not yet come of age. The daring deed the two sisters performed are unparalleled examples of courage-deeds that even men are not bold enough to perform.

(3) Hazrat Abdur Rahman bin Auf says that during the battle of Badr he was standing in the rank. He looked right

and left and found himself flanked on either side by two Ansari lads (local boys belonging to Madina as distinct from the immigrants of Makkah). One of the boys winked at me and asked, "Uncle do you recognize Abu Jahl?" Hazrat Abdur Rahman replied, "Well, I do. But what have you to do with him?"

The boy said, "I have come to know that he vilifies the Holy Prophet (S.A.W.). By God! If I happen to see him, he will find it difficult to get rid of me till I kill him." Hazrat Abdur Rahman says that the lad was elated. Then the other lad expressed similar sentiment.

After a little while, says Hazrat Ibn Auf, Abu Jahl was seen moving about among the enemy ranks.

I said to the boys, "Look lads, Abu Jahl is there — Abu Jahl the man whom you were just enquiring about. No sooner did the boys hear me than they unsheathed their swords and ran up to Abu Jahl, whom they struck repeatedly till he was reduced to nought. Having performed this deed they returned to the Prophet (S.A.W.) with the news of their slaying of Abu Jahl. The Prophet (S.A.W.) asked who of the two killed Abu Jahl. Both of them replied in unison, "I have killed him."

The Prophet asked them if they had cleaned their swords. The boys replied in the negative. Hazrat Ibn Auf says that the Prophet (S.A.W.) looked at the swords of both and said, "Really both of you have killed him."

The Prophet (S.A.W.) then equally divided Abu Jahl's arms and armour between Ma'az bin Amr bin al-Jamooh and Ma'az bin 'Ifra.

(4) According to a tradition narrated by Ibn Abi Sheba Imam Sha'bi, a woman gave his son a sword to fight in the battle of Uhd but he was too small to hold it. The woman then tied the sword to his shoulder with a rope and took the boy to the Holy Prophet (S.A.W.) and told him that her son would fight in the battle. The Prophet (S.A.W.) said to the boy, "My dear son, attack the enemy from this side and then from that."

The boy was injured during the fighting. He was brought to the Holy Prophet (S.A.W.), who said to him, "My dear son, you were, perhaps a little upset." The boy replied, "Not at all."

The following tradition is quoted by Ibn Sa'd in his *Tabaqat* and also by Bazzaz and Ibn Athir in *Kitab-ul Asasa* with reference to Sa'd bin Abi Waqqas

"I ((*Hazrat Sa'd*)) saw 'Umair bin AbiWaqqason the day of the Battle of Badr hiding before the Prophet's inspection of the Muslim army. I asked him what was wrong. He replied that he was hiding lest the Prophet (S.A.W.) should send him back, but he wanted to fight so that he may, by the grace of God, die a martyr."

Hazrat Sa'd adds that 'Umair was presented to the Prophet (S.A.W.). As he was too young, the Prophet (S.A.W.) sent him back. But 'Umair was so grieved that he started crying. Thereupon, the Prophet (S.A.W.) allowed him to fight. According to Hazrat Sa'd 'Umair was then too young to bind his sword belt without Sa'd's help. He fought and fell a martyr. He was only sixteen years old.

These striking examples from history bear a testimony to the fact that the sons of the Prophet's companions were extremely brave, always ready to rush into the battlefield. These virtues were imbibed in them as the result of the training by the Prophet (S.A.W.) and breeding in the environment of Muslim homes and a society composed of valiant individuals. In fact, the Muslim mothers themselves encouraged their sons to participate in Jihad and die as martyrs. Whenever they heard the news of the martyrdom of any of their sons they used to thank Allah for that. There was one such mother who uttered the following immortal words on the martyrdom of her sons:

"All praise be to Allah by Whose grace I have been honoured by the martyrdom of my sons and I wish that He may bless me with a place by them in the blissful life in the Hereafter."

The parents themselves trained their children in riding, in the arts of war and performing perilous deeds. Because of such training the youngsters used to march along with the warrior men before they came of age. They accompanied grown up Muslims in their pursuit of the means of livelihood or joined the warriors in the battlefield.

It will not be out of place to cite the example of a

young boy who said to his father, "Please let me go out and move about in the wide world in order that I may pave the way for a respectable station in life and attain a high status." The boy addressed his parents in the following couplets that are expressive of his pride, self-respect and yearning for honour and greatness:

1. Put saddle and bridle on the mare.
2. Then put a helmet on my head and armour on my body and give me a sword.
3. If I do not explore the avenues of livelihood in my boyhood, when am I going to do it?
4. I will wander in the immensity of the earth in quest of lawful and not unlawful living.
5. It is quite possible that the journey into the wide world will relieve me starvation or bring me on the verge of death.

That was, then, the ideal training imparted to our forbears which inculcated the above virtues in them in their boyhood and the same virtues were successively transmitted from generation to generation.

They were taught in their early years the arts of archery, swimming and riding. Riding also included the game of polo. They were not caressed and spoilt. They were not allowed to grow introvert. They were conscious of their responsibilities and obligations in their childhood.

They were inured to rough life and trained in the various arts of horsemanship and sent on long journeys.

They were taught to mix up and spend their time with their first cousins and other close relatives. They were taught and made to bear in mind the accounts of the daring deeds of warriors and heroes and Muslim conquerors and leaders. In other words our forbears imparted to their children comprehensive training and imbued in them sterling qualities. Says a poet:

The khittineza tree grows in the land where its sapling grows.
The date tree grows in the date garden.

When the present day guardians, tutors and parents

start treading in the footsteps of our valiant and fearless ancestors and inculcate in the children the virtues mentioned, ridding its mind of phobias, cowardice and sluggishness, our new generation will be free of perplexity and gain self-confidence. It will shake off fear, lethargy, timidity and ridden of ignominy and will instead become brave, courageous and resolute and attain the heights of glory. It will then conform to the following verse of the Holy Quran:

"All the might belongeth to Allah and His messenger and the believers; but the hypocrites know not." (63 : 8)

(3) Inferiority Complex.

This psychic state is also found among the children. It is either innate or developed during illness, or acquired as the result of wrong training or of poverty. This is a mental abnormality fraught with serious consequences. It causes a complex in the child's mind and he starts behaving immorally. Finally he sinks into a life of disgrace, misery and crime.

When a remedy for any psychosis is suggested in the life of Islam, it is necessary to investigate the causes thereof. We therefore, expect that the parents and guardians would take all the prescribed preventive measures and strictly adhere to the methods of treatment, and thus rid their children of inferiority and other psychosis so that their training may be completed on the right lines and they may grow up to be men of good character.

The causes of inferiority complex among children are as follows:

1. Their contempt and insult.
2. Excessive checks as well as excessive caressing.
3. Preference of one child to another.
4. Physical deformities.
5. Orphanhood.
6. Poverty and pauperism.

We propose to deal with the causes at length and then proceed to suggest remedy for them.

1. Contempt or scornful treatment

The child develops inferiority complex and immoral propensities as the result of unwarranted indignities they suffer at the hands of parents.

We often hear that whenever children incidentally

commit any mistake, the parents start broadcasting it. If the child is once guilty of telling a lie, they call him a liar. If he gives a slap to his younger, he is dubbed as a mischievous fellow. If he snatches the apple from his younger sister, he is proclaimed to be a cheat. If the child happens to take out the pen from his father's pocket, he is dubbed as a thief for good If he is asked to bring water which he does not for some season or other, he is called lazy. In other words the parents all the time insult the child in the presence of his brothers and sisters for a trivial mistake he commits for the first time.

Many examples may be cited to illustrate how disdainful treatment is meted out to children. These include calling them with insulting and derisive nicknames or use contemptible words to address them in the presence of brothers, sisters relatives and friends or strangers whom they may never have seen before. Such treatment compels the child to think that he is a debased and mean fellow and is as worthless as waste paper. This mode of thing causes complexes in his mind with the result that he too begins to regard people disdainfully. He develops introversive abnormality and seeks escape from the realities of life. He is stricken by defeatism, instead of facing the problems of life and fulfilling his responsibilities.

It may well be judged from what has been said above what a severe punishment we inflict upon the child for his neglegible mistake and how cruelly we treat him. It is because of our injudicious attitude towards the children that they develop personalities inconsistent with the social norms and become a bundle of vices and a symbol of immorality.

After meting out such a wrongful treatment how can we expect that the children would conduct themselves in conformity with the moral norms and respect their parents when they grow up. If the parents sow in their minds the seeds of wickedness, disobedience and rebellion, they cannot expect anything good from them.

Once a man came to Hazrat 'Umar bin Khattab and complaind to him of his son's disobedience. Hazrat 'Umar sent for the boy and rebuked him for disobeying his father in violation of the latter's rights.

The boy asked the Caliph, "O Chief of the believers, does the son have no rights to his father?"

Hazrat 'Umar replied, "Why not?"

"What right does the son have to his father?" enquired the boy.

"He should choose a good mother for his son i.e. should marry a virtuous girl so that his offspring may turn out to be virtuous. He should also choose a good name for the son and teach him the Holy Quran.

The boy said, "My father did nothing of the sort. As for my mother, she is a negro woman. She was formerly a Zoroastrian. He has nicknamed me magian-born. Moreover, he has not taught me a single word of the Holy Quran."

Hazrat 'Umar then turned to the father and said, "You have come to complain of the boy's disobedience. But it is you who have first violated his rights and that is why he has distressed you."

Once a father taunted his son referring to his mother and said, "Do you dare disagree with me — you being the son of a slave girl?"

The father enquired in what respect she was better. The son replied, "Because she married free man, exercising the right to choose a husband wheress you exercised your right wrongly with the result that slave girl gave birth to me."

Doubtless, the parents do not mean to insult their children when they rebuke them. They simply want to set them right and teach them manners. But there can be no denying of the fact either, that disdainful attitude and derogatory way of talking to children in itself proves to be a blunder, as it leads to a sin or offence.

But an offence or mistake should not be rectified by violence or rebuke, for violence, rebukes and threats adversely affect the child's psychology and individual behaviour. Consequently he grows up to be a foul-tongued person and an idiot habitually deviating from the social and moral norms. This is a great wrong done to the child; for by giving him wong training we crush his individualities and do a great harm to his psychology. Some people do such a wrong intentionally, while others do it unwittingly. Whatever the case may be, their treatment produce pernicious effect on children. The parents, therefore, are advised to treat the child well and impart to him the best possible training which would make him grow to be a balanced and intelligent personality, capable of functioning in every field of life in a balanced, judicious and consistent manner.

How is a child to be corrected from the Islamic viewpoint when he commits a fault or behaves insolently? The answer to this question is as follows:

We should warn the child in a soft and compassionate manner and try to convince him by giving cogent reasons that he has been guilty of a fault which he should never commit again and that he has done something of which no serious and sensible person would approve. If this instructive mode of speaking to him makes him realize his mistake fully, it may be presumed that he has been set right as desired and his deviant behaviour has been corrected. But if the child is not susceptible to the instructive mode referred to then he should be subjected to other methods of correction which we will discuss under the head of training by punishment or reform in another Chapter of this book.

The right method of correction and teaching manners is the one which the Holy Prophet (S.A.W.) himself adopted. His method of correction was polite and gentle as may be seen from the following traditions:

(1) Imam Ahmed quotes a tradition with reference to Abu Umama and substantiated by authentic proofs. The tradition runs as follows:

A young boy called on the Holy Prophet (S.A.W.) and said, "O Prophet, would you allow me to commit fornication?"

The companions who were present on the occasion shouted at the boy for such impertinence. The Prophet (S.A.W.) said, "Bring him to me.Come, draw close to me." The boy did accordingly and sat down close to the Prophet (S.A.W.).

"Would you like your mother to commit adultery?" enquired the Prophet (S.A.W.).

The boy replied in the negative. The Prophet (S.A.W.) said, "Well then, other people too would not like their mothers to commit adultery."

The Prophet (S.A.W.) asked again, "Tell me if you would like your daughter to commit adultery."

The boy's answer was in the negative again.

The Prophet, "Other people in the same way would not like their daughters to commit adultery."

The Holy Prophet (S.A.W.) then went on to refer to paternal and maternal aunts to the same effect to receive answers from the boy in the negative.

He then put his hand on the boy's chest and prayed to Allah to purify his heart, forgive him and protect his private part from sin.

When the boy rose to leave, his heart was filled with hatred for adultery.

(2) Imam Muslim quotes the following tradition in his collection Sahih Muslim as narrated by Hazrat Moawia bin Al Hakam Al *Lalmi*. Says he:

"Once when I was offering prayer with the Holy Prophet (S.A.W.) one of us sneezed all of a sudden and I said: May God have mercy on me.

The people present at the moment stared at me. I asked them why they were staring at me like that. They started striking their thighs with their hands. I felt that they wanted me to keep quiet, so I kept quiet.

When the Prophet (S.A.W.) finished saying prayers, he called me. Well, I never saw a better teacher before and after him. He neither rebuked me, nor struck me nor reproached me. What he simply said was : Talking like ordinary people during the prayer is disallowed. Prayer consists of only praise of Allah, profession of His greatness and the recitation of the Holy Quran."

(3) Imam Bukhari cites the following tradition narrated by Abu Huraira (R.A.A.):

"An Arab made water in the mosque. People wanted to beat him. But the Holy Prophet (S.A.W.) asked them to leave him and throw a bucketful of water over the spot saying: You people are meant to make things easy and not to create difficulties."

The Prophet has given the following advice about softness of speech:

(i) According to Hazrat Aisha (R.A.A.) the Holy Prophet

(S.A.W.) said, "Allah conducts Himself softly and likes softness in every affair of His." (*Bukhari–Muslim*)

(ii) Hazrat Aisha (R.A.A.) narrates another tradition wherein she quotes the following words of the Holy Prophet (S.A.W.):
"Softness beautifies the thing in which it is found and mars the thing from which it vanishes." (*Muslim*)

(iii) Hazrat Jareer bin Abdullah reports the Prophet (S.A.W.) to have said, "Whoever is devoid of softness is devoid of goodness."

The whole foregoing discussion may be epitomized in a few words. Insulting the child all the time particularly in presence of other people causes inferiority complex in him. Such a complex takes root deep in his mind. This is the main and pernicious cause of the child's moral degradation and psychological deviation.

In order to rid the child of inferiority complex it is necessary to convince him of his misconduct by giving cogent reasons in such a soft and compassionate manner that he abstains from repeating his mistake. The guardians and tutors should make it a point not to rebuke the child in the presence of other people. They should rather adopt judicious method to correct and reform him right from the very beginning of his deviation. The Prophet (S.A.W.) also approves of the best possible way of reformation training and correction of moral aberration.

2. Rebuking and checking the child frequently or caressing him in reason and out of reason would result in his moral and psychological aberration often causing in him serious inferiority complex. He begins to think that he is no more than a bundle of vices and consequently looks at life with contempt. In other words life becomes miserable for him.

In normal circumstances excessive rebuking and shouting or excessive caressing makes the child shy and depressed. He would be devoid of manliness, courage and self-confidence. He becomes inconsistent, irresolute and always lags behind the boys of his age group.

Some of the signs of inferiority complex resulting from frequent rebuking and shouting are as under:

He sees other people making progress while he himself lags behind.

He sees other people demonstrate courge and boldness but he himself is frightened and exhibits timidity.

He sees other people taking active part in movements and jehad while he himself remains passive and inert.

He sees other people meeting with each other and attending social functions while he himself is in solitude engrossed in his own self.

He sees other people smile in difficulties while he himself complains and sheds tears in the face of difficulties.

It is evident that a child in such a state of mind and behaviour can never be a normal person and useful member of the society. He can never look at life with optimism and can never grow up to be a self-consistent and self-confident personality.

It so being the case, why do we rebuke children without any shyness or reason and mete out cruel treatment to them? Who is to be blamed most in this respect? It is the mother who meticulously looks after her child and takes too much precaution to protect him whenever there is smallest harm to be feared. This impedes the development of self-confidence in the child. Mothers who always carry their children in their laps and thus give them a sense of security from themselves, bring up the children on the wrong lines. Such mothers are mostly ignorant of Islamic way of training. These mothers commit the following mistakes:

1. The mother knows that the child can do such and such work, but out of compassion and love for him she would not allow him to do it.
2. Whenever the mother is free, she lifts up the child and keeps him in her lap. She does not leave him alone. She always him in her bosom whether or not there is any reason for it.
3. The mother does not allow the child to be out of her sight for a single moment lest the child should come to any harm.
4. She does not try to stop the child when he happens to break or damage household articles. If he drags the table or spoils the walls of the house, she takes

nò notice of it.

The parents will be particularly found checking the child or exhorting him frequently when they are blessed with an offspring after a long time after marriage or after many a miscarriage or when the son is born after the birth of many daughters or gets a new life after a protracted illness.

Islam has suggested the following remedy for this wrong attitude of the parents.

(a) If the parents have strong faith in the efficiency of Allah's Will, their mode of training the children would automatically accord with the demands of such faith. Parents whose belief in the divine will is weak should be induced to have a strong faith in the all-pervasiveness of the divine will. They should believe that the children's sickness and health is in Allah's power and whatever pleasure or pain is experienced owes itself to His Will only. It is Allah Who gives them offspring and deprives them of any offspring. Richness and poverty too must be attributed to His choice only. Everything takes place as the result of His Will.

In order to have a strong faith in the necessitarian principle of predestination or the all pervasive divine will, the parents should ponder over the following verses of the Holy Quran :

(1) "Naught of disaster befalleth in the earth or in yourselves but it is in a Book before We bring it into being — Lo! that is easy for Allah. That ye grieve not for the sake of that which has escaped you, nor yet exult because of that which has been given. Allah loveth not all prideful boasters. (57: 22-23)

(2) Unto Allah belongeth the sovereignty of the heavens and the earth. He createth what He will. He bestoweth female offspring upon whom He will, and bestoweth male offspring upon whom He will. (42:49)

(3) We will, of course, put you to test by a certain degree of fear by some poverty and by the loss of some wealth, lives and fruits. And O Muhammad! to those who are patient and who say whenever some evil befalleth them, that we all belong to Allah and are to return to Him, give this tiding that blessings will be showered upon them from Allah. And it is they who are truly

guided. (2: 155-157)

(b) If the child is found to be susceptible to exhortation and instruction, the guardian is advised not to abandon him to do as he chooses and if he is being reformed as the result of leaving him free, then corporal punishment is not advisable. In case if the guardian fails in his efforts to reform the child and if all the methods of correction such as subjection to to discipline, reproach, rebuke and admonition have been tried in vain, the guardian may inflict corporal punishment on him provded that he does not cause to grievous injury thereby. Detailed discussion to this effect is to follow under head "Punish to Reform", in a Chapter of this book entitled "Effective Methods of Training the Child."

(c) The child should be trained to hard-working and hold and develop self-confidence and accept responsibilities. Such training should commence in his early years so that he may have a strong sense of his self. It will enable him to be conscious of his duties and obligations in the true sense of the terms.

The need to inure the child to hard-working is proved by the following tradition of the Holy Prophet (S.A.W.). It is narrated by Hazrat Mu'az bin Jabal.

Says the Prophet (S.A.W.):

"Avoid to seek comforts. Allah's bondsmen are not comfort-seekers."

The following tradition aims at inculcating self-confidence and the habit of bearing responsibilities as is evident from its general sense.

"Everyone of you is a shepherd and will be held responsible for his charge."

This tradition applies to all the members of the society including men, women, youngsters small children, the ruler and the ruled.

It will not be out of place to mention the advice of Hazrat 'Umar (R.A.A.) as cited by Imam Baihaqi in his *Musnad*.

Says Hazrat Umar:

"Teach your children swimming and archery and mounting the horse by jumping."

It the child is taught archery, swimming and riding at an

early age, he will have self-confidence and a sense of his ego and will also be capable of bearing hardships and making commitments.

There is a tradition narrated by Hazrat 'Ubada bin Samit wherein we find a hint at the need for the moral training of children. It runs as follows:

> "We made a pledge to the Holy Prophet (S.A.W.) that we would obey him in all circumstances good or bad, in adversity and comfort; that we would always speak the truth wherever we may be and that we will never be afraid of censure from any one in vindicating the ways of Allah."

This commitment was not confined to any specific group but was binding upon all the Muslim major and minor, men and women.

We have explained the teachings of Islam in the previous pages in the context of the physical training of the children and relevent training of children under the head of 'Responsibility for Physical Training'. All these teaching aim at inculcating in children self-confidence and the capacity to bear responsibilities and safeguard their trust as well as to make every child realize that he is a man with a distinct individuality and a distinct place in the society.

(d) It is essential for us to follow all the acts of the Holy Prophet (S.A.W.) which he did from his childhood up to puberty as well as during the period of Prophethood; for Allah taught him the best manners and imbibed in him moral excellence, kept him under His observation, and built his character as a special case.

We cite here some incidents of the Prophet's life that will serve as a beacon light to the guardians. These incidents are best examples of placing faith in Allah and the Prophet (S.A.W.), which the new generation should follow as a model.

(i) The Prophet (S.A.W.) used to graze goats in his childhood. Once he said to his companions, "Allah sent no Messenger who did not graze goats. I too did graze the goats of Meccans for a few qirats (a legal tender current in Prophet's days)."

(ii) The Prophet (S.A.W.) used to play with other boys in

his childhood. Ibn Kaseer narrates this tradition. The Prophet (S.A.W.). said,

"I have been myself playing with the boys of the Quraish also. We used to carry stone from one place to another. This was a sort of game during which the boys stripped themselves and were stark naked. They put off their *tahmads* (loin cloth used instead of pyjama to cover the lower part of man's body) placed it on their neck and the stone to be carried was put on this cloth. I was also moving from one place to another like this along with my play-fellows when some one gave me a thump with a force that I felt pain. I did not see the man who struck me but heard him say: "put on your tahmad." The Prophet (S.A.W.) says that he did accordingly and carried the stone on his neck. He was the only boy at the moment who had his tahmad on," added the Prophet (S.A.W.).

(iii) The Prophet (S.A.W.) also participated in the construction work. Imam Bukhari and Imam Muslim narrate that when the new building of Ka'ba was being constructed, the Holy Prophet (S.A.W.) joined hands with the elite of the Quraish in carrying the stones. Hazrat Abbas asked him to put off his tahmad and put it on his shoulder after folding it. The Prophet (S.A.W.) did accordingly but fell down on the ground with his eyes fixed on the sky. After a few moments he got up again and said, "Where is my *tahmad*, where is my *tahmad*?" When he got hold of it he immediately bound it round his body and said, "I have been forbidden to move about naked."

This incident bears testimony to his being innocent before prophethood was hestowed upon him.

(iv) The Prophet (S.A.W.) also went on business tours. We learn from history that he made two such tours. In his first tour he accompanied his uncle Hazrat Abu Talib when he was still a boy. He undertook the second journey at the behest of Hazrat Khadija when he had grown up.

(v) The Prophet (S.A.W.) was extremely bold. It is written in his biographies that in his boyhood he was once asked to swear by *Lat and 'Uzza* (the false gods worshipped by the Arab idolators). He retorted, "Don't ask me to swear by them. By God, I hate nothing more than them."

(vi) The Prophet (S.A.W.) participated in a battle before he came of age. In a biography he has been referred to have been picking the arrows and bringing them to his uncles.

(vii) The Prophet (S.A.W.) was very wise and held firm opinions after careful deliberations. When he grew up, he was assigned the job of deciding a dispute. The Quraish empowered him to decide the dispute relating to the installation of the Black Stone in Ka'ba. His wise decision in the matter pleased all the tribes of the Quraish.

The Prophet (S.A.W.) was an orphan, he was praiseworthy for his sterling qualities and moral excellence. He never lay prostrate before any idol, nor did he ever support pagan ignorance, nor partook of the flesh of any animal slaughtered in the name of a being other than Allah.

Allah Himself imparted him training and taught him manners under His own care. The Prophet (S.A.W.) himself is reported to have said, "My Lord taught me decorum and good manners." *(Narrated by Askari)*

These were a few glimpses of the Holy Prophet's boyhood that bear testimony to his innocence and moral excellence in his young days. The Prophet's boyhood as well as youth provides us a model to be emulated in the training of our children. His life in youth no less than in old age is the ideal for us to approximate to. He is the chief and leader of all those prophets whose teachings the whole of mankind has been commanded to translate into action.

To sum up, unwarranted checks are one of the major causes of deviation in children which results in life-long inferiority complex.

Hence it is necessary that the parents should train their children on the lines chalked out by Islam. According to the Islamic tenets of training, temperance should be observed in loving the children and they should be taught to resign to the Will of Allah when confronted by difficulties and dangers. If the child has reached the years of discretion, he may be punished for the purpose of correction. Besides, the child should be trained in a manner that he develops self-confidence and belief in himself to be capable of bearing responsibilities. Moreover, the training imparted to him should inculcate in him straightforwardness. The last and most important principle is that the children should be brought up according to the Prophet's life preceding the formal commencement of his mission as the Prophet.

As soon as the tutors embark on training the new generation in accordance with the principles mentioned above, they will remove it from aught that undermines human personality and nobility. They will raise the new generation to such a high plane of psychological, moral and intellectual capabilities that every child will be able to live like an honest and upright person.

3. Another factor that leads to inferiority complex is the preference of one child to another. If the parents do not treat all the children equally they develop inferiority complex. The parents are advised to give all the children similar things, treat them equally and love them without discrimination.

Discrimination against any child causes in him moral and psychological deviation, for discriminate treatment results in hatred, fear, shyness, abnormal introversion and the habit of crying. This would ultimately make the children insolent rebellious, quarrelsome and disobedient. As a the result of such treatment, children are frightened at night and develop nervous abnormalities as well as multi-inferiority complexes.

How wise and great guide, philosopher and teacher was the Holy Prophet (S.A.W.) who taught us to be God-fearing in dealing with children and act on the principle of justice and equity in treating them.

Ibn Hibban quotes the following saying of the Prophet (S.A.W.):

> "May Allah have mercy on the father who helped his son in doing good."

The words of the tradition quoted by Mo'jam Al-Tabarani:

> "In giving any thing to your children, equality must be maintained."

There is a tradition relating to Hazrat Noman bin Basheer which has been cited in both *Sahih Muslim and Sahih Bukhari.* Hazrat Noman narrates that his father took him to the Prophet (S.A.W.) and said, "I have given him (Noman) a slave."

"Have you given such a gift to all your sons?" enquired the Prophet (S.A.W.).

Hazrat Noman's father replied in the nagative.

The Prophet (S.A.W.) said, "Then, take back the slave from him."

According to another narrator of the same tradition the Prophet (S.A.W.) asked, "Have you treated your other sons similarly?"

Hazrat Noman's father replied in the negative.

The Prophet (S.A.W.) said, "You should fear Allah when dealing with your children."

Noman bin Bashir (R.A.A.) says that his father took back the slave from him.

There is yet another version of the same tradition:

The Prophet (S.A.W.) enquired, "O Basheer, have you any son other than this one?"

Basheer said, "Yes I do have."

"Have you given similar gifts to them as well?"

The answer to this question was in the negative.

The Prophet (S.A.W.) said, "Then do not call me to bear witness as I do not bear witness for the justification of transgression."

The Prophet (S.A.W.) then enquired, "Will you not be pleased when all your sons mete out equal treatment to you?"

Basheer said, "Why Not?"

The Prophet (S.A.W.) observed, "Well, then, it is not right that you bestow a slave on one son, while depriving others."

Hazrat Anas narrates that a man was sitting with the Holy Prophet (S.A.W.) when his son came to him. He kissed the boy and seated him on his thigh. A few moments later his daughter also came to him. He seated her in front. The Prophet (S.A.W.) asked "Why did you not treat them alike?"

The above traditions of the Holy Prophet (S.A.W.) bear testimony to the need for treating the children equally. They also prove that it is wrong to mete out discriminate treatment to children.

Of course there are some apparent reasons for the disaffection of parents for certain children who are therefore not properly taken care of. The following reasons, for instance, may be given:

1. Because of ignorance the parents do not have as much affection and love for the daughter as they have for the son.
2. The child is not handsome or is not intelligent.
3. Some physical deformity in the child.

But these physical and natural defects do not warrant discrimination against any child.

The parents who treat their children inequitably and thus maltreat them are very cruel indeed.

If a child is female, ugly or not intelligent, it is no fault of his or hers. If a child is naturally fidgety and takes pleasure in making a noise, he is not guilty of any excess. If he develops any physical deformity or has an innate physical defect he is not to blame at all.

If the parents and guardians want to rid their children of or keep them immune from psychological abnormalities and inferiority complex and subjective maladies like jealousy, evil temper, bad faith, there is only one method by which they could do so and that is to act on the following edict of the Holy Prophet (S.A.W.):

"Fear God and mete out just treatment to all your children."

Moreover, the guardians and parents should also be contented with the lot ordained by Allah. It is in His Power alone to bestow sons and daughters. They are under the obligations to imbibe in the children the passions of affection, fraternity, equality and the desire to forgive, so that they may grow up with a sense of social justice, balanced attitude and compassion.

The wisdom of Prophet's saying is unquestionable:

"May God have mercy on the father who cooperates with his son in doing good."

Physical deformities are also a main cause of psychological deviation; for physical handicaps beget inferiority complex and the child develops disdainful outlook on life.

If the child develops any physical deformity in an early age such as loss of vision in one eye, deafness, insanity, senseless volubility or dumbness, the parents, brothers, sisters, other close relatives, members of the family and members of the society at large should treat him compassionately and conduct themselves in such a polite manner that the child is delighted. They should act on the Prophet's tradition which has been narrated by *Tirmizi* and *Abu Dawood.*

"Allah has mercy on those who have mercy on their fellow beings. Have mercy on the people of the earth. the Lord of the heavens will have mercy on you."

Imam Bokhari and *Imam Muslim* cite the following tradition:

> "None of you can be a true believer unless he chooses for his brother what he chooses for himself."

Imam Tirmizi in his *Sunan* and Ibn Hibban in his *Musnad* have cited the following tradition:

> "The person with perfect faith among the believers is he who is morally the best."

If a child with one eye is called one-eyed or a child hard of hearing is called deaf, or one bereft of speech is called dumb or one mentally handicapped is called mad, he will naturally develop inferiority complex and numerous other psychological complications. This would turn him into a pathetic figure moving about with a sense of defeatism and pessimistic outlook on life resulting from the ill-will he hears against the society.

The parents and guardians are, therefore, under the obligation to treat all ailments and physical handicaps of their children judiciously, deal with them compassionately and look after them properly; for according to religion the criterion of a man s value is his morality and not his outward appearance.

The first practical step to be taken in this respect is that parents should treat their handicapped children kindly and affectionately and pay them special attention. They should try to inculcate in such children the feeling that they are as good as others in respect of understanding, intelligence, knowledge and vitality. Such a treatment would mitigate their inferiority complex. In fact it would induce them to play active role in constructive activities with a full sense of confidence.

Secondly, the parents should take it upon themselves to urge upon all their relatives, whether close or remote, to refrain from scorning and insulting any one because of his or her physical deformity and acquaint them with consequences of derisive and insulting treatment of handicapped children; for such attitude produces harmful effects on their mind.

The parents and guardians should also tell their relatives and friends that they should adopt an attitude towards a handicapped person that is based on sincerity, good faith and pure love and respect for others.

The following traditions of the Holy Prophet (S.A.W.) make it clear and enjoin upon the Muslims to abstain from any act that may undermine a believer's personality or result in the disintegration of Islamic society.

The Holy Prophet (S.A.W.) warns against the potential dangers of the tongue in these words:

"A man says something to which he does not attach any importance but which leads him to Hell." (*Bukhari*)

The words of another tradition are as follows:

"A man says something without knowing its full meaning and falls into the abyss of fire as deep as the immense chasm yawning between the east and the west.

The Holy Prophet (S.A.W.) has forbidden to express pleasure on the condition of a Muslim in a manner which implies his insult. *Tirmizi* cites the following tradition:

"Do not be delighted over the distress of your brother-in-faith. Otherwise Allah will have mercy on him and cause distress to you instead."

The Prophet (S.A.W.) forbids even a gesture of contempt.

Hazrat Aisha (R.A.A.) narrates that once she said to the Prophet (S.A.W.), "A woman like Safia suits you (she pointed to the short stature of Hazrat Safia). The Prophet (S.A.W.) replied: 'Aisha, you have said such a bad thing that if it is mixed in water of oceans, it will change their taste."

(*Abu Dawood, Tirmizi*)

The teachings mentioned above are summed up in the following divine decree:

"O believers, no community should deride another community, for it is just possible that the latter is better than the former nor the women should ridicule other women, for it is just possible that these women are better than the former. You should not call each other with disdainful nicknames or bad names. Bad is the name of lewdness after the profession of faith. Those who do not-repent, accordingly, are guilty of transgression." (49:11)

Another precaution to be taken in dealing with the problem of the handicapped children is that they should be provided with good company. The companions chosen for them should be of good moral conduct and commendable habits. They should play with good friends who talk to them with affection and compassion and no hot words are exchanged between them and their friends so that the children suffering deformities may feel that other people love and give them importance and that they are not lacking in any thing.

Avicinna has this to say with regard to the building of children's character and inculcating in them the love of social life:

"The habits and manners of children s classfellows in the school should be commendable; for a child is susceptible to other children's influence and quickly becomes familiar with them and learns many things from them."

The Holy Prophet (S.A.W.) has said:

"A child's keenness, abstinence and cleverness is the evidence of his prospects of growing up as an intelligent person."

To sum up, guardians should leave no stone unturned in curing the deformity and alleviating the suffering of a handicapped child. For instance, he should look at the child compassionately, pay him special attention and keep him away from an environment fraught with contempt, indignity and derision. Besides, he should provide the child the company of good friends. The child would thus be ridded of psychological complications and will become a useful member of the society, capable of contributing his bit towards the promotion of culture and civilization, raising the edifice of Ummah's glory and brighten the future of his motherland.

4. **Orphanhood.**

Orphanhood may also prove to be a serious cause of the

child's moral aberration, specially when he is brought up in an environment wherein there is nobody to take care of him, alleviate his sufferings and to treat him with affection and compassion.

Islam lays special stress on the proper rearing, education training and kind treatment of the orphans, enabling them to become useful members of the society and discharge their duties and obligations in the best possible manner.

The Holy Quran enjoins upon us not to rebuke the orphan and say to him anything derogatory. Says Allah:

As for the orphan, do not oppress him and as for him who asks do not chide him." (93: 9-10)

"Hast thou observed him who belieth religion? That is he repelleth the orphan." (107: 1-2)

The Holy Prophet (S.A.W.) specifically commands to provide for the orphan and take care of him and gives the tiding that whoever treats the orphan kindly will be with the Prophet (S.A.W.) in paradise.

Imam *Tirmizi* quotes the Prophet (S.A.W.) to have said:

"I and the man who provides for the orphan will be together in Paradise." He then raised his forefinger and midfinger to indicate what he meant.

Imam *Ahmed* and Ibn Hibban quote the following tradition of the Prophet (S.A.W.) in their respective Musnads.

"Whoever places his hand on the head of an orphan by way of love and compassion, Allah records one good act to his credit for each of the hair that comes under his hand."

The following tradition has been reproduced in the Sunan *Nasai*.

"I intervene in the matter of two weaker members of the society, that is the orphan and the woman."

(What the Prophet means is that he whoever usurps the rights of the two weaker persons would be regarded by him as sinner and that he would intervene to restore their rights.)

The care of orphan is an obligation on his legal guardians and close relatives. It is their duty to correct the orphans' psychological and moral deviation. Because of close relationship they are bound to treat orphans compassionately.

They should make the orphans feel that they enjoy the same rights as the children of their relatives.

In case if there is no legal guardian or close relation to look after the orphans, then it is the responsibility of the government to care for them and ensure for them an honourable place in the society.

The Holy Prophet (S.A.W.) took special care of the orphans as the head of the first Muslim government established in Madina. He treated them with affection and compassion. Hazrat Aisha (R.A.A.) tells us that on an Eid day the Prophet (S.A.W.) saw an orphan whom he caressed and as a gesture of love and affection, brought him home and said to him, "Will you not be glad if I become your father and Aisha becomes your mother?"

An evidence exists with broken chain to the effect that if a child thrown away by its mother is found alive, it is the responsibility of the Islamic government to provide for and take care of it.

Once a man brought such a child to Hazrat 'Umar (R.A.A.), whereupon he said, "It is our responsibility to bear its expenses and the child is free."

If the orphans and foundlings are brought up in accordance with tenets of Islam they will grow up to be law abiding and peaceful citizens, duly bear. their responsibilities and they will develop no inferiority complex, nor will they harbour any miguiding ideas or suffer from dangerous phobias.

5. Poverty

Another main cause of children's deviation is indigence. If the child in his discretionary years finds his parents hard up and all the members of the family in a state of destitution, the possibilities of his deviation are greater than otherwise. When he sees his relatives, neighbours children, and classfellows better off, such possibilities increase manifold. He would develop inferiority complex and grow morose with a heart greif-stricken, for he neither has meal to his heart's content nor decent dress which he is to wear.

It is no wonder if such a wretch developes psychological maladies. The attitude of a psychologically abnormal child towards the society like this would be one of abhorrence and animosity. He will in fact be victim of serious psychological complications. All his desires would be thwarted and their frustration would result in despondency. His concept of good luck would be replaced by pessimism. [1]

The Prophet (S.A.W.) expresses undeniable truth when he says," It appears that destitution would turn into infidelity."[2] *(Musnad Imam Ahmed and Sunan Baihaqi)*

In fact the Prophet (S.A.W.) used to pray to Allah to protect him against both destitution and infidelity. He prayed in the following words.

"O Lord! I seek thy protection against destitution and infidelity."

Islam prescribes two basic remedies for poverty and distitution:

(1) Respect for man and

(2) The principles of social security.

(1) Respect for man:

Islam enjoins respect for man or the acknowledgement of human dignity by allowing equal status to every human-being irrespective of colour and race. The only critierion of superiority according to Islam is righteousness, good conduct and benevolence. It gives the eternal concept of the scale of preference among human beings in the following words of the Holy Quran:

"O mankind, We have created you by male and female and divided you among small communities and tribes so that you may know one another. Verily noblest in the sight of Allah is one who is more righteous than others." (49:13)

Islam pays little heed to bodies and faces. It fixes its gaze on motives and actions.

The Holy Prophet (S.A.W.) is quoted to have said in *Sahih Muslim* with reference to Abu Huraira (R.A.A.), "Allah does not look at your faces and physique. His attention is

1. Pessimism is a symptom of infidelity. As has been said in the Holy Quran: Do not despair. The infidels lose hope of Allah's blessings. (12: 87).
2. Destitution leads man to infidelity or renunciation of Faith in Allah.

rather focussed on your hearts and actions."

Islam gives a high status to the infirm and the poor and declares that insulting and giving them offence displeases Allah.

According to *Imam Muslim* Abu Sufian came to see Hazrat Salman, Sohaib and Bilal. Some other people were also present on the occasion. All the three of them said to Abu Sufian, "You did not take the swords of Allah from His enemies in the right manner." Hazrat Abu Bakr (R.A.A.) said, "Are you saying this to the chief of the Quraish tribe?"

Abu Bakr (R.A.) then went to the Prophet (S.A.W.) and informed him what happened. The Prophet (S.A.W.) observed, "You have probably offended them and if you have offended them, then take it for granted that you have displeased Allah."

Hazrat Abu Bakr returned to the three companions of the Prophet (S.A.W.) and enquired, "Brothers, have I offended you?"

They replied, "No brother, not at all. May Allah forgive you."

(2) Social Security

The principles of social security as laid down by Islam are far better than those worked out by human ingenuity. The guidance provided by Islam to weed out destitution and indigence from the society is as follows:

(a) It enforces a law to pay Zakat from the government treasury to the deserving individuals. Such individuals are specified as under:

(1) Destitutes.
(2) People without any support or means.
(3) Travellers.
(4) Borrowers for the repayment of their loans
(5) For the release of captives and slaves.

The following verse of the Holy Quran may be cited in this context:

"The alms are only for the poor and the needy, and those who collect them, and those whose hearts are to be reconciled and to free the captives and the debtors, and for the cause of Allah and for the wayfarers; a duty imposed by Allah. Allah is Knower and Wiser." (9:60)

In *Mo'jam-al-Tabarani* the following tradition of the Prophet (S.A.W.) has been reproduced:

"Allah has imposed the duty upon the affluent Muslims to give so much alms out of their wealth which may suffice the needs of the destitutes. When the destitutes have no food and clothing, they will not be able to work. The wealthy only can enable them to work. Look, Allah will call the wealthy to account and inflict severe punishment on them."

(b) Allah does not treat that believer, a Muslim, at all who
goes to sleep having his dinner to his heart's content while he is aware that his neighbour has gone to sleep without having any meal.

Bazzaz and Tabarani both quote the following tradition of the Prophet (S.A.W.).

"A man who has a sound sleep at night after having a meal to his heart's content while knowing that his next door neighbour remains hungry has not accepted my faith."

In fact the Prophet (S.A.W.) describes expression of sympathy with and propitiation and consolation of one's neighbour is one of the best acts that ensures one's drawing closer to Allah.

Tabarani quotes in his Al Mo'jam the following tradition narrated by Hazrat 'Umar and transmitted with broken chain:

"The best act is the propitiation of Muslim, that is, clothe him, gratify his hunger and meet his need."

Alleviation of poor people s sufferings, providing them assistance and seeking their pleasure is one of the most important duties as is evident from a tradition narrated by Abdur Rahman bin Abu Bakr.

"*Ashab Suffa* were poor people. The Prophet (S.A.W.) said whoever has two persons meal, he should take a third person from among *As-hab Suffa*, to partake of it; whoever has three persons meal should take a fourth person and whoever has four persons meal he should take a fifth person and whoever has five person's meal should take a sixth person to prtake of it.

Imam Muslim quotes this tradition as narrated by Hazrat Abu Saeed Khudri.

The Prophet (S.A.W.) said, "Whoever has it surplus means of conveyance should give it to him who has none. Whoever has surplus provisions during a journey should give them to one who has none." The Prophet (S.A.W.) went on to mention quite a number of things, consequently we saw with our own eyes that there was not a single person among us who had superiority over others in any thing (i.e. who had any thing surplus).

(c) The Prophet (S.A.W.) has made the man in authority duty bound to employ any one who is able bodied and capable of work. *Abu Dawood and Nasai* report that a local man of Madina came to the Prophet (S.A.W.) asking for alms. The Prophet (S.A.W.) said, "Havn't you got any thing in your house?

The man replied "Oh yes, I do have a mat of which one half we use to lay on the ground to lie on and the other half to cover ourselves with it. We also have a bowl with which we drink water."

The Prophet (S.A.W.) asked him to fetch both the things to him and the man did accordingly.

The Prophet (S.A.W.) took those things and asked the people present who of them would buy the two things. One of them offered one dirham for both. The Prophet said, is there any one who is willing to pay for them more than one dirham? Another man responded offering two dirhams. The Holy Prophet (S.A.W.) handed over both the things to this man in lieu of two dirhams. Then giving the two dirhams to the owner of the mat and the bowl he told him to buy food for one dirham to feed his family and buy an axe for the second dirham and bring it to the Prophet (S.A.W.). The man complied with the Prophet's instruction. The Prophet (S.A.W.) took the axe from him and fixed a handle to it with his own hand and said to him, "Go and cut wood with it and earn your livelihood by selling it. Look! I don t want to see your face for fifteen days." The man from Madina obeyed the Prophet's command. When he came back after a fortnight he had ten dirham with him. He had bought edibles for some of the dirhams."

The Prophet (S.A.W.) said to him, "This is much better for you than to appear with a black stain on your face on the Day of Judgment."

(3) Family Allowance:

According to Islam the community is under the obligation to bear the expenses of every child born in any family, regardless of whether it is the offspring of the master or the servant, the labourer or the commoner.

Abu 'Ubaid writes in his book *Kitabul Amwal* that Hazrat 'Umar bin Khattab (R.A.A) paid government allowance to the father as well as the son. As the child grew, his allowance correspondingly increased. This practice was continued by Hazrat 'Usman and Hazrat Ali (R.A.A.).

This family allowance was in addition to the spiritual training received by each individual under the Islamic system with result that the spirit of mutual co-operation, help and sacrifice persisted between the individuals of the Islamic society. They cooperated with one another and made sacrifices for their brethren, voluntarily in response to the demands of faith.

Examples may be drawn from history to substantiate what has been stated above. Following are a few instances of mutual co-operation of the members of Islamic society and their sympathy and compassion for each other.

(i) Some people of Madina were having adequate supplies to meet their needs. But they did not know where those supplies came from and who meets their needs. On the demise of Hazrat Zainul 'Aabideen bin Hussain those supplies stopped. It was then those people came to know that Hazrat Zainul Aabidin used to bring and leave the necessities of life at their doors in the dead of night. The evidence of this was the marks found on the back and shoulders of his body after his death. Those marks were imprinted by the bags of provisions he carried for the widows and the needy.

(ii) The annual income of Hazrat Lais bin Sa'd was more than seventy thousand dinars and he distributed the whole of it among the needy people. They used to say that Lais was no longer under the obligation to pay Zakat. Once he bought a house in auction. When his attorney went to take possession of the house he found that it was occupied by orphans and small children. They entreated the attorney to leave that house for them. When Hazrat Lais bin Sa'd received a word of this he sent a message to the children that not only did the house belong to them but that they would also get daily allowance to meet their expenses.

(iii) The great scholar of Hadis, Imam Abdullah bin Mubarak distributed a lot of alms among the needy, whose amount exceeded one lac dinar annually. Once he left on pilgrimage accompanied by his companions. As he was passing by a village, he found a dead bird there. The Imam was advised to throw the dead bird into a sink. His companions were going ahead, but Hazrat Abdullah slowed down his pace and lagged behind them. When he reached the sink, a girl appeared from a house close by and got hold of the dead bird. She told Abdullah bin Mubarak that she and her brothers were destitutes and nobody knew of their indigence. On hearing the account of her plight Hazrat Abdullah ordered all the effects to be given to her. He then asked his attorney how much cash he had with him. The attorney informed him that he had one lac dinars. Hazrat Abdullah asked him to put aside twenty dinars which would sufficice them till they reach the town of Marv and give away the rest to the girl, for that was some thing preferably to the performance of Haj that year. Abdullah bin Mubarak then went back without performing Haj.

As soon as the government assisted by every member of the society starts a campaign against poverty, the society will be purged of destitutes, grow prosperous and enjoy the blessings of peace and security. Each member of the society will be immune from delinquency and psychological deviation. All of us will then see the banner of Islam held aloft in the world and Allah will allow us the occasion to rejoice.

Hitherto we have been discussing the causes and effects of inferiority complex and its cure. Let us now proceed to consider jealousy.

6. Jealousy

Jealousy means to desire that other people's are deprived of the good things of life enjoyed by them. In other words, it amounts to wishing their ruin and downfall. This is social malady fraught with serious consequences. If the guardians detect such a tendency in the child, they ought to do whatever they can to rid the child of it before it assumes serious proportions.

At the initial stage such an ill-will against the members of the society remains concealed as it is not clearly manifest. Consequently the parents and guardians believe that their sons and daughters cannot be jealous. They do not know what jealousy means and, therefore, they cannot think of the presence of such tendency tending in their children.

Hence whoever is responsible for the upbringing of children is under the obligation to take judicious measures to nip this morbid tendency in the bud and train the children on the right lines so that trouble of psychological complications may be forestalled.

What is the remedy for this morbid passion? Before dealing with this question I wish to touch on the factors which fan the fire of jealousy among children. To my mind the factors leading to the development of jealousy are as under:

(a) The child feels that he is not receiving the affectionate treatment which he ought to have been. Nobody holds him dear to his heart. When a new child is born he thinks that his right to affection is bestowed upon it.

(b) Sometimes the parents speak of one child as clever and of another as dull in the presence of children.

(c) Sometimes the parents attach more importance to one child and focus greater attention on him. For instance, they take him in their laps again and again, play with him with good things and nice toys, while depriving other children of their affection. They rebuke the latter instead, and pay them little heed.

(d) They would ignore the mistake of the child that appears lovely to them while shout at another child for the most trivial mistake he may commit as if they were already expecting it of him

(e) The child who witnesses opulence around him in contrast to the life of indigence led by his family at home, he will nourish the feeling of jealousy and malice against the society.

The factors enumerated above are the unmistakable causes of impairing the formation of the child's personality and consequently the children in most cases develop serious inferiority complex or morbid egoism or virulent malice and resentment against the social setup besides other abnorma-lities like discontent, rebellion and lack of self-confidence.

Islam suggests most effective remedy for jealousy. If the guardians resort to the measures suggested by Islam its causes will be removed and jealousy will give in to mutual love, spirit of sacrifice, sympathy and sincerity and candour among the children.

The Treatment of Jealousy

1. Inculcation of the sense of love in the child. This means to make the child realize that he is being loved. This was the Prophet's practice and he used to urge upon his com-panions also to treat the children with compassion and affection.

This is borne out by the following traditions of the Holy Prophet (S.A.W.).

Abdullah bin Buredah quotes his father to have said that as Hazrat Buredah saw the Prophet (S.A.W.) delivering a sermon one day the grand-sons of the Prophet, Hasan and Hussein (R.A.A') arrived. Both of them were wearing red shirts and were stmbling as they walked. When the Prophet (S.A.W.) saw them, he got down the pulpit and seated them in front of him. He then observed, "Allah has truly said that wealth and offspring are seditions. Look! as I was talking to you, I caught sight of these boys coming to me stumbling. I could not forbear the sight of them and stopped my dis-course to raise them up.'

The Prophet (S.A.W.) also used to play with both his grandsons. He got them mounted upon himself and moved with hands and knees. As he moved thus he used to say to them, "The best mount is your mount and you two are the best riders."

Imam Bukhari in his *Adab-ul-Mufrad* quotes with reference to Hazrat Aisha (R.A.A.) that an Arab came to the Holy Prophet (S.A.W.) and said, "Do you kiss your children? We don't kiss ours." The Prophet (S.A.W.) replied:

If Allah has bereft your heart of love and compassion, what can I do.?

In the same book Imam Bukhari quotes a tradition as

narrated by Hazrat Aisha (R.A.A.). It runs as follows:

A woman came to Hazrat Aisha (R.A.A.) who gave her three dates. The woman gave two of the dates to her two children keeping one for herself. The children having eaten both the dates looked expectant at their mother. The woman divided the remaining date into two halves and gave away each of them to the children. When the Holy Prophet (S.A.W.) returned home Hazrat Aisha (R.A.A.) related the incident to him. The Prophet (S.A.W.) said, "Well, this is not something surprizing. Allah has had great mercy on this woman for being so compassionate towards her children."

It must be borne in mind that in order to forestall the development of jealousy in a child, with the birth of the new child the care and affection for the elder one should not lessen in the least in addition to other measures to be taken for this purpose. At the same time the younger should not be under the impression that he is being ignored. If the parents do not take these aspects of the matter into consideration then elder child would feel that the younger one is a hindrance to the love and affection he deserves. Consequently he would begin to be jealous of the younger child and this morbid tendency takes root in his heart deeper and deeper with the passage of time. The mother is specially responsible for the prevention of such tendency.

The training of the elder child must begin much earlier than the birth of the new one. For instance, he should be given a separate bed, or sent to the nursery school etc.

Besides, if there is no harm if the elder child is allowed the opportunity to help in washing, feeding and clothing the younger child. The elder one shoud also be provided the opportunity to play with the younger one. But care should be taken that he does not trouble the younger child. When the mother takes the younger child into her bosom to suckle, the father should play with the elder one, talk to him and make him feel that the parents take care of him with unabated affection and compassion.

The main purpose of these precautions is to make the elder child realize that he is being loved by the parents, he is the object of their desires and he shares with the other children all compassion and affection of the parents.

The Holy Prophet (S.A.W.), the first patron of mankind has drawn the attention of Muslims to this importnat matter. It is incumbent upon all the parents and guardians to breed their children in accordance with the principles laid down by him so that the children may develop self-consistent and integrated personalities, with love and affection and the spirit of sacrifice for each other. Such training would exclude the possibility of the nourishment of jealousy and malice in their hearts.

2. Equal Treatment with Children.

It goes without saying that if the parents mete out just and equitable treatment to their children, they will never be jealous of each other and the hearts will be free of malice and animosity. Such a treatment woud rather foster harmony, understanding and love between them and the whole atmosphere of home will be imbued with sincerity and affection.

It is for this reason that the Prophet (S.A.W.) has urged upon the parents to treat all their sons alike with justice and equity. He did not like those who discriminated between their children.

3. Anger

This is a passive state of mind. It is a feeling experienced by the child at the initial stage and it persists throughout his life.

If a man is irritable right from his birth, he should not be treated to have acquired a vice; nor should this habit be regarded as undesirable emotionality. Allah has created men with a variety of dispositions and different degrees of feelings. This is divine wisdom which has kept in view the collective good.

It is anger that motivates man to protect himself as well as defend the Ummah and guard it against aggression. It is the severe indignation at work behind the urge to counter the conspiracies and machinations against Islam and defend the frontiers of an Islamic country. Had Allah not imbibed this sacred passion in man, no believer would have been enraged over the sacrilege of divine sanctity or over blasphemy; nor would he have expressed ingination over the nuisance caused by the enemy, nor his pride would have been aroused if the enemy had usurped the territory of his homeland.

Such anger (which is a sacred passion) is evident from the practice of the Holy Prophet (S.A.W.) himself.

We read of incident in *Sahih Bukhari* that bears testimony to the Holy Prophet's sacred passion. Once a man came to the Holy Prophet (S.A.W.) to recommend waiving a divine *hadd* in a certain case. The Prophet's face was reddened with indignation. He then expressed his sacred passion in the oft quoted words:

> "Verily the generation preceding you was destroyed because the people belonging to it did not take a thief to task if he happened to he strong but punished one who happened to be weak. By God! If Muhammad's daughter had committed theft I would have amputated her hand."

Educational psychologists and sociologists say that the anger which is tantamount to a vice is the expression of such resentment as produce pernicious effects. Anger aroused by laughter or anger which overwhelms a man to lose sight of public interest can on no account be approved of. Such an emotional upsurge disintegrates the Ummah and does away with bonds of mutual affection, sincerity and fraternity among the members of the society.

It is for this reason that the Holy Prophet (S.A.W.) praises those who suppress anger and exercise restraint when provoked.

Hazrat Imam Bukhari says that a man asked the Prophet (S.A.W.) to provide him guidance. The Prophet said, "Do not be angry." The man repeated his request twice and again the Prophet (S.A.W.) exhorted him each time not to be provoked.

In *Musnad Imam Ahmed bin Hanbal* we come across the following tradition:

> "Hazrat Abdullah bin 'Umar asked the the Holy Prophet (S.A.W.) what protected him from Allah's wrath. The Prophet (S.A.W.) replied that the thing which saved him from Allah's wrath was that he whould not lose temper."

There is another tradition to the same effect.

> "The man who eschews the expression of indignation despite his capacity to do so, Allah will call him on the Day of Judgment in the presence of all the people and say to him, "Take any house you like." *(Bukhari)*

It has been stated in *Sahih Bukhari* and *Sahih Muslim* with reference to Hazrat Ibn Masood (R.A.A.) that the Prophet (S.A.W.) said to his companions, "Whom of you do you regard as a valiant man champion?" The companions replied, "Well, the man whom nobody can knock down." The Prophet (S.A.W.) said, "The brave man or champion is rather he who controls his rage."

In the Holy Quran too the Muslim men and women have been urged to restrain anger, express good reaction and ignore the foibles of the ignorant so that the bonds of mutual cooperation and affection are strengthened in the Muslim society. We quote here a few relevant verses of the Holy Quran.

(a) "The good deed and the evil deed are not alike. Repel the evil deed with one which is better, then Lo! he, between whom and thee there was enmity will become as though he was a bosom friend." (41:34)

(b) "The faithful slaves of the Beneficent are they who walk upon the earth modestly and when the foolish ones address them answer: peace." (25:63)

(c) "Those who spend in ease and adversity in the way of Allah, those who control their wrath and are forgiving toward mankind, Allah loveth the benevolent." (3:134)

(d) "Those who when they are wroth forgive." (32:37)

But the anger which makes negative impact on human personality, disturbs his mental poise, vitiates his character and which is detrimental to national integration and weakens mutual bonds of the individuals, then such a passion should be nipped in the bud so that the child is ridded of it before he reaches the age of discretion.

The best way to do this is to keep the child away from the provocatives.

Somebody expresses the truth when he says:

"A dirham spent on prevention is better than hundreds of dirhams spent on treatment."

If hunger makes the child angry, then he should be fed at the right time. Negligence in this connection would cause him physical and psychological ailments. What a great sin do those parents commit who fail to make arrangement for their children's meal at the proper time! Abu Dawood quotes the following tradition of the Holy Prophet (S.A.W.):

It is a sin big enough for a man to lose one nourished at his table (that is, he fails to give him at the proper time)".

If the child remains irritated because of illness then he should be provided medical treatment.

"There is medicine for every disease. If the medicine is suited to the disease then the patient recovers by the Will of God." (*Muslim, Ahmed*).

If the child is provoked by frequent rebukes and is insulted without rhyme or reason, the parents should be cautious in speaking to him and should refrain from using derogatory language. This would inhibit morbid impact upon the child's mind. This precautionary measure is also a method of imparting sound and good training to the child.

Ibn Majah cites the following tradition of the Prophet (S.A.W.) with reference to Hazrat Ibn Abbas:

"Teach manners to your children and inculcate virtues in them."

Ibn Hibban quotes another saying with regard to children's training:

"May Allah have mercy on the parent who has helped his son in a good deed."

Sometimes the child acquires the habit of talking frowningly from his parents. The parents should, therefore, take care that they speak in the presence of children in a serious and dignified manner and refrain from losing temper, as Allah commands his good servants:

"Those who control wrath and forgive and Allah likes the benevolent." (3: 134)

Moreover, the Holy Prophet (S.A.W.) has said:

"A brave man is one who controls his rage."

Unwarranted lavisning of affection on the child and making him accustomed to luxuries and comforts also incites anger. The parents are advised to be moderate in their treatment of children along with the expression of natural love and affection as well as spending money on them. The following advice attributed to Hazrat Ali (R.A.A.) should be kept in view.

"Should you love your dear one, then love him (or her) in a slow-moving way. May be that he hates you at some stage later. If you dislike any one, then dislike him in a moderate way. May be that he becomes your good friend at some stage."

The best way to pacify an angry child is that the parents should endeavour to act according to the practice of the Prophet (S.A.W.):

There are four phases according to the Prophet's way of life for the treatment of an irritable child.

In the first phase the posture in which the child is angry should be changed. Says the Prophet (S.A.W.):

> "If some one is angry while standing, he should sit down. If he is pacified well and good; otherwise he should lie down."

The second phase is to perform ablution when angry. Abu Dawood reports the Prophet (S.A.W.) to have said:

> "Indignation emanates from Satan. Satan has been created with fire which can be extinguished with water. Hence when you get angry you should perform ablution."

The third phase is to be quiet when angry.

Hazrat Imam Ahmed reports the Prophet (S.A.W.) to have said that one should observe silence when angry.

The fourth phase is to seek Allah's refuge from the cursed Satan.

It has been mentioned in both *Sahih Bukhari* and *Sahih Muslim* that two persons started reviling each other in the presence of the Holy Prophet (S.A.W.). One of them was reddened with indignation and was abusing the other. I know for certain that if he had recited the formula:

> "O Allah I seek Your refuge from the cursed Satan" his anger would have been allayed.

These then are some of the Prophet's sayings about dealing with anger.

It is incumbent upon the parents and guardians to teach decorum to their children and pupils. Thus it is hoped that they would develop disposition and learn to be patient, and control their wrath.

Imam Ahmed quotes the Prophet (S.A.W.) to have said, "Listen, the emotion of anger is like the smouldering fire within the breast of man. Don't you see that the veins of his throat are swollen and his eyes are aglow. Whoever experiences such an emotional upsurge within himself, he should lie down and cling to the ground."

The sum and substance of the foregoing discussion is that if the parents keep their children away from the stimuli arousing anger by acting according to the methods prescribed by the Holy Prophet (S.A.W.) and teach them to control their temper by demonstrating the detrimental effects of anger, the children grow meek, mild, patient and develop balance of mind and self-discipline. Such children would typify the sterling moral qualities, decorum and character as envisaged by Islam.

What the guardians, parents and tutors need most is to keep in view the principles of training and discipline bestowed upon us by Islam and the Holy Prophet (S.A.W.). They will thus realize the importance of their duties and obligations and discharge them appropriately.

Thus trained, the members of the new generation would bloom with fully developed personalities, with purity of soul and nobility of character. Their minds will be free from all kinds of psychical ailments and complexes. If the reformers try their level best and the tutors fulfil their obligations in the right way, the task in question will not be a difficult one.

* * * * *

CHAPTER XI

RESPONSIBILITY FOR SOCIAL TRAINING

By social training is meant cultivating decorum and habit of abiding by the principles of civility in the child at the early stage of his life. The springs of these sterling qualities lie deep in the eternal beliefs of Islam. Training the child on such lines is designed to make him decorous and capable of interacting with other members of the society decently, to help him develop a balanced personality, foster the growth of mature thinking and to enable him to act wisely and judiciously.

It is undeniable that this is a heavy responsibility resting on the parents and guardians in respect of training and refinement of children. In fact social training of kids is the essence of all the aspects of their training. We have already dwelt on, for instance, religious, spiritual, moral and psychological training etc. The climax of the entire process of cultivation is social training; for it pertains to the child's behaviour and direct experience or intuition, which enriches him with qualities like adherence to his duties, decorum, balance of mind, maintenance of good social relations and the appropriate pattern of interaction.

The parents and tutors, therefore, should always be ready to impart social training to their children, which constitutes one of their principal responsibilities. This is how they are expected to contribute towards the formation of an Islamic social system based on faith and morality, wherein social training occupies a very important position and special measures are adopted to foster the sublime values of Islam. It is not difficult for Allah to set up such a society.

To my mind there are three practical methods of training children.

(I) Cultivation of spiritual potentials.
(II) Respect for the rights of others.
(III) Consciousness of values and social criticism.

(I) Cultivation of Spiritual Potentials

Islam has formulated the rules of imparting training to all the individuals including the minor and the major, the young and the old, man and women in consideration of the sublime spiritual and psychological principles. These rules are all based on the eternal precepts of children's training. Unless these precepts are translated into practice, a Muslim's personality cannot be perfect and he can never be a true Muslim. These precepts in themsevles constitute everlasting human values as well. Islam has bestowed upon us its invaluable teachings in order to inculcate only these fundamental values or spiritual potentials in us, so that the task of social training may be accomplished in letter and spirit and sacred environment may be created to foster mutual cooperation, establish strong social bonds and affection between individuals and the spirit of constructive and self-criticism is engendered.

Islam wants to imbibe the following spiritual principles in the human soul:

Taqwa or the state of mind generated by the profound consciousness of faith.

Such a faith is linked with a sense of Allah's presence and his fear. This involves the apprehension of incurring Allah's wrath and punishment for any act of disobedience as well as unshakable confidence of His forgiveness. This is how the Ulama define pure and uncontaminated faith. According to them "You should not be seen by Allah at a place where He has forbidden you to be and see you at a place where he wants you to be, (i.e. refrain from committing acts which have been probibitted by Him and do acts enjoined by Him)."

It has been recorded that Hazrat 'Umar bin Khattab (R.A.A.) asked Hazrat Ubaiy bin Ka'b (R.A.A.) about *Taqwa.* The latter replied, "Haven't you ever happened to pass through a thorny way?"

Hazrat 'Umar replied in the affirmative. Hazrat Ubaiy

further enquired, "How did you walk through such a path ?"

"Well I rolled up my clothes and moved on very cautiously."

Hazrat Ubaiy bin Ka'b observed, "That is what *taqwa* is."

Syed Qutb Shaheed, writes in his commentary of the Holy Quran (see *Fi zilal-il-Quran*, vol-I, P.40).

"This then is *taqwa* . . . which is another name for the sensitivity of conscience and the crystalline thinking i.e. awakening of conscience and right-thinking; constant fearing of God; ceaseless cautiousness and treading the thorny path of life with the greatest caution. What are the thorns? The desires, temptations aspirations, fears and phobias; pinning false hopes on the person who has no power to fulfil them and be scared of the person who can neither do harm nor good. These are the thorns and there are countless other thorns besides."

Apart from the fact that *taqwa* imbues man with the fear of Allah and the sense of His perpetual presence, it constitutes in itself the fountainhead of all the cardinal virtues and social morality. It is the only means by which we can guard ourselves against evils, sins, and thorns of inequity. In fact, *taqwa* is the prime factor that inculcates in the individual collective consciousness and perception and by virtue of which social bonds between the individuals are established and strengthened.

The Prophet (S.A.W.) once repeated thrice "*Taqwa* is here." He most probably meant that *taqwa* is the very essence of social training. It demands that man's sense of self-respect is not to be injured and that no harm should be done to him.

We cite a few examples here of the impact made by *taqwa* on the character of an individual:

(a) Abdullah bin Dinar relates the following incident:

Once I set out for Mecca along with Hazrat 'Umar bin Khattab (R.A.A.). At the nightfall we came across a shepherd on our way. Hazrat 'Umar said to him, "O Shepherd, will you sell us one of the goats out of your flock?"

He told the Caliph that he was just a slave.

Hazrat 'Umar wanted to put him to test and said to him,

"You can tell your master that the goat was eaten by a wolf."

"But Allah is Omnipresent. What am I tell to Him, then?" retorted the shepherd.

Hazrat 'Umar burst into tears. He took the shepherd along with him to his master, bought him and said to him setting him free, "What you said, got you freedom and it will also get you freedom in the Hereafter."

(b) The story of a mother and her daughter is well-known. The mother wanted to mix water in the milk in order to earn more profit. The daughter reminded her that the Caliph had forbidden to sell adulterated milk.

The mother said, "The Ruler of the believers is not here to see what we are doing."

The daughter retorted, "If the Ruler of the believers is not there to see us the Lord of the believers' Ruler is there and does witness us."

In the light of the examples cited above, it is absolutely necessary that the upbringing and training of our children should be based on *taqwa.*

Fraternity

Brotherhood or fraternity constitutes psychological correlation which generates in the individuals of the society compassion, sympathy, love. Respect for others and inculcates profound consciousness of fraternity among those imbued with Islamic faith and *taqwa.* When such a deep sense of fraternity is created in a Muslim, he is saturated with the spirit of cooperation sacrifice and compassion and possesses the virtue of forgiving in spite of having the power to retaliate. This would be his positive attitude. His negative attitude, on the other hand, would be to abstain from such acts that might result in damage to life and property of others or injuring their sense of self-respect. The demands of kin or true brotherhood that Islam induces to establish have been mentioned in innumerable verses of the Holy Quran and the Traditions of the Holy Prophet (S.A.W.).

(i) "The believers are not else than brothers." (49:10)

(ii) "We will strengthen thine arm with thy brother." (28:35)

(iii) "And remember Allah's favour unto you: how ye were enemies and He made friendship between your hearts so that ye became as brothers by His grace." (3:103)

Some traditions pertaining to the subject under discussion i.e. fraternal correlation of Muslim, are as under:

(i) "A Muslim is the brother of another Muslim. He does not wrong to his brother, does not leave him without support nor insults or disdains him. It is an evil enough for a Muslim to scorn a Muslim brother. Life and property of every Muslim is unlawful for another Muslim and the seat of *taqwa* is here." The Prophet (S.A.W.) is said to have repeated the last words thrice pointing to his chest (meaning heart). (*Muslim*)

(ii) "None of you can be a true Muslim unless he or she likes for his or her Muslim brother what he or she like for himself or hereself." (*Bukhari and Muslim*)

(iii) "In mutual affection, sympathy and compassion the believers are like the body. If any part of the body is unwell, the whole body is sleepless and suffers from fever." (*Muslim and Ahmed*)

(iv) "Allah will say on the day of Judgment: Where are those who love one another in due respect for my Majesty. I will take them under My shadow this day when there is no other shadow other than Mine."

It was the result of such mutual affection and love for the sake of Allah that the members of Islamic society demonstrated for centuries unparalleled pattern of interrelation to which the history bears it out when the Muslims set examples of mutual cooperation, sacrifice and social security.

(i) Once famine broke out during the caliphate of Hazrat 'Umar (R.A.A.). In the meantime a trade caravan of Hazrat 'Usman (R.A.A.) arrived with a hundred camel load of food and clothes. The local merchants came to purchase those things. Hazrat 'Usman asked them how much profit would they allow him. They offered five percent. Hazrat 'Usman observed, "I have found one who will give more profit. They said that they had no knowledge of any merchant who would offer more profit than they had. Hazrat

'Usman said, "I have found one who will give me seven hundred dirhams in lieu of one dirham and that One is Allah." So saying he recited the following verse of the Holy Quran:

> "The likeness of those who spend their wealth in Allah's way is as the likeness of grain which growth seven years, in every ear a hundred grains. Allah giveth increase manifold to whom He will. Allah is all-embracing, All-Knowing." (2:261)

He then said to the merchants, "O tradesmen, I make you bear witness that I give the entire quantity of wheat, olive oil and fat comprising the merchandize brought by this caravan to the needy and the destitutes in your presence. This is a gift from me to the Muslims."

(ii) Imam Bukhari quotes the following remarks of Hazrat Abdullah bin 'Umar in his *Adab-ul-Mufrad*.

"We have seen those days when no Muslim had greater right to money than his Muslim brother."

We should also try to create such an atmosphere of fraternity and breed our children in such atmosphere.

Compassion

Compassion is another name for living conscience, refinement of mind and tenderness of heart. It is transmuted into affection and sympathy for others. A person with such noble passions shares others sufferings and is kind to them. He tries to do every thing to console them. A heart filled with compassion cannot forbear to see a believer in trouble. He would never cause trouble to any one, nor commit an offence. A compassionate heart is the spring of good, well being and security for others.

The Prophet (S.A.W.) has said that Allah shows pity on one who shows pity on others. The relevant tradition has been quoted by Imam Tirmizi, Abu Dawood and Imam Ahmed in their *Jame'e Tirmizi, Sunan Abu Dawood and Musnad* respectively. It runs as follows:

"The Merciful has pity for those who show pity on others.

Have pity on the people of the earth so that the Being who is in the Heaven may have pity on you."

The Prophet (S.A.W.) describes pitiless people as unfortunate. *Tirmizi, Abu Dawood* and others quote then following tradition to this effect:

"Compassion is taken out of the heart of only the unfortunate person."

A believer's compassion is not confined to the believers alone. It extends to the whole of mankind. It is the gushing spring of pity and kindness. Once the Holy Prophet (S.A.W.) said to his companions:

"You can never be a believer until you do not be kind and compassionate."

The companions replied, "O Holy Prophet, we are all compassionate and take pity on others."

The Prophet (S.A.W.) observed, "The compassion you have for one another is no compassion. By compassion is meant universal mercy and kindness."

This universal mercy embraces the animals besides the human beings. Only a believer can have pity for animals and can fear Allah on their account. Only a believer can feel in his heart of hearts that Allah will call him to account if he disregards the right of any one and causes him trouble.

The Prophet (S.A.W.) once declared above board that the doors of heaven were opened for a whore who gave water to a thirsty dog. For this act of goodness Allah forgave her sins. On the contrary the doors of Hell for another woman were opened because she kept a cat bound without giving anything to eat and drink and the cat finally died. She did not feed the poor creature herself; nor let her off to eat and drink.

Once Hazrat 'Umar (R.A.A.) saw a man dragging a goat by the leg to carry it for slaughtering. He said to the callous person, "Woe be to you! Drive it to death in a proper manner."

Sacrifice

This consists of a conscious state of mind which involves the spirit of preferring others' interests and welfare to one's own.

The spirit of sacrifice is a sterling quality provided that it aims at seeking Allah's pleasure. Its real motive is sincerity of faith and purity of soul. It is the strongest pillar of social security and purity of soul. The Quranic description of fraternity, sympathy, spirit of sacrifice, decency and mutual affection that characterized the conduct of the local people of Madina, called the Ansars, provides us with sufficient guidance:

> "Those who entered the city and the faith before them love those who flee unto them for refuge, and find in their breasts no need for that which hath been given them, but prefer the fugitives above themselves though poverty become their lot; and whoso is saved from his own avarice — such are they who are successful."
>
> (59:9)

This was the spirit of sacrifice and collective compassion demonstrated by the Ansars by all their acts. The history of mankind has no parallel of such acts of sacrifice and collective compassion.

We quote here a few examples of sacrifice made by the members of the Islamic society:

(1) Imam Ghazzali relates an interesting incident showing the spirit of sacrifice demonstrated by the Prophet's companions. Hazrat 'Umar (R.A.A.) is reported to have narraated that the head of a goat was presented to one of the companions of the Prophet (S.A.W.). He said that another companion needed it more than he. So it was sent to him. This companion in his turn sent it to yet another companion whom he thought needed it more than himself. Finally the goat's head returned to the first companion after changing as many as seven hands.

(2) Another astonishing incident of sacrifice, which according to the statement of Qurtubi, has been narrated by Hazrat 'Adi (R.A.A.) is as follows:

Hazrat 'Adi says, "On the day of the Battle of Yarmook I set out in search of my first cousin with a little water I had at the moment. I was saying to myself that if my cousin was still breathing I will cause him to drink the water. At last I found him lying seriously wounded. I asked him if he would drink water. He nodded. But at that very moment he heard the groan of another wounded Muslim. He made a sign bidding me to go to him. I found the man to be Ibn Hisham (R.A.A.). I asked him if he would like to have some water. He too nodded his assent. But suddenly he heard another wounded person groaning. He also made a sign signifying that I should take care of him. But by the time I reached the wounded Muslim, he was dead. Then I retraced my steps to Hisham who too was no more. Finally I returned to my cousin who had also breathed his last."

The above incident bears it out that each of the companions of the Holy Prophet (S.A.W.) wounded on the battlefield preferred the other to himself for drinking the water offered to him when he was breathing his last. This is an example of great sacrifice unparalleled in the history of mankind.

We must strive to inculcate such spirit of sacrifice in our children.

Forgiveness or Mercy

This is a psychical condition in which a person forgives the man who does wrong to him, condones the latter's transgression and forgoes his right to retaliate in spite of his ability to do so, provided that the wrong done by the aggressor is not detrimental to or constitutes descreation of any sacred place of Islam; for this is a serious crime. Forgiving it would be tantamount not only to an affront to one's self but also to a manifestation of one's lack of courage and helplessness. This is something which no one would like for himself.

Forgiveness qualified by the above condition is a cardinal virtue signifying one's strength of faith and refinement in conformity to the principles of Islam.

We have been commanded in the Holy Quran to forgive. This command has been repeated time and again in the Holy Book. Some of the relevant verses are cited below:

"To forgo (forgive) is nearer to piety. And forget not kindness among yourselves. Allah is Seer of what you do." (2:237)

"The good deed and the evil deed are not alike. Repel the evil deed with one which is better, then lo! he, between whom and thee there was enmity will become as though he was a bosom friend." (41:34)

"The bondsmen of Allah the Beneficent walk on earth in humility and when some ignorant person tries to pick up quarrel with him, they say to him, salam!" (25:63)

"Those who control their wrath and are forgiving towards mankind." (3:134)

If a believer's mind is enriched with goodness self--possession, restraint, forgiveness, slow-going and sociability, he will become a model to be emulated by others. In fact such a believer would be angel moving on earth by virtue of his cleanliness and purity of soul.

We cite here a few examples to illustrate the self-passion restraint and forgiveness that characterized the conduct of our virtuous forbears.

(1) There is a well-known incident pertaining to Hazrat Zain-ul-'Abideen. Once, while he was on his way to the mosque someone reviled him. His slaves rushed to beat the man but the Imam stopped them and turning to the man he said, "I am worse than what you have just said. Whatever you know about me is much less than what you do not know. If you want to know the things about me of which you are ignorant, I will tell you." The man who called him names felt ashamed of himself. The Imam took off his shirt and gave it away to the man along with an amount of one thousand dirhams. When he took shirt and the cash, he went his way saying, "I bear witness that this young man is a descendant of the Holy Prophet (S.A.W.).

(2) Another tradition about Imam Zainul-'Abideen is oft quoted. One of his slaves was pouring water from a lota (a pot with a spout resembling a kettle) to help the Imam perform ablution. He dropped the lota injuring the Imam's foot. Seeing the injury, the slave said "My lord, Allah has said that righteous people control their wrath."

The Imam said, "Well, I have controlled my anger."

The slave added, "Allah says that they forgive the people."

The Imam said, "I have condoned your fault."

The siave said further, "Allah like those who do good."

The Imam said, "You have been set free for the sake of Allah."

The companions of the Holy Prophet (S.A.W.) acquired the sterling qualities of forgiveness, leniency and self-possession by following the practice of the Holy Prophet (S.A.W.). It was for this reason that they reached the acme of moral excellence which is unattainable by any person high or low.

Abu Dawood narrates the following tradition of the Holy Prophet (S.A.W.):

"Whoever controls his rage in spite of his ability to give vent to it, would be called by Allah on the Day of Judgment in the presence of all the people and will tell him to choose any of the Hoors with wide beautiful eyes."

Another tradition of the Holy Prophet (S.A.W.) as narrated by 'Ibada bin Samit has been cited in *Mo'jam-Al-Tabarani.* It runs as follows:

The Prophet (S.A.W.) said to his companions, "Shall I tell you of the thing by virtue of which Allah exalts a man and raises his rank?"

"Do tell us what it is," replied the companions.

"Exercise restraint and maintain composure when any one talks to you rudely. Forgive him who does wrong to you. Be generous to him who deprives you of what is due to you. Whoever severs relation with you maintain links with him."

The moral to be drawn from the traditions quoted above is this that we must also train our children in such a way that they become model of self-possession, restraint, leniency and forgiveness.

Courage

This state of mind is an excellent quality which springs from the intensity of faith in Allah. The fountain-head of courge lies in the same teachings to which the unshakable belief of a Muslim owes its origin. A Muslim with such a dauntless courge resigns himself to the decisions of Allah and is fully conscious of his responsibilities. The degree of the strength of his courage will be commensurate with the degree of the soundness of his training.

Hence the valour, courage and frankness of a beliver will be proportional to the strength of his faith, the illumination of his soul with truth, the unshakability of belief in Allah's omnipotency and degree of the consciousness of his responsibilities.

We find all these virtues in the personality of Hazrat Abu Bakr (R.A.A.) who is next only to the Holy Prophet (S.A.W.) in respect of the strength of faith. It was his intensity which forced a stubborn person like Hazrat 'Umar (R.A.A.) to admit that if the faith of Abu Bakr is weighed against we faith of the entire Ummah, it will prove to be much heavier.

We cite here a few incidents to highlight some of the aspects of Hazrat Abu Bakr's personality.

1. On the day of the Holy Prophet's demise the entire Ummah was stunned. Every body was stupefied by news of his passing away. Even Hazrat 'Umar was so much agitated that he threatened to behead the man who said that the Prophet (S.A.W.) was no more. On this juncture it was Hazrat Abu Bakr who proclaimed at the top of his voice, "The man who worshipped Muhammad (S.A.W.) should know that Muhammed (S.A.W) is dead and the man who worshipped Allah should know that Allah is Alive and will never die." He then recited the following verse of the Holy Quran:

> Muhammad (S.A.W.) is but a messenger, messengers the like of whom have passed away before him. Will it be that, when he dieth or is slain, ye will turn back on your heels? He who turneth back doth no hurt to Allah, and Allah will reward the thankful." (3:144)

2. On hearing of the news of Prophet's demise, a large number of people who had embraced Islam superfluously turned apostates and refused to pay Zakat to the Islamic government. The prejudices of pagan ignorance were revived. After the Prophet's death the Muslims were, as depicted by Hazrat Aisha (R.A.A.), like the wet goats on a rainy night. Things came to such a pass that the Muslims advised the Caliph that as it was not possible to fight the whole of Arabia, he should go and

remain in peace at home, close his doors and worship his Lord till he meets with his death.

Hazrat Abu Bakr's humility was personified. He was tender hearted and always moved to tears with a sense of Allah's presence. He was mild, kind and compassionate. But on that occasion he was a different man. He was enraged like a tiger and said to Hazrat 'Umar (R.A.A.), "Should we become tyrant in ignorance and cowards in Islam?" The revelation of Allah's message was complete and came to an end. Can religion be tampered with while I am alive? By God! If they do not give me the piece of rope which they used to give to the Holy Prophet (S.A.W.) even then I will fight them. As long as the sword in my hand remains intact, I will wage war against them." On hearing this Hazrat, 'Umar (R.A.A.) said, "Allah made Abu Bakr's heart adamant in his stand about war and I was convinced that he was right."

That is why saying boldly what is right and true has been described as the highest form of *jihad.* In this connection *Abu Dawood, Tirmizi* and Ibn Majah *quote the following tradition of the Holy Prophet (S.A.W.):*

"Saying a word of truth in the presence of a tyrant ruler is the highest form of *jihad.*"

And for the same reason the man who dies as a martyr while upholding truth has been described as the head of the martyrs.

Imam Hakim reproduces a saying of the Holy Prophet (S.A.W.) in his *Musnad* which runs as follows:

"Hamza bin Abdul Muttalib is the head of martyrs and the man who stood before a tyrant king and preached him to do good acts and abstain from bad acts and was slain by the king."

For the same reason the Prophet (S.A.W.) got a commitment from his companions that they would speak the truth wherever they might be.

Imam Muslim records the following statement of Hazrat 'Ibada bin Samit:

"We made a pledge on the Prophet's hand that we would obey in comfort and difficulty, whether we are delighted or disgusted. We also made a pledge that we would make sacrifice for others and would not protest against the people in authority unless we have a solid proof that they were guilty of acts amounting to infidelity. Also we made a commitment that we would speak the truth wherever we might be and will never be afraid of censure from any critic in any matter pertaining to Allah."

Hence Allah's praise for those who convey their Lord's message to others and never fear any one other than Allah:

"(There were the people) who delivered the messages of Allah and feared Him and feard none save Allah. Allah alone is sufficient to guard." (33:39)

It is, therefore, parent's special responsibility to imprint indelible impressions of pure faith and *taqwa* on the hearts of the children and to imbue them with the spirit of fraternity, love, mercy sacrifice and restraint. They should be inspired to do good eagerly and inculcate in them the sterling qualities of being outspoken and truthful. There are other psychological principles besides that should be given due importance.

When the child grows up and treads the difficult path of life such training would enable him to bear the responsibilities resting on his shoulders smoothly with all his heart and duly fulfil his obligations towards others.

Guarding the Rights of Others

We are now in a position to discuss the social rights which the children are to be acquainted with and taught respect and develop the habit of discharging them as duties.

Those social rights are as follows:

(1) The Rights of Parents, (2) The Rights of Kinsmen, (3) The Rights of Neighbours (4) The Rights of Teachers (5) The Rights of Friends and (6) The Rights of Elders.

We proceed to discuss these rights in details.

1. The Rights of Parents

One of the most important duties of the parents and the tutors is to acquaint the child first of all with the rights of the parents. They are, for instance, to be told to do good to their parents, obey every genuine or legitimate order that they give him, treat them kindly, serve them, look after them when they are old, talk to them in a low and soft voice (should not speak aloud) and when the parents are dead the child/children should pray to God to have mercy upon them.

We cite below the Holy Prophet's sayings about the kind treatment of the parents under different heads. The guardians and the tutors should not only make the children commit these sayings to memory but also make them act upon those sayings.

(a) The pleasure of parents delights Allah.

In his *Al Adab-ul-Mufrad* Imam Bukhari quotes the following tradition with reference to Ibn Abbas:

"The believer who looks after his parents day and night, Allah opens two doors of Garden on him. If one of the parents is alive, then He opens one door. If he displeases one of the parents, Allah will be displeased with him until he has propitiated the offended parent. The Prophet (S.A.W.) was asked if Allah will be displeased with him seven if the parent has done wrong to him. The Prophet (S.A.W.) replied in the affirmative."

(b) Kind treatment of parents preferable to Jihad.

Imam Bukhari states with reference to Hazrat Abdullah bin 'Umar that one day a man said to the Holy Prophet (S.A.W.):

"Can I fight in the way of Allah?" The Prophet (S.A.W.) asked him if his parents were alive. The man replied in the affirmative. The Prophet (S.A.W.) then, told him to go and serve them heart and soul.

(c) Praying for Allah's forgiveness and mercy after their death and having respect for their true and sincere friends.

This has been enjoined by Allah in the following words:

"And lower unto them the wing of submission through mercy, and say: My Lord! Have mercy on them both as they did care for me when I was little." (17:24)

Imam Bukhari quotes the following statement of Hazrat Abu Huraira (R.A.A.):

"A man will be exalted after his death. He will say to himself, "O my Lord! How have I been raised to such a high status." Allah would say, "Thy son has prayed for thy forgiveness."

The following tradition has been given in *Sunan Abu Dawood, Sunan Ibn Majah and Musnad Hakim:*

"Malik bin Rabia said that as we were sitting with the Holy Prophet (S.A.W.), a man belonging to a family of Bani Salama came to him and asked, "Am I responsible for doing any good to my parents after their death as well?" He said, "Yes, pray for them. Pray for their forgiveness. Fulfil their promises. Respect their sincere friends and mete out kind treatment to those who are related to you by being kinsfolk of your parents."

There is another tradition to the same effect quoted in *Majama-'ul-Fawaid* with reference to Hazrat Anas (R.A.A.):

"The Prophet (S.A.W.) observed: A good act is this that you do good to the sincere friends of your father."

(C) Mother is to be preferred to father

Imam Bukhari quotes Hazrat Abu Huraira to have narrated that a man came to the Holy Prophet (S.A.W.) and said, "O Holy Prophet (S.A.W.), who is most entitled to my kind treatment?" The prophet (S.A.W.) replied, "Your mother." He asked again, "Who has the greatest right to my kind treatment?" The Prophet (S.A.W.) replied, "Your mother." The man asked further, "Whom am I under the obligation to treat the best after my mother?"

"Your father" was the Prophet's (S.A.W.) reply.

We find a tradition in the Commentary *Tafseer Ibn Kaseer* narrated by Ibn Suleman Ibn Buraida which he quotes with reference to his father:

A man helped his mother to take rounds of Ka'ba as a part of pilgrimage by lifting her up. He asked the Prophet (S.A.W.), "Have I fulfilled my duty to my mother." The Prophet (S.A.W.) said, "No, not even to a single pang she had to endure when she gave you birth."

There is yet another tradition narrated by Hazrat Buraida as cited in *Majma-'ul-Fawaid:*

A man came to the Holy Prophet (S.A.W.) and said, "O Holy Prophet (S.A.W.)! I seated my mother on my neck and carried her for a distance of about two miles on a ground which was so hot that even if a lump of flesh had been put on it, it would have been roasted. I want to know if I have done justice to her service of which I was under obligation?" The Prophet (S.A.W.) replied that the trouble he took in her service was probably equal to a single pang of child birth she endured in begetting him.

There seems to be two reasons for which Islam treats mother as preferable to father:

The first reason is that, that the mother had to bear the child for nine months, endures the pangs of child-birth, meticulously takes care of it and breeds it. The father had to take much less trouble in this connection. This has been explained in the Holy Quran in the following words:

> And we have enjoined upon man concerning his parents- his mother beareth him in weakness upon weakness, and his weaning is in two years — give thanks unto Me and unto thy parents. Unto Me is the return. (31:14)

The second reason is that the mother is far more fond of the child and has much compassion and affection for it than the father. Sometimes the son takes advantage of the intensity of mother's love and gets easy going and seeks comfort. For this reason the *Shariah* specially enjoins upon the children that they should mete out better treatment to the mother than the father, prefer her to the latter and obey her. They should not neglect their duty to the mother and should always be mindful of the respect and kind treatment due to her.

Mother's love can well be judged from the fact that however disobedient and rude the son may be to her, the mother forgets all his faults and misbehaviours when she finds her in a predicament or confronted with difficulties.

How to mete out kind and respectful treatment to parents.

(1) One should not walk ahead of them.

(2) One should not call them by using their names.

(3) One should not sit before they are seated.
(4) One should not feel bored or vexed by their exhortation.
(5) One should not eat any edible of which they seem to be fond of. Leave it for them.
(6) One should not sit before them at a higher place.
(7) One should not oppose their instructions or whatever they say.

We have derived all the above points from the following verse of the Holy Quran:

"Thy Lord hath decreed, that ye worship none save Him, and that ye show kindness to parents. If one of them or both of them attain old age with thee, say not 'Fie' unto them nor repulse them, but speak unto them a gracious word. And lower unto them the wing of submission through mercy and say! My Lord! Have mercy on them both as they did care for me when I was little." (17:23-24)

The saying of the Holy Prophet (S.A.W.) to this effect should also be kept in view.

(1) Whoever stared at his father angrily, ill-treated his father.
(2) Hazrat Aisha narrates that a man called on the Holy Prophet (S.A.W.). He was accompanied by an old man. The Prophet (S.A.W.) asked him who the latter was. He said that the old fellow was his father. The Prophet said, "Do not walk ahead of him, nor sit before he is seated. Never call him by his name and never reproach him."

We cite a few examples to illustrate how our forbears resepected their parents.

(1) It has been mentioned in the book *Oyûnul Akhyar* that 'Amr bin Zaid was asked how his son treated him. He said, "Well, he walked behind me in the daytime and ahead of me at night. He never climbed the room under which I have been.

Abstinence from Disobedience of Parents.

The Arabic word *'Uqooq'* signifies disobedience including defiance of parents' instructions and not to fulfil one's obligations regarding them. Thus if the son looks askance at his father and stares at him angrily, it would be tantamount to disobedience and insolence on his part.

If the son regards himself as equal to his father, this too would amount to insolence.

If the son considers it unnecessary to kiss the hands of his parents as a mark of respect or pay them due respect, he will be guilty of insolence.

The son should not be too proud to feel ashamed of talking about his father. This would be his unworthiness. He should, in particular, not be ashamed of mentioning his father in social functions.

An unworthy son is also one who does not bear the expenses of his poor parents and thereby compels them to go to the court to force him to fix their allowance.

The most odious disobedience is that the son talks rudely to the parents, is niggardly towards them, injures their pride by his foul tongue and insults them.

The Prophet (S.A.W.) has forbidden to disobey the parents and told a defiant son that disobedience of parents is a great sin that invalidates all the great acts and Allah takes on him the vengeance of his parents sooner or later.

Imam Bukhari and *Imam Muslim* quote the following tradition as narrated by 'Abdullah bin 'Amr bin 'Aas:

The Holy Prophet (S.A.W.) said: "Abusing one's parents is a major sin."

Abdullah asked, "O Holy Prophet, (S.A.W.), how can a man abuse his parents?"

"Yes, he can, To revile another person's father amounts to abusing one's own father. To revile another person's mother is to abuse one's own mother." observed the Prophet (S.A.W.).

Imam Ahmed and others quote a tradition narrated by Hazrat Mo'az bin Jabal according to which the Prophet (S.A.W.) forbade him to abstain from ten things, two of which are as under:-

1. Ascribing partners to God even if you are burnt alive or slain.

2. Disobedience of parents even if you have to abandon your wife and children and material possessions.

According to *Imam Hakim* and *Allama Isbahani*, Hazrat

Abu Bakr reports the Prophet (S.A.W.) to have observed: "Allah lays down as much punishment for every sin as He chooses till the Day of Judgment, except disobedience of one's parents. Allah awards the punishment of this sin to the son during his life and in this world".

The sum and substance of what has been discussed above is that those reponsible for breeding and training the children are under the obligation to acquaint them with the following precepts of morality and decorum:

(1) Obedience of parents is consistent with the obedience of Divine commands.

(2) The parents should be addressed in the most respectable manner.

(3) When the parents come before the children, they should immediately stand up as a mark of reverence.

(4) They should kiss the hands of their parents every morning and every evening.

(5) They should guard the honour, venerability, reputation and wealth and property of the parents.

(6) The parents should be given whatever they ask for.

(7) Their advice should be sought in every matter.

(8) The children should frequently pray for Allah's forgiveness for their parents.

(9) If the parents have guests with them, the children should sit by the door and should watch their looks. May be that the parents happen to talk about some secret matter or make a clandestine gesture to the children without letting the guests know what they have in mind.

(10) Without being asked by the parents, the children should act in a manner that they are delighted.

(11) The children should not speak aloud in their presence.

(12) They should not interrupt while they are talking.

(13) If the parents do not allow, the child should not go out of doors.

(14) If the parents are asleep, he should not disturb them.

(15) The son should not prefer his wife and children to his parents.

(16) If the parents could not do as he wishes, he should not reproach them.

(17) He should not laugh in the presence of parents with-

out any reason.

(18) He should not take food from their plate to eat.

(19) He should not go to sleep without the permission of parents as long as they remain sitting.

(20) He should not stretch his legs before them.

(21) He should not move to take meal before the parents have taken.

(22) He should neither enter the room, or house, before them, nor walk in front of them.

(23) He should respond as soon as the parents call him and go to them.

(24) The compassions of the parents should be respected during their lifetime and after their death.

(25) The company of person who does not behave as indicated above is to be shunned.

(26) One should pray for one's parents, particularly after their death. As prayer is beneficial to them, one should pray frequently. The words of the Quran for such prayer are as under:-

O Lord, have mercy upon them as they nourished and brought me up when I was a child. (17:24)

2. The Rights of Kinsfolk or Zawil-Arham.

Kinsfolk are enumerated below in order of close relationship:-

(1) Parents

(2) Paternal grand-father and grand-mother as well as maternal grandfather and grand-mother.

(3) Brothers and sisters

(4) Paternal uncles and aunts

(5) Sons and daughters of brothers

(6) Sons and daughters of sisters.

(7) Maternal uncles and aunts.

Also the close relations of the above kinsfolk in order of importance.

The Shariah treats all the kith and kin or *Zawil Arham* mentioned for the following reasons.

(a) The Arabic word 'Rahm' (mercy) is derived form 'Rahman' (Merciful — name of Allah). This is proved by the following tradition of theHoly Prophet (S.A.W.).

"Allah says: I am Allah and I am Rahman. I have created

'rahm'. I have derived the noun rahm from My name (Rahman). Whoever metes out affectionate treatment to one's kinsfolk, I will join him and whoever ceases treating them with affection and compassion I will abandon him."

The purpose of originating *'Rahm*, from Rahman is to establish the relationship of mutual compassion and bonds of affection between one another. This derivation induces to maintain the bonds of affection, compassion and close relationship with one's kinsfolk.

(b) Kinship owes its origin to a man's relationship. For this reason the Holy Prophet (S.A.W.) has emphasized time and again compassionate treatment of one's kith and kin and urges abstinence from giving up such treatment.

The two reasons referred to above induces man to acknowledge the rights of kinsmen and compassionate treatment of them from the core of his heart and inculcate in him the sense of fraternity.

In view of the facts explained above it is incumbent upon the guardians and parents to imbibe in the child respect for and consciousness of the rights of kinsfolk so that the child may develop the habit of mixing up with people and the quality of sociability as soon as he reaches the age of discretion. His personality under such training will be imbued with love, and affection and he will establish such strong bonds of love and compassion with other people as if they are members of his own family. If the child is trained in his early childhood in the manner indicated above, his mental qualities will mature. He will be accustomed to mete out compassionate treatment to others, respect the elders, take pity upon the younger people, try to console the suffering, will have sympathy for those confronted with difficulties and will help the destitutes.

It is obvious that development of all these sterling qualities in the child requires thorough training in an organized manner.

We cite here a few relevant verses of the Holy Quran:

(1) "Fear Allah in Whom ye claim your rights of one another and toward the wombs that bare you." (4:1)

(2) "Give the kinsman his due and the needy and the way farer, and squander not thy wealth in wantonness." (17:26)

(3) "And serve Allah. Ascribe nothing as partner unto Him. Show kindness unto parents, and unto near kindred and the orphans and the needy and unto the neighbour": (4:36)

As opposed to strengthening the bonds of kinship and kind treatment of the kinsfolk, the Holy Quran enjoins that the bonds of kinship should not be broken and describes the reverence of the relation of kinship as the cause of disruption on earth. The person guilty of this would be doomed to perpetual damnation and would be liable to be given the worst abode in the Hereafter. Says Allah:

"And those who break the covenant of Allah after ratifying it, and sever that which Allah hath commanded should be joined, and make mischief in the earth; theirs is the curse and theirs the ill-abode." (13:25)

"Would ye then, if ye were given the command, work corruption in the land and sever your ties of kinship? Such are they whom Allah curseth so that he deafendeth them and maketh blind their eyes." (47:22-23)

This then is the fate and the tragic end of the oppressors and transgressors. It is, therefore, incumbent on the guardians to warn their children and wards against the horrible catastrophe resulting from severing kinship and ill-treatment of parents and also tell the children the reward of meting out kind treatment to their parents.

The reward for doing good to kinsfolk and its salutary effects have been dwelt upon by the Holy Prophet himself. We adumbrate them here under various heads for the parents and guardians so that they may urge upon the children to mete out kind treatment to their kinsfolk both in their childhood as well as when they grow up.

(i). *Imam Bukhari* and *Imam Muslim* quote the following tradition of the Holy Prophet (S.A.W.):

Whoever believes in Allah and in the Day of Judgment, should honour his guest. Whoever believes in Allah and in the Day of Judgment should mete out kind treatment to his kinsfolk and whoever believes in Allah and the Day of Judgment should speak kind words or keep quiet."

(ii). Prolongation of life and increase in income.

Imam Bukhari and *Imam Muslim* cite the following saying of the Prophet (S.A.W.) with reference to Hazrat Anas (R.A.A.).

"Whoever wants increase in his provisions and prolong ation of life, should treat his kinsmen kindly."

(iii). To avert tragic death.

Abu Ya'la quotes a tradition narrated by Hazrat Anas (R.A.A.). It runs as follows:

"The Prophet (S.A.W.) said that by charity and benevolent treatment of kinsmen, life is prolonged as tragic death is averted by Allah and He also keeps man away from undesirable and forbidden things.

(iv). Increase of population and wealth.

According to *Tabarani's Mo'jam* and as quoted by *Imam Hakim* with reference to Hazrat Ibn Abbas (R.A.A.) the Holy Prophet (S.A.W.) said: "It may be that Allah may not have looked at a nation because of indignation on its emergence, but Allah multiplies its population and increases its wealth. While asked the reason for this the Prophet (S.A.W.) said: Owing to benevolent treatment of kinsfolk among the individuals of that nation."

(v) Forgiving sins and mistakes

Ibn Hibban and *Imam Hakim* both quoted the following tradition in their respective Musnads as narrated by Ibn 'Umar (R.A.A.). According to this tradition a man came to the Holy Prophet (S.A.W.) and said, "I have committed a major sin. Is it possible that my repentence is accepted? The Holy Prophet (S.A.W.) asked the man if his mother was alive? He replied in the negative.

"Is your maternal aunt alive?" asked the Prophet

(S.A.W.) again.

The man replied in the affirmative.

The Prophet (S.A.W.) said, "Mete out benevolent treatment to her (that is, serve her).

(vi) Leniency in accountability and guarantee of entering the Heaven.

Bazzaz, Tabarani and *Hakim* cite the following tradition narrated by Hazrat Abu Huraira.

The Holy Prophet (S.A.W.) said, "Allah will be lenient in calling to account a person with three qualities and will be merciful enough to allow him a place in the Heaven. The companions present enquired about those three things. The Prophet (S.A.W.) said, "Be generous to him who deprives you, mete out benevolent treatment to the kinsman who severs kinship with you and forgive the man who does wrong to you. If you develop these three habits, then Allah is sure to let you enter the Heaven."

Imam Bukhari and Imam Muslim quote another tradition narrated by Jubair bin Mut'im.

(vii). Guarantee of getting highest ranks on the Day of Judgment.

Bazzaz and *Tabarani* record the following tradition of the Prophet (S.A.W.) as narrated by Hazrat 'Ibada bin Samit:

The Prophet (S.A.W.) said, "By virtue of what does Allah raises ranks in the Hareafter?" The companions replied, "Allah and the Messenger know better." The Prophet (S.A.W.) himself mentioned the reasons for raising the ranks by Allah and said, "Speak softly to the person who speaks to you rudely, forgive the man who does wrong to you, be generous to him who deprives you and treat the kinsman kindly who severs relation with you."

When the children are told about the advantages of treating kinsmen kindly, they will certainly be filled with affection and spirit of benevolence for their kinsmen. They will acknowledge the respect due to them because of their age and will fulfil their obligations with regard to them. They will share their kinsmen's happiness and sorrow, support the suffering and the poor. I swear by my life! that this is the culmination of goodness and kindness with kinsmen.

In the present day world we badly need tutors who could

acquaint the children with these things and turn them into noble and edified persons by inculcating moral excellence.

3. The Rights of Neighbours

Apart from other rights, it is essential for the parents and guardians to attach special importance to the rights of the neighbours. The question arises; who are the neighbours?

All the people living to the right and left and above and below your house are your neighbours. This relationship of neighbourhood extends to forty houses. Every inmate of these houses is your neighbour. You have rights to them as they have rights to you. We have derived this meaning of neighbourhood from the following tradition which *Tabarani* has quoted in his Mo'jam with reference to Hazrat Ka'b bin Malik (R.A.A.). According to this tradition a person came to the Holy Prophet (S.A.W.) and said, "O Holy Prophet (S.A.W.), I live in the area inhabited by such and such tribe. The man who is troubling me most is my closest neighbour."

The Prophet (S.A.W.) sent a word to Hazrat Abu Bakr, Hazrat 'Umar and Hazrat Ali (A.A.A.) to come and stand at the doors of the mosque to proclaim:

> "O ye people: Listen, Neighbourhood extends to forty houses. The man by whose mischief his neighbour remains in a state of constant fear will never enter the Heavens. According to Islam there are four fundamental rights of the neighbour, which are as follows:
>
> 1. The neighbour should nto be troubled or harassed.
> 2. If some one troubles the neighbour, the later should be extended support.
> 3. The neighbour should be treated kindly.
> 4. If the neighbour does wrong to you and shows bad temper, you should exercise restraint and pardon him.

We discuss the above rules of conduct with regard to the rights of the neighbour under four different heads:

1. Relieving the neighbour of trouble.

By trouble is meant distress, suffering etc. This rule involves protection of neighbour against adultery, theft, abuse, and slander or scandal. Serious offences among these include adultery, theft and defamation. The Prophet (S.A.W,) urged upon his companions to abstain from the above offences while exhorting them to do good acts and refrian from bad ones.

As for the act of afflicting with the hand and foul tongue, the following saying of the Holy Prophet (S.A.W.) provides sufficient guidance:

"By God he is not a believer! By God he not a believer! By God he is not a believer!"

The companions asked him whom he was speaking of.

"The man from whose nefarious acts his neighbour is not secure." observed the Holy Prophet (S.A.W.).

(*Bukhari and Muslim*)

2. Helping and supporting the neighbour.

Protection of the neighbour and saving him from wrongful treatment is a trait of the people with purity of soul. In fact, Islam treats it as one of the greatest virtues. A man's act to deliver his neighbour from affliction, is indicative of his courage and boldness. The Arabs are well-known for their pride in extending help and support to their neighbours. Numerous proofs of this are found in their verses. Whole collections of poetical works are replete with the examples of their assitance lent by them to the neighbours.

As regards the importance of extending help to the neighbour and guarding him aganst ill repute and oppression, we cite here a tradition of the Holy Prophet (S.A.W.) reported by *Imam Muslim* and *Imam Bukhari* to have been narrated by Hazrat 'Umar.(R.A.A.).

The Holy Prophet (S.A.W.) according to this tradition said, "A Muslim is brother of another Muslim. He neither does wrong to him, nor leaves him helpless. The man who meets the needs of his brother and relieves him of distress, Allah will relieve him of the hardships he may have to suffer on the Day of Judgment. One who provides clothing to the Muslims will on the Day of Judgment be provided with clothing by Allah."

When one Muslim enjoys so much right to another Muslim, then he is under greater obligation with regard to his neighbours for neighbours have specific rights and duties to each other.

3. Kind treatment of the neighbour.

By Kind treatment of the neighbours does not merely mean that he should not be troubled and defended against disgrace and wrongful action. It also signifies expression of sympathy when he is in distress, congratulated on his success and on occasions of festivitities, ask after his health when he is ill, and in the light of one's own knowledge acquaint him with whatever benefits him in this world and in the Hereafter and to be the first to greet him. One should as a rule try to maintain the best relations as far as possible and honour him.

We have drawn this conclusion from a tradition quoted by *Kharaitee* and *Tabarani* with reference to Hazrat 'Amr bin Shoaib. According to this tradition the Prophet (S.A.W.) said, "If any one has shut his door against his neighbour because the latter poses a threat to his family and belongings, such a neigbour is not a Momin (believer) and he is also not a Momin from whose mischief his neighbour is not secure. Do you know the right of a neighbour? When he seeks help from you, go to his help, when he is sick, visit him to ask after his welfare, if he is successful or has the cause for happiness, congratulate him. If he is in trouble, console and support him. When he dies, attend his funeral. Do not build your house so high without his permission that he is deprived of fresh air. Do not trouble your neighbour with odour of the dish you cook. Send him some of the food you prepare for yourself. Also send some of the fruits you purchase. Should it not be possible, then bring them concealed. Do not let your child to go out of the house with any fruit. This would make the neighbour's child angry."

Hazrat Mujahid relates that once he was with Hazrat Abdullah bin 'Umar. One of his slaves was skinning a slaughtered goat. He instructed the slave to distribute the meat beginning with his jew neighbour. He repeated again and again the following tradition of the Holy Prophet (S.A.W.):

"Gabriel impressed upon me the importance of the right of the neighbour so frequently that I started believing that he would give him the right of inheritance."

(Bukhari and Muslim)

4. Endurance of suffering inflicted by the neighbour.

The greatness of a man consists in alleviating the suffering of his neighbour, providing him protection, going to his rescue if he is being tortured and meting out kind treatment to him as far as possible. But there is yet another thing which exalts a man and that is to forgive the wong done by the neighbour. Ignore his faults and exercise restraint when one is troubled by him. The fault committed by the neighbour unwillingly should particularly be forgiven, provided that he is sorry for the act wrongly done by him.

Hareeri writes in his *'Maqamat'*, "I am mindful of the welfare of my neighbour even if he is doing wrong to me."

No doubt the man who exercises restraint in response to misbehaviour and does good in response to the harm done to him and forgets the excesses committed by his neighbour is a high class man and will find himself exalted on the Doomsday.

Bazzaz and *Tabarani* quote the following tradition of the Holy Prophet (S.A.W.) with reference to Hazrat 'Ibada bin Samit (R.A.A.).

The Prophet (S.A.W.) said to his companions, "Shall I tell you something, by virtue of which Allah will raise man's ranks?"

"Please do tell us" answered the companions.

"Whoever behaves with you rudely, treat him in a dignified manner and maintain your composure. Whoever oppresses you, forgive him. Whoever deprives you, be generous to him. Whoever severs kinship with you, treat him kindly."

The guardians are advised to make the child familiar with the virtue and blessings of treating kindly with the neighbours as soon as he reaches the age of discretion, so that he may be able to learn the importance of conducting himself with other people in a nice and judicious manner, be mindful of the welfare of his neighbours, alleviate their sufferings, protect them against oppression, do good to them and endure whatever wrong he has to suffer at their hands.

There are two things essential to accustom the child to

look after the rights of the neighbours:-

(a) To exhort the child verbally from time to time.

(b) To train the child to deal kindly with other children of the same age group.

Trained on this pattern, the child woud like to mix up with other people. He will develop social and sociable character in the right sense. He will be free from morbid introversion and shyness. His individual existence will be his identity. He will have a prominent personality. He would develop such a sterling quality as a result of the way he is socially trained. Such a training would enable him to reform the various aspects of his life.

The guardians should train the child on the lines chalked out above and turn him out as the most likeable personality of the community.

4. The Rights of Teachers.

One of the most important rights of which the guardians and the tutors ought to be acquainted with is the right of the teacher to be respected and esteemed by his pupils. The guardians and parents should impress upon the minds of their offspring the importance of the teacher's rights so that the child may grow up as a man with due respect for his guardians and tutors. If the teacher himself is a virtuous man imbued with the depth of faith and moral excellence, the child would automatically develop good character under his influence.

The Prophet (S.A.W.) has given the guardians special instructions for training the child to revere and honour the teachers and scholars. It is, therefore, incumbent upon the pupils to respect the rights of the teachers and revere them.

We cite here a fews sayings of the Holy Prophet (S.A.W.) in this context:-

(a). "The man who does not respect his elders, does not have compassion for the younger people and does not respect the rights of our scholars, does not belong to my Ummah."

(Narrated by Hazrat Ibada bin Samit and quoted by *Tabarani*, *Ahmed* and *Hakim*).

(b). "*Imam Tabarani* quotes in his *Al Mo'jam-ul-Awsat*,

a tradition narrated by Hazrat Abu Hurairah. According to this traditions the Prophet (S.A.W.) said, "Acquire knowledge, develop dignity and self-possession for the acquisition of knowledge and respect the person from whom you acquire knowledge."

(c) *Tabarani* has cited in his *Al Mo'jam-ul-Kabeer* the following tradition narrated by Abu Umama:

The Prophet (S.A.W.) said, "Only a hypocrite can insult three persons:

(i) The Muslim who is hoary or grey-headed.
(ii) Scholar.
(iii) A just ruler.

(d) The pupil should sit respectfully before the tutor, calm and humble. Listen attentively to what the teacher says, with his gaze fixed upon him. He should be all attention to him and should never look right and left or up and down.

The pupil should abstain from any act in the presence of the teacher that is incompatible with decorum, discipline and modesty.

Hazrat Ali (R.A.A.) explains the rights of the teacher to be respected by the pupils in the following words:

"The right of a teacher demands that you should greet him respectfully while greeting others in an ordinary manner. Sit in front of him. Do not make signs in his presence nor quote the remarks of any one opposed to the opinion of the teacher. Never backbite in the presence of the teacher. Do not find faults with the teacher. If he commits a fault, readily accept his excuse. You are under the obligation to esteem the teacher for the sake of Allah. If the teacher requires anything, then try to be the first to meet his need. Do not whisper in his class. If the teacher exhibits sluggishness, do not try to activate him. You should never be contented with the company of the teacher, for the teacher is like the date tree. You should wait for a bunch to fall in your garment."

Hazrat Ali's exhortation is quite adequate for the guidance of a student.

When the student goes to the teacher, he should be well-dressed in every respect. He should wash, put on clean or fresh clothes, particularly when he is going to attend his class or accademic gathering; for an academic gathering or attending a lecture or class is tantamount to worship.

When the student is with the teacher, his mind should be free of wordly worries and he should be well-composed so tht he is capable of bearing in mind whatever the teacher imparts to him and thus be able to add to his knowledge.

If the teacher is absent from his place, the studnet should not go back. He should instead wait for him in order to be able to benefit from him. He should not knock at the teacher's door for the purpose of his giving the teacher the trouble of coming out. If the teacher happens to be asleep, the pupil should wait till he wakes up or should go back and come again after sometime in order to learn his lesson.

According to a tradition Hazrat Ibn Abbas (R.A.A.) used to go to acquire knowledge from Hazrat Zaid bin Sabit (R.A.A.) and sit at the latter's door till he woke up. Ibn Abbas (R.A.A.) was told that Hazrat Zaid would be awakened and informed of his arrival. But Ibn Abbas asked the people not to do it. He often stood at the door for a long time in the burning sun.

It does not befit a student to repeat the same question again and again, of which he already knows the answer, nor is it proper for him to further enquire into any point which he has comprehended. Thus Imam Zahri has said that repetition of the same thing again and again is like bearing a heavy stone.

The student should concentrate on what the teacher imparts to him and try to bear in mind the significance of every point. He should be careful of this in particular. It does not behove a student to be engrossed by the thought of something else and trouble the teacher to repeat the point he may have missed. This amounts to disrespect. He should be all attention and keep up presence of mind right from the beginning of the lecture.

In case the student happens to be sitting at a distance from the teacher and therefore the latter's voice is not clearly audible to him, he should respectfully beg to be excused and request the teacher to repeat and explain whatever he may have missed during the lecture or the lesson.

There are the modes of behaviour which every child should learn from his teacher or guardian. They are the essence of moral training and also constitute social rights.

If the child is acquainted with the modes of conduct referred to in his early years, he will realize the rights of teachers and guardians when he has grown up and will owe gratitude to those who have a share in building his character.

There are not two opinions about the principle that the child's moral and social training should be given preference to his academic and cultural training, for moral virtues are of primary importance and the academic problems are of secondary importance.

5. The Right of Friend.

The guardians should also urge upon the child to have an honest friend and a virtuous companion. The companions play an important role in moral improvement of a child. If he can find well-behaved and upright friends, his behaviour will certainly improve. Someone has rightly said, "A companion is one who drags his friend along with him."

There is another pithy remark to the same effect:

"Do not ask me who I am, but ask me who are my acquaintances. You will thus be able to know me." (The same idea is expressed in the English proverb in a much better way: A man is known by the company he keeps).

A poet has expressed the same idea in couplet as rendered below:

Do not ask about a man. Ask about his companion. Every friend acquires the modes of his companion's behaviour.

We cite in this context the sayings of the Holy Prophet (S.A.W.) who is the guardian and the tutor of mankind.

(1). Hazrat Abu Musa Ash'ari quotes the Holy Prophet (S.A.W.) to have said, "A good companion may be likened to one who carries musk, while a bad companion may be likened to one who blows in the furnace. The man having musk on his person will either give you musk of his own accord or you will buy it from him, or in any case you will enjoy its fragrance. On the other hand the man who blows in the furnance will either burn your clothes or spread offensive smell."

(2). *Abu Dawood* and *Tirmizi* have cited the following traditions:

"Make friends only with a true believer and only a righteous person should share meals with you."

(3) Hazrat Ibn 'Asakir quotes this saying of the Prophet, (S.A.W.). "Shun the company of a bad man; for a man is known by the company he keeps."

Tirmizi and *Abu Dawood* give yet one more tradition to the same effect:

The Prophet (S.A.W.) said, "A man is like his companion. Any of you must think what sort of acquaintance he has made."

Now the question arises what those rights of companionship are with which the children are to be acquainted with.

Rights of Friendship.

These rights are adumbrated as follows:

1. *Greeting the friend when meeting him.*

Hazrat Abdullah bin 'Amr bin 'Aas (R.A.A.) narrates that a man once asked the Prophet (S.A.W.), "What is the best sign of Islam?"

"Feed the hungry and greet everyone whether you know him or not."

(*Sahih Bukhari and Sahih Muslim*)

According to the collection of authentic traditions compiled by *Imam Muslim*, Hazrat Abu Huraira quotes the Holy Prophet (S.A.W.) to have said:

"You will not enter the Heaven without being a believer and as long as there is no love and affection among you people, you will not become believers. Shall I tell you of the mode of behaviour that may intensify the feelings of affection among you? Increase the practice of saying" *Assalamo Alaikum*" to each other.

2. *Enquiring after welfare.*

Hazrat Abu Musa quotes the Prophet (S.A.W.) to have said, "Go to visit the patient and enquire after his health, feed the hungry, and liberate the captive."

(*Shahih-al-Bukhari*).

According to Hazrat Abu Huraira, the Holy Prophet (S.A.W.) said, "The Muslims enjoy five rights to one another:

(1). Reciprocation of greeting.

(2). Visiting the sick to ask after welfare.

(3). Attending funerals.

(4). Acceptance of invitation.

(5). To pray for Allah's mercy when a Muslim sneezes.

(*Bukhari and Muslim*)

3. *Extending help in Need.*

Hazrat Ibn 'Umar (R.A.A.) narrated the following tradition of the Holy Prophet (S.A.W.):

"One Muslim is brother to another Muslim. He neither does wrong to his brother nor leaves him in the lurch. Whoever helps his brother in need, Allah fulfills his need. The Muslim who relieves his brother of distress or trouble, Allah will deliver his from one of his tribulations on the Doomsday and theMuslim who clothes his brother, will be provided with clothing by Allah (will hide his blemishes) on the Day of Judgment."

(*Sahih Bukhari and Sahih Muslim*)

4. *Sending Presents on Various Occasions.*

Imam Tabarani quotes a saying of the Holy Prophet (S.A.W.) which is as follows:

"Give present to one another and you will intensify mutual affection."

We find in the same book another tradition attributed to Hazrat Aisha (R.A.A.) who quotes the Prophet (S.A.W.) to have said, "O women of believers, give presents to one another, even if the present consists of the hoof of a goat. This would intesify affection between you and rid you of malice."

Imam Malik quotes the following tradition in *Al-Muatta:*

"Shake hands. This act does away with malice. Exchange gifts with one another. This puts an end to animosity."

Believer's rights of perpetual fellowship implies the rights of limited fellowship. Such fellowship includes the companionship of a fellow traveller, class-fellow, one belonging to the same profession, that is a colleague. The Holy Quran treats such companions as fellows at par. The colleague or co-worker should treat his colleagues and co-workers kindly, sympathetically, respectfully. They must have a spirit of sacrifice for the security of one another and must foster the spirit of mutual cooperation. One companion has a right to excellent treatment by another companion.

6. The Rights of venerable Elders.

1. *Who is venerable Elder*

A venerable elder is one who is not only senior in age but also superior in respect of knowledge, righteousness, rank, nobility of character and esteem. If such elders have sincerity of faith and lead themselves on the way laid down by their Lord (that is, Islam), then it is incumbent on others to revere them and acknowledge their superiority and respect their rights. By doing this, they would be acting on the Prophet's (S.A.W.) edicts according to which the elders coming up to standard explained above are superior. Besides, we shall thus be respecting the rights that Islam provides for the elders.

Following are a few relevant sayings of theHoly Prophet (S.A.W.):

(1) *Tirmizi* quotes a tradition narrated by Hazrat Anas (R.A.A.). According to this tradition the Prophet (S.A.W.) said, "If a young man respects an old man because of his age, Allah will provide a man who will respect him when he is old."

(2) *Abu Dawood* and *Tirmizi* quote a tradition as narrated by Hazrat 'Amr bin Shoaib with reference to his grandfather. It runs as follows:

The Prophet (S.A.W.) said, "He is not one of us who has had no compassion for our youngsters and who has not acknowledged the rights of our elders."

(3). According to *Abu Dawood*, Hazrat Abu Musa (R.A.A.) reported the Prophet (S.A.W.) to have said, "To respect an aged Muslim, a man who has learnt the Holy Quran by heart and acts on its instead of being proud of it, and a just ruler is one of the signs of revering Allah."

2. Giving precedence to the elders in every matter. For instance, in congregation older people should be given precedence to the younger. Similarly an elderly person should be chosen to negotiate with the people. As Ibn Mas'ood has said according to Imam Muslim, "The Prophet (S.A.W.)

used to put his hand on our shoulders before the beginning of the congregation and asked us to line up equally and not to be behind or ahead of one another in the row as it is likely to cause discord in your hearts. The Prophet (S.A.W.) also said, "The people who are mature, sagacious and having religious wisdom should stand closest to me followed by others in order of importance.

3. **Mocking and Insulting the Elders is a bad habit.**

Mocking, insulting and afflicting the elders, misbehaving with them and talking to them rudely is despicable.

Imam Tabarani quotes in his *Al-Mo'jam-ul-Kabeer* a tradition narrated by Hazrat Abu 'Umama, wherein the Prophet (S.A.W.) is reported to have said: Only a hypocrite can insult the following three per sons:—

1. An aged Muslim (whose head is hoary)
2. A Scholar.
3. A just ruler.

It is clear from this tradition that according to the Shariah holding the elders in esteem and paying respect to them are the Islamic modes of social behaviour. It is, therefore, necessary for the guardians to teach the children such modes of conduct. But we shall have to inculcate in the children the following qualities.

1. *Modesty.*

This is a quality which induces men to give up bad habits, prevents them from committing any wrong act against elders and also induces them to give whatever is due to others.

2. *Rising to meet a visitor.*

According to the Islamic patterns of social behaviour one must get up to meet any visitor whether he is a traveller, a scholar or an elderly person. This mode of behaviour is a virtue and the child should be accustomed to it. This is borne out by the sayings of the Holy Prophet (S.A.W.) given below:

(1). According to *Imam Bukhari*, *Abu Dawood* and *Tirmizi*, Hazrat Aisha (R.A.A.) is reported to have observed, "I have never seen any one following the example of the Prophet (S.A.W.) more than his daughter Hazrat Fatima (R.R.A.) who emulated her father in rising and sitting and acquired all his habits and manners. When Hazrat Fatima

(R.A.A.) came to visit the Prophet (S.A.W.) he used to rise and move to receive her, kiss her and seated her in his own place. Similarly, when the Prophet (S.A.W.) paid a visit to Fatima (R.A.A.) she also rose to receive him, kissed him and seated him in her own place.

(ii).*Abu Dawood* cites a tradition narrated by Hazrat 'Umar bin Al-Saib. According to him, one day while the Prophet (S.A.W.) was sitting, the husband of his foster-mother arrived. The Prophet (S.A.W.) spread his cloth for the visitor to sit upon. Then came the Prophet's foster-mother. The Prophet (S.A.W,) spread his cloth from the other side for her on which she sat down. She was followed by his foster-brother. The Prophet (S.A.W.) rose from his place and seated his foster-brother before himself (the space where he had been sitting before).

There are, however, certain other traditions that prohibit rising to receive the visitor. But they apply to such visitors as are desirous of being respected and held in esteem by all the other people in order to gratify their ego. Thus it will be wrong to stand up for the reception of a self-conceited person, as it was customary with people in olden days to receive the proud members of aristocracy. The custom in those days was that the haughty noble man used to sit and the people stood around him respectfully.

3. *Kissing the hands of elders.*

It is also a mode of social behaviour that when a child meets an elderly person he kisses the former's hands. This inculcates a sense of respect in the child for the elders and will thereby learn to esteem every one in keeping with his rank, age and erudition. It is necessary for a child's moral improvement and social behaviour that those responsible for his breeding and education should begin acquainting him with the Islamic pattern of social behaviour right from his early childhood.

In a tradition the Prophet (S.A.W.) denounced such a custom describing it as Persian.

Kissing the elder's hands, an Islamic mode of social behaviour has been borne out by a number of traditions and Ulama have also endorsed it.

In this connection the gurardians should familiarize the children with the following precautions:

(a) The kissing should not be too long. This would make the child ignore evils and the purpose of respect etc. wich would cause a great harm to the child's personality in the final analysis.

(b) The limits laid down by Islam for the payment of respect should not be exceeded. For instance, it is wrong to bow or lower one's head while standing and to bow as one does in prayer while kissing the hand of the elders.

These, then, are the basic modes of behaviour whereby the rights of others can be repected. In view of their social importance, the guardians and parents are expected to teach the children the above mentioned Islamic modes of conduct in order to inculcate in them the spirit of respecting the people older than themselves. The child should be told at an early stage of the rights of old people to those who are younger and also how to pay repect and esteem to those who are more educated, and higher in rank and position.

7. Conformity to the Social Patterns of Behaviour.

One of the principles of training the new generation on social principles as laid down by Islam is that the child should be taught the modes of social behaviour in his early years so that when he enters the stage of boyhood, the realities of social life may be comprehensible to him and consequently he will mete out benevolent treatment to the members of the community. His social behaviour would be the embodiment of affection compassion, kindness and moral excellence.

The principles prescribed by Islam in the moral and social training of children aim at achieving the results indicated above.

We chalk out the line here on which social training is to be imparted to children and also point out the responsibilities imposed on parents and guardians.

The following modes of behaviour should be taken into consideration in the social training of children.

(1). Modes of eating.

(2). Modes of greeting.

(3). Modes of seeking permission.
(4) Modes of behaving in a gathering.
(5). Modes of conversation.
(6). The manners of joking.
(7). The modes of congratulation or felicitation.
(8). The modes of asking after the welfare of the sick.
(9) The modes of condolence.
(10). Manners of sneezing and yawning.

We dwell at length on these modes so that they may be indelibly imprinted on the children's minds.

(1) Modes of Eating and Drinking

The parents and gurdians should instruct the children how to eat and also show them the manners of eating by practical demonstration.

(a) Manners of Eating.

(i). Washing both hands before and after eating. *Abu Dawood* and *Tirmizi* both quote the following Hadith with reference to Hazrat Salman Farsi (R.A.A.)

The Prophet (S.A.W.) said, "The blessing of eating consists in performing ablution (partial ablution) both before and after eating.

(ii) Saying *Bismillah* (meaning "I begin with the name of Allah, the Beneficent and Merciful" before beginning the meal and *Al Hamdo Lillah* (thanks giving prayer) after having had it.

Imam Abu Dawood and *Imam Tirmizi* quote Hazrat Aisha (R.A.A.) to have said "Whoever of you starts to have his meal should do it with the name of Allah and should he forget to do so, then he should say I begin with the name of Allah before and after it whenever he remembers to have forgotten it."

According to *Imam Ahmed* and others, whenever the Prophet (S.A.W.) ate anything he used to say the following thanksgiving prayer.

"Allsh is worthy of all praise who gave us to eat and drink and admitted us to the folds of Islam."

(iii) *Imam Muslim* and *Imam Bukhari* quote Hazrat Abu Huraira to have narrated that the Prophet (S.A.W.) never found faults with any edibles.If he felt like having anything, he ate it, otherwise left it.

(iv) *Imam Muslim* has recorded the following statement of Hazrat 'Amr bin Abi Salma (R.A.A.).

"I was still a child and was under the tutelage of the Holy Prophet. (S.A.W.). Once when I was having my meal my hand was moving fast on all sides of the dish. Thereupon the Prophet (S.A.W.) said, "You boy, say Allah's name, eat with your right hand, take your morsels from the nearest place."

(v) It is wrong to eat sitting against the support of anything. Eating with such a posture is indicative of laughter and is also injurious to health. *Imam Bukhari* mentions the following tradition of the Holy Prophet (S.A.W.) with reference to Wahab bin Abdullah.

The Prophet (S.A.W.) said, "I never have my meal sitting against the support of anything."

Imam Muslim quotes Hazrat Anas to have stated that he saw the Holy Prophet (S.A.W.) sitting on his buttocks and eating dates.

(vi) It is commendable to praise the dish or any item of meal. *Imam Muslim* quotes Hazrat Jabir to have narrated that once the Prophet asked one of his wives to bring curry. He was told that there was only vinegar in the house. He asked to let him have it and started eating bread with it. The Prophet praised vinegar again and again while eating it.

According to authentic traditions the Holy Prophet (S.A.W.) talked to his companions while having meals on several occasions.

(vii) It is commendable to pray for the welfare of the host after finishing the meals.

(viii) One should not start eating first in the presence of elders.

Imam Muslim cites a tradition narrated by Hazrat Anas. As the latter has it, "when the Holy Prophet (S.A.W.) finished his meal he licked his three fingers and said 'whenever a morsel falls, one should pick it up, clean it from the side on which it fell and eat it. He also asked us to clean the plate that contained curry with our fingers and lick them. He said you do not know which of your meals is blessed by

Allah."

(b) Manners of Drinking.

(i) One should say *'Bismillah'* and *"Thank God"* before drinking, and should drink with three pauses.

(ii) *Imam Tirmizi* quotes Hazrat Ibn Abbas to have narrated the following tradition:

The Prophet (S.A.W.) said, "Don't drink in a gulp like the camel. Rather drink pausing twice or thrice. When you start drinking it, do it with the name of Allah. When you remove the pots and crockery thank Allah."By removing the pots here is meant when one has had one's drink.

According to Hazrat Abu Huraira as cited by *Imam Bukhari* and *Imam Muslim*, the Holy Prophet (S.A.W.) forbade to drink water from the leather container by putting one's mouth to it (i.e. not to drink directly from the container) for this is incompatible with decorum. Another reason for refraining from drinking directly from the container is to prevent any insect from creeping into the container.

(iii). To refrain from blowing or exhaling into the drinking pot. *Imam Tirmizi* quotes Hazrat Ibn Abbas to have stated that the Prophet (S.A.W.) had forbidden to blow or exhale into the drinking pot. The harm of doing this is obvious from hygienic point of view. Moreover, it militates against collective taste.

(iv). It is commendable to be seated for eating and drinking. Imam Muslim cites a tradition of the Holy Prophet (S.A.W.) with reference to Hazrat Anas wherein the Holy Prophet (S.A.W.) is said to have forbidden to drink water while standing. Hazrat Qatada says, "We asked Hazrat Anas what about eating?" He replied, "To eat while standing is an act worse than drinking."

Imam Muslim states with reference to Hazrat Abu Huraira that the Holy Prophet (S.A.W.) forbade to drink water while standing and that whoever did it unwittingly, vomit it.

But there is also evidence that the Prophet (S.A.W.) also drank water while standing. But he did this in keeping with the occasion. Thus when the situation requires that one should drink while standing one should prefer doing so rather than sitting down to drink.

(v) Prohibition of drinking with pots made of gold and silver.

Imam Bukhari and *Imam Muslim* cite a tradition with reference to Umm Salama (R.A.A.) wherein the Prophet (S.A.W.) is reported to have said, "whoever drinks with silver or gold pot, he fills his stomach with the fire of Hell."

The wordings of the tradition quoted by Hazrat *Imam Muslim* are as follows:

"Whoever drank with silver or gold pot, poured into his stomach the fire of hell." (The reason for this prohibition is that the use of silver and gold is the expression of one's pride and greatness, which injures the poor people's sense of self respect.

(vi) Prohibition of Overeating.

Imam Ahmed, Imam Tirmizi and others quote the following tradition .

The Prophet (S.A.W.) said, "There is no pot worse than the stomach that man fills to the brim. Man should have only as many morsels as are sufficient to keep his back straight. If it is absolutely necessary to eat more than that then should reserve one third of his stomach for food, one third for water and one third for respiration."

The tutors and guardians should teach the children the manners of eating as explained above so that they may learn how to conduct themselves in social life.

(2). Modes of Greeting

There are also modes of greeting. The tutors are required to accustom the children to such modes:

Modes of greeting involve the following elements that have been explained below in order of importance:

(i). Greeting is an injunction of the Shariah. This injunction is contained in the following verses of the Holy Quran:

"O ye who believe! Enter not the houses other than your own first announcing your presence and invoking peace upon the folk thereof." (24:27).

Again,

"When ye enter houses, salute one another with a greeting from Allah, blessed and sweet." (24:61) (ii). The manner of greeting:

The man who is the first to greet should say:

As salamo Alaikum wa Rahmatullahe wa Barakatuhoo

(May you be safe and may Allah have mercy upon you and shower upon you His blessings).

The man greeted should also wish him in the same way using the pronoun in the second person through the man so greeted should be a single person. The words of the reciprocal greetings are the same with only one additional letter at the beginning:

"*Wa 'alaikumus salam wa Rahmatullahe wa Barakatuhoo.*" (And may you also be safe and may Allah have mercy upon you and shower upon you His blessings.)

This method of greetings owes its origin to the authentic traditions of the Holy Prophet (S.A.W.).

Abu Dawood and Tirmizi cite the following tradition as narrated by Hazrat Imran bin Husain:

"A man came to the Holy Prophet (S.A.W.) and greeted him saying *As salamo Alaikum.*" The Prophet (S.A.W.) reciprocated his greeting in the same words. The man then sat down. The Prophet said to him: Ten good acts (to your credit). Another came and greeted the Prophet (S.A.W.) saying '*Assalamo Alaikum wa Rahmatullah*' and sat down. The Prophet (S.A.W.) wished him in the same words and said, ' Twenty good acts (to your credit), then appeared a third man who greeted the Prophet (S.A.W.) saying '*Assalamo Alaikum wa Rahmatullahe wa Barakatuhoo.*' The Prophet (S.A.W.) reciprocated his greeting in the same words. When this man also sat down, the Prophet (S.A.W.) said to him: Thirty good acts (to your credit).

(iii). The conditions and manners of greeting.

One on horseback should greet one on foot. The man on foot should greet one seated. Minority of people should greet majority, and the younger one should greet the older one. This is borne out by a tradition narrated by Hazrat Abu Huraira and quoted by *Imam Muslim* and *Imam Bukhari.*

(iv) The mode greeting Non-Muslim is prohibited. *Imam Tirmizi* quotes a tradition with reference to 'Amr bin Shoaib which was narrated to him by his grandfather. The words of the tradition are, "The Prophet (S.A.W.) said that the man does not belong to us who adopts the fashion of Non-Muslims. You neither imitate the Jews nor the Christians. The Jews salute by signing with fingers and the Christians salute with their palms."

The Prophet (S.A.W.) has given the Muslims a distinct pattern of social behaviour by fordidding them to greet in the fashion of the Jews and Christians.

(v) The Children should be the first to greet.

The children should be taught to greet the elders first. The Prophet (S.A.W.) himself greeted the children when he went past by them. As Muslim it is incumbent upon us to follow the Prophet (S.A.W.) who was the first guide for the whole of mankind.

Imam Bukhari and *Imam Muslim* both quote the tradition narrated by Hazrat Anas wherein the Prophet (S.A.W.) is reported to greet the children as he passed by them and this was customary with him.

(vi). The greeting of the Non-Muslims should be reciprocated only by saying "*Walaikum*" and the Muslims should not greet them first.

Imam Muslim and *Imam Bukhari* quote a tradition to this effect with reference to Hazrat Anas. It runs as follows:

"The Prophet (S.A.W.) said: When you are greeted by the people of Book you should reciprocate their greeting by simply saying '*Walaikum.*'

Besides, there is a tradition in *Sahih Muslim* wherein the Prophet (S.A.W.) is quoted to have said, "You should not be the first to greet the Jews and the Christians."

The children should, therefore, be told not to take the lead in greeting the Non-Muslims.

Ibn Sanni narrates this tradition of the Holy Prophet (S.A.W.):

The Prophet (S.A.W.) said: Whoever receprocated salam, peace is upon him and whoever does not reciprocate not one of us."

Abu Dawood's wordings of the same tradition are: Allah regards that man among human-beings as closer to Him who takes the leading in bidding salam to the people.

The tutors and the guardians should also tell the children of the circumstances wherein it is forbidden to greet. For instance, one busy performing ablution, bathing, taking his meal or fighting in the battlefield need not greet. Similarly a person should not be greeted when he is busy reciting the Holy Quran, remembering Allah, saying *labbaik* during Haj, giving sermon on Friday or delivering a speech in the mosque, teaching Islamic jurisprudence, or any other subject, discussing academic problems, giving a call to prayer (Azan) or saying *'Iqamat'* at the time of prayer, doing personal work or deciding a matter or settling a dispute. If any one greets a person in the circumstances mentioned above, it will not be necessary for the latter to reciprocate his greeting.

The children should be taught the manners of greeting and acquainted with the conditions laid down for it.

(3). Mode of Seeking Permission

There are certain set modes of seeking permission also. The guardians should accustom the children to these modes, enabling to fulfill the requirements mentioned in the Holy Quran. Says Allah:

> O ye who believe! Let your slaves and those of you who have not come to puberty, ask leave of you at three times (before they come into your presence): Before the prayer of dawn and when ye lay aside your raiment for the heat of noon and after the prayer of night. Three times of privacy for you. It is no sin for them or for you at other times, when some of you go round attendent upon others (if they come into your presence without leave). Thus Allah maketh clear the revelations for you. Allah is Knower, Wise.
>
> And when the children among you come to puberty, then let them ask leave even as those before them used to ask it. Thus Allah maketh clear His revelations for you. Allah is Knower, Wise" (24: 58-59)

In the above verses Allah commands the parents and tutors to teach children who have not reached the age of puberty to seek permission to go into the presence of the member of the family on three occasions:

(1). Before the morning prayer; for the people are asleep

in their beds at that time.

(2). In the afternoon when one takes one's meridian nap. At this time one is usually undressed.

(3). After the night prayer; for this is the time of rest and going to bed.

The Shariat's requirement for seeking permission at these three times is necessitated by the fact that grown up men and women do not like the children to be in their presence.

But when the children come of age, they are under the obligation to seek permission at other times as well besides the three times specified above:

"And when the children among you come to puberty, then let them ask leave even as those before you used to ask them."

Then the children are trained on the lines specified by Islam as above, they will grow up to be models of social behaviour.

There are certain other manners and conditions of seeking permission, which are adumbrated as under:

(1). One should first greet and then seek permission.

Abu Dawood states that a man belonging to Banu 'Aamir came to visit the Holy Prophet (S.A.W.) who was at home at the moment. The words in which he sought permission were "May I come in?" The Prophet (S.A.W.) asked his servant to go out and tell the man how to seek permission. "Tell him", said the Prophet (S.A.W.), "Say Assalamo Alaikum. May I come in." The visitor overheard the Prophet's instruction and said, "Assalamo Alikum. May I come in?" The Prophet (S.A.W.) then allowed him to enter.

(2). Introducing One's self

Imam Bukhari and *Imam Muslim* quote Hazrat Abu Musa to have narrated:

"Once as the Holy Prophet (S.A.W.) was sitting at coping stone of a garden well, Hazrat Abu Bakr asked for permission to come. Abdu Musa asked: 'Who is there?' 'This is Abu Bakr' was the answer. Then came Hazrat 'Umar and asked for permission. He too had to tell his name. The next to come was Hazrat 'Usman who asked for permission in the same manner. Abu Musa asked again, 'Who? Hazrat Osman told his name in reply.

Sahih Bukhari and *Sahih Muslim* contain this tradition narrated by Hazrat Jabir. "I went to visit the Prophet (S.A.W.) and knocked at the door. The Prophet (S.A.W.) asked: "Who is it?' I said, 'This is I.' The Prophet (S.A.W.) repeated: 'I', 'I'. The Prophet (S.A.W.) did not like saying 'I'.

(3). Permission should be asked for thrice.

(i) According to *Sahih Bukhari* and *Sahih Muslim* a tradition narrated by Hazrat Abu Musa Al Ash'ari (R.A.A.) is as under:

"The Prophet (S.A.W.) said: 'permission may be asked for thrice. If you get it, well and good; otherwise go back."

One had better wait after the first knock as long as one requires to finish four 'rakats' of a prayer. May be that the man from whom permission sought happens to say prayers or be in the bath room.

(4). The Door should be tapped gently.

Care should be taken not to tap forcefully the door of one's father, teacher or any other venerable elder in particular.

Imam Bukhari quotes a tradition narrated by Hazrat Anas according to which the people used to tap the Prophet's door with their fingers.

(5) When asking for permission, one should stand on a side of the door.

This is necessary as it is possible that a woman appears when the door is opened; for the very purpose of asking for permission is that to avoid the sight of what is behind the door, as the Prophet (S.A.W.) exhorted his companions. Imam Bukhari and Imam Muslim quote the Prophet (S.A.W.) to have said, "Vision is the reason for the need to seek permission."

Hazrat Abdullah bin Busr (R.A.A.) narrates that he heard the Prophet (S.A.W.) say: "Do not enter the houses of others from the front but ask for permission to enter while standing aside. If you are permitted, well and good; otherwise go back." (*Al Mo'jamul Tabarani*)

(6) If the members of the family ask the visitor to go back, he should do so accordingly. Says Allah:

"O ye who believe! Enter not houses other than your own without first announcing your presence and invoking peace upon the folk thereof. That is better for you, that ye may be heedful.

And if ye find no one therein, still enter not until permission hath been given. And if it be said unto you: Go away again, then go away; for it is purer for you."

(24: 27-28)

If the person asking for permission is told to go away, he should not take ill or be angry.

These are the essential rules of seeking permission, which the children ought to be taught by their guardians and parents. This is necessary for the smooth interaction of the members of the society.

(4) Modes of Attending Social Gatherings.

There are also certain modes of attending social functions or gatherings, which the children ought to be acquainted with.

(i) Shaking hands.

According to *Ibn Al Sanni* and *Abu Dawood*, the Holy Prophet (S.A.W.) said, "When the two Muslims meet they should shake hands, praise Allah and prayer for each other's forgiveness so that Allah may forgive them."

Imam Tirmizi and *Ibn Majah* quote Hazrat Braa to have narrated this tradition: "The Prophet (S.A.W.) said: When two Muslims shake hands at the time of meeting, Allah forgives their sins before they separate."

Imam Malik quotes in his *Al Moatta* a tradition of the Holy Prophet (S.A.W.) with reference to Hazrat 'Ata-ul Khorasani (R.A.A.). As Hazrat 'Ata has it, "The Prophet (S.A.W.) said to me: Shake hand with each other. This will rid you of malice. Exchange presents, this will intensify the feelings of affection for each other and put an end to animosity."

(ii) One should take one's seat where the host wants.

This is because the host knows where the guest is to be seated and this is the right of the guest. There is an old saying: "The owner of the house knows who is in his house."

(iii). One should sit in front of the people and not between them.

This is a manifestation of consummate pattern of social life, for if one sits in the middle of the gathering, others would be at one's back, which would cause them inconvenience and they will reprove one in their heart.

Imam Dawood quotes with reference to acknowledged authorities a tradition narrated by Hazrat Huzaifa bin Alyaman (R.A.A.) It runs as follows:

"Cursed is the man who sits in the middle of a circle."

Imam Tirmizi cites an incident with reference to Abu Mijlaz. As the latter has it: "A man sat down in the middle of a circle. Hazrat Huzaifa said: In the words of Muhammad (S.A.W.) cursed is the man who sat in the middle of a circle."

(iv) One should not sit between two men without their permission.

Abu Dawood quotes a tradition to the effect that it is not permissible for any one to sit between two persons without their permission.

(v)One who arrives at the venue of a gathering should sit wherever he finds room.

Abu Dawood and *Tirmizi* quote a relevant tradition with reference to Hazrat Jabir bin Samurah (R.A.A.), who narrates: "Whenever we went to join any meeting of the Holy Prophet (S.A.W.), every one of us sat down wherever he could find a place."

This injunction applies to the person who often attended the meetings. But if the person coming to attend a meeting is a scholar or one holding a high position, then the members of the host family or those present at the moment may give him a place he deserves according to the edict of the Holy Prophet (S.A.W.).

We have already mentioned that when the delegation of Abdul Qais came to visit the Holy Prophet (S.A.W.) he welcomed it, made room for its members and seated on his right side the head of the delegation, Munzir bin 'Aaid. The Prophet (S.A.W.) meted out kind and affectionate treatment to him.

(vi). To refrain whispering to each other in the presence of a third person.

According to *Imam Muslim* and *Imam Bukhari*, the Holy Prophet (S.A.W.) said, "Where there are three of you together, do not whisper to each other without taking into confidence the third person present. This would sadden him."

(Narrated by H. Abdullah bin Masood)

The reason for the prohibition of whispering is that it would cause doubts in the minds of the third person. He would also be grieved by being ignored. However, if there are four or more persons together and two of them talk to each other without being overheard, then whispering in such a case is not forbidden provided that it is not likely to cause any doubts or misapprehension.

(vii). The person who has to leave a meeting on business and who returns later has greater right to the place where he had been sitting than any other person.

Thus *Imam Muslim* quotes Hazrat Abu Hurairah to have narrated that the Prophet (S.A.W.) said, "When any of you leaves a gathering and returns later on, he has greater right to his place."

(viii) Asking for permission before leaving.

As the Prophet (S.A.W.) said, it is because of one's catching sight that permission has to be sought. This rule applies to both coming and leaving. Islam has laid down this rule of seeking persmission for the sake of the sanctity, honour and purity of homes.

(ix) Praying as penitence for the proceedings of a meeting.

Imam Hakim refers to this tradition narrated by Hazrat Abu Hurairah: "Whoever rises to leave a meeting he should say this prayer: 'O Lord! Thou art Pure and all praise is due to Thee. I bear witness that there is no god other than Thee worthy of worship. I beg Thy forgiveness and repent before Thee.' One of the present said to the Prophet (S.A.W.): 'You never said before what you are saying now.' The Prophet (S.A.W.) told him that it was the repentance of what was said in the meeting."

The parents and guardians are under the obligation to teach the children the modes of attending an assembly. They should themselves abide by rules laid down for the purpose and make the children to follow them.

(5) Modes of Conversation or Talk

The parents and guardians should also focus their attention on the modes of talking. They should teach the children talk politely and the modes of talking characteristic of Islamic decorum. When such training begins in the early stage the child will have learnt in his discretionary years how to talk and how to listen patiently. He will also know the delightful mode of talking.

We give here some such modes of talking for the guidance of the guardians and the tutors.

(i) Eloquence.

The style of talking or conversation should be eloquent and the language used should be simple and chaste.

(ii) Talking with a pause.

This is also a civil way of talking. It would enable the person or audience listening to the speaker fully understand what he means. The Prophet's conversation was alternated by pauses. His practice ought to be followed by us all.

Imam Bukhari and *Imam Muslim* quoted a tradition narrated by Hazrat Aisha (R.A.A.) that runs as follows:

> "The Holy Prophet (S.A.W.) did not like you to talk ceaselessly. On the contrary he used to state everything separately. If any one wanted to count the things, she said, could do so.

Imam Ismaeel cites the same tradition with a few other words also. As he has it: "The Prophet (S.A.W.) spoke in such a way that everything was crystal clear to the mind."

Abu Dawood quotes the tradition attributed to Hazrat Aisha (R.A.A.) wherein she says: "His conversation was divided by pauses with the result that every one who heard it could understand what he said clearly.

(iii). Flowery style of speaking should be avoided.

To identify subtleties and talk with affected eloquence is against the good manners of speech. *Imam Abu Dawood* and *Imam Tirmizi* quote Hazrat 'Umar (R.A.A.) to have narrated, alluding to acknowledged authorities, that the Prophet (S.A.W.) observed, "Allah does not like the man or woman who speaks in an affected manner."

By affected manner is meant to move the tongue the way that a cow does while playing with it.

Hazrat Anas narrates a tradition as quoted by *Imam Muslim* and *Imam Bukhari* wherein it is stated: "Whenever the Prophet (S.A.W.) said something he repeated it three times so that one may fully grasp it.

Whenever he visited any family, he talked in a manner that every word he said was comprehensible. His talk was neither verbose, nor wanting in words. It was neither characterised by affected eloquence, nor lacked in real eloquence. He did not like talking by opening one's mouth in an affected manner."

(iv) Talking in keeping with the level of the understanding of the person addressed to.

Islamic modes of talking also include speaking in accordance with the people's culture, level of understanding and age. Says the Prophet (S.A.W.):

"We, the group of Allah's messengers have been commanded to speak to the people keeping in view their level of understanding."

In *Sahih Bukhari* we find this *Hadith* attributed to Hazrat Ali (R.A.A.):

"Talk to the people according to their knowledge and capacity to comprehend. Would you like that Allah and His messenger are repudiated."

In *Sahih Muslim* this tradition of the Prophet (S.A.W.) is given with reference to Hazrat Abdullah bin Masood (R.A.A.):

"If you say to the people a thing incomprehensible to them, it may prove to be trial for some of them or may create trouble for them."

(v) The talk should not overtax the mind or patience of the listener.

Doing justice to conversation is also included in the modes of speech. The talk should not be so lengthy that it bores the listener, nor too brief to overtax his understanding. The style of talking should be charming and interesting.

Imam Muslim quotes Hazrat Tahir bin Samura to have said, "I used to pray with the Holy Prophet (S.A.W.). His prayer was of medium duration. His sermon too was moderate."

(vi). Paying full attention to the speaker.

Paying full attention to the speaker is also a requisite of the Islamic mode of behaviour. This would enable the listener to bear in mind what the speaker says. When the Holy Prophet (S.A.W.) addressed his companions, they attached great importance to everything he said and listened to him spell-bound.

The Prophet (S.A.W.) himself gave full attention to anyone who talked to him.

(vii) The speaker should keep turning to all the audience.

The speaker should cast his glance frequently to all the people attending the meeting. He should not confine his attention to only any one section of the audience lest any individual should have the impression that the speaker was addressing him to the exclusion of others.

(viii). The speaker should have liberal attitude towards the audience, both during and after the speech.

Another requisite of good conversation or talk is that speaker should adopt a liberal attitude towards those present in the meeting, both during and after the speech or conversation, lest they should feel bored.

We find a tradition in *Musnad Imam Ahmed* narrated by Umm Darda. She says, "Abu Darda used to smile while talking. I told him to refrain from smiling, or else the people might think that he was mad. Abu Darda said, "I have never seen or heard the Prophet (S.A.W.) talk to the people without a smile." So whenever Abu Darda spoke he smiled following the example of the Holy Prophet (S.A.W.).

Imam Muslim narrates a tradition with reference to Hazrat Sammak bin Harb wherein the latter is reported to have said, "I asked Tahir bin Samura if he attended the meetings of the Holy Prophet (S.A.W.). Hazrat Tahir replied in the affirmative and told me that the Prophet (S.A.W.) never rose from the Musalla (Carpet used for prayer) on which he led the morning prayer till the daybreak. His companions talked to him while he remained seated. They used to relate the anecdotes of the days of pagan ignorance and laughed while the Prophet (S.A.W.) smiled."

These then are the Islamic modes of speech and conversation which the children ought to be accustomed to.

(6) The Mode of Being Humorous

A toiling and serious Muslim's life will be delightful if it is reasoned with jest, laughter, witty remarks and sweet conversation.

How nice does a Muslim really look when he enchants the people with his exquisite and delightful conversation. Islam too expects the Muslim to be loving, humorous, mirthful, smiling and laughing, jovial, polite with excellent habits, so that all the people may praise his character and modes of social behaviour and that he may attract the people by his sweet personality and the people may like to sit around him. Islam wants the children to be trained on such a pattern that the people are pleased by their behaviour. Complaisant pattern of behaviour is absolutely essential for the formation of a good social set up.

But it does not behove a Muslim to adopt whatever humorous attitude he chooses. In fact, there are certain modes of humorous behaviour which a Muslim should cling to.

(i) Excess of humour is forbiddin

As an after effect of too much joking one is dejected. Excess of joking also intensifies humility and people younger in age take liberties with their elders on account of it. It was for this reason that Hazrat 'Umar (R.A.A.) observed, "Whoever laughs too much does so at the cost of his dignity and whoever is in the habit of making fun, is slighted."

(ii)Jest should not aim at distressing any one.

One may joke with the members of one's family, relatives, brothers and intimate friends provided that the joke should not be in the nature of mockery designed to insult or distress anyone.

We cite here the tradition of the Holy Prophet (S.A.W.) wherein distressing fun is forbidden.

We come across a tradition in *Sunan Abi Dawood* and *Sunan Tirmizi* with reference to Abdullah bin Saib. It was told to him by his father as narrated by his grandfather. The latter, according to the tradition heard the Prophet (S.A.W.), "None of you should take away anything belonging to your brother-in-faith by way of jest. If anyone has taken the lathi of his brother, he should return it to the owner."

In Sunan *Abu Dawood* there is a tradition attributed to Abdur Rahman bin Abi Laila who heard it from the Prophet's companions. It runs as follows:

"Once we were on our way accompanied by the Holy Prophet (S.A.W.). One of the companions fell asleep. Another companion strode towards dragging a rope with his hand. The touch of the rope terrified the former. The Prophet (S.A.W.) observed: It does not behove a Muslim to frighten another Muslim."

During the Battle of Trenches (Khandaq) Hazrat Zaid bin Sabit (R.A.A.) was carrying stones along along with other Muslims. As he was doing this he felt drowsy. Ammara bin Hazm stealthily drew near him and picked up his arms unawares. But the Prophet (S.A.W.) checked him form such an act.

According to a Hadith cited by Imam Yazid, *Tabarani* and *Ibn Hikam*, Hazrat 'Aamir bin Rabia narrates that a person took away the shoes of another person unawares and hid it by way of jest. When the Prophet (S.A.W.) was informed of this incident, he said, "Do not terrify and harass a Muslim. This is a great sin."

The man is a great sinner indeed who ridicules and backbites by way of jest and does not only turn his target into a disdainful figure but commits a profane act. Such a person is undoubtedly guilty of an unlawful act, whether he knows it or not.

(iii). Abstinence from lying and fabrication.

In social functions jolly people sometimes tell comic stories, arousing laughter and delighting those present. But such stories are fictitious and give the illusion of truth. Islam forbids telling lies and taking the people in. The Prophet (S.A.W.) warns the man who is guilty of telling tales and deceives the people by fictitious stories for fun only.

Abu Dawood, *Imam Tirmizi* and *Imam Nasai* and *Imam Baihaqi* quote *Buhz bin Hakim* to have said that his grandfather heard the Holy Prophet (S.A.W.) observe: "Woe be to the man who makes the people laugh by telling lies. Woe be to him! Woe be to him!"

Imam Ahmed and *Abu Dawood* quote Hazrat Nuwas bin Sum'an to have narrated this tradition:

"The Prophet (S.A.W.) said: "The biggest breach of trust is that you tell your brother a lie giving him the illusion

Imam Ahmed and Imam Tabarani quote the Prophet (S.A.W.) to have said with reference to Abu Huraira, "A man's faith cannot be complete until he gives up telling lies by way of jest or in disputes, even if he ordinarily speaks the truth.

A very bad western custom which has crept into Muslim society is the joke of April Fool which consists of utter falsehood. This custom is absolutely incompatible with the Islamic pattern of social life. The custom of taking the people in by the custom of April Fool is unlawful. It consists of an evident lie and a sinister joke.

As the Companions of the Prophet (S.A.W.) were guided by his practice in all aspects of their life, they bore in mind all his sayings with regard to jest as well and acted accordingly. We cite here a few traditions that refine our sense of humour and teach us how to make jokes.

(i). In *Sunan Abu Dawood* a tradition is quoted with reference to Hazrat Auf bin Al Ashja'e, wherein Hazrat Auf is reported to have said, "I went to see the Prophet (S.A.W.) when the Battle of Tabook was being fought. The Prophet (S.A.W.) was in a tent at the moment. I saluted him and the Prophet (S.A.W.) reciprocated and said, 'Come in.' I asked him, "Shall I enter with the whole of my body?" The Prophet (S.A.W.) said, 'Do enter with the whole of your body."

(ii). According to Hazrat Hasan Basri as quoted by *Imam Tirmizi* an old woman came to the Holy Prophet (S.A.W.) and beseeched him for praying to Allah to let her enter the Garden. The Prophet (S.A.W.) said that no old woman would enter the Heaven. The woman returned crying over her fate. The Prophet (S.A.W.) then asked some one to tell her that she will not enter the Heaven as an old woman. Says Allah:

Lo: We have created them a (new) creation and made them virgin, (56: 35,36).

What the Prophet (S.A.W.) meant was when entering the woman will be young.

It is incumbent upon the parents and gardians to be conscious of the Prophet's mode of being humorous in the light of the above traditions, and also train the children accordingly, so that they may follow the example of the Prophet (S.A.W.) in their social behaviour.

(7) Modes of Felicitation

The children should also be taught the manners of congratulation in the course of their social and moral training. This is necessary to inculcate in them love for the society and strengthen their bonds of affection with their kinsmen, friends and others whom they brush their shoulders with. There are numerous occasions on which we congratulate one another. The guardians and parents should get their children and pupils visit the people who would warmly felicitate them on religious festivals and occasions of festivities. This would imbue them with the warmth and pleasure of felicitation and they would thus be accustomed to congratulate one another on such occasions.

As every good act ensures a reward in the Hereafter, congratulating a Muslim, pleasing and treating him politely and affectionately is reckoned as an act that brings him closer to Allah. With Allah it is the most desirable act after the essential duties. In fact, it is the cause of getting one's sins forgiven, and thereby paving the way for one's entry into Heaven.

We now proceed to deal with some modes of felicitation.

(a) The incident relating to Hazrat Ka'b bin Malik's repentance, its acceptance and the people's felicitation to him has been stated in both *Sahih Bukhari* and *Sahih Muslim*. It is as follows:

Hazrat Ka'b bin Malik said: I heard someone crying loudly, O Ka'b bin Malik! There is something for you to be delighted. Then came the people with good tidings. I set out to visit the Holy Prophet (S.A.W.). On my way I met with people in groups after groups congratulating on the acceptance of my repentance. They said: Congratulations! Allah has accepted your repentance.' At the last I arrived at the mosque. There I saw the Holy Prophet (S.A.W.) surrounded by a cluster of people. Talha bin Abdullah came running to me, shook hands and felicitated me. When I greeted the Holy Prophet (S.A.W.), his face was glowing with joy. He congratulated me in these words: Good tiding to you of the best day in your life since your mother brought you forth.

(b) Use of Polite Language for Extending Felicitation and Benedictory Formula.

The Prophet (S.A.W.) exhorts to use delightful and kind words for congratulation. It is necessary for a Muslim to learn by heart the benedictory formulae for the purpose suited to the occasion. We reproduce below such formulae recited by the Holy Prophet (S.A.W.) and quoted by our righteous forbears.

1. Benedictory Formula to be recited on the birth of a child.

« بورك لك بالموهـوب . وشكرت الواهب ، ورزقت برّه ، وبلغ أشدّه »

May thou be blessed in what Allah has bestowed upon their. Thank him for what He has bestowed upon thee. Thou hast been bestowed upon a good soul. May this child grow and come of age and complete the full span of life.

The man who is felicitated should reciprocate the above benedicite by invocation of blessings in the following words:

« بارك الله لـك ، وبارك عليـك ورزقك الله مثله »

May Allah bless you with abundance of blessings and bestow upon you, too, a child like this.

The two formulae reproduced above have been cited by Hazrat Hasan al Basri (R.A.) with reference to Hadrat Husain bin Ali (R.A.A.).

2. Welcoming a travelling person on returning home.

On such an occasion felicitation consists of the following words:

« الحمد لله الذي سلّمك ، وجمـع الشمل بـك وأكرمك »

All praise is due to Allah who has protected you, brought you back to your family and bestowed upon you His favour and kindness.

(8) To felicitate one returning from Hajj.

It is commendable that a person returning after performing pilgrimage is felicitated in the following words:

« قبل الله حجك ، وغفر ذنبك ، وأخلف نفقتك »؛

May Allah accept your Hajj, forgive your sins and bestow upon you more than what you have spent.

(9) Felicitation on Wedding.

Abu Dawood and *Tirmızi* etc. quote this tradition with reference to Hadrat Abu Huraira (R.A.A.) wherein the benedictory formula to be used in congratulating on the occasion of a marriage:

"The Prophet (S.A.W.) used to felicitate a person on his nuptial, while praying for his material welfare, offsprings and happy relations between the man and wife:

« بارك الله لك ، وبارك عليك ، وجمع بينكما في خير »

May Allah bless you abundantly and keep you united in goodness.

(10) Congratulation on the Occasion of Eid.

It has been stated in *Al Maqasid* that Khalid bin Me'dan met Wathila bin Asqa (R.A.A.) on Eid day. He felicitated bin Asqa (R.A.A.) in the following words:

« تقبل الله منا ومنك »

"May Allah accept from me and from you too."

Wathila (R.A.A.) repeated the same words. These benedictory words of felicitation are traceable to the Holy Prophet (S.A.W.). In the light of this tradition it is commendable for Muslims to congratulate each other on the occasion of Eid in the words mentioned above.

(11) How to honour the benefactor?

The benefactor should be thanked in the following words:

« بارك الله لك في أهلك ومالك ، وجزاك الله خيراً »

May Allah bless you and your family and may bestow on you a better compensation than the good you have done."

The man to whom good is done should invoke the blessing of God for his benefactor in the following words:

« مَنْ صُنِعَ اليه معروف فقال لفاعله : » جزاك الله خيراً «

"May Allah compensate you with a better reward." If he does this he will say enough in praise of his benefactor.

The better way of felicitating and thanking is to use the words of prayer and benediction in accordance with the Prophet's tradition. If any one is desirous of congratulating or thanking in the best possible words, he should, in any case, make sure that he does not use the words of Non-Muslims, nor resorts to the pagan ways so that his Islamic identity may be manifest.

(12). Words of thanks to be used while accepting presents etc.

The Prophet (S.A.W.) specially urged on the Muslims to give presents on various occasions like the birth of a child, or one's returning home from a journey or bringing home one's wife after the wedding.

Imam Tabarani and *Hasan-al-Askari* quote Hadrat Aisha (R.A.A.) to have advised the Muslims: "Exchange gifts among yourselves and make migration your peculiarity. Your sons will be esteemed. And ignore the faults of your elders."

Imam Tabarani cites a tradition in his *Al-Mo'jam* with reference to Hadrat Aisha (R.A.A.) wherein the Holy Prophet (S.A.W.) is reported to have said:

"O believing women! Send gifts to each other even if the gift be the hoof of a goat. This increases mutual affection and does away with malice."

We find with broken sequence a tradition narrated by Hadrat Abu Huraira (R.A.A.) in Imam Bukhari's *Adabal-Mufrad* and the *Musnad* of Imam Ahmed wherein the Prophet (S.A.W.) emphasizes the importance of exchanging gifts as this puts an end to animosity and pacifies anger.

Imam Tabarani quotes in his *Al Mo'jam-ul-Awsat*, Hadrat Aisha (R.A.A.) to have narrated (here too the chain of narration is broken) that the Prophet (S.A.W.) said, "Exchange gifts between yourselves as it increases mutual affection."

As exchange of gifts between the members of the society has in general been so greatly stressed, such an exchange of gifts and presents increases the bonds of love and unity and every indivdual of the Islamic society will be imbued with affection and good will.

The guardians and parents are advised to introduce this Islamic custom in their families so that the children may realize the importance of exchanging gifts.

Inquiring about the Health of the Sick.

The children should also be trained to share the grief and distress of others. When this quality is inculcated in them, they will develop affection and compassion for the people as well as the spirit of sacrifice. If such a sterling quality is imbibed in the children in their early years, it will become their second nature. They will never ignore the right of anyone, nor will shirk the fulfilment of obligations imposed upon them. They will, on the contrary, share the sufferings and grief of the members of the society as well as their joys and pleasures. This is what Islam aims at in the formation of a welfare society and the training of the offsprings. It is one of the basic principles of Islamic ethics.

In view of what has been stated above, Islam does not only enjoin upon the Muslim to visit the sick to enquire about their health but gives it the status of worship. It is also the right of one Muslim to another.

Imam Bukhari and Imam Muslim quote a tradition attributed to Hadrat Bara bin 'Aazib (R.A.A.) wherein the Prophet (S.A.W.) is to have enjoined upon us to visit the sick for asking about their health, join the funeral of a Muslim, say the prescribed formula when a Muslim sneezes, help the suffering and oppressed, respond to the call of a Muslim and introduce the custom of greeting one another.

It was in pursuance with these injunctions that the companions of the Holy Prophet (S.A.W.) took active part in welfare work and tried their utmost to secure a place in the Garden for themselves by adhering to all principles of good including visits to the sick.

(I) When and How to visit the sick for enquiring about their health.

(1) Visiting a sick person should not be delayed.

There is a saying of the Prophet (S.A.W.) to this effect: "When a Muslim is taken ill, visit him and enquire about his health."

It is evident from this *Hadith* that a sick man should be visited in the beginning of his illness.

However, there are some traditions according to which the sick man should be visited three days after his falling sick. Those traditions are as follows:

Ibn Majah and *Baihaqi* state that the Prophet (S.A.W.) used to pay a visit to a sick person three days after he fell sick.

Imam Tabarani states in his *Al Mo'jam-ul-Awsat* with reference to Hadrat Ibn Abbas (R.A.A.) that visiting the sick three days after the beginning of ailment was the practice of the Holy Prophet (S.A.W.).

A'mash narrates that he and his associates used to gather together every day. If any companion of theirs was absent for three days, they enquired about him. If it was found that he was indisposed, we visited him to ask about his health.

The author of the book concludes after putting all the traditions together that if the disease was acute, the sick person should be visited promptly, but if the illness is slight then one should pay a visit to him three days after start of his ailment.

(2). Enquiring about health in keeping with the disease.

If the disease is serious and the ailing person, particularly a woman, need someone to attend to him or her, visits to the sick person should not last long so that he may not be disturbed. But if visit to the sick is a solace to him, then the visitor may remain with him for some time.

It is preferable to visit a sick person every other day, provided that he is getting better. Says the Prophet (S.A.W.): "Visit the sick after proper intervals, so that mutual affection may increase."

(*Bazzaz, Baihaqi, Tabarani and Hakim*)

Imam Bukhari and *Imam Muslim* quote a tradition with reference to Hazrat Aisha (R.A.A.) according which: Whenever the Prophet (S.A.W.) visited any ailing member of his family to enquire about his or her health, he used to pat the sick person with his right hand and say the following prayer:

"O Allah! O Lord of mankind! Remove his ailment, restore his health, for Thou art the One who bestoweth remedy. Remedy is that which Thou bestoweth and which roots out the disease."

(3) It is commendable to enquire after the condition of the sick.

Imam Bukhari quotes Hadrat Ibn Abbas (R.A.A.) to have narrated that Hadrat Ali (R.A.A.) left the Prophet (S.A.W.) and went out when the latter was on his death-bed. The people asked him about the Prophet's health. Hadrat Ali (R.A.A.) replied that he was recovering, by the Grace of God.

(4) It is commendable to sit at the head of the sick person and enquire about his health.

Abu Dawood quotes a tradition attributed to Hadrat Ibn Abbas (R.A.A.) wherein it is narrated that whenever the Prophet (S.A.W.) visited a sick person, he sat beside his head and repeated the following words seven times:

« أسأل الله العظيم ربّ العرش العظيم أن يشفيك »

'I pray to Allah the Most High, Lord of the great Throne to restore your health."

If the ailing person's process of death is prolonged, then the above words had the soothing effect upon him.

(5) Praying for recovery and long life as a solace to the sick is commendable.

According to tradition cited by *Imam Tirmizi* and *Ibn Majah with* reference to Hadrat Abu Saeed Khudri (R.A.A.), the Prophet (S.A.W.) said, "When you visit a sick person, console him by praying for his long life. Although this produces no effect, yet the prayer does please the patient."

(6). If the ailing person is in the throes of death.

The patient should be asked to say the *Kalima Tayyiba* (i.e. there is no god but Allah).

According to Abu Sa'eed Khudri (R.A.A.) as quoted by *Imam Muslim*, the Prophet (S.A.W.) said, "Ask the dying man among you to say, there is no god but Allah."

Imam Abu Dawood and *Hakim* quote Hadrat Mo'az bin Jabal (R.A.A.) to have narrated:

"The Prophet (S.A.W.) said: The man whose last words are *La Ilaha Il-lallah* will enter the Heavens."

In view of the great stress laid by Islam on visiting the sick for asking about their health, every tutor and guardian is expected to accustom their pupils and wards to these Islamic patterns of social behaviour so that they may grow up to be the model individual of the future.

II. Modes of Condolence.

By condolence is meant to share the grief of the bereaved people and try to arrange their anguish by soothing words and say the words spoken by the Holy Prophet (S.A.W.) on such occasions to help them bear their loss.

Condolence of death and for that matter expression of sorrow over material loss is a commendable act. A Non-Muslim under the protection of Islamic state also deserves condolence and expression of sympathy over his loss.

According to Hadrat 'Amr bin Hazm (R.A.A.) as quoted by both *Ibn Majah* and *Baihaqi*, the Prophet (S.A.W.) said:

> "It can never be that Allah does not exalt the person who expresses sympathy with his brother-in-faith in distress."

Imam Tirmizi and *Baihaqi* quote Hadrat Abdullah bin Masood to have narrated this tradition:

> "The Prophet (S.A.W.) said: Whoever expresses sympathy will earn as much reward as the person in distress for patiently bearing his loss.

Condolence should be offered to all the relatives of the deceased whether they be grown up people or children as well as all the members of the bereaved family including both men and women. (However, condolence can be offered to a young woman only by her *mehram*, i.e. the man for whom she is forbidden). Condolences may be offered before the burial of the deceased or for three days thereafter.

(1) It is commendable to prepare meal for the bereaved family.

The Islamic *Shariah* treats it commendable to prepare meal to feed the bereaved family; for this constitutes a good act that relates to the reinforcement of social relationship. The bereaved family members are busy to prepare for the funeral of the deceased and are also overwhelmed by grief. It is therefore, commendable to arrange for their meals. This is testified by a tradition quoted by *Ibn Majah* and *Imam*

Tirmizi with reference to Hadrat Abdullah bin Ja'far (R.A.A.), wherein the Prophet (S.A.W.) is reported to have said, "Prepare meal for the family of Ja'far (R.A.A.). They are overwhelmed by a tragedy which allows them no time for anything else."

All the authorities on Islamic Shariah are unanimous that preparing meals for those who come to visit to offer condolences is abominable. They refer to a tradition narrated by Ibn Jareer (R.A.A.) to substantiate their position, "We all went together to the house of the deceased and prepared meal after the burial."

The feasts held during the time of condolence is extremely a sinister custom consisting of an innovation inconsistent with Islamic principles. There is no divine injunction to justify such feasting. The person visiting to offer condolence is under the obligation not to participate in a feast that is inconsistent with the Prophet's practice and the Islamic modes of conduct.

(2). How to reciprocate sentiments expressed in condolence.

If the members of the bereaved family are condoled by quoting the verses of the Holy Quran or in the words used for the purpose by the Prophet (S.A.W.), they should listen to them attentively and express humility.

One should not be guilty of sin by smiling, laughing, talking nonsense or indulging in irrelevant talk. This would cause distress to a bereaved person and is also a violation of decorum. The best way to condole the death of any one is to pray to Allah for the forgiveness of the deceased, expression of sorrow on his death and praising his virtues. This was the practice of our forefathers. Imam Dawood, Imam Nasai and Hadrat Abdullah bin 'Amr bin al 'Aas (R.A.A.) quote a lengthy tradition wherein it has been mentioned among other things that the Prophet (S.A.W.) asked Hadrat Fatimah R.A.A.) "O Fatimah! why have you come out of your house?"

Hadrat Fatimah (R.A.A.) replied, "I have been to the bereaved family of the deceased, prayed that his soul may rest in peace and offered condonence."

(3). If one sees something improper while offering one's condolence, one must counsel its prevention.

It sometimes happens that a bereaved person does indecorous acts when people offer condolence to him. For instance, he picks up the photograph of the deceased and embraces it; or people smoke tobacco while the Qari recites the verses of the Holy Quran; or melancholy tunes are on; or the visitors who come to express sympathy are feasted or many other things forbidden by the *Shariah* are done. In such cases the person offering condolence should apprise the people of the teachings of Islam and exhort them to abstain from such forbidden acts.

There cannot be the least doubt that the task of enjoining good requires didactic and judicious way of saying things, such as suits the occasion. Such an effective manner of exhortation opens the eyes of the wrong doer and he readily accepts counsel. In other words, wisdom expressed softly, changes a person completely and joins the ranks of the good and believing bondsmen of God. Says Allah:

> "Call the people to the path of thy Lord in a wise and most instructive manner and discuss with them in the best possible way." (46:125)

These then are the modes of condolence prescribed by Islam. The guardians are under the obligation to teach them to their children.

(III) Modes of behaviour at the time of sneezing and yawning.

The compulsory modes of behaviour to be taught to children also include those to be observed at the time of sneezing and yawning.

(1) How to behave when one sneezes.

The Prophet (S.A.W.) commands to observe the following modes of behaviour when sneezing.

(a) Praise of Allah and seeking His mercy.

This is apparent from the life of the Holy Prophet (S.A.W.) *Imam Bukhari* quotes a tradition narrated by Hazrat Abu Huraira (R.A.A.) wherein the Prophet (S.A.W.) observes: Whoever of you sneezes should say: "*Al hamdo Lillah* (All praise is due to Allah). And if any brother-in-faith who happens to be with him at the moment should say: "*Yar hamu-Kumul lah* (May Allah have mercy on you.) The person sneezing should reciprocate the sentiments of his companion by saying: *'Yah-di-kumul-lah'* May Allah keep you treading the right path and edify your heart.")

(b) If the person sneezing does not say: Al Hamd-o-lil-lah.

the person present should not say *Al Hamd-o-lil-lah.*

This instruction is contained in a tradition quoted by *Imam Muslim* with reference to Hadrat Abu Moosa (R.A.A.).

However, there is no harm if other people present say *Al-Hamdo-lil-lah.* in order to remind the sneezing person.

(c) Putting hand or handkerchief on the mouth while sneezing or trying to sneeze without making a noise.

There is a tradition quoted by *Abu Dawood* and *Tirmizi* with reference to Hadrat Abu Huraira (R.A.A.) wherein the Prophet (S.A.W.) is said to put a piece of cloth on his mouth while sneezing and thus prevented his sneezing from being heard.

According to Hadrat Abdullah bin Zubair (R.A.A.) as quoted by Ibn Al-sani, the Prophet (S.A.W.) said, "Allah does not like the noise made while yawning and sneezing."

(d) 'Tashmit' or saying Al-hamdo-lil-lah should not exceed three sneezes.

If a person sneezes continuously, any one present should say *Al-hamdo-lil-lah* only three times.

The above words are not to be repeated more than three times. According to a tradition quoted by Ibn Al-sani with reference to Hadrat Abu Huraira (R.A.A.), the Prophet (S.A.W.) said, "If any one of you is the person who happens to be with him should say *Al-hamd-o-lil-lah.* if he sneezes twice and thrice, the same words should be repeated each time, but if he goes on sneezing, *tashmit* should not be said, as the man suffers from cold."

Majority of *ulama* are of the opinion that though *tashmit* is not commendable after three sneezes, the person sitting with the man sneezing should pray for the health and welfare of the latter.

(e) How to react to the sneeze of a Non-Muslim.

According to a tradition quoted by *Abu Dawood* and *Tirmizi* with reference to Hadrat Abu Moosa Ash'ari (R.A.A.), the jews used to sneeze in the presence of the Holy Prophet (S.A.W.) intentionally hoping that the Prophet (S.A.W.)

would pray for Allah's mercy upon them by saying *yar-hamu-kumullah:* But the Prophet (S.A.W.) reacted to their sneezed by saying: *yah-di-kum-ullah wa asleh ba-lakum* (May Allah lead you to the right path and correct your condition.)

The words of '*tashmit*' are not to be said when a stranger or a young woman sneezes.

Tashmit in such cases is unnecessary according to a large number of *ulama*. However, *tashmit* in the case of an old woman is not forbidden.

Allama Ibn Jauzi narrates with reference to Imam Ahmed *bin Hanbal*, that once a devout person happened to be sitting with the Imam, when the latter's wife suddenly sneezed. The man said: "May Allah have mercy on thee". The Imam observed, "This fellow who has devoted himself to worship is totally ignorant. He does not know so much as not to *tashmit* when a female stranger sneezes."

(2) Manners of Yawning.

(i) Yawning should be avoided as far as possible.

According to a tradition quoted by *Imam Bukhari* with reference to Hadrat Abu Huraira (R.A.A.), the Prophet (S.A.W.) said, "Allah likes sneezing but dislikes yawning. When any of you sneezes, he should say *Al-hamdo-lil-lah* and the person present at the moment should pray for Allah's mercy upon him by saying *yar-ham-o-kum-ullah.* But yawn-is caused by the Devil. Whoever feels like yawning he should try to avoid it; for when any one of you yawns, the devil laughs."

(3) If yawning cannot be avoided, one should put one's hand on the mouth, because the devil finds his way into you. Many an Ulama and scholars say that, the hand should be put on one's mouth even if one has to yawn during the prayer (but this should not be done more than three times, as it would vitiate one's prayer).

The Muslims are under the obligation to adapt themselves to all the modes of conduct relating to eating, drinking, greeting, asking for permission, sitting in a gathering, talking, joking, congratulating, condoling, sneezing and yawning — as we have explained above. All the Muslims are obliged to share them without distinction. They are equally important for a child as well as an adult, for a male as well as a female, the ruler as well as the ruled, the rich as well as the poor, the scholar as well as the layman. By moulding their behaviour according to the foregoing patterns the Muslims will emerge as model personalities in spite of their regional, linguistic, social and cultural distinctions.

IV. Observation and Collective Criticism.

One of the basic and most vital principle of the improvement of the child's moral conduct and social behaviour is that it should be impressed upon the child's mind in his early years that it is essential for him to observe keenly every detail of social life. According to the principle in question the child should also be taught the mode of social criticism which should be constructive and based on goodwill. The child should be trained to be bold enough to check any one whom he finds deviating from the social norms.

In short, the child is to be trained in his early years to enjoin good and forbid evil, for these two principles are of basic importance in respecting the public opinion and preventing curruption in the society resulting from moral aberration; for it is by adherence to these two principles that respect for Islamic values and morality can be ensured.

What are the principles of respecting the public opinion and social cirticism? In how many stages is this task to be accomplished? We propose to answer these questions in the ensuing pages.

Respect for the Public Opinion Is a Collective Obligation.

Accoridng to Islam the entire *Ummah* is under the obligation to respect public opinion based on the acknowledged concept of good and evil. It does not discriminate between people belonging to different races and regions in this regard. The rulers, officers, Ulama, the commoners and the elite, men and women, the children and the grown up people, government officials as well as the officers of private organizations and labourers are all equally under the obligation to enjoin good and forbid evil to the best of their respective ability. We cite here some of the relative verses of the Holy Quran:

"Ye are the best community that has been raised up for (the guidance of) mankind. Ye enjoin right conduct and forbid indecency." (3: 110)

The same collective duty of the believers has also been mentioned in this verse:

"And the believers, men and women, are protecting friends one of another; they enjoin the right and forbid the wrong, and they establish worship and they pay the poor-due, and they obey Allah and His messenger. As for these, Allah will have mercy on them. Lo! Allah is Mighty and Wise." (9: 71)

Hence the guardians should inculcate in the children moral courage and boldness both in word and deed. This training would prepare the new generation to shoulder the responsibility of safeguarding the public opinion based on the love of good and hatred for evil and to duly fulfil the obligation of social criticism in view of enjoining the right and forbidding the wrong.

The Rules of Respecting the Public Opinion.

There are certain conditions and modes of enjoining good and forbidding evil which it is incumbent upon the guardians to adhere to as well as teach them to the children. It is absolutely necessary to acquaint each and every Muslim child with the above rules and modes so that he may act accordingly. When he begins his campaign of prevailing upon the people to do good and abstain from evil and thus calling them to the path of Allah, he will gain increasing popularity and his words will be more and more effective.

A majority of Muslim jurists and ulama are agreed on the following principles:

(1) Harmony between word and deed.

Says Allah:

"It is most hateful in the sight of Allah that ye say that which ye do not." (6: 13)

"Enjoin ye righteousness upon mankind while ye yourselves forget to practice it? And ye are readers of the scripture! Have you then no sense?' (2: 44)

(2) The wrong to be forbidden should be one unanimously acknowledged as wrong.

It must be first ascertained that any wrong act which is being forbidden is one treated at such by the ulama and authorities competent to construe the injunctions of Islam.

Any wrong act on which the authorities referred to differ cannot be regarded as wrong under the *Shariah*. Thus a Hanafite should not object to the position of one following Imam Shafe'i. Similarly a follower of Imam Ahmed should not object to one who follows the school of Imam Malik. For all the Imams have tried their level best to arrive at the right injunction by their reasoning.

(3). Opposition to wrong or evil should be gradual.

One who undertakes a campaign against evils must consider himself under the obligation to carry on his campaign gradually and slowly. Hence, he should first find out what evil, wrong act actually consists of. He should next be able to say that any one alleged to be committing an evil act is really committing it. Finally, he should try to prevent him from committing the act in question by arousing in him the fear of Allah and should, for this purpose, try to exhort him in a delightful manner and in a spirit of good-will. If this mode of preaching does not produce the desired result then he should rebuke the evil-doer and threaten him.

(4). The Preacher must be amiable, polite and of mild disposition.

The personality of the man who invites the people to the path of goodness ought to be enriched with the traits mentioned above. Mildness and kind treatment is essential for preventing the common people from wrong conduct; for this manner of preaching is most effective and the preacher also gains popularity among the masses, who readily take his advice. The missionaries, and reformers, as a matter of fact should be outstanding in respect of kindness, politeness and amiability. The Prophet (S.A.W.) himself was soft-spoken, polite and kind and enjoins that preachers must have these qualities.

(5). To be patient in torture.

It is obvious that a social critic and a missionary has to bear various kinds of hardships. The obduracy of the haughty, stupidity of the ignorant, the derogatory behaviour of the scoffers and the like are really torturous. But in every age the prophets, the missionaries, preachers and reformers have had to suffer such afflictions.

The advice of Luqman to his son is also worth mentioning in this context:

O my dear son! Establish worship and enjoin kindness and forbid inequity and persevere whatever befall thee. That is the proof of the steadfast heart. (31: 17)

It is for the reason that those who are suffering afflictions patiently in way of Allah are called to the Road of the Heaven and expiation of the past sins. Says Allah:

"So those who fled and driven forth from their homes and suffered damage for My cause, and fought and were slain, verily I shall remit their evil deeds from them and verily I shall bring them into Gardens underneath which rivers flow — A reward from Allah. And with Allah is the fairest of rewards." (3: 195)

(6) Reinforcement of Religious Ties.

We have dwelt at length on this subject in the present volume at many places, where we have emphasized that the Islamic beliefs should be impressed upon the child's mind before he reaches the age of a early youth, so that faith may be rooted deep in his heart. In this way his links with his religion will be strengthened and he will grow on sound moral lines. He will be an angel in the form of a human-being. He will be looked upon as a pious man.

It is an established fact that the child is prevented from moral deviation by strengthening his bonds with religion, incubating in him the sense of Allah's presence both in his inner self and outward life, making him participate in academic and religious gatherings, offer his prayers regularly, worshpping at the death of night, keeping fasts other than those mandatory, making him mindful of life after death and keep company with good and true Muslims. These acts would be conducive to his full growth as a selfconsistent personality and go a long way in preventing him from deviation from social and moral norms. He will thus become a model of purity and moral excellence.

We relate some incidents from the history of Islam for the guidance of contemporary youth.

(1). Hazrat Yusuf (Joseph A.S.) was in the prime of his youth but could not be enticed by a woman. On the contrary he said, "May God protect me! He is my Lord and He has bestowed upon me a very high position. But He does not side with the transgressors."

The wife of the Aziz of Egypt tried all possible means to entice and lure Hazrat Yousuf (A.S.). She also threatened him but he could neither be taken in nor pressurized. Then she spread false reports among the women designed to bring him into disrepute. In the words of the Holy Quran, "I (the wife of Aziz) endeavoured to entice Yousuf (A.S.) but he escaped. If he does not do as I bid, he will be put behind the bars and thus will suffer indignities."

But Hazrat Yousuf's attention was never diverted from his concern for modesty and chastity. He continued to seek God's help and pray to be protected from the sinister designs of Aziz's wife.

> "O Lord! I would rather prefer prison than do what the people would have me to do. If thou does not avert their perfidious plot against me, then I shall drift toward them and finally become like ignorant people." (12:33)

At this stage the conscience of the believer and the fear of Allah were put to test. Yousuf was being tempted to commit a sin, but the nefarious scheme of the Egyptian women ended in smoke and the faith finally emerged triumphant.

The youths should always keep in view Hazrat Yousuf's example of purity.

(2). During the caliphate of Hadrat 'Umar Farooq (R.A.A.), the husband of a woman had been away from home participating in jihad for a long time. The woman felt extremely lonely and distressed. She was burning with sexual desire. But her strong faith prevented her from going astray. On a dark night as Hadrat 'Umar (R.A.A.) went past by her house he overheard her singing the following couplets.

> "The night has grown long and its darkness has increased, what has kept me awake is that there is no lover with me to enjoy. (i.e., I am awake waiting for my husband). By God, had I not feared painful doom from Allah, ...

The next day Hadrat 'Umar (R.A.A.) went to his daughter Hadrat Hafsa (R.A.A.), who was one of the Mothers of Believers by virtue of being the Prophet's wife. He asked her how long a woman can bear the absence of her husband. Hazrat Hafsa (R.A.A.) told him that she could bear it for a maximum period of four months.

Hadrat 'Umar (R.A.A.) then sent a message to the General Commanding the Muslim forces not to keep any of the soldiers absent from home for more than three months.

In this example we have a woman torn between the fear of Allah on the one hand and sensual and adulterous urge on the other. Faith emerges victorious at the end and the wild demand of nature is subdued.

We have enunciated above, all the Islamic rules and regulations, by following which a young man can attain to the zenith of righteousness, overcome the sensual and devilish urges rather than being subdued by them and can thus play the role of a prophet in goodliness, of an angel in purity, and of our virtuous forbears in chastity and righteousness.

A youth ought to keep himself pure and chaste before marriage and when he can afford to marry, he should lose no time in doing so.

But the youth who does not have the means to marry and abstains from unlawful acts, Allah soon blesses him with the salutary outcome of his righteousness. Says Allah.

> "For a God-fearing person Allah opens up the avenue of livelihood and provide for him from where he cannot imagine to have his livelihood." (65: 2-3)

At another place in the Quran it has been said:

> "Those who cannot afford to marry should adopt the course of purity until Allah bestowes upon them His bounty." (24: 33)

By purity and chastity Islam does not mean self-frustration or self-abnegation; for according to the psychologists thwarting of sexual instinct means looking upon sexual intercourse as a sin, even if it is performed through wedlock. Islam regards such an attitude as monkish. We have already shown under the head of marriage and sexual intercourse that Islam denounces monkish escape from life and legalises marriage by declaring it as a demand of nature. Thus to thwart sensual desires is inconsistent with the teachings of Islam. So if a young man feels disposed to gratify sexual urge, Islam does not teach to seek refuge from such a feeling. Islam rather regards it as a demand of nature and the *Shariah* provides for its legitimate gratification.

It is, therefore, not necessary to prove one's righteousness to the world by frustrating the sexual urge. This urge is but natural. To experience it is no sin. If one thwarts it continuously one would violate the law of nature and consequently one would deviate from moral norms and fall into the abyss of wickedness. The only way to avoid it is to get married.

Islam does not allow to gratify sensual desire at one's sweet will. It rather lays down legal limits within which to gratify it. If such a desire is gratified within the prescribed limits, one would earn reward. But if one gratifies it out of wedlock one would be committing a sin.

The limits laid down by Islam for the gratification of sexual urge are not designed to frustrate it. The limits of the Shariah are one thing and thwarting of sexual instinct is another. The limits in question are intended for maintaining physical delight.

Here the author expresses the view that if a young man cannot afford to marry and is overwhelmed by sexual urge and is also apprehensive of committing adultery and sodomy, then he can legitimately gratify his urge by masturbation. He quotes in support of his view the following principle of Islamic jurisprudence.

> "Of two alternative courses the less harmful one which is also lesser evil should be adopted."

In view of this principle, the author declares adultery and sodomy more injurious and a greater evil than masturbation and as such treats masturbation as legitimate.

Besides, the jurists also hold that to arouse one's slumbeing libido and derive pleasure by masturbation is unlawful. But if one's sexual appetite is so overwhelming that it cannot be controlled and one is at the threshold of debauchery, one can legitimately gratify it by hand, for one would be committing a less harmful sin in order to avoid a bigger sin. In such a case one would neither earn any reward nor incur any punishment. (But if one falls into the habit of hand practice, one would develop physical trouble which would be as painful as any punishment).

Those who level the charge of preaching seclusion and

repression of sexual instinct have no proof to produce in support of their contention. If they maintain that Islam treats gratification of sexual urge as something impure, then this contention too has no grain of truth.

Arguments on the basis of *Shariah* lead us to the conclusion that the guardian should tell his son or daughter all about the demands of sex and in certain cases it is absolutely necessary. The provisions of the *Shariah* in this respect are as follows:

(1). There are numerous verses of the Holy Quran in which matters relating to sexual intercourse, creation of man and debauchery are stated in details. The verses in question are as under.

"(Successful indeed are the believers) who guard their modesty save from their wives or the slave girls that their ight hands possess . . . . and whoso craveth beyond that are transgressors." (23: 5-7)

(2). "It is made lawful for you to go unto your wives on the night of the fast." (2. 187)

(3). "They question thee (O Muhammed) concerning menstruation. Say: It is an illness, and so let women alone at such times and go not in unto them till they are cleansed. And when they have purified themselves then go in unto them as Allah has enjoined upon you." (2: 222)

(4). "Your women are tilth for you (to cultivate) so go to your filth as you will." (2: 223)

(5). "If ye divorce them before ye have touched them and ye have appointed unto them a portion, then pay the half of that." (2: 237)

(6). "Verily we created man from a product of wet earth, then placed him as a drop (of seed) in a safe lodging." (23: 12-13)

(7). "Lo! We create man from a drop of thickened fluid to test him. We make him hearing, knowing." (76: 2)

(8). "And we have enjoined on man the doing of good to his parents. His mother bears him with trouble and she brings him forth with pain and the bearing of him and the weaning of him is thirty months." (46: 15)

(9). "And go not nigh to fornication; surely it is an obscenity. And evil is the way." (17:32)

(10). "And We sent Lot, when he said to his people: Do you commit an abomination which no one in the world did before you? And surely you come to males with lust instead of females. Nay, you are a people exceeding bonds." (7. 80-81)

(11). "Adulterer shall not marry save an adulteress or an idolatress and the adulteress none shall marry save an adulterer or an idolator." (24. 3)

It has been clearly enjoined in these verses that man should protect his private parts and that there are some people from whom he does not have to protect them. Besides, according to these verses a man may do sexual intercourse with his wife at night during the holy month of Ramazan. Again, we are told what is menstruation and that during the period a woman menstruates, one should abstain from her, sexual intercourse is done thorugh the part of a female's body which Allah describes as the field, i.e., the part through which the child comes into the world. Moreover, if a woman is diverced before being touched, half of the amount of her mehr should be paid to her. We are also told what is sperma hominies (man's seed) and how conception comes about. Man is created by the mixing of fluids discharged by males and females. The embryo is formed and grows into a child in the woman's stomach. Again, we are acquainted with the legnth of period for sucking baby, what adultery consists of, which is a major sin. One of the greatests sins is sodomy.

All the information provided by the Holy Quran relates to sex.

(1) The child will not be able to understand the meanings of the versed cited above even when he reaches the years of discretion unless they are explained to him by the parents, guardians and tutors.

No sane person would say that the guardian or tutor would not tell him the meaning which is not clear; for it would be against rules of Islam training laid down by Islam. Says Allah.

"This is a scripture that we have revealed unto thee, full of blessing, that they may ponder its revelations and that men of understanding may reflect." (38: 7)

The Quran treats those as undesirable persons who do not ponder over its revelations. Such people have been described us devoid of spirit, hard-hearted and with minds imperious to word of Allah. Says He:

"So don't they reflect on the contents of the Holy Quran. Have their hearts been locked up?" (47: 24)

In short, the Holy Quran provides us with specific sexual information with which every person should be acquainted, whether he is a child, youth, aged person, man or woman.

The purpose of the Quran in providing such specific information is to let the Muslim know what act is lawful and what act is unlawful and what he should shun and what he should enjoy. Besides, he is told what what he should abstain from and take into consideration while performing sexual intercourse.

The Quranic verses pertaining to sex highlight Allah's attribute of creation and origination. When a Muslim reads them he feels that his faith is reinforced and finds ample food for thought in them. The process of man's creation passes through various stages such as conception caused by the male's seed formation of foetus which is turned into a lump of flesh before a complete human being comes into existence. This process is a marvellous manifestation of Allah's omnipotence.

By pondering on the various stages on man's creation faith in Allah is reinforced and man cannot but admit that all the principles of Islam are eternal, which can be applied at all times, that Islam is the only religion which fulfills all the psychological and physical needs of man and that it remains intact through every revolution and transformation of culture and civilization.

(2) The injunctions relating to sex in themselves are proof enough of the vital need to acquaint a boy in his early youth with every thing about sex so that he may be aware of matters enjoined upon him as well as those he must shun. Besides, he should be able to discriminate between lawful and unlawful.

We have already discussed this question at length while dealing with the need to teach the child matters relating to the age of maturity. The reader is, therefore, referred back to that portion of the present volume.

(3) As sexual intercourse and sexual gratification is indispensable in life, it is therefores essential that boy should be well informed about sex before his wife sets foot in the home. It is for this reason that we have discussed the subject in question at length under the head "Marriage and Sexual Intercourse."

We come to the conclusion, then, that child should be acquainted with all the religious injunctions with regard to sexual intercourse and its natural reguirements. The parents and guardians should discharge their responsibilities in this respect in order to prevent the child form going astray on account of his ignorance.

However, there are two things to be taken into account in this connection.

(a) The child's education should be in keeping with his age. Care should be taken not to apprise the child about the methods of sexual intercourse at the age of ten years, while he is told of nothing at the age of puberty.

(b) It is advisable that the mother should preferably take upon herself the responsibility of providing sexual information to her daughter for the girl can better learn from her mother than any one else. If the mother is not alive, then no other woman can take over the same responsibility.

The information provided by Islam about sex is of immense value. Even the modern experts on sex can learn a lot from it. They should try to seek guidance from Islamic teachings and act upon them in order to regulate sexual desires in accordance with the principles of Islam. We can, then, hope the personality of the modern youth will be salf-consistent, their soul will be pure and their morals will remain un-impaired. The Muslim youths would thus be capable of discharging properly the duty of propagating Islam and uphold the banner of Islam and Allah's unity.

A Word of Advice for the Guardians.

You will have realized the heavy responsibility which rests on your shoulders. You also have fully understood the following pints.

(1) Religious training is the basic function you have to

perform.

(2) Moral training is the vital responsibility which calls for your special attention.

(3) Physical training is the most important means to gain strength. It therefore involves a responsibility that requires determined effort.

(4) Intellectual training is also the the vital responibility as it is fraught whith the wealth of Muslim culture and civilization.

(5) Psychological training is the fundamental requirment of inculcating firmness and balance is children.

(6) Social training occupies an outstanding place among all the responsibilities to the training of children.

(7) Responsibility of sexual training constitutes the most important requirment to be fulfilled by the person on whom the responsibility of breeding and training the children is imposed.

It follows then that you will have to shoulder the over-all responsibility of training the children and to discharge it in the right earnest. You should not neglect or slacken your duty. The out-come of your training will be that your children will be pure like angels, firm and determined like the prophet's companions, brave like lions and bright like the full moon. The greater your dedication and determination in performing this task, the better will it be for the Ummah and more virtuous and better trained will your oppspring be.

Do you know how best the duty of training the children could be dischaged?

To my mind two things of basic importance should be taken into account in this commection.

(1) Full observation of children.

(2) Spending Leisure time usefully.

There are five advantages of their observation.

(a) The faith and morals of the child will be firm, his body strong and his intellect and knowledge will be sound and his psychological and collective behaviour will be perfect.

(b) The child will be safe from bad company and thus there is no likelihood of his going astray.

(c) The child will not be amenable to deviation by deparaving stimuli. He will refrain from watching television and films and from hearing obscene songs. He will not read obscene literature nor sex-inciting magazines and fiction that are prejudicial to human decency and moral excellence.

(d) The child will be immune from misguic ing socialist systems and heathenish beliefs and ideas. His bonds with Islamic faith would be unbreakable.

(2) Spending Leisure Time Usefully.

The guardian should spend his leisure time at home with his children and preach them moral virtues and beliefs. In this way he will be adding to their knowledge, and their morality will inprove.

How good are the parents who spend their spare time in the evenings with children and preach tham goodness under an integrated and systematic programme. Such parents, in fact, deserve great virtue who sit together with their children to inculcate moral excellence in them. They explain to them problems and relate to them instructive stories. They tell them literary anecdotes to delight them and are delighted themselves.

The deeper the parent's interests in the children, the better their children will be. Such children attain to the acme of morality and esteem. Thus the parents breed their children into balanced personalities who grow up to be wise and virtuous.

This is the ideal method of training the young generation and serves as the first brick in the construction of excellent society. Good training is the task of turning out good Muslims.

How cruel are the parents and detrimental to the cause of humanity whose child wastes his precious time in bad company and does not spend his leisure time in a useful maner. His parents do not care if their child idles away his time in hotels or in association with the urchins of the neighbourhood or in witnessing obscene drama.

You may well-judge who else should shoulder the responsibility of training the children if not the parents? It is the parents alone who can impart the right training to their offspring. They alone can turn the child into a sensible, physically strong and energetic man. Again, it is the responsibility of the parents alone to inculcate in the child the passion for acquiring useful knowledge and teach him to take care of other's rights and follow the patterns of social behaviour.

If the father is careless and the mother lacks the interest, who is going to sow the seeds of virtue in the soil of the child's heart?

The poet *Shauqi* has aptly said.

Orphan is not he whose parents died and left him behind in the lurch.

Rather orphan is he whose mother has abandoned him and the father has no time to take care of him.

The parents should look to it whether or not they are discharging their responsibilities properly, for they will be questioned about it on the Day of Judgment and if found guilty of neglecting their responsibilities they may be punished. And the Day of Judgment is the time when neither material possessions would be profitable nor one's sons. Only the people with purity of hearts would escape unpunished.

It would be enough for the parents to set the following verse of the Holy Quran as their ideal.

"O ye who believe ward off from yourselves and your families a Fire whereof the fuel is men and stones, over which are set angels strong, severe, who resist not Allah in that which He commandeth them, but do that which they are commanded." (66: 6)

If the parents keep this verse in view, they will always have the sense of Allah's fear and they would infuse and foster this sense in their offspring and would thus impart training to their children in the best possible manner.

So the parents and guardians should realize their duties and train their children in their spare time. They should be wide awake to the fact that time is sword. If they do not cut this sword, it will cut them off. Duties outnumber the days of man's sojourn in the world. They pass away quickly. If they do not realize the responsibilities imposed upon them and fail tc discharge them duly, then they should be mindful of the fact that death will come to them suddenly and imperceptibly. I should rather say that painful doom will overwhelm them and that there will be no one to come to their rescue. Says Allah.

"Turn unto Him repentant and surrender unto Him before there come unto the doom when ye cannot be helped.

And follow the better (Guidance) of that which is revealed unto you from your Lord before the doom cometh on you suddenly when ye know not." (39: 54-55)

At the end I would like you to make it clear, to the guardians, whether they be the tutors or the spiritual guides and particularly the parents that the Islamic principle of training I have adumbrated above are applicable to the olders and young, the males and the females alike. Particularly so are the principles of collective training.

It is, therefore, necessary that the guardians should first mould their lives according to those principles so that they may serve as models to the children. This is the way to fulfil the obligation with regard to the training of children. First train yourselves and then focus your attention on the training and moral uplift of your children so that the real beliefs and principles of Islam may be translated into action.

Thus trained, the children will be able to solve the knotty problems of life when they grow up and would bear the heavy responsibilities by dint of the strength of faith and spiritual power. In the fulfilment of their obligations their mature intellect, balanced thinking and strong bodies will stand in their good stead.

I, therefore, urge upon the guardians once again that they should make determined efforts to breed and train their children in accordance with the Islamic principles and thus fulfil their obligations in this regard. The Master's Eye is watching. The posterity will reap the fruits of your efforts and achievements. Allah will reward you both in this world and in the Hereafter. A'men.

* * * * * *

CHAPTER XII

RESPONSIBILITY OF SEXUAL TRAINING

What is meant by such training is that when the child comes of age and feels sexual urge and develops a craving for getting married, he should be furnished with detailed information about sex so that when he comes to full puberty, he may be able to differentiate between the legitimate and the illegitimate. This is absolutely necessary to make him realize that he is bound by the Islamic teachings and is thus prevented from being a debauchee and licentious.

The child should be imparted sexual training in phases. In this connection we lay down the following procedure for the guidance of the guardians and tutors:

The First Phase

From seven to ten years; i.e. the years of discretion.

The Second Phase

From ten to fourteen years.

The Third Phase

From fourteen to sixteen years; i.e. the age of puberty. If preparations for the marriage of a boy at this age is under way, then he should be taught the modes of sexual intercourse.

The Fourth Phase

When the boy comes to full puberty, he should be taught the ways of remaining chaste and the morals pertaining to sexual purity. If he cannot afford to marry, the boy ought to learn the morals keeping himself pure.

We propose to acquaint the tutors and the guardians with the proper ways of imparting sexual training to the children. It is necessary to point out that Islam covers all the aspects of sexual training. It does not only provide for such training on moral and psychological plane but also lays down the guidelines for imparting sexual training for the tutors and the guardians. It imposes on them the obligation of imparting such training along with general education so that they may fulfil this obligation with devotion.

The Modes of Sexual Training

(1). Asking for permission.

Here, I want to emphasize here only one point and that is that the child should be accustomed to ask for permission to enter the house of any one at such times when men and women do not like small children to come into their presence. This has been clearly enjoined in the Holy Quran:

> O ye who believe! Let your slaves and those of you who have not come to puberty ask leave of you at three times before they come into your presence. Before the prayer of dawn, and when ye lay aside your raiment for the heat of noon and after the prayer of night. Three times of privacy for you. It if no sin for them or for you at other times, when some of you go round attendent upon others if they come into your presence without leave. Thus Allah maketh clear the revelations for you. Allah is Knower, Wise.
>
> And when the children among you come to puberty, then let them ask leave even as those before them used to ask it. Thus Allah maketh clear his revelations for you. Allah is Knower, and Wise." (24: 58-59)

Allah has laid down the principles of training in domestic life which relate to seeking of permission by immature children from their elders of the family before entering the house.

There are, however, times for the need to seek permission, which are as under:

(i). Before the dawn prayer, because the people at that time are usually asleep in their beds.

(ii). At noon when man takes off his extra clothes while being at home.

(iii). After the Isha (night) prayer, inas much as it is the time to go to bed.

The child is enjoined to seek permission to enter the house at these times, lest he should go into the presence of the members of the family when they do not like to admit any one to come into the house.

When the child reaches discretionary years and comes of age, it is incumbent upon the guardians to tell the child that he should ask for permission before intering the house, as Allah says:

"And when the children among you come to puberty, let them ask leave even as those before them used to ask it." (24: 59)

Any one who fully understands the significance of these rules of training must also be capable of realizing the fact that the verses of the Holy Quran cited above emphasize the need to teach the child to be modest, to accustom him to the modes of social behaviour and acquaint him with the sublime pattern of social life as determined by Islam. When such a child grows up, he will become the model of moral excellence and social behaviour.

How shameful it would be if a child enters the bed room of his parents and finds them in sexual action. When he remembers the spectacle of what he witnesses, he is distracted.

The child who sees such a spectacle of sexual intercourse, his libido would come into play and he will indulge in sexual corruption. As he will have seen the act of copulation and learnt how to derive carnal pleasure, the possibilities of his sexual deviation increase two-fold.

It is, therefore, absolutely necessary for the guardians that no sooner the child enters the age of discretion than they should teach him to take permission before going into the presence of the elders if they want to mould his personality in accordance with the Islamic modes of behaviour.

Rules regarding looking at men and women.

(a). Looking at one with whom wedlock is unlawful.

Every woman who is eternally unlawful for a man is treated as one of those who are tabooed for him.

And every man with whom a woman's wedlock is unlawful is one of those tabooed for her.

On the basis of this the details of the forbidden males and females are as under:

(i). Those under taboo by virtue of descent:

There are seven kinds of tabooed women specified by Allah in the following words:

"Forbidden unto you are your mothers, and your daughters, and your sisters, and your father's. sisters and your mother's sisters and your brother's daughters and your sister's daughters." (4: 23)

(ii) Relationships forbidden by virtue of matrimonial ties. Under this head fall four categories of women:

(a). Fathers wife, as has been specified by Allah in the following words:

"And marry not those women whom your fathers married." (4: 22)

(b) Son's wife or daughter-in-law; as has been enjoined in the following verse:

"(Marry not) the wives of your sons who spring from your own loins." (4: 23)

(c) "(Marry not) your motehrs-in-law."

(d) "(Marry not) your step-daughters under your protection born of your women unto whom you have gone in-but if ye have not gone in unto them then it is no sin for you to marry their daughters." (4: 23)

(iii). Women under taboo are who sucked milk from the same breast. Says Allah again:

"(Marry not) your foster-mothers and your foster-sisters."

Says the Holy Prophet (S.A.W.):

"Just as women are tabooed by virtue of descent, women sucking milk from the same breast are similarly under taboo."

A man under taboo is allowed to look at the body of a woman under taboo from breast up to the head. He may also see her body down to the knees, provided that both men and women are free from lust. But if the male is not confident of controlling his sexual appetite, it is disallowed for a tabooed woman, as a precautionary measure, to look at a man forbidden for her.

On the basis of the principle mentioned above it is permissible for a man under taboo to see the interior and exterior of a woman and her organs of adornment such as the hair of the head, neck, chest, ears, sides, ankle, palm, the part of the leg below the knee up to the foot, face and breast. But it is absolutely forbidden to look at the woman's stomach, back and thigh.

The principle in this regard is laid down in the following verse of the Holy Quran:

"(And tell the believing women) not to reveal their adornment save to their own husbands or fathers or husband's fathers, or their sons or their husbands's sons, or their brother's or their brother's sons or their sister's sons." (24: 31)

Thus when a forbidden male comes to the age of puberty, he is disallowed to look at a forbidden woman who is clad in such short clothes as do not cover her thighs or is improperly dressed, with the complexion of her body or private parts exposed. Similarly the daughter or wife is prohibitted to look at the private parts of a forbidden male, that is, the parts between pubes and the knees, whether the male is his son, brother or father, however confident she may of his sexual insensitivity and even if she has to bathe such a forbidden male during his ailment.

"These are the limits or restrictions laid down by Allah. Do not infringe them. And those who oversteps Allah's limit, such are the great wrongdoers." (2: 229)

(iv) Looking at one's fiancee.

It is permissible for the man who sends the proposal of marriage to have a look at his fiancee. Similarly the girl may have a look at the man betrothed to her. This is necessary for selecting and knowing one's would-be partner of life. We have the instruction of the Holy Prophet (S.A.W.) to cite in this connection which he gave to Mughaiara bin Shu'ba (R.A.A.).

"Have a look at your fiancee. It is better for maintaining the bonds of love between you." (*Sahih Muslim*)

Imam Muslim and *Nasai* quote a tradition wherein it is narrated that a person came to the Holy Prophet (S.A.W.) and told him that he had contracted a woman into marraige. The Prophet (S.A.W.) asked him if he had viewed her thoroughly.

However, there are certain modes of observing one's fiancee. The man seeking the hand of a woman should take them into consideration. The modes in question are as follows:

(a). When a young man once makes up his mind to marry

a girl, he is disallowed to see any parts of her body other than her face and palms.

It is forbidden for a man to shake hands with a woman who is a stranger to him. This is borne out by a tradition narrated by Hazrat Aisha (R.A.A.). The words of the tradition are as follow:

"The Prophet (S.A.W.) never touched a woman's hand while taking pledge of faith from her. This consisted of only talking to her."

(b). The fiancees cannot meet each other in private. Some kinsman of hers should b present during the meeting. The reason for this is that it is unlawful in Islam to meet a woman in private with whom wedlock is allowed. *Imam Bukhari and Imam Muslim* have cited to this effect a saying of the Holy Prophet (S.A.W.) which is as under:

"Listen, no man can meet a woman alone, nor can a woman travel unaccompanied by a tabooed male."

It is absolutely necessary to point out here that Islam loathes the sort of unrestricted freedom allowed to males and females betrothed to each other on the pretext of understanding each other; for it is incompatible with morality and human standards. Such a promiscuity is more harmfull to female than the male fiancee and is likely to bring her into disrepute. It is possible that the engagement is later broken and thus honour and purity of the girl is called into question. This would deprive the girl of all prospects of marriage. The unmarried girl in such a case may be compared to a product whose price has gone down in the market.

(v). Looking at the parts of wife's body.

The husband can legitimately see any part of wife's body lustfully or without lust. For as the man can touch his wife and enter into sexual intercourse with her, then it is the more legitimate for him to see the whole of her body. However, it is better for the couple not to see each other's private parts. Hazrat Aisha (R.A.A.) says , "The Holy Prophet (S.A.W.) passed away. But till then neither he saw the parts of my body nor I saw his." (*Fathul Qadeer, Vol. 8, Kitabul Hazar, Fasl-un-Nazir*).

(vi) Injunction pertaining to looking at women amenable to wedlock.

An adult male is disallowed to look at women amenable to marriage even if she has no appeal for him. But the question arises as to which female is and which male is amenable to marriage?

(a). For a female such males are amenable to marriage whom she could legitimately marry under the Shariah. Such males include sons of maternal uncles and aunts, sons of paternal uncles and aunts, sister's husband (after her death) and the husband of maternal aunt (after her death).

(b). For a male, females amenable to marriage are those women who he can contract into marriage under the Shariah. Such females include the daughters of paternal uncle, paternal aunt, maternal uncle and maternal aunt, widow of paternal uncle and maternal uncle, sister-in-law, the paternal and maternal aunts of his wife.

Male here also includes a boy in his early youth or one who has the sense of discrimination between beautiful and ugly women.

In either case the male is forbidden to look at a woman who he can legitimately marry.

Proofs of the illegitimacy of looking at females described above. Says Allah:

> "Tell the believing men to lower their gaze and be modest. That is purer for them. Allah is aware of what they do. And (also) tell the believing women to lower their gaze and be modest." (24: 30-31)

The above verses of Quran, which are crystal clear, prove it beyond doubt that a male is forbidden to look at a female stranger (including those specified above) or vice versa when such males and females happen to sit at same place, for in such a situation the possibility of iniquity is consiserably increased.

Doubtless, the Islamic injunction to keep one's gaze low aims at bringing into existence a pure society wherein sensual desires are at a low ebb.

Syed Qutb (may his soul rest in peace) writes in his commentary of the Holy Quran that the upsurge of the latent sensual impulses throw a man into the bonfire of sexual appetite which burns unabated with the result that his iniquitous eyes, his gestures inducing sex, the naked beauty and the naked body, all conspire to fan the fire of sexual madness. One of various measures that Islam provides for is that without exciting the sex by artificial methods, a natural sexual relation between the male and the female is established and this relationship is fostered by natural force.

Once there was a common notion that freedom of looking at women, and of conversation between males and females, their mixing up without restrictions, joking and merry making and familiarity with the female's private parts gratify the mind, their sensual desires are freely released instead of being thwarted and thus man is immune from psychological complications. Besides, the intensity of sexual appetite is assuaged and the individual does not fall a prey to morbid introversion.

But the advocates of the foregoing idea completely lost sight of the fact that the natural propensity of the male and the female is the very essence of life. It is through this propensity that Allah has caused flux of life and has declared man his rightful vicegerent on earth. This natural propensity is sometimes dormant and sometimes active. When it naturally comes into play, man is compelled to give vent to it physically in order to gratify himself. If this demand of human nature is not fulfilled, his nerves are fatigued and then he falls a prey to constant trouble.

The Prophet (S.A.W.) has expressed perfect truth in the following words:

"Three eyes will not be able to see the fire of Hell:

(a) The eye which kept vigil on the path of Allah (i.e. remained awake the whole night for the sake of fighting in the way of Allah.)

(b) The eye which kept shedding tears for fear of Allah.

(c) The eye which did not look at forbidden things (i.e. which did not gaze at women or looked at anything obscene).

(vii) How a man should look at another man?

A man is disallowed to look at the body of another man between the navel and knees, whether the latter is a believer or an infidel. However, one may see his stomach, back, chest etc., provided that it does not incite sex.

Imam Muslim quotes the Prophet's saying in this context.

"No man should see the private parts of another man, nor a woman should see the private parts of another woman."

The wordings of the same saying as quoted in Musnad-Imam Ahmed, Sunan-Nasai, Sunan-Baihaqi, Sunan-Ibn Majah are as follows:

"You should always keep your private parts covered from every one save from your wife and the maid which your right hand possesses.

(viii). Private parts in consideration of exposition to vision.

It is unlawful to expose or uncover both the essential and general private parts.

The relevant injunctions in this respect are as follows:

(a) For a male, private parts of another male consist of the portion from the navel down to the knees.

(b) For a female, private parts of another female consist of the portion from the nevel down to the knees, provided that both of them are believing women.

(c) According to one opinion a Muslim woman is enjoined to conceal her entire body from a heathen women with the exception of the palms and the face, while according to another opinion she must cover her entire body from the latter without any exception.

(d) The woman is allowed to keep her face, hands, head, neck and the parts above the feet exposed before the forbidden males. She should cover up the rest of her body before such males; for it is disallowed to see any parts of her body other than those mentioned above.

The doctor however, should fulfil the following conditions in the treatment of the woman:

(1) He should be righteous, honest and just. He should also be a specialist and highly qualified.

(2). He should examine the affected part of the woman's body only as much as it is necessary.

(3). There is no lady doctor available for the treatment of the disease from which the woman is suffering.

(4). The treatment is carried out in presence of the husband or a forbidden kinsman or a reliable woman such as the patient's mother, sister or servant.

(5). If a Muslim doctor is available the woman should not submit herself to the treatment of a non-Mustlim doctor.

When the above conditions are fulfilled, the doctor is allowed to touch the private parts of a woman; for Islam is a religoin that removed every difficiulty faced by man and provided every possible facility to him,

(ix) To, see while deciding a case or giving evidence.

It is permissible for a judge or witness to see the face and plams of woman involved in case if such an act is likely to result in corruption; for in such a case the use of vision is designed to prove the truth and do away with the wrong.- It is, therefore, lawful for the judge as well as the witness to see a fermale stranger wearing a veil, During the legal proceed, ing the woman appearing in the court will be asked to remove the cover from her face so that it may be ascertained if she is really the woman involved in the case and not some other person. This would make the proceeding free of doubt and would also save a lot of time.

The woman is allowed to unveil herself on such occasions because Islam gives due importance to the milieu and fully respects the values of life. It safeguards the tegitimate interests and the rights of the indviduals.

The parents and guardians are advised to follow themselves the precepts of looking at woman and as described above and then train their children accordigly, if they are desirous that their children should also learn the prescribed modes of looking at children, possess sterling moral qualities, their Islamic identity is projected and their social behaviour is praiseworthy as the result of Islamic training. Allah will reward them on the Day of Judgment when no material benefit would accrue, nor would one's sons would be of any help.

(3). Guarding the child against sexual inducements.

One of the most important responsibilities of the parents and guardians according to Islam is to guard their offsprings against anything that may incite the children's sex or is detrimental to their morality. Precautions in this regard should begin from ten years up to the age of puberty.

The educationists unanimously are of the view that the age mentioned above is the most critical phase of an individual's life. If the parents and the guardians are well-versed in the way the child is to be bred and trained, how he is to be presented from going astray, and how he is to be saved from corruption, the children would grow on sound moral grounds and their modes of behaviour would be superior to others. They will, in short, be imbued with the spirit of Islam.

The following verse of the Holy Quran teaches us that we should guard our children from sexual stimuli.

> And tell the believing women . . . . .to draw their veils over their bosoms, and not to reveal their adornment save to their own husbands, or fathers or their husband's fathers, or their sons, or their husband's sons, or their women or their slaves, or male attendants who lack vigour or children who know naught of women's nakedness. (24 : 31)

It may be inferred that the child in his early years is not susceptible to sexual inducement by the things peculiar to the females, particularly their private parts. In this phase of life their mixing up with the females is not open to objection. But when the child is nearly nine years old, he should be prevented from associating with the females; for at this age the child comes to be conscious of the beauty or ugliness of the woman and is sensually induced at the sight of any sexual stimulus.

Abu Hakim and Dawood quote the Prophet (S.A.W.) to have said, "Order your children to say Prayers when they reach the age of seven years and beat them if they do not say prayers at the age of ten years. At this stage separate their beds also."

Hence the parents, tutors and the guardians are under the obligation according to the Shariah to separate the beds of their children when they are ten years old. The idea underlying this Islamic injunction is that at this stage of life beginning about the tenth year the sex of children is naturally incited when they see the private parts of each other when awake or asleep and are thus likely to fall a prey to sexual corruption.

The injunction in question also bears it out that Islam instructs the guardians and parents to adopt precautionary measures and positive approach in the training of their children. It particularly calls upon them to guard the children against debauchery so that they may grow up to be good Muslims.

In the light of the injunctions and traditions mentioned above it is incumbent upon every tutor and guardian to curb the sensual impulses of the child so that he may not indulge in immoral acts and irretrievably fall into the abyss of wickedness.

There are two ways to check the sexual urge of children: (1). The internal method and the (2) external method.

(1) The Internal method:

It is the duty of the guardian to translate into practice the Islamic principles for guarding the children against sexual stimulation.

(a) One of these principles for instance, is that the child should not go to his parents or elders at the time of their rest and sleep without obtaining their permission.

(b). The children should be prevented from witnessing such scenes on television at home as may incite their sex. In homes with TV sets the children's morals are jeopardized.

(c). If the child is allowed the opportunity to collect nude pictures, books of erotic fiction or cassettes of sensual songs, he is bound to be sexually corrupt. It is, therefore, the duty of the parents to check the almirahs of their children, keep an eye on their activities and adopt effective measures to guard them against corruption.

(d). The children in their early youth should never be allowed to make acquaintances with boys and girls of the same age group living in the neighbourhood on the pretence of doing their school work or preparing for the examination together with them. Otherwise they would be sexually induced as the result of their association with such boys and girls. If they are allowed the freedom to associate with the latter they will be irretrievablly spoilt and incorrigibly corrupt.

(2). External Method

This is as important as the internal method; for there may be innumerable causes of depravity. Some of the sexual stimuli are enumerated below:

1. *Cinema and stage Drama.*

Both of these things are full of sexual stimuli. sensual inducements and glimpses of sexual immorality

The Cinema and the stage drama today have become decadent causing debauchery, sexual immorality and leading to the violation of chastity. They have actually become a permanent source of earning and their organizers or com*Panies* are busy vying with one another to gain success. In this competition all sorts of people are involved including jews and other Non-Muslims as well as the so-called Musalmans who nevertheless identify themselves with Islam.

2. *Obscene Costume*

It is impossible that the boys in their early youth do not run after women appearing in obscene costume, not to speak of indulging in the pleasure derived from such voluptuous sight. It is a deluge carrying away with it all the moral values. How can the juveniles withstand the force of its current? Their nerves and morals are bound to be affected by it and they will become good for nothing, incapable of working hard and doing anything constructive.

As the result of moral aberration the women today have invented new vogues of constume. They will never give up these vogues whatever corruption they may result in. These women have turned themselves into marketable commodities by making themselves attractive from both within and without. But they actually present a sight worse than the animals.

But Islam requires its woman to lead her life within the moral and social limits laid down for her and thus ensure the establishment of a stable and peaceful society. She must live in such a serious and dignified manner that the juveniles and the unmarried people are constrained to respect her. Her dress and *chadar* should be the guarantee of her honour and dignity. The woman who does not possess such qualities should be declared a deviant from the essetnaials of Islam. Such a woman becomes iniquitous and a slave of her desires as against the following divorce injunctions.

> "No believing man and no believing woman has the right to prefer anything in their affair to what has been decided by Allah and His Messenger."

We have dwelt at length in this section on some of the

most dangerous factors leading to the moral deterioration of children and the serious consequences ensuing therefrom.

Hence the parents and guardians should realize their responsibility and keep a strict vigil on the activities of their children and act in conformity with both the external and internal methods we have suggested above.

But the question is if vigilance alone will serve the end or will other positive measures would be necessary for the reformation and disciplining of children?

To my mind there are three positive measures which the parents and tutors may adopt to fulfil their responsibility of training the children in the best possible manner.

They are as follows:

(1). Teaching and Exhortation.

(2). Warning against prohibited acts.

(3). Reinforcement of religious ties.

We discuss these measures in the ensuing pages:

1. Teaching and Exhortation

There can be no two opinions about the fact that the growing moral deterioration in the society today is the result of the joint conspiracies of Judaism, Communism, Christianity and Imperialism. If this fact is impressed upon the child's mind in his early years, he would abstain from debauchery and carnal pleasures by virtue of his strong moral sense and religious consciousness.

The anti-Islamic forces referred to, have resorted to certain means for the annihilation of Islamic culture and social life. They include sex-incitements, cinema, stage play, magazines with obscene contents, newspapers, television, nude pictures, obscene dress, prostitution dens both public and clandestine etc. etc.

These elements are busy wrecking the morals of humanity through sex and woman all over the world. The Jews and the Masons say that it is necessary for them to get hold of the woman. They maintain that the day when she stretches out her hands to them, they would secure the unlawful forces marshalled on the side of religion.

(1) Conspiracies of the Imperialists and the Christians

One of the champions of imperialism maintains that wine and woman would cause more destruction to the *Muslim*

Ummah than a thousand guns of artillery and, therefore, he suggests that the Muslims should be immersed in wine and sex.

In a conference of Christian missionaries held at Jerusalem, one of their prominent leaders observed that they are succeeding in bringing forth a group in the Islamic countries which is absolutely ignorant of its relation with Allah. In other words, the new generation of Muslims has been moulded perfectly in accordance with the requirements of imperialism — a generation that sets no value on great deeds but loves leisure and comfort and whose aim in life is to indulge in debauchery. The present day Muslim youth receives education to gratify his sensual desire and acquires material means only to achieve this end. If he is appointed to a high office, he spends all his income on carnal pleasures.

(2) The conspiracies of Communists and Materialists

We will discuss in the context of the consciousness of responsibility what communists have written in their secret documents. However, it would not be out of place here to cite one of their observations:

"We have achieved complete success in the popularization of the media that demolish the edifice of religion, such as erotic fiction, stage drama, subversive lectures, magazines, newspapers and books. The sole purpose of all these instruments is to disseminate atheism and ridicule the champions of religion. They invite the people to learn science for its own sake and give it the status of God Almighty.

It is a pity that they have succeeded in their designs. We find our boys and girls who speak our own language, identify themselves with Islam and yet are crazy for the gratification of sensual desires. They have fallen into the abyss of blindfold imitation, self-deterioration and licentiousness. They are obsessed with sex and are busy contaminating themselves with debauchery and deriving pleasures from obscene plays and films or frequenting places where masculine pride, manliness and human decency are extirpated.

It is, therefore, incumbent upon parents and guardians to inculcate religious and political consciousness in the children so that they may be able to comprehend the machinations of anti-Islamic forces. They should also be warned that if they contaminate themselves with the filth of immorality, deviate from the ethical norms and tend to be licentious, they will be implementing willingly or unwillingly the nefarious plans of the jews, communists, imperialists and the christian missionaries and will be reckoned among those who are instrumental in their success.

To my mind, meaningful religious and political instructions profoundly affect the intellect and the intuition of children, making them abstain from obscenity and prohibited things.

2. Warning against serious Consequences of Misdeeds

I am of the opinion that the most effective way of preventing children from unlawful acts and indulgence in debauchery is to warn them against serious consequences of such acts. By this method all the deadly results of licentiousness and debauchery are depicted before the child.

It was the horrible consequences of debauchery which the President of USSR Mr. Khrushchev realized and declared in 1962 that the future of Russia was in danger. He said that future of the Russian youths was uncertain as they were obsessed with sex and that they lacked strength of character.

At about the same time the President of the USA Mr. John F. Kennedy warned that future of America was in a jeopardy because the American youth's personality is disintegrated and inconsistent, who, being obsessed with sex, is incapable of shouldering any responsibility. Mr. Kennedy added that six out of seven young men who offer themselves for recruitment in the military service are physically unfit. Their excessive indulgence in debauchery wrecks their health, both physical and mental.

This pestilence of licentiousness that broke out and became virulent in the western and eastern countries also struck the Islamic societies. We often hear about the prostitution dens, gambling houses and cabarets which have sprung up in the Islamic countries also and that the governments of these countries are in the know of it.

We are pained to learn that in Islamic countries too young girls are brought and sold and that adulteresses are employed to run this business. The people who are responsible for such a diabolical business have no fear of God, nor is there anyone to call them to account.

Besides, there are innumerable young men who seek to gratify their sexual appetite by illegitimate means and who are addicted to liquor with impunity.

These are facts known to all the Muslims whether they happen to be close by or at distant places.

3. Collective Dangers

It is an established fact that the wicked youth do equal harm to themselves and their family by indulging in debauchery. In fact the impact of their wickedness on the community as a whole is more horrible. Some of the harmful effects of debauchery are as follows:

(1). Families are on the decline for a young bachelor who gratifies his sexual appetite like a beast by unlawful means, thinks of neither building up of a family of his own nor of producing good and righteous children. The same also holds good in the case of an adulteress. She has no desire of being pregnant. In order to keep her immune from the physical and psychological effects of pregnancy she does not want to give birth to a child. She wants to avoid begetting a child by whatever method she could do it.

(2). The new babes are ill-treated. In societies where the people try to escape from wedlock and where they are fond of leading licentious life children have no value. There is no respect for the nobility of descent at all. No greater wrong can be done to children than this sort of sordid attitude.

Is it not a great wrong to deprive the child of parental love? Such a child is reared at the hospital and has no experience of love and compassion.

What a great cruelty it is that when the child reaches the age of discretion he comes to know that he is the illegitimate son of some one.

The child consequently develops various complexes and sometimes takes to dishonest and immoral practices. Generally such a child bears ill-will against both the individuals and the community. In fact the very existence of an illegitimate boy or girl poses a constant threat to the peace and tranquillity of the entire community.

(3). The adulterer and the adulteress both are damned;

for such men and women are deprived of the blessings of a happy life. They do not have the opportunity to earn in a dignified manner. Bonds of mutual affection and compassion stem only from conjugal relations. But a society devoid of the very connection of wedlock is deprived of these blessings. A community lacking in moral strength and is a victim of moral degeneration is absolutely a stranger to the happiness resulting from conjugal relation and respectable means of livelihood.

(4). Debauchee is unconscious of the significance of helping the kinsmen and respect for kinship. For when a bachelor gratifies his sexual desire by unlawful. means or by fornication, he is degraded in the eyes of his relations. Everyone curses and cold-shoulders him. In this way rebellion and defiance takes root in the psychology of the aberrant. This causes hatred for him among the members of the family. Next to attributing plurality to Godhead, the biggest sin is disobedience of the parents.

Apart from the collective dangers and the harmful effects mentioned above, there are other consequences of adultery, too, which the wise and sane people can well realize.

(5) *Economics Disadvantages:* There can be no two opinions about the fact that those who indulge in debauchery often avoid legitimate wedlock. Such people are addicted to fornication and sodomy. It is these people who are responsible for the economic crisis of a people. The reasons for this are as follows:

(a) They are sluggish since their energy is on the wane.

(b) Their output diminishes.

(c) They adopt methods of earning livelihood disallowed by the law.

(6) *Religious Harm:*

The unmarried person who does not abstain from unlawful things, nor does suppress sexual temptations, develops four vices according to the Holy Prophet. Says the Holy Prophet (S.A.W.):

Abstain from adultery, for it is pregnant with four vices:

(a) It deprives the face of its attraction (The adulterer

does not have dignity).
(b). It reduces means of livelihood.
(c). It incurs Allah's displeasure.
(d). It turns man into eternal hell.

(Al Mojam-ul-Awsat-ul-Tabarani)

From the above lines the reader may have seen how horrible and tragic are the consequences of debauchery. It undermines a man's health and wrecks his morality. His psychology and intellect too are badly affected. His faith is also vitiated. Besides, the debauchee's family comes to grief. Such a person is also a burden on the society and its economy.

The guardians and parents should, therefore, impart sexual training to their children with meticulous care.

Religious training goes a long way in the discipline and moral behaviour of the child; for when the child is trained to have firm faith in Allah and is imbued with His fear at all hours, he will naturally grow up to be an honest, righteous and God-fearing man. He will never be overcome by sex and consideration of material interest. The Devil will not be able to dominate him. No sinister wishes will rise from the depth of his baser-self to lead him astray. If any rich and high ranking woman tries to entice him, he would say that he is afraid of Allah. If the Devil tries to misguide, he would say to him that he cannot succeed in prevailing upon him to do as he wishes. If bad companions induce him to be immodest and do forbidden acts, he would tell them that he would not be a party to what the ignorant people do.

I pray to Allah that He may motivate all the Muslims to train their children on the lines chalked out by Islam, so that they may be successful on the Day of Judgment. Allah may provide them an opportunity to see that their endeavours have borne fruit and the new generation is adhering the tenets of Islam, moulding their lives according to the principles laid down in the Holy Quran, waging war in the way of Allah and have reached the acme of moral excellence and decency. This will give a great pleasure to the believers.

The child should be well-acquainted with the duties and the Prophet's practice etc. with regard to purifying bath when such a bath becomes obligatory for him so that he may be thoroughly familiar with the procedure of purifying himself when he is unclean. We give below the duties laid down for and the Prophet's practice pertaining to purifying bath.

(I). Obligations relating to purifying bath.

Says Allah:

"If you are unclean, then take purifying bath." (4: 43)

But any part of the body which is likely to be harmed in washing such as the interior of the eye etc. and any part which is not likely to be damaged by washing is to be purified; as for example the mouth and the nose.

Imam Abu Dawood and *Imam Tirmizi* quote the Prophet (S.A.W.) to have observed; "Every hair is contaminated and, therefore, you should fully moisten it (clean it by rubbing) and purify your skin by thoroughly rubbing it."

According to these injunctions of the Shariah it is obligatory to wash all the parts of the body provided that it causes no harm; for instance it is necessary to wash the navel. The woman should wash the exterior of her womb thoroughly. She should also pour water below the uterus. Moreover, it is obligatory to wash the exterior of the ears and the armpits.

(II). Prophet's practice with regard to ablution and the procedure thereof.

First both the hands should be washed and then the private parts are to be washed and purified. Then ablution or *wuzu* should be performed as is done for saying prayers. But the feet should not yet be washed, as they are to be washed at the end of the bath. This should be followed by pouring water over the whole body. This process is to be repeated thrice. The feet then should be washed at place where the water does not remain blocked but flows away.

III The Prophet's practice with regard to bath are as follows:

(1). It must commence with *Niyat* (intention). *Niyat* is to be followed the recitation of

(2). *Bismillah*

'I begin with the name of Allah the Beneficent and Merciful.'

(3) Rubbing the teeth to cleanse them.

(4). Cleaning the beard by passing the fingers into it and likewise cleaning the inner portions of the fingers by passing them into one another.

(5). To rub as many parts of the body as possible.

If a man under the obligation to bath is as far away from water as it may take him half an hour to reach it, or in case if water is near at hand but the man is sick and a bath would aggravate his malady, or there is no facility to warm the water in winter or the danger of an attack by the enemy is looming large, or the water available is so scanty that if he takes bath no water would be left for drinking, then *tayammum* (dry abultion) is permissible.

(IV). The procedure of Tayammum (dry ablution): Beat the hands twice on clean sand, stone or soil. Beat it once and wipe the face with it.

Beat it a second time and wipe both the hands from the fingers up to the elbow.

Says Allah:

> "If you cannot find water, then betake yourselves to pure earth, then wipe your faces and your hands." (4: 43)

It has been stated in a tradition of the Holy Prophet (S.A.W.):

> "*Tayammum* consists of striking the hands twice (on pure earth). Striking first is designed for wiping the face, Striking a second time is designed for wiping the arms up to the elbows."

In *tayammum* too, *'niyat'* is essential, and is meant for the worship whcih is not possible without ablution. *Tayammum* performed in lieu of *wuzu* or bath is governed by th same rule.

The child should be fully apprised of acts unlawful in the state of pollution. This is necessary for preventing him from doing anything forbidden in such a state.

For women in a medical handicap or subject to a prohibitory injunction of the Shariah as well as polluted males and females the following acts are forbidden:

(I). A woman during the period of menstruation or during the puerile period of forty days after the child-birth is forbidden to offer prayer or keep fast. Later on she is to keep fast to atone for missing the Ramadan fast on account of her handicaps mentioned above. But she has not been enjoined to offer prayers in lieu of those she omits during the periods in question.

In all the six authentic books of traditions Hazrat Aisha (R.A.A.) quotes of the Holy Prophet (S.A.W.):

"When you have monthly period, you are enjoined to postpone fasting to a later date and to give up offering prayers with no condition to offer them later on."

(II). It is unlawful for a polluted man and woman and for a woman having monthly course to enter the mosque. This injunction is contained in a tradition quoted by Abu Dawood wherein the Prophet (S.A.W.) is reported to have said: "I do not treat as lawful the entrance in a mosque of a polluted man and woman or a menstruating woman."

(III). It is unlawful for a polluted man and woman to move round the Ka'ba because Ka'ba is also a mosque.

It is forbidden to recite or read the verses of the Holy Quran when one is polluted or discharging menses or during the puerile period of forty days following the child-birth.

Iman Tirmizi and *Ibn Majah* quote a tradition with reference to Ibn 'Umar (R.A.A.) wherein the Prophet (S.A.W.) is reported to have said that a woman discharging menses and a polluted man should not recite any verse of the Holy Quran.

This injunction, however, applies to reading the Quran with the intention of reciting it. If one reads the verses of the Holy Book with the intention of praising or remembering Allah, he may legitimately do so. Thus it is not objectionable to recite

A menstruating woman or a polluted male as well as female may recite the words of the Quran as a matter of necessity, excuse or for purpose of teaching. The jurists are unanimous on this point.

I request the guardians and parents to acquaint the children with these injunctions as soon as they reach the age of discretion; for it is at this stage that the worship of Allah becomes incumbent upon them. Hence it is essential for them to be aware of the lawful and unlawful acts. They should also be well-acquainted with the Shariat injunctions relating to sex and the demands of human nature. It is not enough that they learn the Islamic injunctions with regard to the beginning of adolescence but also try to develop religious acumen. They should try to take lead in the acquisition of knowledge.

The Prophet (S.A.W.) has rightly said: "Allah bestows religious acumen on any one to whom He wants to do good."

* * * * * *

Muslim Children - How to Bring up?

MUSLIM CHILDREN-
HOW TO BRING UP?

Translated by
S. Zakir Aijaz

Vol. III

KITAB BHAVAN
New Delhi-2 [India]

Kitab Bhavan
Publishers, Distributors, Exporters & Importers
1784, Kalan Mahal, Darya Ganj
New Delhi - 1100 02 (India)

Phone : (91-11) 23277392/93, 23274686, 30906494
website : www.kitabbhavan.com
Email : nasri@vsnl.com
Fax : (91-11) 23263383

First Edition 1995
IInd Reprinted 2006

ISBN : 81-7151-135-X (Set)
ISBN : 81-7151-202-X (Vol. III)
Code No. : ZZZ054

Published in India by :
Nusrat Ali Nasri for Kitab Bhavan
1784, Kalan Mahal, Darya Ganj
New Delhi - 1100 02 [India]

Printed in India at :
Nice Printing Press
Khureji Khas, Delhi-110051

Muslim Children-How to Bring up?

Vol. III

CONTENTS

MUSLIM CHILDREN - HOW TO BRING UP?

Vol. III

Moral Training of the Muslim Youth

The present volume comprises three sections on the training of children.

1. Effective Methods.
2. Fundamental Rules.
3. Some Vital Suggestions.

THE EFFECTIVE METHODS OF TRAINING THE CHILD

The obligations imposed on parents and guardians in this regard have already been mentioned in Volume II of this book. They relate to (a) religious (b) intellectual (c) moral (d) psychological and (d) social training.

These are undoubtedly the most important obligations to be fulfilled by the parents and guardians. How lucky and happy will those parents or guardians be indeed, who will reap the fruits of their endeavours in the Hereafter!

The parent or guardian who imparts necessary training to his child should try his level best to,foster the growth of his offspring's intellectual potentialities. In order to achieve this objective the parent or guardian is advised to adopt the following methods:

1. Demonstration by example.
2. Development of habit.
3. Exhortation.
4. Observation.
5. Punishment.

1. Demonstration by Example

The most effective way of bringing up the child to be a good individual and a social and sociable personality is by one's own example. The parent or guardian is the ideal person for the child. He tries to follow the example of his parent or tutor in every matter. In other words the child's mind, word and deed are reflective of the parent or guardian's personality. That is the reason why the example of the parent, guardian or tutor is regarded most effective in making or marring the child. If the former is honest, upright, polite, kind-hearted, bold and righteous, the child will grow to be like him and the other way round.

It is easy for them to teach the child the tenets of good conduct. But he will assimilate them only when the tutor himself translates them into action.

Allah has revealed unparalleled injunctions for the guidance of mankind. Whenever He wanted to send anyone to be His Messenger, he selected for the job a person who was the wisest and morally the best so that the people might take inspiration from him, follow him, receive from him the knowledge of various things, acknowledge the truth of what he says, inculcate in themselves all his virtues and tread in his footsteps.

Hence prophethood is something obligatory and not acquired. Thus He chose Muhammad (S.A.W.) the son of Abdullah to be the guide of Muslims till the Day of Resurrection, the beacon light for the whole of mankind.

> "Verily in the Messenger of Allah ye have a good example"
>
> (33:21)

Allah has framed the entire Islamic system in the figure of the Holy Prophet (S.A.W.) so that posterity might follow him as the living example of moral excellence.

It is an obligation imposed by Allah upon His chosen servant. He does not bestow this position on anyone in view of his prayers and self-abnegation.

No sacrifice was too great for him in his mission for the propagation of Allah's faith. He passed many a sleepless night and denied himself all the comforts of life in carrying out his sacred mission. He did not rest till a large number of people embraced Islam, although he received divine instructions not to be dismayed and to slow down his missionary activity. There is a number of verses in the Holy Qur'an to this effect:

> "If they believe not in this statement, that thou (Muhammad) wilt torment thy soul with grief over their footsteps."
>
> (18:6)

> "Thou (O Muhammad) guidest not whom thou lovest, but Allah guideth who He will."
>
> (28:56)

> "Let not thy soul expire in sighings for them! Allah is aware what they do."
>
> (35:8)

Despite these instructions the Prophet (S.A.W.) demonstrated unparalleled perseverence, steadiness, patience and industry in his missionary work. This is how great prophets strive in the way of Allah until they bring the whole nations into the fold of divine faith.

It is difficult to deal with the Prophet's sublime character in all its aspects. We shall try to highlight here some of his outstanding virtues under different heads. Allah says:

> "The Prophet's life is the best model for you."
>
> (33:21)

1. Generosity and Munificence

The Prophet (S.A.W.) was generous without starving himself. He was more generous during the holy month of Ramadhan than other months.

Hafiz Abul Shaikh quotes Hazrat Anas to have narrated

that if anyone asked of the Prophet (S.A.W.) for something, he never disappointed him. Once a man asked him for his help. The Prophet (S.A.W.) gave him such a big flock of goats that it would have filled a chasm between two hills. The man went back to his tribe and said to them, "Embrace Islam all of you. The Prophet is so bountiful that he does not seem to be apprehensive of starvation."

2. Abstinence

Imam Ahmad quotes Hazrat Anas to have narrated this Tradition:

"Hazrat Fatima (R.A.A.) offered a piece of barley bread to the Holy Prophet (S.A.W.). He said to her, "This is the first meal your father has had after three days." This is the height of self-denial unattainable by ordinary human-beings. That was quite natural as he obeyed all the divine commands in letter and spirit. Allah addresses him in the following words:

> And strain not thy eyes toward that which we cause some wedded pairs among them to enjoy, the flower of the life of the world, that We may try them thereby. The provision of thy Lord is better and more lasting (20:131)

It must be borne in mind that the Prophet (S.A.W.) did not deny himself the comforts of life because of poverty. Had he desired comforts and luxuries, he would have had plenty of them. But his abstinence was designed to provide us guidance in many ways.

First the purpose of his abstinence was to teach the Muslims to co-operate among themselves and make sacrifices to help each other.

According to *Imam Behaqi,* Hazrat Aisha (R.A.A.) is reported to have stated that the Prophet (S.A.W.) never had his meals for three consecutive days to heart's content. Had we wished we would have fully gratified our appetite but the Prophet (S.A.W.) preferred others to himself.

By his abstinence and self-abnegation the Holy Prophet(S.A.W.) has taught his followers that the Muslim *Ummah* should content itself with the basic necessities of life; for, if they indulged in luxuries and worldly pleasures they would neglect the imperative duty of upholding the Unity of Allah. He feared that luxuries and comforts might destroy the *Ummah* just as it had destroyed other nations.

3. Politeness and Humility

The Prophet (S.A.W.) was so polite and humble that he was always the first to greet others. During conversation he paid full attention to the man he talked to, whether young or old.

When he shook hands with any one he did not take away his hand until the other did.

When he wanted to attend a function or gathering, he would not like to sit at an important place. He used to go for shopping, and carried himself the things he bought. He said that he had greater right than any one else to carry his own goods. He never considered it below his dignity to work like an ordinary worker. He worked like a labourer in building the Holy mosque at Madinah. He also dug ground during the Battle of Trenches. He accepted the invitation of every free man or slave. He was also magnanimous enough to forgive those who apologized. He himself put patch on his clothes, mended his shoes, helped his wives in household jobs, tethered his camel, and shared his meal with his servant. He fulfilled the needs of the poor and did not mind sitting on the ground with them. He strictly followed the divine command:

"And lower thy wings (in kindness) to those believers who follow thee."

(26:215)

4. Benevolent to Enemies

Abdur Rehman-Al-Uzzal writes in his book Batil Ibtal (P.55)

"The Arabian peninsula never witnessed a more magnanimous conqueror marching into Makkah as the head of a great army. The whole city was at his mercy. But he forgave all its people and treated them with utmost benevolence. The chieftains of Quraish were people whose tyranny knew no bounds and who had tortured Muslim ruthlessly. But he declared general amnesty for them after the conquest of the city. This was of course at variance with the general practice of conquerors. The history of mankind bears testimony to the fact that when a conqueror enters the captured country, he massacres the vanquished mercilessly."

The Prophet (S.A.W.) gathered the citizens of Makkah and posed the following question to them:

"What treatment do you people expect of me today?"

All of them answered in a chorus, "You are a venerable brother and the son of a venerable brother."

The Prophet (S.A.W.) graciously declared, "You may go as all of you are free (meaning thereby none of you will be called to account today)."

5. Valour in Highest Degree

He was matchless in valour, too. The highest degree of valour that is needed in a soldier is to be found only in the life of the Holy Prophet (S.A.W.). We cite two incidents that bear testimony to his unrivalled bravery.

1. Once the residents of Madinah were terrified by a mysterious scream. Some people plucked up their courage to proceed in the direction from where they heard the outcry to find out what caused it. They met with the Prophet (S.A.W.) on the way who was coming back after satisfying himself that there was nothing serious. He was the first among the people of the city to proceed towards the spot in order to find out what actually happened. He was riding on the back of Abu Talha's horse with sword hanging from his neck. He tried to compose the horrified people by proclaiming that there was nothing to worry about.

2. In the Battle of Hunain the people took to flight deserting the Holy Prophet (S.A.W.). He rode a mule and repeated the following sentences again and again:

> "I am the Prophet and this is no falsehood. I am the grandson of Abdul Muttalib."
>
> He was the only warrior among the Muslims who could confront the enemy close to his ranks.

I have selected only these two incidents from the history of Islam to illustrate the matchless valour of the Holy Prophet (S.A.W.). In the first incident the Prophet (S.A.W.) led the van in reaching the danger spot and in the second we find him standing in the battle-field firm like a rock while others turned their back leaving him alone.

6. Political Acumen

The Prophet (S.A.W.) was extra-ordinarily successful in every field. It is common knowledge that he was peerless not only in moral excellence but also in political sagacity. He had the full grasp of every problem in all its details. We cite only one out of innumerable incidents from history which would bear testimony to his political acumen and skilful handling of a difficult situation.

After the Battle of Hunain the Prophet (S.A.W.) distributed booty among the people of Quraish but gave nothing to the Ansar (the natives of Madinah). Consequently the Ansar started grumbling. One of them is quoted to have said, "By God! the Prophet (S.A.W.) has defected to his compatriots." The Prophet (S.A.W.) came to know about it. He called a meeting of all the people and said to them:

"O company of Ansar! I have been apprised of something strange. Why should you have such a grievance? When I came to you, were you not misguided? Allah led you to the right path. You were then destitutes and Allah bestowed upon you wealth. You bore animosity against each other and Allah imbibed affection in your hearts."

The Ansar replied, "We are indebted most to Allah and His Prophet (S.A.W.). These two are the only source of grace and kindness."

The Prophet (S.A.W.) demanded answer to his question.

The Ansar said, "What answer can we give? We are indebted to Allah and His Prophet (S.A.W.) alone.

The Prophet (S.A.W.) retorted, "Listen! If you wanted to say something, you would have said it. Had you spoken the truth, it would have been endorsed. For instance, you could have said that when I came to you, I was being repudiated by others and you were the people who acknowledged the veracity of my message; that I came to you having been defeated and you helped me; that I was expelled from the city and you gave me asylum; that I was penniless and you allowed me to share your possessions. O Ansar! Don't you see that I have consoled a people by giving them a little wealth in order that they may embrace Islam, while I was satisfied with your faith. Would you not like if other People take away from your Prophet the gifts of camels and goats while you carry away with you the Prophet himself?" Added the Prophet, "By God, had there been no emigration, I would have been one of the Ansar. If others move into one dale and the Ansar into another, I will accompany the Ansar. O Allah! Have mercy upon the Ansar and also on their sons and grandsons."

This speech deeply moved the Ansar whose eyes were wet with tears. They said, "We are content with whatever the Prophet (S.A.W) gives us." Every word of the Prophet's speech was permeated with sincerity and fraught with veracity and penetrated deep into the hearts of the Ansar making them pure and impeccable like the cherubim. It was thus that the Holy (Prophet (S.A.W.) nipped in the bud a serious trouble that was brewing among the Ansar and inspired them by his speech. His soul-stirring speech brings home to us the judicious manner in which he gathered the people, consoled and taught them to unite under the banner of Islam.

Had the Prophet not been endowed with such sterling qualities including political wisdom and unifying power, he would never have been able to establish Islamic government in Madinah and could never have brought the whole Arabian Peninsula under his rule.

7. Firmness and Constancy

The most outstanding quality of the Holy Prophet (S.A.W.) was firmness and strength of character. We refer in this context to the firm stand he took when his uncle Abu Talib was about to withdraw his support for him. It testifies to his perseverance, constancy and unshakable faith. He said to Abu Talib, "O my uncle! By God! If these people (the pagans) put the sun on my right hand and the moon on my left and ask me to give up my mission, I will never yield. In that case Allah will either ensure the ascendancy of his faith or I will sacrifice my life for its sake." Having said this he rose with tearful eyes.

Abu Talib was deeply moved by his determination and dedication to his mission. He observed speaking to the Prophet (S.A.W.) aloud, "O my brother's son, do what you will. By God! I will never leave you alone. He then recited a few Arabic verses which are translated as under:

1. By God, the enemy never reach you as long as I am alive.

2. Carry on your mission. No harm will come to you. May you be blessed with the propagation of the faith and be gratified.

3. You have invited me to embrace the faith and think that you are my well wisher. You are truthful and also trust worthy.

4. You have presented a faith which is better than all the other faiths.

5. Had I not been apprehensive of taunts and censure, you would have found me professing (your) faith inevitably.

Nobody could have shown greater degree of constancy and firmness of faith than the Prophet (S.A.W.) did in the presence of his uncle. The ordeal he had to face was the most severe a man could endure and he faced it with indomitable courage. He obeyed this divine decree both in letter and spirit:

"Then have patience (O Muhammad) even as the stout of heart among the messengers (of God) had patience." (46:35)

The contemporary missionaries of Islam also need such constancy and determination.

Nobody can do justice to all the sterling qualities of the Holy Prophet (S.A.W.). His virtues described above are no more than just a drop in the ocean. Allah Himself has said about him

> "You occupy (O Muhammad) the highest moral position."

No greater tribute can be paid to him than this Divine Praise.

The upshot of the foregoing discussion is that one's example of moral excellence exercises great impact on the minds of those whom one brushes one's shoulders with. This alone was the secret of the dissemination of the message of Islam in the four corners of the world.

Every Muslim man and woman should bear it in mind that if they want Islam to regain its glory in the world they will have to present exemplary character in every sphere of life. They can guide the nations of the world only when they inculcate in themselves virtues like complaisance fairness, in dealings, business honesty and the life. It is only thus that we can serve as the true missionaries of Islam and strive for the welfare of mankind.

In other words Islamic training and promotion of Islamic values require Practical examples that produce deep impression on the minds of the people. In fact, moral virtues are absolutely essential for furtherance of social welfare. They continue to exercise impact on posterity.

That is the reason why the Holy Prophet (S.A.W.) wanted every parent to be a living model of moral excellence himself before they start training the children. The children imitate every act of the parents. Thus if the parents bear exemplary character, their offspring will grow on sound moral basis and will acquire sterling qualities in their impressionable years.

If the parents want to imbibe in their children truthfulness, honesty, modesty, kindness and aversion to falsehood, they should demonstrate these virtues by their own behaviour and active participation in noble tasks. If the child sees his parents tell lies, commit breach of trust, lack constancy, behave in a shameful manner, he will never grow up to be a good man. If he hears his parents talk blasphemously and use foul language, he will never learn to be soft-spoken. The child whose prents are prejudiced, irritable and susceptible to pressure will never develop a balanced personality. The child who observes his parents' wrongful and offensive behaviour will never learn the meaning of magnanimity, love and friendship.

If the parents' conduct is exemplary, their children will naturally develop good character. Obversely if they conduct themselves immorally, they gradually deviate from the moral norms and will finally disobey their parents and revolt against them.

A poet poses the question.

Can such children be expected to develop good character as suck the milk of lewd woman?

But the parents will be wrong if they think that they have fulfilled their obligations with regard to the training of children by their own examples. They must rather try to make the children tread in the footsteps of the Holy Prophet (S.A.W.). For this purpose it is necessary to relate to the children the events of the Prophet's life including those of the wars he waged against the pagans and thus help them develop his habits and virtues. *Imam Tabarani* narrates the following tradition of the Holy Prophet (S.A.W.) to this effect:

"Imbibe three qualities in your children:

a. The love of the Prophet (S.A.W.),

b. The love of the members of his family,

c. The habit of reciting the Holy Qur'an.

The parents are advised to choose such schools for their children whose atmosphere is healthy so that the child may have good associates. This will provide him the right spiritual, moral, physical, social and individual training. In a good school the child will not be induced to deviate from the moral and social norms nor would his mind develop complexes. He will be physically strong, spiritually sound and intellectually mature.

If the father, however, pleads that the entire society is rotten to the core and corroded by ignorance and in such a milieu it will be extremely difficult to create healthy atmosphere for the child, we would agree with him. The contemporary society is really corrupt and misguided. Nevertheless, the father is under the obligation to strive heart and soul to provide the right moral and spiritual training to the child. He will have to work hard to foster his intellectual, psychological and social growth on the right lines. He will have nothing to be ashamed of in the Hereafter if his child goes astray despite his efforts to bring him up aright.

I am of the view that the example of parents, good companions, the teacher and the eldest brother goes a long way in making the child a useful member of the society. If the parents are determined to impart the right sort of training to the child, they can create for him such an atmosphere in which he will grow up to be a virtuous person.

The parents should bear it in mind that the training and moral uplift of the eldest child has far-reaching effects on the training of the younger ones. The younger son looks upon his elder brother as the model to be followed and, therefore, he imitates the latter as the model to be followed and, therefore, he imitates the latter and tries to develop all his habits. If the eldest son is corrupt and vagrant, the younger ones are sure to follow his example and will thus go astray.

Hence it is incumbent upon the parents to focus their attention on the training of the eldest son first and then to take care of the younger son. If the former is bred on the right lines, the younger sons will automatically get the right training. Allah himself patronizes the righteous people.

The Holy Qur'an describes those people as undesirable whose words do not accord with their deed. The following verses of the Qur'an apply to parents and guardians who are responsible for the upbringing and training of children:

> "O ye who believe! Why say ye that which ye do not? It is most hateful in the sight of Allah that ye say that which ye do not."
>
> (61:2-3)

> "Enjoin ye righteousness upon mankind while ye yourselves forget to practise it? And ye are readers of the scripture. Have ye then no sense?"
>
> (2:44)

These verses are addressed to those who set bad example.

We would in this context refer to Hazrat Umar's admirable practice.

Before he ordered others to do or refrain from doing

anything, he used to advise the members of his own family. He gathered them together and addressed them in the following words:

"I am going to call upon the people to do this and not to do that. I swear by Allah that I do not want any one of you to do what I prohibit other people; nor do I want to omit what I enjoin upon others. Otherwise I will inflict on you exemplary punishment."

Having said this, he used to go out and call upon the people to do or not to do a certain thing. Not a single citizen would disobey his orders in view of the example he set by enjoining upon the members of his own family what he enjoined upon them.

What all the parents and guardians have to learn from these verses and events is that it is they themselves who play the basic role in the moral uplift of children. The pattern of their life serves as a model in children's refinement.

No exhortation and sermonization would produce the desired results in the training of children unless the parents, guardians and the tutors conduct themselves in an exemplary manner. It is they whose manners and habits are imitated by the children. They fall under the category of those mentioned in the following verses of the Holy Qur'an:

"Those are they whom Allah guideth, so follow their guidance."

(6:91)

2. Development of Habit

It is an established fact according to the Islamic *Shariah* that the child is born with Faith in Divine Unity, God's Existence and an Islam ass the right path. This is clear from the following verses of the Qur'an:

The nature (framed) of Allah, in which He has created man. There is no altering Allah's creation. That is the right religion but most men know not.

(30:30)

According to a tradition cited in the *Sahih Bukhari*, "Every child is born in conformity to divine nature" viz. with belief in the Godhead and Divine unity.

In order to keep the child in tact on the innate natural pattern, his training should commence in his early years by inculcating in him good habits, teaching him good manners and subjecting him to discipline. He would be imbued with the *Shariah* proprieties as he grows up.

It is an established fact that if the child is trained on the Islamic pattern and is also placed in a healthy and pious atmosphere, he would develop an exemplary character. The Islamic pattern of training is indicated in many traditions of the Holy Prophet (S.A.W). For example some of them are cited below:

1. "It is better for a man to teach his sons better manners than to do an act of pure charity."

(Tirmizi)

2. "The father gives no better gift to his son than good training."

(Tirmizi)

3. "Teach your offspring and members of family good conduct and manners."

(Musnad Abdur Razzaq and Musnad Saeed Bin Mansoor)

4. Inculcate three virtues in your offspring:

a. Love of your Prophet (S.A.W.). (b) Love of the Prophet's Family. (c) The habit of reciting the Holy Qur'an.

(Mo Jam-al -Tabarani)

The Prophet (S.A.W.) tells us what healthy and good atmosphere is. We cite the following traditions in this context:

Every child is born on the pattern of Islamic nature (that is with Islamic disposition). Later his parents convert him into a Jew, Christian or Zoroastrian."

(Bukhari)

It follows from the foregoing tradition that if the child is fortunate enough to have such virtuous parents as could instil in him the Islamic faith and enrich him with the teachings of Islam, then he will grow up to be a true Muslim. In other words the family circumstances and the home atmosphere exercise great influence on the child's training.

Maintenance of link with faith

This is the fundamental principle of training. It requires that the Muslim should be able to feel the pleasure of meditation in his heart of hearts constantly (that is, he should be mindful of the Master's eye at every moment) and should always be conscious of Allah's glory and never for a moment be unmindful of fearing and respecting Him. It is characteristic of a true Muslim to make himself ever stronger individually and psychologically, strengthen his will and avoid indulging in sensual pleasures. On the contrary, he tries to mould his life according to the Prophet's practice. He never allows scepticism to vitiate his faith. A true Muslim's way of life is outlined in the following verses of the Holy Qur'an:

> "Who is better than Allah for judgment to a people who have certainty (in their belief)?"
>
> (5:50)

A true Muslim evaluates his deeds by this criterion:

"And whatsoever the Messenger giveth you take it. And whatsoever he forbiddeth abstain from it."

(59:7)

"But nay O Muhammad! By thy Lord, they will not believe (in truth) until they make thee judge of what is in dispute between them and find within themselves no dislike of that which thou dicidest, and submit with full submission."

(4:65)

The various forms of worship and the basic Islamic beliefs undoubtedly perpetuate the blissful state of meditation. They include prayers, remembrance of Allah, recitation of the Holy Qur'an and pondering over its verses in the peaceful hours of the night, constant awareness of Allah's Greatness, the belief in the torment to be suffered in the grave, the belief in the Hereafter and the horrible scene of Resurrection. All these things foster the growth of a consistent personality, striking a fair balance between the claims of the world and the Hereafter. Such a person does justice to all and strictly adheres to the following edict of the Holy Prophet:

"You have your duty towards Allah, towards yourself and towards your family. So fulfil your duties to all."

No dispute will ever arise between them. Saturated with the fear of Allah they would not possibly have borne animosity against each other. As they fulfill their duties to all, they will not go astray.

The best way to persuade grown-up people to abstain from forbidden things and cause them to hate sin is to highlight evil.

Bringing evil into relief and expose it to disgrace is such an effective method of reformation that has been adopted in the Qur'an itself to cause aversion among Muslims to the customs of pagan ignorance.

For instance, when prohibition was enjoined on the Muslims', verses were revealed from time to time wherein the harm and evils involved in drinking were highlighted and they were told that liquor produces harmful effects on human beings and mars the moral, collective and religious behaviour of mankind.

3. Change of Environment

Change of environment is as effective in the reformation and training of an adult as the two methods dealt with above. Had it not been so the Prophet (S.A.W.) would not have been commanded by Allah to migrate to Madinah; nor would the Prophet (S.A.W.) have advised his companions to follow suit.

The purpose of migration was to impart training in an environment where forbidden acts and sins are not committed. It was designed to set up a government under the divine Shariah and to reform the Muslims in a milieu dominated by Islam, wherein the divine decrees revealed in the verses of the Holy Qur'an are in force.

It is incumbent on the tutors of the adults to adopt the Islamic methods of training if they want the individuals of the *Ummah* to lead a peaceful life. Says Allah.

> "Say: This is my way; I call on Allah with sure knowledge, I and whosoever followeth me. Glory be to Allah - and I am not of the idolators.
>
> (12:108)

There are two methods of reforming the minors:

1. Exhortation

2. Habituation

By exhortation is meant the theoretical method of training and by habituation is meant the shaping of the minor's personality. It is the practical method of training.

As the child is naturally susceptible to exhortation and habituation, the tutors and parents should exhort him to do good acts and accustom him to good things right from the years of discretion.

The child is a trust in the custody of his parents. His pure heart is like a fine essence. If the child is helped to form good habits and is taught goodness, he will go up to be a well-bred and well-trained person with an awareness of this world as well as the Hereafter.

We would like to furnish here some valuable information about the exhortation and habituation of children.

(a) The Holy Prophet (S.A.W.) advises us to teach the child the *Kalima.*

"There is not God but Allah and Muhammad is His Prophet."

"*Imam Hakim* quotes in his Musnad the following tradition of the Holy Prophet (S.A.W.) with reference to Hazrat Ibn Abbas:

"Teach your children the *Kalima* as soon as they begin to talk."

This is the theoretical aspect of instruction. The practical aspect requires that the child should be mentally prepared for believing in his heart of hearts that there is no creator, no inventor, no object of worship other than Allah. This requirement of training is fulfilled by natural phenomena like flowers, the sky, the earth, the ocean and man himself. At the sight of other created-beings, the idea of Divine Unity should strike him of its own accord. He should be driven to the conclusion that the real Creator of all things is Allah alone.

Next the child should realize as a result of the tutors training that the sensible things with which the universe is fraught have not come into being by themselves. They are no creators and no inventors in themselves. They are all state without any intrinsic virtue. It, therefore, follows that there is a Being which has created them and that is no Being other than Allah Himself.

Having trained the child thus, the guardians should try to make him ponder over the realities of the heaven and earth and bring into play his potentiality to infer that Allah alone is the Creator of the universe so that the child may come to believe in this ultimate reality. They should then direct the child's thinking from the sensible to the rational, from the particular to the general and from the simple to the complex. Consequently the child would have firm faith in Allah's Being both intuitionally and intellectually.

(b) The Prophet (S.A.W.) has enjoined on the parents and teachers to exhort and teach the children to offer prayers when they are seven years old. *Imam Hakim* and *Imam Dawood* report with reference to Hazrat Amr bin-al-'Aas the Prophet (S.A.W.) said, "Instruct your children to offer payers when they are seven years old and when they reach the age of ten years, beat them for failing to do so. Also separate their beds."

Acting on the principles of exhortation and habituation laid by the Holy Prophet (S.A.W.) would foster the child's development of consistent personality and make him a true Muslim with unshakable faith.

If the guardians and parents strive hard to train and edify, the children will grow up to be the soldiers of Islam and by virtue of their unshakable belief they will prove to be the missionaries of Islam and will acquire the qualities of the veterans of Islam. The entire Muslim *Ummah* will be proud of them and the Islamic society will become a heaven of peace and tranquillity because of their moderation.

If the conduct of the child is moulded in accordance with moral principles, he will acquire moral excellence. This may be done by the following methods:

The child's moral spirit should be spurred by delightful talk. He should be given presents from time to time. Sometimes he should be induced by the lure of good things and at others he should be frightened by the dangerous consequences. Rebukes and punishment may also be resorted to whenever it is considered necessary to prevent the child from moral aberration.

By these methods of reformation and disciplining the inherent capacities of the child will be developed and he will grow up to be a refined and decent gentleman with balanced personality. He will thus endear himself to the people who will regard him with respect.

Didactic Approach (Exhortation)

Didactic approach is of vital importance in the spiritual training, moral refinement and improvement of collective behaviour of children. Preaching and instruction lead the child to understand the nature of things. It induces him to acquire good habits and take interest in the basic principles of Islam. This method has been adopted in the Qur'an too, wherein human beings have been frequently addressed in a didactic and instructive manner.

A few verses of the Holy Book are cited here in which instructive style has been adopted:

> "And remember when Luqman said unto his son when he was exhorting him : O my dear son! Ascribe no

partners unto Allah. To ascribe partners unto Him is a tremendous wrong.

(31:13)

"And Luqman said, "O my dear son! Anything though it be but the weight of a grain of mustard-seed, and though it be in a rock or in the heavens, or in the earth, Allah will bring it forth. Lo! Allah is Subtle, Aware.

"O my dear son! Establish worship and enjoin kindness and persevere whatever may be fall. Lo! that is of the steadfast heart of things."

(31:16-17)

The Holy Qur'an abounds in verses that contain a call to turn to Allah and guidance for the individual and the society. In these verses the didactic style is of the essence. A careful study of the Qur'an would reveal that in these verses the following styles have been used:

1. Exhortation to fear Allah.
2. Narration of the events of the past.
3. Preaching and Instruction.
4. Instruction to have goodwill towards others.
5. Counsel to tread the right path.
6. Inducement by giving tidings of good consequences.
7. Warning against bad results.

All these are the seven modes of refinement and reformation found in the Holy Qur'an.

Every intelligent person knows it full well that the Holy Qur'an attaches vital importance to didactic approach for the disciplining of the human mind and for persuading man to tread the right path.

We have quoted at many places in this book the verses of the Holy Qur'an to substantiate the fact that pure and meditative minds are susceptible to instruction and exhortation couched in effective style. It tends to take advice quickly and accept guidance from the revealed injunctions.

These were the methods of training the adults.

We proceed to discuss now the modes of training the minors. It may be mentioned here that the child is born on natural pattern. His mind is pure and uncontaminated, free from the sinister influence of paganism. He does not commit sin either. That is why exhortation and advice make deep impressions on the child's mind.

The parents and guardians will have to adopt the Qur'anic method for the training and reformation of their minor children. If they want their children to grow as balanced and consistent personalities with maturity of intellect and sterling qualities, they ought to follow the Qur'anic method in the moral training of children. We would like to quote here some of the verses of the Holy Qur'an in which the didactic mode is manifest so that the guardians may benefit from them and train the children accordingly.

The Qur'an has adopted many modes which fall under the following heads:

(a) Instructive Method

Involving leniency or expression of dislike. This way of exhortation is extremely effective and penetrates deep into the heart. Such verses are put in the mouth of the Prophets. The Qur'an addresses the people of every region and all mental levels:

1. Mode of addressing; the son:

"And Luqman said exhorting his son: O my dear son! Do not assign a partner unto Allah."

Noah addresses his son in the following words:

"O my son! Come ride with us and be not with the disbelievers."

"He said, O my dear son! Tell not thy brethren of thy vision, lest they plot a plot against thee."

(13:5)

And this is what Abraham said to his sons and also Jacob:

O my sons! Allah hath chosen for you the true religion; therefore cling to it and die as Muslims."

(2:132)

2. The people of the Book are addressed in the following style:

(i) O people of the Book, come to an agreement between us and you, that we shall worship none but Allah and we shall ascribe no partner to Him and that none of us shall take others for lords beside Allah. And if they turn away, then say. Bear witness that we are they who have surrendered unto Him.

(3:64)

(ii) O people of the Scripture! Now hath Our messenger come unto you, expounding unto you much of that which ye used to hide in the scripture, and forgiving much. Now hath come unto you light from Allah and a plain Scripture, whereby Allah guideth him who seeketh His good pleasure unto paths of peace.

(5:15)

The Holy Prophet (S.A.W.) attaches special importance to instruction and exhortation. He calls upon the parents and the missionaries of Islam to adopt didactic method of education and training and tries to impress upon the mind of every believer to consider himself a missionary of Islam wherever he is and in whatever environment he is placed and should continue to perform his function as such. It is quite possible that his advice and exhortation imprints deep impression in the mind of someone and rids many a people of ignorance and iniquity.

There exist innumerable other Traditions on this subject. The parents should act upon them in order to reform themselves as well as to train their children. The Prophet's mode of advice and exhortation is the best method of training and reformation because of its variety and merits.

The guardians should address the children in a manner that may create in them the urge to act on the right lines and be conscious of their mistakes. This would not only purify their souls but also make their minds susceptible to instruction. Thus they would meditate over the God head. Having created such a state of mind in the children, the guardian would be able to make them pledge that they would acknowledge Islam as the code of their life and try to put it into practice, and thus inculcate in themselves the same moral virtues as required by Islam.

(b) Question and answer method

The Prophet (S.A.W.) used to preach his companions by question-answer method and brought into play their mental potentialities.

We cite here some instances from the collections of the Prophet's Traditions:

(i) *Imam Ahmed* quotes this Tradition with reference to Hazrat Abdullah bin Amr Bin al 'Aas.

I (Abdullah) heard the Prophet (S.A.W.) say : Do you know who a Muslim is?

"Allah and His Messenger know better," I replied.

"A Muslim is one from the harm of whose tongue and mouth other Muslims are safe," observed he.

He asked again, "Do you know who a Muslim is?"

The companions said, "Allah and His Messenger know better."

He observed, "A Muslim is one who is regarded by other Muslims as the custodian of their lives and property."

He then referred to a Muhajir and said, A Muhajir is one who abandoned evil and abstained from it."

(ii) *Imam Muslim* mentions a Tradition in his collection as related by Hazrat Abu Hurairah. It runs as follows:

The Prophet (S.A.W.) asked his companions, "Do you know who is a poor fellow?"

"We regard him as a poor fellow who does not possess wealth," replied the companions.

The Prophet (S.A.W.) observed, "But in my *Ummah* a poor fellow is he who will appear on the Day of Judgment with the observance of religious duties to his credit including the saying of prayers of five times, fasting during the month of Ramadhan and the payment of poor-due; but at the same he would have abused some person, calumniated another person, usurped the possessions of yet another, shed the blood of still another without any reason and beaten still another person. The good acts of such a man would be distributed among those who may have suffered at his hand while the misdeeds of the latter would be imputed to him and he will be hurled into the Fire."

(c) Commencing instruction with swearing by the Name of Allah

This is designed to make one realize the importance of giving up wrong-doing and of doing good deeds. We cite a couple of relevant Traditions in this context:

1. According to *Imam Muslim* the Prophet (S.A.W.) is quoted to have observed, "I swear by Him Who possessed my soul that you will never enter the Heaven until you become true believers and you can never become true believers until you establish strong bonds of affection among yourselves. Shall I not tell you to do something which intensifies affection among you? Universalize the practice of Islam among yourselves."

2. *Imam Bukhari* gives this Tradition with reference to *Abu Shuraih* wherein the Prophet (S.A.W.) is quoted to have said, a By God! the man is faithless, By God! the man is faithless, By God! the man is faithless." When asked who the man was. He said, "The man whose malignity disturbs the peace of his neighbour."

This was a mode adopted by the Prophet (S.A.W.) for the instruction of his companions. The books of Hadith abound with the examples of such instruction.

(d) Delightful Instruction

Delightful mode of exhortation stimulates the mind and creates interest and removes boredom.

An example of delightful exhortation is provided by a Tradition mentioned by *Abu Dawood* with reference to Hazrat

Anas (R.A.A.). According to this tradition a man came to the Prophet (S.A.W.) and asked for a camel as gratis so that he may load it with household goods. The Prophet (S.A.W.) said, "Well I am going to make you ride the offspring of a female camel."

The man said, "But what can I do with the young one of a female camel?"

The Prophet (S.A.W.) replied, "A female camel begets only the offspring of a female camel."

The Prophet (S.A.W.) humorously explained to him that a camel remains the offspring of a female even when it grows up and is able to carry burden.

It is necessary to point out that preaching or instruction is effective only when the preacher is sincere, compassionate and devout—one whose soul is pure. If a preacher does not possess these qualities, he will be accountable to Allah for preaching deceitfully.

(e) Instruction by Illustration

In order to make his point crystal clear during his sermon the Holy Prophet (S.A.W.) cited the examples of things commonly observed and easily comprehensible to the audience.

Imam Nasai quotes this tradition with reference to Hazrat Anas (R.A.A.): The Prophet (S.A.W.) said: The true believer who recites the Qur'an is like a lime whose smell and taste both are pleasant; a believer who does not recite the Qur'an is like a date which is sweet but has no smell; an iniquitous fellow who recites the Qur'an is like the flower of *'Nazbo'* which emits fragrance but is of bitter taste; and the iniquitous fellow who does not recite the Qur'an at all is like the fruit of *'indrain'* which is of bitter taste and has no fragrance and a bad companion is like a blacksmith who blows the furnace. Its smoke will certainly be a nuisance to you, even if you are fortunate enough to avoid its soot."

These similes and examples used by the Prophet (S.A.W.) to illustrate his points are extremely effective in persuading the people to do good and abstain from evil. They are quite intelligible to the audience as they are drawn from common observation.

(f) Exhortation by reference to prohibited things

The Prophet (S.A.W.) used to take a forbidden thing in his hand and prohibit by showing it to the people in order to cause hatred for it. Such a demonstration would unequivocally prove it to be unlawful and human nature would develop aversion to it.

Imam Dawood, Imam Nasai and *Ibne Majah* quote Hazrat Ali (R.A.A.) to have stated that the Holy Prophet (S.A.W.) took silken cloth in one hand and gold in the other and then raising both the hands announced, "The use of both these things are forbidden for the men of my *Ummah* while it is lawful for the women."

There, then, were the various modes of exhortation and instruction which the Prophet (S.A.W.) adopted for the guidance of the grown up people, training of the youngsters and leading both the elites and commoners to the right path.

We have described quite a few effective modes of instruction and exhortation. As has been mentioned the Holy Prophet (S.A.W.) adopted a variety of methods for the guidance and edification of the people: Sometimes he would relate didactic stories, and at others he would resort to the question-answer method. On some occasions he was in raptures and on others he was humorous, or drew figures on the ground, or demonstrated something practically or resorted to didactic method quoting the verses of the Holy Qur'an in support, or explained things profiting by a suitable opportunity. If a question was put to him, he sometimes answered it by asking an important question himself. Sometimes he prohibited an act verbally and on others he tried to cause aversion for something with reference to common observation.

The parents and guardians should adopt the same methods of instruction as the Prophet (S.A.W.) did. For the Holy Prophet's sermons and preaching did not stem out of his personal desires. He was taught manners and rules of propriety and exalted to the highest degree of morality by Allah. He grew and received his training entirely under God's care and was guarded by Him Alone. Every word and act of such an exalted person always conforms to the Will of Allah. Thus all the acts and words, likes and dislikes of the Holy Prophet (S.A.W.) were subject to the Divine Will. Therefore, they constitute everlasting code of life for the whole of mankind and his character will serve it as the beacon light till the Day of Judgment.

Allah Himself guarantees the eternal glory and the good repute of the Holy Prophet (S.A.W.):

> "Verily in the messenger of Allah ye have a good example from him who looketh unto Allah and the Last Day, and remembereth Allah much."
>
> (33:21)

> "Whosoever obeyeth the messenger, obeyth Allah."
>
> (4:80)

We would like to impress upon the parents and guardians that if there is a discrepancy between their word and deed and if they do not themselves adhere to what they teach, their instruction and exhortation will fall on deaf ears.

Nobody would respond to their call. On the contrary they will come under fire and all the people will mock them and will have a very low opinion about them.

> A word that does not come from the heart produces no effects on the hearts. An insipid sermon or instruction does not move the audience.

A good father and a good mother sit together with their children and relate to them interesting incidents and didactic anecdotes and foster their intelligence and wisdom by illuminating conversation. Sometimes they tell them stories, and at others some incident from which a moral can be drawn. Sometimes they recite didactic poetry to them and at others the verses of the Holy Qur'an. They also encourage debates among the children on different subjects. In other words they resort to different methods for the training, reformation and edification of their children. That is how they refine and discipline their children spiritually, psychologically and morally. At the same time good parents also exhort their children to pay full attention to their studies.

By training their children in different ways, the parents are satisfied in heart of hearts. They are also reassured that their children pass most of the time usefully.

If the children or pupils are trained and disciplined in the manner indicated above regularly every day, one will before long find in them glimpses of good character and righteousness. It is the pupils of today on whom the hopes of nations future is pinned and who are expected to accomplish the tasks of glorifying Islam.

The parent or tutor is therefore, advised to imitate the Qur'anic mode and teach the child in a didactic manner alternated by exhortation and inducement. As the last resort he may also admonish and warn him.

Apart from the methods mentioned above, directly addressing the child would also stir his feelings. For instance the guardian should address the child by saying: "O my child!" This way of addressing would induce him to promptly take the advice. At many a place in the Holy Qur'an this mode of addressing has been adopted. Besides this, the following other methods have been adopted in the Holy Book at many places:

1. Instructive manner of telling anecdotes.

2. Moral teaching by exhortation and advice.

3. Use of imperative expressions or words to stress Islamic injunctions.

4. Negative Interrogation.

5. Rational reasoning.

6. Transformation of outlook on the basis of observation.

7. Guidance to the system on the basis of the *Shariah* rules.

These methods have been adopted in the Holy Qur'an at innumerable places. There are other methods of instruction too which have been derived from the Holy Book.

It remains to be seen now how the parents and guardians adopt the Holy Prophet's instructive methods. A few questions come to our mind in this connection.

1. Do the parents or guardians elaborate the instructive elements while relating anecdotes?

2. Do they talk about useful things in question-answer method?

3. Do they keep in view the boredom of listeners and confine themselves to important subjects while exhorting and preaching them in a single sitting?

4. Do they adopt the swearing method?

Do they try to create interest during their conversation?

5. Do they dominate the minds of the children while instructing or exhorting them?

6. Do they draw a diagram to elucidate their point?

7. Following academic phase of training, what method do they adopt for practical demonstration?

8. How do they profit by current events and context for making effective their instructive discourse?

These are the questions to which the answers of the parents or guardians must be in the affirmative; for all these modes of reformation and instruction over their origin to the Holy Qur'an and the Traditions of the Prophet (S.A.W.).

The parents and guardians are advised to use the Qur'anic method of addressing the common people; for the Qur'an is the Book that can never be susceptible to falsehood and is the revelation of Allah Who is Wise and Praiseworthy. They are also advised to imitate the Holy Prophet's mode of instruction and exhortation because the Prophet (S.A.W.) was impeccable and whatever he spoke was pure, without a tinge of beastly desire and whose perfection as a man is unattainable by any other human-being. Allah himself praises the prophet by saying:

"O Prophet! Thou possessest great moral qualities."

"O Prophet! We have sent you as a blessing for the universe."

The Prophet himself says: "My Lord has taught me manners and excellent manners."

4. Vigilance (Observation)

This way of training means that in the religious education and moral refinement of the child every act of his is to be watched and all his psychological and collective tendencies are to be carefully observed. Besides he should be questioned with regard to his physical training and progress in his studies.

It is the basic method of training by which the child may be helped to develop a balanced personality that enables him to do justice to the deserving, bear his responsibilities independently and duly fulfil his obligations. It is by this method that man becomes a true Muslim and can play an effective role in the glorification of Islam and which can be relied upon for the establishment of a stable Islamic state whose magnificence and cultural splendour may serve as a beacon light to other nations. The comprehensive tenets of Islam and its everlasting principles of life require that the parents and guardians should attach special importance to the care and observation of their children. They should keep an eye on the children's behaviour along with providing guidance in every walk of life. That is how they will be able to fulfil their overall responsibility of training the youngsters.

A guardian should be fully conscious of the fact that watching the child carefully is one of the fundamental principles of training. If the guardian keeps an eye on the activities and behaviour of the child he will come to know of his weaknesses. When the guardian finds that the child is desirous of doing something good, he should appreciate it and encourage the child. But if the child is disposed to do something wrong, the guardian should prohibit him and acquaint him with its evil consequences. If the guardian or parent does not pay attention to the child and watch him carefully, he will inevitably deviate from the moral norms and go astray. Thus he is bound to ruin himself.

The Holy Prophet (S.A.W.) who was our first teacher and guide has handed down to us the pattern of training and reforming his companions. He used to ask them questions and enquire about their affairs. If any one of them was guilty of any thing wrong, he asked him to be careful in future. If he found any of his companions doing a good deed, he encouraged him. The Prophet (S.A.W.) was also nice and kind to the poor and the needy. He taught manners to the children and illuminated the ignorant with knowledge and wisdom.

The sense of responsibility with which the Holy Prophet (S.A.W.) performed the task of training and edifying his companions may well be judged from the following Traditions:

(1) Collective Training

Imam Bukhari and *Imam Muslim* state with reference to Hazrat Abu Saeed Al Khadri that the Prophet (S.A.W.) said to his companions to refrain from holding meetings on the thorough-fares. The companions replied that those meetings were absolutely essential for them as they exchanged views in them. The Prophet (S.A.W.) said that if they did not acquiesce in giving up meetings, then they should avoid encroaching on the right of the way. They enquired what was meant by the right of the way. The Prophet (S.A.W.) repled, "Lower you gaze, remove nuisance, reciprocate greetings, enjoin good and forbid evil."

(2) Abstinence from what is unlawful

Imam Nawawi quotes Hazrat Ibn Abbas in his *Riadh-us-Saleheen* to have stated that once the Prophet (S.A.W) saw a man wearing a gold ring which he took off from his finger and threw it away. Having done so he said, "One of you has taken a bit of fire and put it on his hand!" He then went away. Those present asked the man to pick up the ring and try to derive some other benefit from it. The man said, "By God! I will never pick up the ring which the Prophet (S.A.W.) has cast away."

(3) Disciplining the Children

Imam Bukhari and *Imam Muslim* quote Hazrat Umar bin Abi Salamah to have said, "I was a child under the tutelage of the Holy Prophet (S.A.W.). During the supper my hand was moving all over the plate. The Prophet (S.A.W.) admonished me saying: O child! Begin with the name of Allah, eat with your right hand and take you morsels from the part of the pot which is closer to you.

(4) Guidance for the elders

Imam Behaqi and *Imam Dawood* quote this Tradition as narrated by Hazrat Abdullah bin 'Amr (R.A.A.): Once my mother called me when the Prophet (S.A.W.) was present at our home. He asked her what she wanted to give me. My mother replied that she intended to give me a date. The Prophet (S.A.W.) replied, "Had you not given him any thing, a lie would have been entered in the record of your deeds."

(5) Moral Training

Imam Bukhari and *Imam Muslim* quote Hazrat Abu Bakr to have stated, "They were talking about a person in the presence of the Holy Prophet (S.A.W.). Another persons praised him. The Prophet (S.A.W.) said: "You have cut off the head of your comrade." He repeated this remark time and again and then said: If any one must praise a person at all he should say: I think he is like this and like this (Provided that he is really so). As for the rest Allah knows better."

Nobody can, added the Prophet (S.A.W.), "prove himself to be chaste and immune before Allah".

(6) Individual Training

According to *Imam Bukhari* and *Imam Muslim* Hazrat Noman Basheer stated that his father took him to the Prophet and said, "I have gifted a slave to this son of mine." The Prophet (S.A.W.) asked him if he had gifted a slave to each of his other sons as well. Hazrat Basheer replied in the negative. The Prophet said, "Then take back the slave from him." According to another Tradition the Prophet (S.A.W.) asked Hazrat Basheer if he had meted out the same kind of treatment to all his sons. Hazrat Basheer replied in the negative. Thereupon the Prophet observed, "Fear God and do justice among your children." Hazrat Basheer took back the slave accordingly. In yet another Tradition the Holy Prophet (S.A.W.) is reported to have observed, "Do not make me bear witness; for I do not bear witness where wrongful treatment is involved."

(7) Physical Training

According to *Imam Bukhari* the Holy Prophet (S.A.W.) used to go to the groups of his companions practising archery and said to them by way of encouragement, "Shoot the arrows. I am with you."

This holds good in case if praise engenders haughtiness. Otherwise there is no harm in praising. The Prophet (S.A.W.) himself praised his companions in their presence. For instance he said to Hazrat Umar "When Satan sees you going one way, he leaves it and takes another way." (i.e. Satan cannot stand in his way).

(8) Missionary training and exhortation to be kind to the common people

Imam Bukhari and *Imam Muslim* quote a Tradition

wherein Hazrat Anas is reported to have said, "Once I was going along with the Prophet (S.A.W.) who happened to cover himself with a Najrani sheet of cloth with thick fringes. An Arab seized the cloth and roughly pulled him. I raised my eyes and saw the marks of the fringe of the cloth on the Prophet's neck. The Arab then said to him, "Give me something out of your possessions." The Prophet (S.A.W.) turned to the man, gave him a broad smile and ordered that something should be given to him.

We have cited some living examples to illustrate the Holy Prophet's practice of keeping an eye on the individuals of the society in order to instruct and reform them. They bear testimony to the fact that the Holy Prophet (S.A.W.) took keen interest in the training of the people, looking after their affairs as well as in their edification.

You may have also seen from the Traditions mentioned above that the Holy Prophet (S.A.W.) did not only provide guidance to the grown up people but also kept in view the training and reformation of the youngsters. He did not confine his attention to the improvement of only one aspect of human personality but attached equal importance to all its aspects. He tried to refine the psychological, physical and social aspects of the individual alike.

We now proceed to discuss the Holy Prophet's guidance and teachings specifically aimed at the improvement of the woman's standard of living and giving her what is due to her.

(i) According to a Tradition quoted by *Imam Nasai* and *Ibn Majah* a young girl called on the Prophet (S.A.W.) and complained that her father had contracted her into marriage with his nephew, so that he might conceal his weakness although she was not willing to marry the man. The Prophet (S.A.W.) sent for the father of the girl and called upon him to give his daughter full freedom to choose a husband for herself. The girl said that she now regarded as legitimate whatever her father had done. But she added that what she really meant by preferring the complaint was to demonstrate that the fathers had no authority in matters of the daughters' wedlock.

(ii) Imam Bukhari tells us that Hazrat Sabit Bin Qais was a virtuous Muslim but was ugly and of dark complexion. His wife complained to the Prophet (S.A.W.) that she was unhappy because of Sabit's habits but that she could not disobey her husband as a Muslim woman. The Prophet (S.A.W.) asked her, "Are you willing to return the orchard he has given to you?" She replied in the affirmative. The Prophet (S.A.W.) then sent for Sabit and asked him to divorce her. Hazrat Sabit divorced her accordingly.

(iii) According to a Tradition narrated by *Bazzaz* and *Tabarani* a woman named Zainab was famous as a 'Lady Preacher'. She came to the Holy Prophet (S.A.W.) and said, "I have come to you as a representative of women. Allah has enjoined Jehad as a duty on menfolk. When they fight in the way of Allah, Allah rewards them and when they fall martyrs in the battlefield they are alive in the presence of Allah, Who provides food for them. We womenfolk look after them. Are we not entitled to any reward?"

The Holy Prophet (S.A.W.) said to her, "Tell every woman you meet, the obedience of the husband and recognition of his rights entails a reward equal to that of jehad. But only a few women would do this."

The method adopted by the Holy Prophet (S.A.W.) for the observation and taking care of the individuals of the society is the most effective method for the reformation of the society and will for ever serve us the best guide for the parents and tutors. He calls on every parent and tutor to strive heart and soul for the due fulfilment of their obligations with regard to the training of the children. He is desirous of paying full attention to the development of the child's intellectual potentials, personal dignity and moral uplift, besides imparting to him good training in other respects.

If keeping an eye and careful observation is effective in the training improvement and guidance of the grown-up people, it will prove to be the more efficacious in the training and reformation of the youngsters. Impressionable as the child is both mentally and physically, he is much more susceptible to process of edification and instruction. His mind is uncontaminated with sinister propensities. The grown-up people possess such potentialities to a much lesser degree. Hence it will be easier to turn the child into a good man spiritually and morally, provided given proper and congenial environment, receive good training both at home and at the school and his social behaviour is checked and disciplined. As opposed to a youngster, the training and improvement of a grown-up person is much more difficult. If he is already misguided and depraved, it will be still harder to retrieve him. A poet expresses the fact in the following couplet:

> Teaching manners are effective in an early age. It is useless to try training and disciplining old people. Tender and delicate branches can be easily twisted at will, but a straight wood will remain straight.

Every parent, guardian or tutor is under the obligation to follow the Prophet's basic method of training the individuals of the society.

They should endeavour to make the best use of it with full determination in order to discipline and reform the children, to establish an excellent society and to set up a truly Islamic government.

It is necessary to emphasize that the parents and guardians should not pay attention to any one aspect of the child's training to the exclusion of other aspects. They should rather try to foster the growth of his personality as a whole. He should be subjected to spiritual as well as intellectual, moral as well as physical and psychological discipline simultaneously, so that no aspect of his character remains weak, and he develops a balanced and consistent personality to be able to do justice to every one.

(1) Taking care of Religious Training and Education

It is incumbent upon parents or the guardian to look into the kind of beliefs and ideas taught to the child at the school, what sort of education he is receiving and what he is learning outside the school. If he finds that what he is being taught and what he is learning is good and satisfactory he should thank God. But if he finds something wrong with the kind of education he is receiving, it becomes necessary for him to teach him Divine Unity and try to strengthen his religious beliefs, so that the child's mind may not be poisoned by atheism and anti Islamic ideas.

The parent or guardian should also keep a watch on the sort of books and magazines the child reads or the sort of T.V. programmes he views. If the books and magazines he reads contain atheistic material, it should be ensured that they are not brought into the house. The parent should impress on the child that such books and magazines vitiate one's faith and weaken the bond of a Muslim with his religion.

The parent or guardian is also advised to observe the sort of company the child moves in. If his friends and companions consist of subversive, misguided and irreligious elements, he should sever his relations with such fellows and provide him the company of good and righteous friends which may reform him and strengthen his faith.

Besides, the parent or guardian must ascertain whether or not the child has links with any group or organization with atheistic ideas and beliefs. If he is found to have such links, he should be judiciously exhorted to cut off his relations with it. He should more carefully observe the child's activity and advise him now and then to keep off the subversive group until he is fully convinced that the child has developed a tendency towards truth and has returned to the right path.

(2) Taking care of Moral Training

The parent or guardian should focus his attention on the following aspects of the child's moral training.

(i) Truthfulness

If the child does not do what he says, does not keep his promise, tries to cheat in every matter and is regarded in the society as a fraud, hypocrite and a liar, the parent or guardian should first rid him of the habit of telling lies and inculcate honesty and truthfulness in him. They should have long conversations with him and explain to him the dire consequences of telling lies and hypocrisy, so that the child might give up the habit of lying and playing false to the people. But if he is left free to do so he will develop the habit of telling lies and will come to be regarded by Allah and His servants as a big liar.

(ii) Trust

Sometimes the children develop the habit of stealing. For instance, they pick up and keep the money dropped by their brothers and sisters or steal a friend's pen. This is the beginning of the habit or larceny. It is incumbent on the parents and tutors to nib such a habit in the bud. They should tell the child that stealing is strictly forbidden by Islam and that such an act, amounts to illegitimately taking away something belonging to others. Inculcation of aversion for stealing in the child is as important as imbuing him with the fear of Allah. It would reform the child, otherwise he will get into the habit of committing breach of trust and defrauding the people and a stage will be reached at which everyone will be scared of his fraudulent mentality and bad conduct and regard him as a criminal.

(iii) Decency of Language

It is also necessary for the parent or the guardian to take care of the way the child talks. If he uses foul language without any rhyme or reason, he should be judiciously prevailed upon to abstain from it. The parent should first try to find out first the causes of his being foul-tongued and then strive to remove those causes. When this is done, the child should be told in a persuasive manner that foul language is unbecoming in a civilized man and that decency requires refinement of speech. The manner of exhortation should be so effective that the child develops of his own accord aversion for abuse and inculcates in himself moral excellence.

It is also necessary for the refinement of the child's speech to prevent him from moving in bad company; for the first and foremost factor affecting the child's habits is the company of his friends. He is naturally inclined to acquire the habits of his friends.

The child who is brought up caressingly and is accustomed to comforts and luxuries, will be fond of obscene music, acquire feminine habits and manners, frequent at places of ill-repute, mix up with female strangers, view shameful programmes of TV, till late night, read as a pastime sex-inciting magazines, novels and short stories and see pornographic pictures. Such a child will be a profligate whose personality will remain under developed. He will be susceptible to all kinds of evil. He will never make himself a virtuous person. It is, therefore, incumbent on the parents that no sooner they observe such vicious tendencies in the child than they should try to dissuade him from the evil course. This may be done by advice, exhortation, inducement and admonition. The parent or guardian is under the obligation to leave no stone unturned for the reformation of the child, otherwise he will grow up to be a bad character.

There are not many fathers who keep their children under constant observation and see when they arrive from the school, what they read and write and check them unawares and try to find out what the child furtively holds in hands and looks at and whether or not what he looks at is a pornographic picture or an obscene magazine or if he is found to be writing something furtively, whether or not he is writing a love-letter to his girl friend. Every father is advised to check unexpectedly the activities of his child.

There are not many fathers who meticulously check the movements of their daughters and try to ascertain judiciously their daughter goes to the school when she leaves home or return home straight from the school. Some parents who are neglectful of their children come to know all of a sudden that their daughter frequents places where her chastity is violated and honour is in a jeopardy or that she has illicit relations with a profligate. A number of such incident have come to our knowledge which are too shameful for us to hear.

Only a careful vigil on the movement of the child will enable the parent or the guardian to learn all about his behaviour and to prevent him from deviation.

It is essential to keep a vigil on the activities of the child from cultural and academic viewpoint. The child should be told the kind of knowledge which it is his duty to acquire and what kind of knowledge it is imperative for him to enrich himself with.

Every parent must know how far his child has acquired knowledge to fulfil his imperative duty. Whether or not he had learnt to recite the Holy Quran, acquired the knowledge of injunctions relating to worship, is capable of distinguishing the lawful from the unlawful. The parent must also try to find out if the child knows the essential facts of the Holy Prophet's life and if he has fully familiarized himself with Islamic etiquette as well as with the temporal and spiritual affairs.

These are the things about which the Muslims will be called to account. If any one fails to discharge his obligations mentioned above he will be responsible for it before Allah. The parents should take care to adopt such a method as would be conducive to the building of the child's character on Islamic lines and persuading him to act on the Shari'ah.

If the child is found to be learning the sciences that fall into the category of Mandatory branches of knowledge such as medicine or engineering, he should carefully watch his progress. Trained and educated in this way, he would be able to serve the *Ummah* more effectively and could add a new chapter in the development of Islamic culture. The parent should make every possible effort to enrich the child with the best knowledge and expertise. But he should also take care that acquisition of mandatory knowledge (the knowledge of medicine, engineering etc.) does not make him unmindful of imperative knowledge. He should first make the child concentrate on imperative duty and then stress the importance of mandatory duty or at least try to strike a fair balance between the two so that it is possible for him to acquire both kinds of knowledge satisfactory or else he will be accountable to Allah.

(iv) Food for Thought

The parent or guardian should also take into account his relation with religion and with the Islamic system of government. Does he recognise the Qur'an as the basis of spiritual life and as a law. Does he believe in the Holy Prophet (S.A.W.) as his guide? Does he take pride in the Islamic history? Does any spiritual and intellectual relation subsist between him and the Islamic culture? Is he enthusiastic about the missionary movement of Islam?

All these qualities can be engendered in the child only when he is kept under constant observation and a real interest is created in him in thought provoking books and Islamic literature. Besides he should be imbued with eagerness to listen to inspiring lectures on Islam. It is advisable to set up a small library of books on Islamic subjects as well as books written to refute anti-Islamic literature.

By adopting the above methods the child's bonds with Islam will be strengthened as the result of reading atheistic literature and books written by anti-Islamic missionaries. The children thus educated would devote themselves wholeheartedly to the building of Islamic society.

The father of a Muslim child will be saddened indeed to find that his son is busy studying the ideas of western philosophers and great eastern thinkers while he knows very little about the history of Islam, the great Muslim scholars, Muslim conquerors and ulama.

It will really pain the father of a Muslim child that his son is impairing his personality by learning modern sciences with alien culture, western and eastern thought as well as modern social philosophies which have vitiated his identity with the result that he has developed aversion for his religious forbears and Islamic history.

Under these circumstances, it is more necessary to orientate the child's thinking in the right direction. This would strengthen his faith and he would develop a consistent Islamic personality. For this purpose it should be impressed upon his mind that Islam is an all-inclusive system of life comprehending all the aspects of life including the method of government; that it is a legacy to be proud of and that it is the beacon light guiding to the path of glory.

In order to foster, the healthy and balanced growth of a child's mind and help him grow as a right thinking man, every thing exerting scathing influence should be kept out of his reach. Aversion for all such things should be engendered in him. He should be told of the possible sinister effects of those things on human mind.

In the light of the arguments advanced above, it is incumbent upon the guardians to find out if the child is addicted to liquor; for the effects of drinking liquor are ruinous. This habit damages the nervous system. Sometimes the drunkard has fits of hysteria and finally goes mad.

The guardian should also see if his child is addicted to masturbation. This is a habit that results in many a disease at one and the same time. He may develop TB, loss of memory, absence of mind simultaneously. The victim is generally nervous, restless, constipated, depressed and stricken with phobia.

Smoking is also a bad habit. It also weakens the memory and the capacity of thinking. It is, therefore, absolutely necessary to prevent the child from developing this habit.

The guardian should also see to it that the child does not see pornographic films and nude pictures. This badly affects the child's thinking and he gets gradually obsessed with sex. It also weakens his memory and damages his health. Hence the guardian should train him in a manner that his thinking is not tampered and he does not swerve from the right path. Reason is the distinguishing characteristic of man which lends him honour and dignity. It is manifest in the manner of his speech and conduct. The greater the attention to the cultivation of the child's intellect, the more balanced personality he will develop.

(v) Physical Fitness

The guardian or parent should supply the child with wholesome food, good clothing and spacious house, so that his body is immune from diseases and is not debilitated by various epidemics.

(vi) Health Care

The parent or guardian should also see how far the child adheres to Islamic principles. He should be occasionally advised to refrain from over-eating, otherwise he will impair his health by falling a prey to recurrent diarrhoea. Eye should also be kept on the quantity of water he drinks. It must be noticed whether or not he drinks in three or four draughts. If he gulps it in a single breath, he should be asked to refrain from doing it. He should also be prohibited to drink water while standing.

The child should also be habituated to sleep on his right side and should not go to sleep immediately after his meals.

If any one in the house is down with an infectious or contagious disease, the children should be isolated from such a sick person.

The children should, moreover, be taught how to keep good health. For instance they should be prohibited to eat unripe fruits. They should be asked to wash the vegetables before eating them, wash hands before eating and as required by Islam not to blow into the plates etc.

The child should be accustomed to regular physical exercise daily. Also, interest should be created in him riding by acquainting with its advantages. He should be brought up as a hardworking with masculine virtues and not as one accustomed to comforts and luxuries.

Use of Narcotics, smoking, masturbation and sodomy are moral crimes that cause deadly diseases like cancer, cardiac problems, impairment of liver resulting in a number of diseases with the possibilities of making a man impotent. Moreover, pressure on the veins of body increases. Consequently, the doctors warn against the above sinister habits.

If the parent or guardian sees symptoms of such habits from the child's appearance, he should consult a physician without fail, as the Holy Prophet (S.A.W.) has observed:

> "O bondsmen of Allah! Get medical treatment. There is no disease created by Allah for which He has not created cure as well."

Accordingly to this saying of the Holy Prophet (S.A.W.) the parents and guardians are expected to adhere to Islamic injunctions as to precautionary measures and medical treatment so that physical fitness may be ensured and the body may be immune from temporary or permanent ailments.

(vii) Observation of the psychological aspect of child's behaviour

If the child is found to be shy, constipated, inclined to introversion and aloofness, then the parents should try to inculcate boldness in him, rid him of maladjustment and seclusion, and foster growth of mental maturity. He should be asked to move in the society of other children. If he is found to be suffering from phobia and cowardice and to have developed defeatism instead of having the courage to face hardships and adversities, the parents should strive to imbibe in him confidence and perseverance and to encourage him to be dashing and brave, so that he may boldly grapple with difficulties and confront dangerous situations cheerfully.

In this connection the mother should in particular be cautious. She should not frighten the child with the stories of monster, devil, Jinnee, fairies etc., which cause fear in him and he is all the time under the influence of a mysterious phobia.

The parents should also see whether or not the child is developing inferiority complex. If they find symptoms of it, they are advised to remove the cause of this abnormality judiciously by instruction and exhortation. If the complex is result of insulting attitude or hatred, the child should be called in an affectionate and civil manner which may make him feel that he is being respected.

In case the inferiority complex stems out of excessive attachment and cares, the parents should give him proper training to rid him of the complex. He should be chastised or treated leniently as necessary.

If an orphan develops inferiority complex, his guardians should met out affectionate treatment to him so as to make him feel that he is being kindly treated.

If poverty is the cause of inferiority complex, patience, firmness and self-confidence should be inculcated in him enabling the child to chalk out his own line in life and strive to achieve his aims in order to rise to the level of rich people.

If the child develops inferiority complex because of jealousy, he should be treated most affectionately and should be meted out same treatment as is meted out to his brothers so that he may not feel that what is due to him is given away to others. Besides, other causes of jealousy should be removed.

If the child is irritable and is angry over trivial things, then the causes of his resentment should be removed.

(a) If the cause of anger is sickness he should be taken to some specialist for examination and medical treatment.

(b) If hunger irritates him he should be given meal at proper time.

(c) If the child is angered because of unwarranted rebuke, then the parent should not talk to the child in a manner that makes him feel that he is being insulted or shouted at.

(d) If the inurement to comforts has made the child peevish, he should be treated in the same way as other children are treated.

(e) If derision is the cause of child's anger, then the child should be protected from whatever wounds his pride.

It is necessary for the parents or guardians to act on Islamic principles to their children also so that they control their anger and may not lose their temper when they are provoked.

(viii) Observation of the child's Social Behaviour

The parent or guardian should also take care whether or not the child's social behaviour fulfils his obligations towards other people.

If the child fails in fulfilling his obligations towards his mother, brother, sister, a close relation, neighbour, tutor or any respectable elderly person, he should be apprised of the consequences of his misbehaviour towards or mal-treatment of the persons mentioned above. He may probably realize his mistake, be cautious in future and abstain from violating their rights and duly fulfil his obligations.

Doubtless if the child is kept under constant observation and is warned every now and then against misdeeds, his mind will be vigilant and he will be wise. He will consequently grow up to be civil, respectful and virtuous. Such a person will neither violate the rights of others, nor insults any one nor will be guilty of dereliction of his duty towards any body.

It is also necessary to see whether or not the child observes social decorum. If the child is not careful about the manners of eating, greeting, joking, talking, sneezing, congratulation condolence etc., the parent or guardian should teach him such manners and try to inculcate in him all the virtues of social life. By a ceaseless process of training, reformation, refinement and exhortation, the child can be invested with the quality of dealing with others in a polite manner, respecting the elderly people and give every body his due indiscriminately.

If the child is egoistic and headstrong, the parent or guardian should try to instil into him the spirit of sacrifice. Should he be nourishing hatred for others, it should be transmitted into love and goodwill. If he is unconscious of what is lawful and what is unlawful, the parent should exhort him to fear Allah and warn him against the painful doom in the Hereafter so that the sense of Allah's presence and His fear may be ingrained in the depths of his heart and consciousness. If the child is hurt or falls sick, it should be impressed on his mind that it owes itself to the will of Allah and that one should submit to His will. This is how faith, fear of Allah and the sense of His presence is imbibed and reinforced. Similarly the spirit of sacrifice, fellow feeling love and good faith is instilled. Bred thus, the child grows up as one capable of fulfilling his duties towards himself and other servants of Allah besides towards Allah. He will turn out to be a temperate and righteous person as well as prove to be wise and prudent. The People will honour and respect him.

(ix) Observation of Spiritual Aspect

To imbue the child with a perennial sense of Allah's presence and the state of contemplation it should be impressed upon him that Allah is constantly listening to what he utters and seeing what he does. Allah knows full well even whatever he does furtively, whatever he conceals and whatever he whispers. He is wide awake to the sinning of the eyes and the good or bad sentiments the heart is filled with. For this purpose it is also necessary to develop in the child the consciousness of the fact that nothing in heaven and earth can remain hidden from Allah.

This mode of feeling and thought and spiritual attitude can only be cultivated by exhorting him to have firm faith in Allah and His omnipotence. He should be told to turn to Allah in adversity. This would inculcate in him the fear of Allah and induce him to do good deeds. The greater the fear of Allah in a man, the more would he develop the capacity of serious thinking. His mind would be saturated with the contemplation of Allah.

The kind of training underscored above should be imparted to the child in his early impression. For training at that stage of life is more useful than at others.

The parent or guardian is advised to imbibe in the child humility, fear of Allah and the eagerness to serve Him by inducing to study the universe and see for himself with his inward eye the glory of the Creator. The mind is convinced of His glory of its own accord by pondering over every thing in the universe big or small, living or inanimate and over the trees, the flames of various hues exhalting fragrance and all the wonderful created phenomena. Consequently the human mind would exult, after pondering over God's creation in the worship of Allah and obedience of Him.

In order to strengthen the state of humility and fear of

Allah in the child's heart, he should be exhorted to offer prayers five times a day and listen to the Holy Qur'an in all humility and sincerity. When the child is invested with these qualities, he will join those near and dear to Allah and shall have no fear in the Hereafter. These are the virtuous people who will enter Gardens specially prepared for them and who have alluded to in the following verse of the Holy Qur'an:

> Lo! Verily the friends of Allah are (those) on whom the fear (cometh) not, nor do they grieve. Those who believe and fear Allah.
>
> (10:62,63)

The parent and guardian should also focus attention on imparting to the child the training of worship. When the child attains the age of seven years he should be exhorted to offer prayers according to the following edict of the Holy Prophet (S.A.W.):

> "Exhort your child to offer prayer when he attains the age of seven years."

On the analogy of this edict the jurists enjoin that the child should be accustomed to keeping fast during the holy month of Ramadhan and in the process he should, to begin with, fast for a few days according to the strength and stamina to bear hunger and thirst. Similarly he should be given the practical training of the various phases of Hajj. Besides he should occasionally be made distribute alms among the needy and spend money in the way of Allah so that he may be used to pay the poor-due readily.

In addition to the above training the parent or tutor should take the child with him for attending religious gatherings and meetings wherein the divines throw light on academic and Juristic problems. The parent should also narrate to the child the life stories of virtuous people and great and sincere ulema. A tutor should be arranged for him who could teach how to recite the Holy Qur'an and acquaint him with its meaning with commentary. All this would imbue him with sincere desire for prayer and worship and his mind will be illuminated by contemplation and remembrance of Allah, his soul will be purified and his consciousness and feelings will undergo a radical change as soon as he hears the verses of the Holy Qur'an. He will be enraptured when events of the pious people's life are related to him and he will be thrilled when the feats of the Prophet's companions are related.

The parent or guardian should also observe how much and how long the child is affected by the psychological and spiritual discipline and what kind of change is effected in him by the disciplining process. This task is as important as the preparation of the child for missionary and political work. The parent should take care to strike a fair balance between the psychological and spiritual disciplining and training for political and missionary work in order that the child may be as much equipped for a crusade against oppression and infidelity as is necessary to be prepared for resistance against temptations and sensual desires. He should attach equal importance to both. When the parent or guardian is neglectful of his duty to enjoin good and forbid evil, the child is bound to be introverted, lonely and irresolute. He will accept the status quo and will turn his back on the battlefield. He will submit to an unjust and tyrant ruler.

A balanced training of war on the one hand and crusade against desires can only inculcate in the child the spirit of fulfilling his obligations towards others. It is this spirit which would enable in man the sense of God's presence and to discharge his responsibility for the establishment of the kingdom of God on earth. By virtue of such a training he will be capable of crushing everyone who rebels against Islam. A child who receives the balanced training of self-discipline and crusade against the disbelievers will be able to hold the Holy Qur'an in one hand and the sword in the other. He will be capable of enforcing Islam as a balanced system of worship and government.

The guardian should also make the child learn by heart all those prayers which the Prophet (S.A.W.) used to say; for instance the prayers said in the morning and evening, at bedtime and at the time of rising; those said at the time of taking one's meal and having one's fill; the prayers of judging augury, of asking for rainfall, for the rise of moon, for recovery from illness and the prayers said in sickness and sorrow. These prayers are to be found in the collections of Hadith.

When the child learns the above prayers by heart, he will be more God-fearing and develop the habit of self-criticism. Repetition of prayers every now and then plays an important part in the development of the child's spiritual attitude, determination of social behaviour and building of his character as a whole. Consequently there is a salutary change in the child's word and deed by virtue of his purity of soul. He becomes an angel in the human form.

5. Punishment

Infliction of punishment should be the last resort in the reformation of the child. Before resorting to this remedy there are some stages of reformation and correction which ought to be passed. It is quite possible that the child mends his ways as the result of exhortation and rebuke without being subjected to corporal punishment and becomes an upright person.

The parent or guardian is like a physician as Imam Ghazzali has said. As the physician does not treat all the sick people alike for fear of aggravating the disease, so also the parent or guardian does not adopt the method of rebuke and censure to the exclusion of all the other methods; for this method of correction may spoil the child. In other words the mode of reforming the child should conform to his condition. If the child commits a misdemeanour, its motives should be determined first and then his age and level of intelligence as well as his environment should be taken into consideration; for all these factors exercise great influence on his thinking. A careful study of these factors would go a long way in determining the causes of the child's deviation and he will make the right decision as to the most effective method of correcting the child and thus rid the child of the habit of moral aberration and psychological abnormality.

The Holy Prophet (S.A.W.) has suggested effective remedies for the correction of the child's individual and collective behaviour. The parent or guardian should adopt the methods prescribed by the Prophet (S.A.W.) in this respect for they constitute the best possible modes of training the child and turning him into a righteous Muslim.

The methods suggested by the Prophet (S.A.W.) for the reformation of the child are as under:

1. Warning on Mistake and Providing the Right Guidance

According to *Imam Bukhari* and *Imam Muslim* Hazrat Umar bin Abi Salamah narrated that he was under the tutelage of the Holy Prophet (S.A.W.). Once during the supper I moved my hand all over the plate. The Prophet (S.A.W.) said: O child! Begin with Allah's name. Eat with your right hand and take morsels from the part of the plate which is closer to you.

What we find in this Tradition is that the Prophet (S.A.W.) exhorted and admonished Umar Ibn Abi Salamah in superb manner and thus corrected him.

2. Mild Warning against a Mistake

Imam Bukhari and *Imam Muslim* quote a Tradition narrated by Hazrat Suhail bin Sa'd (R.A.A.). According to this Tradition a beverage was offered to the Holy Prophet (S.A.W.). He took some of the drink. There was a boy sitting on his right and grown-up people on his left. The Prophet said to the boy, "Shall I give this drink to the grown-up people?" This was a kind and effective manner of guidance. The boy replied, "O No. By God! I will never prefer anyone to myself in whatever I get from you." The Prophet (S.A.W.) then put the bowl in the hand of the boy. This boy was none other than Abdullah Bin Abbas (R.A.)

This Tradition proves that the Holy Prophet (S.A.W.) taught the boy to prefer grown-up people to himself in drinking the beverage as it was a preferable course of action. Hence he sought permission of the boy. So teaching him in a kind manner he said to the boy, "Do you permit me to give it to all these people?"

3. Drawing Attention by Suggestion

Imam Bukhari cites aTtradition narrated by Hazrat Fazl bin Abbas. Hazrat Fazl was riding on camel's back behind the Holy Prophet (S.A.W.), when a woman belonging to Khus'am tribe appeared. Fazl began looking towards her and the woman towards him. The Prophet (S.A.W.) noticed this and turned Hazrat Fazl's face in the opposite direction. The woman said, "Allah has imposed Hajj as an imperative duty upon His servants. My father is now too old to ride a camel. Shall I perform Hajj on his behalf?" The Prophet (S.A.W.) replied in the affirmative. This incident took place on the occasion of the Prophet's last Hajj.

In this Tradition the Holy Prophet (S.A.W.) corrected the wrong act of looking at a stranger female by turning Fazl's face in the opposite direction. Fazl also was impressed by this act of the Prophet (S.A.W.) and was careful for the future.

If the parent or guardian inflicts punishment on his erring child in the presence of his brothers and sisters, it will not only go a long way in reforming him but would also produce salutary effect on the other children as well and they will correct themselves.

We expect the Muslim parents and guardians to follow the methods of training and reformation adopted by the Prophet (S.A.W.). They will alternate mild exhortation with a frown followed by censure. If a milder mode of reformation does not prove effective, then a harsher mode should be adopted. If censure does not serve the purpose, then the child should be chastized. But care should be taken that corporal punishment should not result in a permanent scar on the body. Corporal punishment should be given in the presence of the other members of the family.

If corporal punishment effects salutary change in the child's behaviour and he is consequently reformed, then the parent or guardian should treat the child with affection and kindness. He should smile when he looks at the child so that he may feel that the punishment he was given was designed to reform him and ensure a better life in this world as well as in the Hereafter The Prophet (S.A.W.) treated his companions in a similar manner.

For instance *Imam Bukhari* and *Imam Muslim* quote a Tradition wherein it has been stated that Ka'b bin Malik did not participate in the Battle of Tabook without any lawful ground. The Holy Prophet (S.A.W.) ordered his boycott for fifty nights together. He was accordingly totally boycotted. Nobody would either sit with him or greet him with the result that life became a bit too distressing for him. But when the Prophet (S.A.W.) announced the acceptance of his repentance, Ka'b says that he set out with the intention of paying a visit to the Prophet (S.A.W.). On his arrival at the Prophet's place I saw crowds of people coming to congratulate him on the acceptance of his repentance. When he entered the mosque he found the Prophet (S.A.W.) sitting there. Hazrat Talha bin Ubaid rushed towards him and congratulated him with a warm handshake.

Hazrat Ka'b says, "When I greeted the Holy Prophet (S.A.W.), his face was red with exhilaration and he congratulated me in these words: "You should be delighted on this best day which has come in your life for the first time after your mother gave birth to you." I asked him: Was it you or Allah who accepted my repentance? He said: No, it is Allah who has accepted it. The Prophet's face was glowing like the moon which led us to conclude that he was delighted.

When the child finds that the parents have, after punishing him, adopted affectionate attitude as before and chastisement was designed only to reform or correct him, he does not develop any complex; nor does he deviate from moral norm. He rather appreciates the affectionate and merciful behaviour of the parents, he tries to develop the qualities of righteous people.

If Islam has laid down punishments, it has also prescribed certain conditions lest chastisement should assume vindictive character. What it actually aims at is to reform the child. The conditions referred to are as under:

(1) Punishment should be inflicted only after all the methods of exhortation and censure are tried.

(2) Punishment is not to be inflicted in rage. This poses the threat of causing serious injuries to the child. The parent or guardian should always bear in mind this edict of the Prophet (S.A.W.) as quoted by *Imam Bukhari* 'Do not be angry.'

(3) Punishment should not be inflicted on the sensitive parts of the body, like head, face, chest and stomach, *Abu Dawood* quotes the Prophet (S.A.W.) to have said, "Do not hit the face." In this connection we would like to refer to the case of the woman named Ghamidia. The Prophet (S.A.W.) ordered her to be stoned on charge of adultery but at the same instructed the people to stone her with small pebbles equal to pieces of gram, taking care not to hit her face. It may be noted that stoning is such a severe punishment that it results in the death of the offender. But the Prophet (S.A.W.) asked the people not to hit her face. Hence it is necessary to see that the face of the child is not hit while he is being chastized. The reason is that the face and the head are the centre of sensation. It is quite possible that the injury caused to the head or the face may result in the paralysis of a sensory organ or nerve. In such a case punishment would turn into an irreparable loss. The victim's audition, vision etc. may be affected.

Striking at chest and stomach is also prohibited for fear of causing death. The Prophet (S.A.W.) enjoins: 'Do not harm, nor be harmed yourself.'

(4) Initially punishment should be very light so that the body may not be tormented. Beating should be done with one's hand, foot or a stick when the child is minor. He should not be struck more than thrice. When the child attains the age of majority and it is found that beating him three times does not serve the purpose, he may be beaten ten times at the most. The Prophet (S.A.W.) is reported to have said that with the exception of the hudood laid down by Allah, the strokes inflicted as a punishment should on no account exceed ten.

(Tradition as quoted by Imam Ibn Taimiyah).

(5) The child should not be punished until he is ten years old as the Prophet (S.A.W.) has enjoined: "When the

child is seven years old, ask him to say prayers and when he is ten years old, beat him if he does not say prayers."

(6) If the boy is guilty of a misdeed for the first time, he should be allowed a chance to repent it, to be cautious in future and begs to be forgiven. He should not be given any punishment at this stage. This course of action is much better than beating the child and creating a scene.

(7) If it is necessary to chastise the child the parent should himself give him the beating. This task should not be assigned to his brother, sister etc; otherwise, ill-feeling would develop between them.

(8) On the child's attainment of majority, it is found that ten strokes do not produce the desired effect, more that ten strokes may be inflicted. The parent or guardian may torment the body of such a child by beating him again and again until he is completely reformed.

The five methods of training with which we have dealt in this book are as follows:

(1) Example (2) Habit (3) Exhortation (4) Observation and (5) Punishment.

We briefly discuss them here once again by way of recapitulation:

1. Practical Example

Demonstration of good character by example inculcates in the child cardinal virtues. He would try of his own accord to imbibe in himself moral excellence by emulation. Unless the parent or guardian presents himself as a model of sterling qualities, the child cannot be reformed.

2. Inculcation of Good Habits

By inuring the child to do good deeds, desirable results

may be achieved. Under this method the child is kept under constant observation and is continually instructed and exhorted. This method is indispensable for training the child on the right lines.

3. Exhortation

The child is deeply impressed by instruction, exhortation, narration of didactic anecdotes, inspiring dialogue, discussion and conversation. Exhortation is the essence of training without which one cannot hope to reform the child; for by exhortation alone can the child's mode of feeling and thinking be transformed. Without exhortation his heart cannot be imbued with compassion and his latent feeling cannot be stimulated.

4. Observation

Observation is absolutely essential for the building of the child's character and helping develop a consistent personality by learning good manners and morals. By keeping him under constant observation he can be turned into a good citizen and a useful individual of the Muslim Ummah. Observely, if left unobserved he will develop sinister habits and fall irretrievably into the abyss of depravity. In the ultimate analysis, such a child will grow up to be an incorrigible offender.

5. Chastisement

This method would make the child desist from bad acts and give up sinister habits. It inculcates in him an aversion for sensuality, forbidden activity and everything immoral. Without punishment no change can be effected in the child. He would rather be incorrigibly accustomed to the commission of crimes sins and unlawful acts.

We urge upon the parents and guardians to adopt the

methods of training explained above. If they are really serious about the development of their children into good individuals and excellent citizens of the nation to be proud of. Says Allah:

> "And say (unto them): Act Allah will behold your actions and (so will) His messengers and the believers." (9:105)

The Basic Rules of Training

Islam is a comprehensive system consisting of basic principles of life. These principles include the rules of training that can help the child develop a complete and consistent personality. The Islamic principles of training relate to all the problems of training including the intellectual, spiritual, psychological and social training.

The above principles of training are simple and clear with noble aims. If the parents, tutors and guardians train the new generation on the lines laid down in these principles a pleasant revolution will be brought in the human societies and the decadent Muslim society can be reformed and regenerated. The individual's moral condition and beliefs can be raised up to the highest level. Their bodies will be enriched with vigour and vitality, their minds will develop into full maturity and their personalities will be imbued with dignity, propriety and civility Thus the *Ummah* will be revived and will regain its high and distinct position by which it was conspicuous in the past. Without emulating the models of our righteous forbears and following the examples of the Holy Prophet's companions we cannot regain our past glory.

Before dealing with the basic principles of the child's character-building, we would like to touch upon the qualities required in the parent or the tutor. If the latter is devoid of the requisite qualities, his training will not be effective and his exhortation will fall on deaf ears.

THE ESSENTIAL QUALITIES OF PARENT OR GUARDIAN

1. Sincerity

The parent ought to have sincerity of purpose. He should perform the task of training for the sole purpose of seeking Allah's pleasure. He must be sincerely interested in the training of the child at every stage including command and prohibition, exhortation, observation and punishment.

Sincerity demands that training should be constant. The child should be kept under unceasing observation. The parent or the tutor will thus be able to earn the favour of Allah and will rise to the height of truth in His presence.

2. Righteousness (*Taqwa*)

This is another distinguishing quality of a parent or tutor. Religious scholars define righteousness as follows:

> "Allah does not see you in a state forbidden by Him and He does not find you absent from doing whatever has been enjoined to do."

According to other *Ulama* "righteousness is the attempt to escape Allah's punishment by good deeds and invert as well as overt fear of Allah."

The meanings of both the definitions of righteousness are identical, i.e., endeavouring to escape the divine punishment under the influence of the contemplation of Allah, sincerely abiding by His commands in letter and spirit and always thinking of doing the lawful and abstaining from the unlawful.

A conversation between Hazrat Umar bin Khattab (R.A.A.) and Hazrat Ubai bin Ka'b testifies the above interpretation of the term *taqwa*. Hazrat Umar asked Hazrat Ubai bin Ka'b what taqwa exactly means, he latter replied, "Have you ever passed through a thorny way?" Hazrat Umar (R.A.A.) answered in the affirmative. Hazrat Ubai bin Ka'b inquired, "How did you manage to pass through it?" "Well," replied Hazrat Umar, "I gathered my clothes cautiously and tried to tread it." Ubai bin Ka'ab observed, "That is exactly what taqwa is."

There are innumerable verses of the Holy Qur'an wherein righteousness has been enjoined in the sense explained above. We cite here a few verses by way of illustration:

> "O you who believe, fear Allah as He ought to be feared."
>
> (3:102)

> "O ye who believe, fear Allah and speak words straight to the point."
>
> (35:70)

> "O ye who believe, fear Allah. And let every soul look to that which it sendeth on before for the morrow."
>
> (59:18)

> "O mankind! Fear your Lord. Lo! the earthquake of the Hour of Doom is a tremendous thing."
>
> (22:1)

> "Whoso believeth in Allah and the Last Day is exhorted to act thus. And whosoever feareth Allah, He will appoint a way out for him and will provide for him from a quarter whence he hath no expectation."
>
> (65:2-3)

It goes without saying that if the parent or the tutor is not righteous and ignores Islamic principles in his dealing with the child, the latter is bound to deviate from the moral norm and will sink deep into the quagmire of depravity. A parent or tutor who is a debauchee and addicted to prohibited things and who is incapable of differentiating between good and evil is not qualified to train the child. He cannot inculcate the fear of Allah and the sense of His presence in him which prevents man from doing evil acts. A child under the tutelage of such a wicked fellow cannot develop moral sense and does not have the twinge of conscience to desist from misdeeds.

The parent and guardian should realize that unless he himself is upright, he cannot train his child on the right lines and make him tread the right path and lead a life of chastity. For further details the reader is referred back to the section of this book entitled "Practical Example."

3. Knowledge

The parent or guardian should be well-versed in the Islamic rules of training. He should be fully aware of what according to Islam is lawful and what is unlawful. Besides, he should be well acquainted with the basic principles of morality. Without acquaintance with all these rules and principles the parent or guardian will not be a good judge of things; whereas sound judgment is absolutely essential for one who imparts training to the children. He can do justice to his job only when he has the requisite knowledge as mentioned above and can train the child on the lines determined by the principles derived from the Qur'an and the *Sunnah*.

A child under the tutelage of one ignorant of the principles of training will develop complexes and deviate from the social and moral norms. He will be as worthless as anything in a dust bin. He cannot be depended upon in any field of life. A man cannot cultivate a virtue in others which he does not possess himself. It may easily be judged from this that an ignorant father is devoid of mercy for his children. A child under the tutelage of one swerving from the path of *shariah* will grow up to be a brute and a savage. The parents or guardians who do not discharge their obligation of training the children on the right lines will have a very hard time on the Day of Judgement. On that day their possessions, property and children will be of no avail to them and Allah will command: "Keep them on standing. They shall be questioned."

4. Restraint and Self-possession

Restraint and self-possession is the essential requisite in the parent or guardian for crowning his efforts with success in the training of children and reformation of the society. He must have a balanced temperament and poise. It is restraint and sobriety of the tutor which impresses the child and makes him assimilate his teaching, imbibes in him decorum and purges him of vices and bad habits.

That is the reason why Islam lays great emphasis on restraint and sobriety. There are innumerable verses of the Holy Qur'an and Prophet's Traditions to this effect, which would impress on the parents and missionaries that restraint is one of the cardinal virtues that exalts man to the highest degree of refinement and propriety.

5. Sense of Responsibility

The parent or the tutor ought to realize his responsibility for the intellectual, social, moral, religious, physical and psychological training of the child in his heart of hearts. This realization can force him to take care of the child and attend to his training and reformation on the right lines. The parent must be absolutely sure that the least negligence on his part in the improvement and disciplining of the child would gradually make him go astray and a day will come when he will be found among the habitual and incorrigible vagrants and bad characters. At this stage the child will be post reformation and improvement. The father then will repent his negligence but his repentance will be of no avail.

In the context of the parent's sense of responsibility for the training of children, I consider it necessary to mention the premeditated plans for causing corruption and disruption in the Muslim Ummah aimed at undermining the personality of the individual and the destruction of the Muslim society as a whole. This is necessary to make the parent or the guardian realize the vital importance of their obligation as to the moral training and reformation of the children at home.

By the above plans we mean the conspiracies formed at the clandestine centers of Zionism, Freemasonary, Christianity and Communism designed to undermine the Islamic beliefs. In order to fulfil their designs these anti-Islamic forces have made use of atheistic concepts, encourage use of liquor, worship of misguiding phenomena and blind-fold emulation.

These diabolical elements have used the woman as the primary tool to serve their ends. She is the most effective means of treachery and debauchery. She constitutes the feeble emotional component of the society which falls a prey to every kind of nefarious propaganda and readily acts on every misguiding programme without giving any thought to it. This is the most effective element in subverting morality.

Now we touch on every such plan which has been prepared to undermine Islam.

CONSPIRACIES OF THE CHRISTIANS

1. Destruction of the Holy Qur'an

The Christians believe that the Qur'an is the fountainhead of the Muslims' strength and that by acting on its injunctions they will regain their past glory and power. This is what some of the Christian leaders and missionaries have to say about the Holy Qur'an:

(1) The British statesman Gladstone declared in the House of Commons raising up a copy of the Qur'an in his hand that as long as the Muslims had that book close to their heart, Europe could never triumph over the east, nor could she ever have peace.

(2) A Christian missionary says that the Muslims of Arabia could be divorced from Muhammad and his faith and westernized only when they lose sight of Mecca and the Qur'an.

(3) Another bigoted Christian missionary Ketley comes out with the suggestion that the Qur'an itself should be used against Islam, for it is the deadliest weapon that Islam possesses. By using it to serve the purpose of Christianity, Islam can be weeded out. It is imperative that the Christian missionaries should impress upon the Muslims that what is valid and correct in Islam is not something new. It embodies what revealed before the Qur'an came into existence and whatever is new in it is incorrect.

(4) At a function held in connection with the centenary celebrations of the French occupation of Algeria, a French official emphasized the need of divorcing the life of Muslims from the Arabic Qur'an. He was of the view that French could subdue the Muslims only when they alienated the Arabs from Arabic.

We relate an interesting incident in this context. The French devised a subtle strategy to eradicate the love of Qur'an from the hearts of the Muslim youths. They picked out ten Algerian girls and put them in modern French schools where they were dressed in the French costume, taught French manners and language and were thus turned into ultra modern French girls. On the girls' completion of education after ten years a function was arranged to which ministers, journalists and intellectuals were invited. When the function commenced all the French gentlemen present were taken aback at the sight of the girls appearing before them clad in the Islamic dress of their homeland. The journalists could not forbear asking the minister for French colonies, "What has French achieved in Algeria during one hundred and twenty-eight years of her rule?" The minister is reported to have replied, "What can I do? The Qur'an is more powerful than France."

2. Stamping out the Islamic mode of thinking and cutting off the Muslims' relation with Allah

This was aimed at alienating the Muslims from Islamic system and imbibe in them ungodly outlook on life and licentious attitude. This was considered to be the only way to divorce the Muslims from Islam. Addressing the Jerusalem Conference of Christian missionaries held in 1935, Samuel Zedmer declared that the function assigned to those missionaries was not merely confined to bringing the Islamic countries under the influence of Christian states. According to him these states would rather be honoured by their association with the Christian powers. He urged upon the missionaries to take a step forward and lead the Muslims away from Islam so that they might have no relation with Allah whatsoever. He said that if they succeeded in this mission, they would be leading the van of Christian imperialism into the Islamic countries. He told them that they had already succeeded in prevailing upon the Muslim intellectuals to tread the path they had laid down and that they had produced a generation of young Muslims that did not have any relation with Allah and had dissociated the Muslims from their religion without bringing them into the fold of Christianity. They had thus brought a generation which was absolutely in accord with imperialistic designs. It had no lofty ambitions and loved a life of ease and sensual pleasures. This new generation of Muslims was obsessed with sex. It was the fruit of the missionaries' endeavours that an educated young Muslim was interested only in the ways and means to gratify his sexual appetite. He acquired wealth for the sake of carnal pleasures alone. Zedmer described their campaign as a success in all respects.

A Christian priest Simon says that unity of the Arab world is the hope of the Muslims all over the world. They have the co-operation of the Arab world in their struggle to get rid of the domination of Europe. According to him propagation of Christianity is the only effective way to arrest the expansion of their movement for Islamic unity. He urges upon the Christian missionaries to strive to divert the attention of Muslims from Pan-Islamism.[1]

Lawrence Brown expresses the fear that if the Muslims are united under the Arabian rule, they will pose a serious threat to the world. He, therefore, underlines the need to divide them so that they may sink into insignificance.[2]

In 1907 a great conference of European powers was held which was attended by their eminent statesmen and political leaders. The British Foreign Secretary presided over it. In his inaugural address he said that European civilization was threatened with disintegration and that it was, therefore, incumbent upon the European leaders attending the conference to devise ways and means to safeguard their

1. *Kaifa Hamdath-ul-Khilafah, P. 190.*
2. *Kaifa Hamdath-ul-Khilafah, P. 190.*

civilization before it was too late. The conference continued for nearly a month during which a number of issues were discussed. The participants reviewed the situation arising out of the external dangers confronting the declining civilization of the west and came to the conclusion that the gravest danger of them all is the world of Islam. The conference consequently thrashed out a programme to offset the centripetal trend among the countries of the Middle East. They regarded Middle East as the only potential danger to the future of Europe. In order to counter this threat they decided to implant an anti-Muslim Jewish state east of Suez. Accordingly the British busied themselves to extend full co-operation to the Zionists and came out with the proposal of carving out a Jewish state in Palestine.

3. Deterioration of Muslim Women

For this purpose Christianity attached special importance to the emancipation of Muslim women. They provided opportunities for a full-scale debate on the equality of sexes. In meetings and seminars the rights of women were freely discussed and upheld and conditions were created for the violation of Islamic laws relating to polygamy and divorce. In this way doubts were instilled into the minds of Muslims whether the Islamic *Shari'ah* was capable of meeting the demands of modern age. The Christian ecclesiast Zedmer who sends out religious missions all over the world has published a pamphlet entitled "The Islamic World Today" in which he says that there has been no better belief in the past than the Islamic principle of Divine Unity. It was by dint of this doctrine that Islam brought under its sway the continents of Asia and Africa and was able to enforce its laws and injunctions among two hundred million people. Besides, Islam has been able to forge unity among the Muslims through the strong bond of the Arabic language. Thus it has erected a lofty edifice below which the woman is growing under the yoke of man's tyranny. The said enemy of Islam, however, ended his address on a note of hope. He solaced the Christian missionaries by saying that they need not be dismayed because the emancipation of women would eat into the wharp and woof of Islamic society like white ants.[1]

In an article published in the 15th September issue of the magazine "Al 'Alameen", a French writer Aine Lome writes, "Apart from the results achieved by the training of Muslim boys on western lines, the education and training of Muslim girls in the Convents run by the Christian nuns would serve as a more effective means of achieving the purpose for which we have been working heart and soul. In fact, I am of the view that training and education of Muslim girls in western type schools is the only way to stamp out Islam."

Again, a Christian woman missionary Anne Mclligan gives an account of the efforts to misguide the Muslim girls of Egypt in these words, "We have managed to gather together at the girls colleges of Cairo the daughters of Pashas and Begs. There are no other institutions in which girls can be brought together in such a great number under the Christian influence. Hence the Christian mission colleges are the shortest way to storm and conquer the citadel of Islam."[2]

These then are the Christian plans to erase the Islamic beliefs from the minds of Muslim boys and girls.

It may be seen from what has been stated above that the first and foremost desire of Christianity is to cut off the golden thread of Islam which binds together the Islamic communities all over the world. This is how the leaders of Christian church want to translate into reality their nefarious designs against the Muslim *Ummah*. The Christians are determined to disintegrate and corrupt the families of the

1. *Al-Ghazath 'Alal 'Alame Islami.*
2. *Al-Ghazath 'Alal 'Alame Islami.*

Muslims so as to misguide and deviate every Muslim boy and girl from the Islamic norms.

Having been acquainted with the evil designs of the enemies of Islam, the Muslim parents ought to realize the urgency of their responsibility for the right training and education of their offspring.

THE JEWISH AND MASONIC CONSPIRACIES

The Jews have adopted subtle snd treacherous methods of dominating the world. Their main objectives are as follows:

(i) Splitting up the people of the world into factions. Exploitation of one people for deceiving another. Causing conflicts between them as well as among various factions and communities.

(ii) Vitiation of peoples' beliefs. Leading them away from the path of Allah by subverting the standards of conduct and by the misconstruction of their religious principles.

The motive behind all their plans is their evil designs to deprive the peoples of the world of their prestige and glory and bring them under the perpetual domination of the Jews. What they want is that no non-Jewish nation be allowed the opportunity to wield power and has a distinct identity of its own. Among organizations set up by the Jews to split up other nations, the Free-Mason Association occupies the central position.

Masonic Schemes and Conspiracies

1. The sole purpose of the views advocated by the Jews in their protocols is to undermine the beliefs, conscience and outlook of the non-Jewish people. They have been supporting

every subversive philosophy that acts at the very roots of religious beliefs and cardinal principles of morality.

2. The Jews have also supported Freud's views who looks at every aspect of human life from sexual angle and preaches the cult of libido-worship.

3. The Jews have also given wide publicity to the views of Karl Marx who attempts to revolutionize the modes of human thinking and feelings; rejects all the true religions as nonsense and attacks the belief in the Existence of God. When asked what he would substitute for God, Marx replied, "Stage Drama. The common people will be attracted to it to such a degree that they will forget God."

4. Besides, the Jews subscribe to Nietzche's philosophy, which declares all the moral values as false, and upholds hedonism. He is of the view that pleasure ought to be sought even if one has to commit murder, shed blood or indulge in subversive activities.[1]

5. The Jews are also all praise for Darwin's theory of evolution, which the scientists have rejected as worthless.

6. But the Jews have now risen to such a position that all the world's media of communication are under their control which they are using to deprave mankind. They control cinema, radio and television. They also sway over all the masonic organizations of the world. There is also a network of masonic institutions spread in every part of the world. These institutions have bought traitors of every country to popularize obscenity and diffuse western culture, arts and sports. These institutions on their part have treacherously contrived to install the Jews in important positions in various countries on the pretext of their

1. *The author seems to have misunderstood Nietzche. Nietzche is a vitalist thinker who preaches the will-to-power. Hedonism seems to be alien to his system of thought. Translator.*

specialization in psychology and radiology. Most of the professors heading the departments of these two subjects at the universities of western countries including the USA are Jews. Even at the universities of the east, majority of professors teaching the above subjects belong to the Jewish community. As the result of this great achievement the Jews have succeeded in undermining both faith and morals of innumerable people all over the world. They have thus deceitfully gained the control of ninety per cent of the academic institutions in order to be able to guide the entire world in the fields of philosophy, psychology and sociology.

THE IMPERIALIST PLANS

The imperialist forces have colluded with the Christian Church and the orientalists in order to wage a systematic war against the Muslims and make them ignore Jihad (which is one of the main pillars of Islam) and to corrupt the Islamic Society by leading it away from the moral norms and causing in it lecherous tendencies. This warfare of imperialism against Islam aims at diverting the Muslims from their beliefs. It is an attempt to see that they nourish no idea of pure and chaste life and indulge in debauchery as the ultimate purpose of life. In short it aims at keeping them in a state of depravity so as to render them incapable of endeavouring to attain a higher position in life or of conveying to them the message of Islam that invites mankind to a sublime system of life.

We quote in this context some statements of the imperialists: One of the champions of imperialism says, "Liquor and a singing girl—the two things are much more powerful to destroy the *Muslim Ummah* than a thousand canons. So make the *Muslim Ummah* indulge in carnal pleasure."

The parents and guardians are advised to guard

against the activities of foreign agents in their respective countries who are in league with the various communist, Christian, Masonic and imperialist organizations. They are busy spreading the germs of infidelity and immorality in the Islamic society everywhere in the world. The parents and guardians ought to know that the above forces opposed to Islam have produced anti-social elements in every country who translate their programmes into practice. They adopt a variety of strategies to perform the task assigned to them. Apart from their fundamental principles, their organizations have assumed different forms.

To achieve their ends they help young people in securing high offices after completion of their education. When these young men associate themselves with some organization or other, they get highest position.

The Fundamental Rules of Training the Children

These rules fall under two heads:

(1) Establishment of Links

(2) Prevention

ESTABLISHMENTS OF LINKS

It is an established fact that if the child's mind illumined with faith and is given spiritual, intellectual and ideological orientation, he will acquire full training right from the age of discretion which will stand him in good stead when he is grown up and his personality will develop the traits of calm and self possession as well as piety emanating from faith. By dint of these virtues he would be able to overcome ignorance and superstitions, while his mental training would make him repulse irreligious ideas and misguiding notions. In fact he would pose a challenge to every one antagonistic to Islamic system How is such a state of mind cultivated?

The real way of doing this is that the child is moored fast to religion and is persuaded to accept in his heart of hearts the Islamic order including its forms of worship, moral principles, laws, code of conduct, the institution of Jihad, missionary obligations, the Holy Qur'an as revealed Book and the basis of Islamic system, the significance of thought, culture and wealth. The guardian should see to it that the child is brought up and trained in a manner that he grows up to be a righteous Muslim. If these religious moorings of his personality are strong he will certainly grow up to be a true Muslim.

We proceed to explain the links mentioned above:

1. The Moorings of Belief

In our discussion of the parent's responsibility for the training of children, we have already shown that when the child attains the age of discretion, it is essential for him to learn the fundamental elements of faith i.e. belief in invisible realities; for instance, beliefs in the existence of Allah, Hell and Heaven, Day of Resurrection, Life in the Hereafter, and in everything which is proved beyond in life in true traditions and pieces of intelligence handed down from generation to generation.

Hence it is the duty of every parent, that he should impress upon the mind of the child the essentiality of faith in the existence and unity of Allah as well as in the existence of angels, revealed books, His messengers, man's freedom of will limited by the will of Allah. It must also be impressed upon the kid's mind that angels named *Munkir* and *Nakir* will call every deceased person to account after burial, that the torment of the grave is inevitable, that one will have to come to life again after death in this world and to account for his deeds and that Hell and Heaven do exist etc. ete. By imbuing the child with firm faith in the realities mentioned above and by ingraining in his heart the belief in the Unity of Allah, the following states of mind can be cultivated in him:

(a) Contemplation on the sense of Allah's constant presence.

(b) Fear of Allah.

(c) Humility for bowing before Him and abiding by His mandates and prohibitions.

(d) Propensity for looking towards Him in afflictions and tribulations.

(e) Sense of pride stemming from faith and light of conscience. If one's heart is illuminated with faith and conscience, all the social evils, mental complexes and bad habits are weeded out.

(f) Sense of moral and spiritual wellbeing.

(g) Intellectual maturity and the habit of conducting one's self aright.

2. Spiritual Relationship

The parents and guardians should try to inculcate in the child inner purity and awareness. Men's heart should be the source of faith and sincerity. Keeping this in view Islam tries to establish many spiritual links so that man may concentrate on the development of the purity of heart and conscience.

Islam adopts the following methods for imbibing these virtues:

Regularity of Worship

Imam Hakim and *Abu Dawood* quote a Tradition as narrated by Hazrat Amar bin al 'As wherein the Holy Prophet (S.A.W.) is reported to have said, "Order your children to say prayer when they are seven years old. If they fail to do so at the age of ten years beat them up and separate their beds."

On the analogy of the injunction relating to prayer, the child should be trained to keep fast provided that he is physically fit. If the father is affluent, he should send his son to perform Hajj. Also the child should be taught to distribute the poor-due. This is how practical training is to be given to the child which would inure him to various forms of worship.

It should also be impressed upon the child that the concept of worship in Islam is not confined merely to prayers, fasting, hajj and the distribution of the poor-due. In fact, any act done in the manner prescribed by Allah for the purpose of seeking His pleasure constitutes worship. It may be asserted in the light of this basic principle that if one keeps in Allah's pleasure in business transactions, abstains from everything unlawful and earns one's livelihood by the sweat of one's brow, such a business and such an earning assumes the character of worship. One who conducts himself thus would be included among true believers who meticulously adhere the prescribed forms of worship.

Hence every parent or guardian is under the obligation to acquaint the child with everything about good and evil. The child should be explained what is right and what is wrong. This way of instruction and exhortation should continue till the child is accustomed to abide by the principle of legitimacy. This mode of instruction is exactly in conformity with the edicts of the Holy Prophet (S.A W.). Ibn Kaseer and Ibnul Munzir quote in their Musnad the following Tradition:

"Obey Allah. Avoid to defy His command. Instruct your children to do what is enjoined and refrain from what is prohibited.

Such a conduct would be a guarantee of their safety from the Fire."

The parents and guardians should make sure that the child would be grateful to Allah and act on His injunctions when he is accustomed to worship Him. Otherwise there is no likelihood of his growing up as a virtuous gentleman with a balanced personality who could be expected to behave in strict accordance with moral and social norms.

It the parent or guardian arranges for the training of his child properly from the very beginning and make his mind worship oriented, he will turn out to be the true believer as depicted in the Qur'an.

Learning the Haly Qur'an

According to Hazrat Ali (R.A.A.) the Prophet (S.A.W.) said, "Inculcate three virtues in your offspring: The love of your Prophet, The love of your family and the habit of reciting the Holy Qur'an. To be sure, those who habitually recite the Holy Qur'an (and act upon it) would move in the enviable company of the prophets and saints on the Day of Judgment. On that day there will be no shadow other than that cast by the Empyrean."

(Musnad Ahmed)

The mosque is the social institution of the Muslims where they acquaint themselves with the problems of their brothers-in-faith in east and the west. They come to know about the conditions, difficulties, tribulations and aspirations of the Muslims all over the world. Had there been no mosque, the Muslims would have been isolated from one another. The mosque is the centre from where the Muslims shower blessings on their brethren by extending sympathy and demonstrating love and compassion to them. If there is no mosque the Muslims can never have such a brotherly atmosphere.

The parents are expected to strive hard to accustom their offspring to walk to the mosques and realize the importance of imparting to them spritual and intellectual training. In this way they would forge unity among the individuals of the Ummah.

In view of the vitality of remembering Allah, it is necessary for the parent or guardian to inculcate in the child the consciousness of His glory so that he might fear Allah both outwardly and inwardly. The child should always be mindful of Him and revere Him whether sitting, standing, walking or going on a journey or is at home or at the market place or asleep or awake. In this way the child will develop such virtues as have been described by Allah in the following words:

> "They only are the (true) believers whose hearts feel fear.
>
> When Allah is mentioned and when the revelations of Allah are recited unto them they increase their faith and who trust in their Loard."
>
> (8:2)

No doubt when the habit of remembering Allah takes firm roots in the psyche of the child and he grows up in an atmosphere of meditation and dedication, he becomes humble, worshipful, righteous, mentally balanced and polite. He will refrain from committing sins and will never disobey Allah.

The Sense of Allah's Presence

We quote some verses of the Holy Qur'an in this context:

> "The mightly, The merciful who seeth thee when thou standest up (to pray) And (seeth) thine abasement among those who fall prostrate (in worship)."
>
> (26:218-219).

> "He is with you wheresoever ye may be"
>
> (57:4)

> "Nothing in the earth or in the heavens is hidden from Allah."
>
> (3:5)

When a guardian trains his ward or child so as to inculcate in him the sense of Allah's presence and the fear of Allah as well as the habit of being accountable to himself, all these states of mind are bound to exercise a deep impact on the child's action, thinking and consciousness and his whole behaviour will consequently be subject to the will of the Lord of the worlds and his every intention and every act would be imbued with sincerity.

Sense of Allah's presence, self-accountability, and fear of Allah are the virtues which would enable a child to get the right spiritual training and his personality would develop in conformity to the divine method. Such a child would undoubtedly tread the straight path and can be clearly distinguished from others.

These then were some of the principles for the moral, spiritual and religious training of a Muslim that have been laid down in the divine law and the Islamic system.

It is an established fact that if the child is accustomed to worship both in word and deed, to recite the Holy Qur'an and ponder over its verses, remembers Allah continuously, frequents the mosque regularly, says the *nafl* prayers with a gusto and to call himself to account with a sense of Allah's presence, he is bound to be conscientious, right-minded and imbued with sincerity and firmness of faith. Such a child will be distinguished by his righteousness and humility in the presence of Allah.

Children with unblemished character cannot be brought up without following the mode of training laid down by Islam. The parents and guardians should therefore, train their children according to the Islamic pattern of training. It is this spiritual method alone by which faith, piety, meditativeness, fear of Allah, trust in Him and the habit and deeds can be imbued in the kids. In fact it is impossible to refine the social behaviour of the child, reform his conduct and character and train him psychologically without following the Islamic method.

3. Shaping the Mode of Thinking

The child's personality can thus be transformed only when his training and education begins at home. For this purpose there must be a library—at home with a good stock of thought provoking books on various subjects like the Shari'at, history, literature and instructive story books written by the Ulema, scholars and Jurists. Care must be taken in the selection of books for the library. It should have books that present Islam in its true form and present it in exactly the same way as the Prophet had done it. The books so chosen should explain Islam in the same light as its is evident to have been done by the companions of the Holy Prophet (S.A.W.) their followers and the successors of the latter.

In selection of books, Ulama with sincerity of faith and the modern scholars with true beliefs should be consulted lest the books brought into the house would be such as are written by a writer under the spell of non-Muslims idea although they may contain detailed discussion on Islamic subjects. The writer in question may hold that whatever the orientalists and the occidentalists have said is true and reproduces in his book whatever they write, which actually constitutes a bundle of lies that have nothing to do with Islam. A writer of this sort labours under the misapprehension that he is doing a great service to Islam by writing such a book. Ahmed Ameen Misri, Taha Husain, Husein Haikel, Khalid Mohammed Khalid, Muhammed Fareed Wajdi, Jalaluddin Kashk etc. are among writers of this kind.

Social Relationship

Under the head of responsibility for social training we have already emphasized the heavy responsibility to be shouldered by the parents and guardians with regard to teaching the children etiquette and impressing upon them the vitality of observing social decorum. The parents and guardians are under the obligation to acquaint the children with the modes of acting on psychological principles as required by the everlasting Islamic beliefs. They are the basic requirernents of the Islamic spirit of fraternity so that the child may be distinguished by his moral excellence, commendable social behaviour and wise conduct.

We made the following suggestion in the context of effective social training.

1. Imprinting good psychological principles on the child's mind.
2. Safeguarding the rights of others.
3. Observance of general social decorum.
4. Speculation and social criticism.

We dwelt on the nature of impact made by taking into consideration the four points mentioned above in the moral amelioration and social behaviour of the child. That is the procedure laid down by Islam. Now the question arises as to what actually is the social relationship. What is the significance of such a relationship in the training of the child. We now proceed to answer these and related questions.

Development of the child's Social Relationship.

This means that when the child begins to understand the reality of things, the guardian should strive to develop his relation with good social environments so that he may be psychologically purified and his faith strengthened, his mind may be enlightened with fruit bearing sciences, and he may grow up to be a virtuous person with his mind illuminated with Islamic teachings and filled with a zest for the propagation of Islam and a strong and vigorous body.

Good Company

Good company provided to the child in his early years will have a deep impact on his religious, psychological, moral and social behaviour. Thus good company is the most important means of the child's training and moral uplift. It lends spiritual lustre to his personality. Fruit bearing knowledge, good manners and moral excellence of an individual owe themselves to good company alone.

It is necessary for the guardian to ensure beneficial social environment for the child's growth. Such an environment is specified as follows:

1. The home environment.
2. The company of the residents of neighbourhood.
3. The company of the worshippers in the mosque.
4. The company of the school fellows.

1. By the home environment is meant the company of brothers, sisters and close relatives; for the child first of all rubs his shoulders with them. They are the first whom he gets to know, acquire their ways and establishes relationship with them. Hence the parent or guardian is under the obligation to watch the child constantly and see how he stands with his kith and kin and how he behaves with them.

It is common knowledge that the eldest child is the criterion of good and evil for his brothers and sisters. If the child, whether boy or girl is allowed the full freedom to associate with whatever sort of boys and girls he chooses, such a child is bound to develop bad habits, and younger brothers and sisters will follow his or her example.

(b) Company of the children of neighbourhood.

By this is meant the milieu constituted by the people belonging to the family, tribe and neighbourhood. It is in the company of these people that the child grows up.

It is an established fact that in every village or town whether civilized or backward, numerous urchins will be found who receive no training and education and lack good manners. They are foul mouthed and insult indiscriminately every one they come across, regardless of his status and sex.

This is a vice which every parent or guardian ought to root out. We have discussed it at length under the head "Obligations Regarding Moral Training."

(c) Company of mosque-going children. This means that the parent or guardian should associate his child with kids who regularly go to mosque of the neighbourhood and join congregations there. I am of the opinion that the child who is accustomed to join the congregations in the mosque of his own accord or at the behest of his parents is blessed with the true spirit of faith and obedience to Allah. He accepts without question every mandate and prohibition imposed by Islam. It is only from a child trained on such lines that good conduct and benevolence can be expected.

(d) Company of school fellows and colleagues.

This means that the child should associate with his class fellows at the school and the boys of his age group. If he needs help in his studies, he should seek it from good-natured and virtuous boys. If the child is employed in a mill or factory, he should try to establish relations with good people.

We would like to make a special mention of girl students here. Girls are generally sentimental and as such can easily be led astray. They are diverted by the worldly attractions and can be quickly taken in. In other words they are more susceptible to the influence of misleading environment than the boys. If they are not imbued with the love of religion and not wise enough to realise the consequences of deviant behaviour, nothing can prevent them from going astray.

For these reasons the training of girls call for greater attention, so that their faith may not be shaken and they may not be depraved. Care must also be taken to prevent them from establishing links with anti-religious organizations, which will deprive them not only of the blessings of Islam but also of feminine decency. It is of course for this reason that Islam makes it obligatory for the parents to ensure that she grows up in an environment free of vices and create at home cleanly atmosphere so that she may be immune from everything causing moral aberration.

No doubt if the child can have the company of good boys in his school, his character will remain intact and his Islamic identity will not be marred. He will consequently conduct him self in a consistent and polite way. It will not be out of place here to quote observation made by Avicenna:

"The child should have well-mannered companions in the school; for a child learns a lot from another child and tends to acquire the latter's habits and is acquainted with him quickly."

Hence the parents are advised to live upto the Islamic principles and adopt Islamic principles of training if they want to save their children from moral and religious deviation.

4. Missionary Training

One of the ways to foster the growth of the child's balanced personality and refinement of his social behaviour is that when he attains the age of discretion and begins to realize his responsibilities, he should be associated with the propagation of religion as well as with some missionary movement designed to espouse the cause of Islam. Such a relationship aims at imbibing missionary spirit in the child as well as the courage to uphold truth so that he may be bold enough to fulfil all the requirements of propagating Islam. Trained thus, he will not be afraid of censure from any quarter, nor is hindered in his mission by the difficulties of life and any mishaps that may befall him.

When a guardian fills the heart of a child with the hope of a bright future, the child is bound to embark on missionary work and leaps into the battle field to fight in the way of Allah like a valiant soldier.

In order to inculcate in the child firmness and spirit of action and sacrifice, historical events such as the following may be narrated to him:

(a) He should be told that the Holy Prophet (S.A.W.) faced great hardships and endured tortures for the propagation of Islam. Innumerable events to this effect may be found in the biographies of the Holy Prophet (SAW.).

(b) The child should also be acquainted with the events of the great sacrifices made by the companions of the Holy Prophet (S.A.W.). For the children may be told that they duly fulfilled the requirements of Jihad and embarked on missionary campaign with unshakable faith. This phase relates to the Makkan period of the Prophet's life. Their position was never enfeebled nor did they exhibit any weakness. In fact the more they were tortured the more their faith was strengthened. They bowed their heads before Allah with increasing humility. Ibn Masood speaks of these companions in the following words: "If anybody is desirous of following the practice of the Holy Prophet (S.A.W.) he should tread in the footsteps of his companions. They possessed purity of the heart of the highest degree, had the deepest knowledge of Islam and were the simplest and the least formal. They are unsurpassed in treading the right path with perseverence and in self purity. Those were the people whom Allah chose to be the associates of the Holy Prophet (S.A.W.) and to lay the foundations of Islam. Therefore acknowledge the excellence of the Prophet's companions and follow their example. All of them tread the straight path."

5. Physical Training

One of the golden principles laid down by for the betterment of the individuals of the Ummah relates to physical training and hygiene. According to Islam it is essential for physical fitness to do work involving hard labour, receive military training and physical exertion in the form of exercise at one's leisure time. A perfect blend of work and commendable games is a distinguishing feature of the sublime and eternal teachings of Islam, which not only calls for the purification of heart and head, but also attaches due importance to physical training and health

The child should be urged to pay proper attention to physical training and take care of his health; for physical training and exercise in the early years and adherence to the principles of hygiene produce good effects not only in his body but also on his mind. He would be active and energetic.

We touch here on some of the teachings of Islam with respect to physical exercise and military training, which would drive home to sensible people that Islam is the eternal divine faith and it calls upon the Muslim to acquire honour, power and fight in the way of Allah. Says Allah:

> "Make ready for them all thou canst of (armed) force and of horses tethered, that thereby ye may dismay the enemy of Allah and your enemy."
>
> (8:60)

The parent or guardian who brings up and trains the child and focusses his attention on the child's health and physical growth is at the same time undet the obligation not only to acquaint him with the methods of physical exercise but also imbibe in the child the gusto for military training so that he may develop a strong body and be physically fit for war and for enduring the hardships involved in the heavy responsibility of life in the future. If needs be, he would readily take up arms to wage war in the way of Allah and for the domination of Islam. Trained in the manner indicated above, the child would be fully prepared to fulfil his obligation of fighting in the way of Allah. This kind of training would make the child self-accountable and cultivate in him sincerity of purpose. He would realise that the aim of physical exercise and military training is to mould him as a Muslim according to the saying of the Holy Prophet (S.A.W.):

> "A strong believer is better than a weaker one and dearer to Allah."

The Holy Prophet (S.A.W.) has also said, "May God bless the man who demonstrates his strength in the presence of others."

The child must also realise that the main purpose of all his physical exercise and military training is to prepare himself for fighting in the way of Allah and for espousing the cause of Islam. Says Allah:

> "Make ready for them all thou canst of armed force and of horse tethered that thereby ye may dismay the enemy of Allah and your enemy."
>
> (8:60)

If the child is motivated by his pure and true passion in his interest in military training and acquisition of greater strength, it would mean that he has established intellectual and spiritual links with Islam and that Jihad in his mind has come to acquire the meaning of deterring the enemy and sacrifice one's life if needs be. His liking for physical and military training would also suggest that to understand full well the importance of doing every day work whole heartedly. When he adopts such an attitude towards Islam and Jihad, it must be presumed that he has become a soldier of Islam who does everything for the good of world, fights for the sake of Islam and is imbued with faith, morality, sense of honour, optimism and the desire for the victory and glorification of Islam.

In the foregoing pages we have touched on certain links and have shown what positive impact those links make on the training, development, behaviour and refinement of the child. We now proceed to explain the basic rules of the child training, namely the doctrine of warning.

Warning against the evil consequences of deeds is a basic factor which guards the child's mind against misguiding ideas and concepts, fosters his faith and consciousness and enables to counter the fallacious idealogies of subversive and misguided people.

There are two purposes of warning:

1.Persistent warning engenders in the child aversion of evil and disruption and he shrinks from the very idea of deviation.

By highlighting the evil consequences of aberration, subversive thinking and atheism, the parent or guardian fully realizes his responsibility with regard to the training of the child and he never tires of striving to exhort him for keeping away from subversive ideas, evils and disruption.

Let us now review this subject as a whole. By an intensive study of the Holy Qur'an and the Traditions of the Prophet (S.A.W.) we have come to the conclusion that there are innumerable verses of the Holy Book and the Traditions which contain warning against evil and elucidation of false and subversive concepts. Some such verses and Traditions are cited below:

Qur'anic Verses

(1) Do not set up and other god with Allah: or else you will sit condemned and forsaken.

(17:22)

(2) Do not tie your hand to your neck nor open it wide, or you would sit rebuked and dejected.

(17:29)

(3) Do not kill your offspring for fear of starvation and destitution. We provide for you as well as for them. Infanticide is a great sin.

(17:31)

(4) Do not go near adultery. It is nothing but debauchery and an evil way.

(17:32)

(5) Do not take any life which has been tabooed by Allah. We give upper hand to the guardian of any oppressed person who is slain. The guardian should not overstep the limits in slaying the killer. Lo! he will be helped.

(17:34)

(6) Do not go near the property of the orphan. You may make use of it in a legitimate manner till he (the orphan) comes of age. Fulfil the pledge. You will be questioned about it.

(17:31)

(7) Do not probe what you do not know. Verily, the ear, the eye and the heart all of them will be questioned.

(17:36)

(8) Do not walk proudly on earth. You can neither tear the earth nor conquer the lengths of mountains.

(17:37)

(9) Every evil act is abhorrent in the eyes of thy Lord.

(17:38)

Traditions

(1) Do not lie, for a lie negates the faith.

(Musnad Imam Ahmad, Sunan ibn Majah, Tirmizi, Abu Dawood)

(2) Refrain from swearing frequently while selling your goods. The goods are certainly sold but you will be deprived of blessings later.

(3) Do not nourish misapprehension, for it is the worst form of falsehood; do not probe, nor pursue any one, nor compete with any one out of lust for wealth, nor be jealous, nor bear ill-will, nor hate one another. O servants of Allah, be brothers to one another. No one of you should make

proposal for the marriage with a woman whose hand has already been sought by your brother till the latter marries and subsequently divorces her.

(4) Refrain from laughing too much. This depresses the heart and the shine of the people destined for entering the garden would vanish.

(Ibn Majah)

(5) Abstain from wearing the costumes of the Persians.

(6) Shun bad company for this would become your identity.

(7) Avoid being niggardly to the degree of meanness, for the people in the past were destroyed on account of it.

There are innumerable sayings of the Prophet (S.A.W.) to this effect in the various collections of Traditions wherein shunning the evil and everything disruptive has been enjoined.

This principle of warning is not the product of educationists mind nor is it a theory expounded by the social philosopher. It is rather a tenet given to us by only the Holy Qur'an. In fact we have got all the principles of building the individual's character and amelioration of the society from the Qur'an and the Sunnah.

Says Allah:

"This Qur'an provides guidance to what is strong and straight."

(17:9)

And the Holy Prophet (S.A.W.) says:

"It is incumbent upon you to follow my sunnah and my companions, practice. Hold fast to my sunnah."

(Abu Dawood, Musnad Ibn Hibban)

Exhortation to Keep away from Atheism

By atheism is meant to deny the Existence of God as well as to deny all the Divine Shariats brought by the prophets of Allah and looking with contempt at all the virtues and scheme of values derived from divine revelation.

Atheism is a form of apostasy but more harmful. This will be clear from the ensuing discussion.

We deeply regret to point out that in the present day world, the big powers are patronising atheism and are trying to impose upon their sattelites by force. Sometimes this is done by exerting pressure and sometimes by coercion and sometimes by the use of force.

Agents of big powers are active in every country who are busy disseminating atheistic ideas inviting people to deny divine religions and the greatness of Prophets.

We see that powerful countries which champion the philosophy of Karl Marx and Lenin use their resources to propagate atheism particularly in Islamic countries. They are aware that the Islamic laws have a force which leads man to the path of cultural and academic progress and that these laws are all embrasive and capable of application at all times. That is why they are everlasting. They do not contain any quality of worldly laws.

If we take stock of the anti-religious activities of big powers we will find that they have had recourse to various methods to propagate atheism in the world particularly in Islamic countries.

These champions of infidelity and atheism have strengthened ungodly doctrines by taking advantage of scientific theories. For instance, the Jews strongly supported Darwin's theory of evolution and gave it world-wide publicity. They themselves were aware that the theory in question was fallacious but they declared it to be correct in order to misguide the Muslims. Darwin's theory deals with the origin of life and tells us that human life originates from the lowest form and develops into the highest to take human form.

But this theory stands totally rejected today.

Similarly, the Freudian doctrine of libido has been harped upon. According to it every human act is traceable to sexual stimulation. The sole purpose of giving publicity to such doctrine is to deny the existence of God.

The parents and guardians should bear it in mind that our boys and girls are playing the role of translating the Jewish plans into action intentionally or unintentionally by indulging in adultery and debauchery, by their fondness for stage-shows and films and adopting obscene fashions. It is, therefore, incumbent on parents and guardians to prevent their children from going to cinema, night clubs and similar places of entertainment, for these centers of entertainment are working to the Jewish conspiracies a success. Some people say that nothing can be an impediment to the Muslims' going to see films and stage-shows since they are highly informative and beneficial.

We reject this contention on the following grounds:

1. In the cinemas and stage-shows men and women sit together and Islam prohibits such mixed gatherings.

2. In historical films and plays in particular women without pardah appear before the audience. Besides, one sees obscene scenes in them. Islam, to the contrary, prohibits witnessing such scenes as are voluptuous and sex-inviting.

3. In films and plays one sees immodest spectacles. These are symptomatic of depravity and lead to further moral

deterioration. The Muslims are prohibited to go to such places where obscene films and plays are displayed, for they create doubts in the minds of the audience. The Prophet (S.A.W.) says whoever nourishes doubts gets into what is declared unlawful.

4. All these centers have such an attraction that if once a person enters them he would not cease going to them. He will get into the habit of frequenting the above centers of entertainment. For the first time, of course, a Muslim would feel ashamed of himself. Subsequently he will have no pangs of conscience in visiting those places. Consequently he would deviate from the moral norms.

However, a Muslim can legitimately see such films and plays as are displayed by a religious instruction to enlighten him by providing historical and other useful information, free of forbidden scenes, in order to reform his individual and social behaviour. Films and plays devoid of such qualities are unlawful and it is a great sin to watch them.

Wisdom of Declaring game of chance unlawful

(1) In playing the game of chance man believes that livlihood is entirely dependent upon fate and chance. It is not earned by the sweat of one's brow.

(2) Game of chance destroys flourishing homes, pockets are emptied, rich people are ruined and respectable people are disgraced. We have seen with our own eyes that owing to the game of chance many respectable people were ruined and disgraced.

(3) Game of chance engenders ill-will and hatred between those who participate in it and the players to extort money from each other.

(4) Game of chance also stands in the way of Salath

and remembrance of Allah. The gambler develops bad habits and generally lacks good manners. Imam Behaqi writes that the Holy Prophet (S.A.W.) once passed by some people who were playing game of chance. He observed, "their hearts are unaware while their hands are busy and tongues active in uttering nonsense."

(5) Gambling is a habit which devours both time and labour. It makes man lethargic and obscure. It is a habit by which man becomes good-for nothing. No constructive work can be expected of such a worthless fellow.

(6) Gambling deadens man's conscience. A gambler who is poor acquires money by hook or by crook, no matter if he has to resort to violence, theft, bribery or deceptive means.

(7) Habit of gambling leads to psychological abnormality and nervousness. The nerves are ruined and he feels ill at ease all the time. Gambling engenders ill-will and animosity in the heart of the gambler.He either starts committing crimes or commits suicide; or else he goes mad or develops some incurable disease.

No wonder if as Professor Qardadi has observed that those fond of the game of chance stake their honour and the interests of their motherland in order to gratify their lust for wealth.

Blindfold Imitation among Muslim Women

1. Most of the Muslim women go out of their homes wearing such dresses as do not properly cover their bodies. Their faces are unveiled. They show off their beautiful parts and make up. The Holy Prophet (S.A.W.) has observed about such women that they will neither enter the Garden nor will even smell its fragrance.

2. When a close relation dies, the women wear black dress as the Christians do.

3. In the wedding ceremonies the women gather together to witness the dance and listen to the songs of the singing girls.

4. Muslim women in the excitement often swear by beings other than Allah.

5. They appear before the strangers of the other sex with open faces and hair hanging undone. For instance they do not cover themselves properly in the presence of the husband's younger brother or their first cousin. The typical specimen of blindfold imitation of non-Muslims are our young men who imitate women or follow the fashion of black beetles or hippies and eunuchs. Some of our youths maintain that the Holy Prophet (S.A.W.) grew long hair which hung beneath his ears and, therefore, the objection of the ulema to the fashion of black beetles carries no weight.

The answer to this question is that it is true that hair of the Prophet (S.A.W.) were so long that they fell beneath his ears but he never appeared in public bare-headed and always wore a turban which was the crown of Prophethood and a trait of Islamic culture.

It is incumbent upon the guardians and parents to point out to their children the sinister aspects of the tendencies indicated above, which undermine human personality and deprive the youngsters of deceney and human dignity. It is also necessary to tell the children that because of the baneful impact of blindfold imitation the honour and prestige of the entire Muslim Ummah is jeopardized. It is hoped that the Muslim children will tread the right path as the result of right training and instructions, use their common sense and will not be taken in by alien elements.

Shunnnig Bad company

The main cause of a child's moral and psychological deviation is bad company. If the child is dull and without firmness of faith and has developed undesirable habits he will be all the more susceptible to the baneful effects of bad company. He will easily adopt vulgar habits and develop most despicable qualities.

Guarding against bad Habits

In dealing with the responsibilities for moral and physical training we pointed out that children are exposed to the dangers of developing certain bad habits and that the parents and guardians should guard against them. If the child has actually developed a bad habit he should be acquainted with its harmful consequences. The vices we identified with regard to moral training are as follows:

(1) Telling lies

(2) Stealing

(3) Abusing and

(4) Moral aberration and Depravity.

The bad habits indicated in connection with the physical training are as under:

(1) Smoking

(2) Hand Practice

(3) Addiction to Drugs and Intoxicants and

(4) Adultery and Homosexual practices.

According to the moralists and experts of training the habits and vices mentioned above are the worst forms of moral deviation. If the parents and teachers do not exhort the children to avoid these vices and do not keep an eye upon them the children are bound to fall into the abyss of depravity and it will then be impossible for the parents and teachers to retrieve them and bring them back to the right path. Such children would pose a serious threat to peace and tranquillity and to the entire social set up. The people do not cease complaining of their evil deeds and crimes and seek refuge from the harm such young people do (The fatal disease of AIDS has now spread in America like an epidemic. From the latest reports of the mortality caused by the disease, it is borne out that humanity is greatly indebted to Islam for warning against the evils in question).

It is absolutely necessary for the parents and teachers to study carefully the measures suggested in this book for the physical and moral training of children. The parents will thus realize the serious consequences of lying, stealing, abusing and moral deviation. They will also learn of the baneful effects of masturbation addiction to narcotics, adultery, sodomy on the physical, psychological, social and economic aspects of life. Familiarized with all the serious consequences of the habits mentioned above the parents and guardians would be in a position to exhort children to avoid developing those habits and warn them against the harm caused by them.

The parents and guardians are advised to consult some medical specialist if they are not satisfied with the health of the child so that he may tell them the kind of serious diseases resulting from the bad habits he may have developed. The child should be verbally apprised of those consequences or should be provided with medical journals containing the findings of the specialist's research and calling upon them to avoid the diseases resulting from sexual aberration. If the guardians make it a habit to act on the advice given above, they will certainly be immune from moral deterioration and refrain from doing anything injurious to health. The child will thus not only abstain from harmful acts but also advise others to abstain.

If you want your offspring to be righteous, you should never neglect their physical and moral health and fulfil their obligations in this respect meticulously.

7. Prohibition of Unlawful acts[1]

The most important thing which the children should be prohibited by the parents is whatever is unlawful. The scholars of jurisdence define the unlawful as follows:

"Any act which the Shariah strictly forbids. Any one who does not give it up has been given a warning of painful doom in the Hereafter besides laying down punishment in this life as well. Such acts include murder, adultery, drinking, gambling, usurping aught belonging to the orphans, loading the dice while weighing and measuring less."

It is incumbent upon the parents and guardians to guide the children in the light of the Holy Qur'an and familiarize them with the difference between the lawful and the unlawful and exhort them to abstain from the unlawful while adhering to the lawful. Doubtless, the children will be prone to the impact of instruction of the parents and they will abide by the parents and they will abide by the limits laid down by Allah.

Islam declares certain things unlawful in respect of adornment costume and appearance.

1. The use of silk and gold is unlawful for males.

2. It is unlawful for men to appear like women and vice versa.

---

1. *Our discussion of this subject is based upon Professor Al-Qardhawi's Book " Al-Halal Wal Haram."*

3. Ostentatious dress is unlawful.

4. Defacement of God's Creation is unlawful.

5. Shaving beard is unlawful.

6. Use of silver and gold plates, dishes etc. is unlawful.

Imam Muslim quotes the Holy Prophet (S.A.W) with reference to *Hazrat Umme Salamah* (R.A.A.) as saying, "Whoever eats and drinks from the vessels made of gold, surely fills his belly with the fire of hell."

7. Prohibitions of Pictures:

Imam Bukhari and *Imam Muslim* both cite a Tradition narrated by Ibn Masood (R.A.A.) wherein the Holy Prophet (S.A.W.) is reported to have said that on the day of judgement the person drawing or painting pictures will undergo the most painful torments.

Imam Muslim and *Imam Bukhari* quote a Tradition cited by Hazrat Ibn Umar (R.A.A.). According to this Tradition the Holy Prophet (S.A.W.) said, "Those who draw or paint pictures will be tormented on the Day of Judgment and would be called upon to instil life in their pictures.

Photographs are as unlawful as the hand-mark pictures. But if urgency or expediency so demands, one can have one's self photographed. For instance photos are required for identity cards, visiting cards, passports, etc. Photos of criminals and suspects are also required to apprehend them (such as those posted in Police stations). Besides, photos are necessary to fulfil certain other formalities or requirements. This injunction as to the legitimacy of photographs is in conformity with a principle of Islamic jurisprudence which lays down that necessity justifies forbidden things.

The current custom of decorating the Muslim homes with pictures of ancestors or family members is a vestige of the period of pagan ignorance or rather idol worship which Islam came to weed out. Hence it is incumbent upon the heads of the families to cleanse their homes of such reminiscences of pagan days.

Binding the Amulet

Imam Ahmed and *Imam Hakim* Narrate a Tradition about *Hazrat Aqaba bin Aamir.* According to this Tradition, *Hazrat Aqaba* brought a party of ten persons to the Prophet (S.A.W.) for admitting them into the fold of Islam. He initiated nine of them on his hand, with the exception of one. The companions were curious about this matter. The Prophet (S.A.W.) said that there was an amulet bound round his arm. The man cut off the amulet and the Prophet (S.A.W.) then admitted him into the fold of Islam. Afterwards the Prophet (S.A.W.) said, "Whoever binds amulet, believes in partnership with Allah."

Bad Omens

Seeking as well as giving bad omens is also unlawful. Thus *Imam Buzzaz* and *Imam Tabarani* report the Holy Prophet (S.A.W.) to have said, "Whoever gives bad omen and for whom bad omen is given, both are not of our community."

Sense of Racial Superiority

Those who boast of the superiority of race and descent are found in every age. Such people are insensible and ignorant of religion. A man's sense of racial superiority is of no avail to him if he deviates from the straight path to which Islam guides mankind. Says Allah:

"And when the trumpet is blown there will be no

> kinship among them that day; nor will they ask of one another."
>
> (23:10)

The Holy Prophet (S.A.W.) has expressed great displeasure for those who boast of their descent and regard others as inferior to themselves. The Prophet (S.A.W.) has said, "The people will either have to desist from boasting of their forbears, who have been reduced into ash by the fire or will be baser in the presence of Allah than the cowdung insect. Allah has done away with the haughter of pagan ignorance and the pride of descent among you. Men are of only two kinds: believer and God-fearing on the one hand and wicked and unfortunate on the other. All human beings are the progeny of Adam and Adam was made of dust."

The basic human rights in his last sermon are given in the following Tradition:

Imam Behaqi in his *Musnad* quotes the Prophet (S.A.W.) as saying:

> "O mankind! Your Lord is One, your father is one. Listen! No Arab is superior to non-Arab, nor is any non-Arab superior to an Arab, nor a coloured person to a white one. The test of superiority is righteousness."

Mourning over the Dead

One of the pagan customs which Islam strove to do away with was mourning over the dead. The people overstepped the limits in observing this custom. In giving vent to their sense of shock and grief they used to slap themselves, tore off the collar and scratch their faces. This was a pagan custom handed down from generation to generation. But the Prophet (S.A.W.) expressed his aversion for this form of mourning. According to a Tradition cited by *Imam Bukhari* with reference to *Hazrat Abdullah bin Masood* the Holy Prophet (S.A.W.) said, "The man who slaps himself, tears off his collar and moaned as the people did in the era of ignorance does not belong with us."

But if tears trickle down one's eyes as the result of excessive grief without moaning and without manifestation of mourning there is no objection to it. This way of expressing sorrow is legitimate, since it is in natural conformity to the Islamic principles and consistent with the demands of human nature.

These are the rules which constitute the fundamental teachings of Islam. By observing these rules the guardians can successfully reform their children, improve their morals and beliefs.

By the methods suggested in them the task of the child's physical training can be effectively accomplished and his character can be built in the best possible manner.

Winding our discussion on the subject we consider it necessary to tell the reader that the desired results could be achieved only by translating all the rules and principles into practice. If the guardians follow some of the rules relating to books and warning leaving others, it is possible that the child may develop a tendency of moral, psychological and intellectual aberration.

The questions arises here as to how many children in Islamic societies are there who have established their links with mosque, the tutor and spiritual guide and virtuous friends.

Answer to this question is disappointing. The position is most deplorable indeed. False belief and ideologies have taken root in the minds of the Muslim youth today. For instance they have taken it for granted that Islam is confined only to mere belief and forms and worship and has nothing to do with the problems of government, political system and the ways of life.

A segment of our youths has developed the most dangerous tendency of moral aberration. They claim that liquor is lawful. The existing way of using TV is legitimate. Money transactions to a certain extent, too are lawful. They also think that there is no harm in listening to obscene music. It is, according to them actually legitimate to do so.

Some of the youths are suffering from psychological and nervous diseases. The main cause of this is their wrong training and wrong guidance. For instance, they are consistently advised to lead the life of seclusion with the result that they do not come out of the four-walls of their homes. They are like the monks who spend the most precious years of their lives in places of worship.

It is therefore, necessary for the parents or guardians to strike a fair balance between the rules of links and warning when acting on them and keep a strict vigil on all the activities of the child so that whenever he is found developing a tendency to deviate, he is set right there and then. If his belief goes wrong he is brought to reason without loss of time and faith is rekindled in his heart. He is warned on the spur of the moment against the consequence of bad habits.

SOME ESSENTIAL PROPOSALS ON TRAINING OF CHILDREN

The proposals we present here are indispensable to the training and upbringing of the child. We have tried to explain herein all the aspects and methods of training and discussed fundamental points relating to the moral, intellectual and psychological davelopment of the child's personality. We have shown here how the individual and social behaviour of the child could be reformed alongwith the physical training so that he grows up as a self consistent personality and lives up to Islam.

The Muslim *Ummah* will be proud of such an individual.

My proposals are as follows:

1. The child should be induced to learn the best possible things.

2. His natural capacities should be observed and developed.

3. The child should be provided with the facilities of sports and healthy entertainment.

4. The atmospheres of home, mosque and school should be harmonized.

5. There should be maximum rapport between the child and the guardian.

6. The principles of training should be adhered to at all hours.

7. The child should be provided with opportunities for profitable activities

8. The child should be continually induced to apply himself to his studies.

9. The child should be made to realize the responsibilities imposed upon him by Islam.

10. Spirit of Jihad should be imbibed in him.

We propose to discuss these suggestions:

11. The child should be induced to learn what is best. This means he should be prevailed upon to learn the best means of earning one's livelihood.

The parent should allow the child to work freely, whatever the nature of the work, whether it is industrial or commercial work or it is concerned with agriculture.

Learning and taking interest in different trades is among the most honourable means of earning one's livelihood by the sweat of one's brow for they are the ways and professions of the prophets, by which they earned their living.

Work is of supreme importance according to the universal principles of Islam. The worker occupies respectable position under the Islamic system. According to Islam working with one's hand and earning one's living thereby is the best means to gain Allah's favour.

Denunciation of Idleness and Idle People

Imam Ibn Jauzi has it that *Hazrat Umar bin Khattab* (R.A.A) one day passed by certain people who were idle. He asked them what the matter was with them. They said, "We trust in Allah and resign ourselves to destiny." Hazrat Umar (R.A.A) said, "You are liars. The man who trusts in Allah is he who sows the seeds in the land and leaves everything to Allah. None of you should say sitting idle at home: O Allah: Send me food, although he knows that the heaven does not pour gold and silver."

Islam denounces idleness and lethargy and calls upon mankind to earn their living by the sweat of their brow.

But no job-oriented profession can be adopted at a tender age. It is more profitable at this stage to receive education Professional training produces deeper impact on the mind after the completion of education. Hence the parent and guardians are advised to arrange for the child's preliminary education in the beginning. When he matriculates, his professional training should begin, making him learn useful trades. But this phase of learning should precede the teaching of the Holy Qur'an. He should also be acquainted with the rudiments of the Shariah, history and geography. This would imbibe in him interest in his job which he would accomplish by hard work.

We quote here the observation of Avecinna. He says that when the child has learnt the recitation of the Holy Qur'an along with the grammar of the Arabic language, the guardian should select for him a suitable profession or trade keeping in view his aptitude. For instance, if the child happens to have an aptitude for Arabic literature, his learning of the fundamentals of Arabic should follow the teaching of the writings of the Arab orators as well as the Arabic idioms and proverbs. Besides, he should be taught mathematics and secure a job for him in the secretariat. Also,the child should be taught calligraphy. Similarly if the child chooses some other profession instead of acquiring proficiency in Arabic writing he should be helped to learn that profession.

Before we decide to impart training to children, we should divide them into two categories (a) Those who excel in education and (b) those who lag behind.

(a) Child who excels others in learning is obviously intelligent. If such a child continues learning his art and trade at his leisure hours, he will not feel overworked. It is, therefore, advised that the child should be imparted basic training of some profession or trade. Says a sage, "Skill in handicraft ensures immunity from destitution."

Hazrat Umar (R.A.A.) says: "When I am impressed by the appearance of someone I enquire what he does. When the people tell me that he does not do anything then his image in my eyes is tarnished .

(b) Children with average or below the average intelligence quotient lag behind. Such children should first be taught the rudiments of religion and then put on some job or taught technical or industrial trades. When the guardians realize that a certain child does not do well in education, they should lose no time in arranging for his training in some skill. It is wrong to force a dull boy to continue his education.

We have found children who are neither educated nor skilled when they grow up. This is because their father thrust education upon them notwithstanding the fact they have no talent for education. Such children grow up to be the dependant of their relatives or live on the help or alms of others, or else they begin treading the path of crime and disturb the peace of law abiding citizens. Thus by degarding human dignity, they turn out to be a disgrace to humanity. Such children do not grow up to be self consistent and are a potential danger to the social set-up.

If such tendencies are observed in a child, it is incumbent upon the parents to impart to him training in some useful trade and thus enable him to shoulder the responsibilities of life and surmount the difficulties he may confront.

A young girl should be given such technical education as is suited to her temperament and specific functions. For instance, she should be taught house-keeping, domestic economy etc., should be taught how to bring up children and what constitute the virtues of a good wife. She should also be taught sewing and other task related to house-keeping.

Islam does not impose any functions and responsibilities other than those indicated above.

Islam does not compel the woman to learn any lucrative jobs that are inconsistent with feminine decency, and physical structure. In fact such jobs are forbidden for women by Islam. Hence under the normal conditions it is not becoming in a woman to learn the art of war, architecture and the like.

The natural function of a woman is reproduction. This function cannot be performed by her if she works in an office or a factory. She is duty-bound to look after her husband, children and domestic affairs.

It is not advisable for the woman to step out of domestic sphere and elsewhere as this might disrupt the society. In fact the woman is disallowed by Islam to mix up with men and work shoulder to shoulder with them.

Sensible people are aware that women are not permitted to seek sources of income outside their homes in order to make them useless. The purpose of doing so is to secure respect for her and safeguard her position as a fair sex. No religion other than Islam takes into account human nature in every sphere of life.

No husband would like his wife to busy herself with such tasks as are inconsistent with the duties and obligations for which she has been created. None of us indeed would persuade himself to put his wife, daughter or daughter-in-law on hard job that would mar her beauty, delicacy and cause them various kinds of diseases. The honour and decency of one's wife, daughter etc. is the most cherishable thing and no one would like it to be violated.

The sum and substance of the foregoing discussion is that handicraft and cottage industry and expertise in professional work is the most legitimate and undefiled means of earning one's living. It is incumbent upon us to foster the professional capacities of our children and draw their attention to the importance of being true to one's salt by earning their living through legitimate means. It is thus that we imbibe confidence in them and enable them to stand on their own legs. This is how they would be able to lead a dignified and honourable life.

Children's Natural Aptitudes

One of the important matters on which the parents should focus their attention is the child's aptitude. They should try to find out the kind of trade and profession to which he is naturally inclined. They should determine him the particular job for which he is endowed with specific capacity and which he can adopt as the means of earning a living.

It is a fact that children are different in respect of talents, aptitudes and temperaments. Sensible parents are those who educate and train their child according to his aptitude and provide congenial atmosphere for fostering his capacities.

If the child is intelligent and wants to prosecute his studies at higher level, he should be encouraged to do so and provide him all the educational facilities so that he may achieve his purpose.

If the child possesses average intelligence and is inclined to learn some trade, the parent should help him in learning it.

However, if the child is dull, then the parent should train him according as he is capable. In such a case the child's temperament and his physical and mental limitations should be taken into consideration.

This is exactly what Hazrat Aysha (R.A.A.) meant when she said, "The Holy Prophet (S.A.W.) has enjoined upon us that we should give the respective position they deserve."
(Sahih Muslim and Sunan Abu Dawood)

Individual capacities are not correlative. Hence selection of subjects for each child should conform to his natural and physical predilections. If a child has talents for literature, poetry or journalism, he will never be able to get distinction in engineering, medicine or maths and the other way about.

It cannot be said that an intelligent boy will get distinctive position in all subjects. Such a child can get distinction only in subjects for which he has a liking and natural aptitude. It is not possible that he will mark in subjects for which he has no liking at all.

If the child is interested in hard and laborious jobs or business instead of education his father would be best advised to arrange for his training in the field of his choice so that he may grow up to be a skilful craftsman or a good businessman. This would not only benefit him but also be contributory to the growth of his country's economy. But if the father cares little for the boy's natural inclinations, latter will be shocked and frustrated with the result that relations between the child and father would be strained and they will finally go to the lengths of exchanging hot words and the child would separate from the parent and refuse to obey him. The father would be entirely blamed for all the consequences of this state of affairs.

If the parents and guardians do not fulfil their obligations of imparting full training to the child his faith is bound to be marred by wrong beliefs and he is bound to deviate from social norms. Consequently no method of reformation would do him any good.

To sum up, if it is incumbent upon the parent to impart physical and moral training at home, he should simultaneously be sent into the undefiled atmosphere of the mosque for his spiritual training and discipline. It is also necessary that the environments of the mosque is conducive to the intellectual and religious development of the child's personality.

If it is learnt that the child is not being taught religion and the basic injunctions of the Islamic Shariah at the school, then the father should take it upon himself the responsibility of the child's comprehensive training and establish his link with Islam and make him meet the demands of Islam with respect to worship and morality. The father has to bear heavy responsibility in such a case and he should have courage enough to fulfil this responsibility. He will have to devote a considerable part of his precious time to the training of his child and impart to him profitable knowledge. Besides, the child should be sent to the mosque and placed under the tutelage of some spiritual mentor. Moreover, he should be provided the company of good company as well as linked with some mission devoted to the propagation of Islam. If a Chinese wall of Islamic beliefs, ethics and etiquette surround the child, he will never be affected by the onslaught of atheistic idealogies and moral aberration.

The need to establish strong link between the child and the guardian

The educationalist, the psychologists and sociologists all agree that there should be a close and strong relationship between the guardian and the child. In other words, this is one of the fundamental principles of the child's training, which should be properly translated into practice in order to develop the full personality and build strong moral character of the child.

The scholars and wise men are convinced that if the parents and the teacher are hard upon the child, his training on the right lines is impossible. It is therefore incumbent upon the parents and tutors to behave kindly towards the child, expressing love and affection for him and adopt positive measures for the creation of benign atmosphere in order to establish rapport and close relation with him. The examples of such measures are as follows:

1. The parent or guardian should always smile in the presence of the child and should never be serious for a single moment.

2. The child should be given a present when he achieves a distinct position in education. In this context we cite a Tradition mentioned by Imam Tabarani in his *Al-Mo'jam* with reference to Hazrat Aysha (R.A.A.):

"Exchange presents with one another for it adds the bonds of affection among you."

3. The child should be given the impression that the parent or the guardian loves him to the highest degree. Hazrat Anas (R.A.A.) is quoted by Imam Behaqi as reporting the Prophet (S.A.W.) to have observed, "Whoever begins his day's business without caring for the Muslims, does not belong with us."

4. The child should be treated kindly and spoken to in a benign and affectionate manner. According to a Tradition as narrated by H. Abu Huriara and quoted by Imam Tirmizi, Imam Nisai and Imam Hakim with reference to authentic sources that the truest and most staunch believers are they who treat the members of the family kindly.

5. Helping the child in something good that he may be doing also exercises salutary impact upon him. According to a Tradition narrated by abu Ash-Shaikh the Prophet

(S.A.W.) said, "MayAllah have mercy on the father who helps his son in doing good."

The positive methods of the Prophet (S.A.W.) for the affectionate treatment of the people in general, maintaining friendly relations with them and making them realize that special attention is focussed on them, as we have dwelt would make it clear to a sensible person that there are certain essential principles of training the child on the right lines in order to build his Islamic character and inure him to the ethos of Islam. Those principles are as under:

Strong bonds of affection, friendship and understanding is to be established between the child and the guardian so that the desired effects of education and training are produced on the child and the guardian may reap the advantages of his labour. When the child under his tutelage joins the ranks of the righteous, he will be filled with a profound sense of gratitude towards Allah.

The only way to make the children act on their guardian's instructions and advice readily, and thus reform themselves, is the adoption of the method of training and education given by Islam, i.e. affectionate treatment of the children as was the practice of the Holy Prophet (S.A.W.) and his companions.

6. Training of Daily Routine

The guardians are advised to impart to the children the religious training of daily routine, so that they may be accustomed and feel spiritually bound to it. The Islamic instructions in this respect are as under:

(i) Morning Routine:

On waking up in the morning the guardian should utter the name of Allah and ask the children to do the same. Allah likes his servants to begin their day's routine with His name.

It was customary with the Holy Prophet (S.A.W.) to recite the following supplication on waking up in the morning:

"All praise is due to Allah who has been gracious enough to revive us after death and to Him we have to return.

(Bukhari and *Muslim)*

The other supplication the Prophet (S.A.W.) used to recite on waking up as quoted by Abu Dawood is as follows:

"There is no God worthy of worship other than Thou. Thou art pure. O Allah! Thy attributes are excellent. I ask for Thy mercy O Allah! Bestow upon me more knowledge and having guided me aright let my heart not deviate. Verily Thou art the one who Bestows in abundance."

Use of water is necessary after use of toilet tissue paper. The use of both is preferable. According to Imam, Ibn Maja and Imam Hakim, Hazrat Anas (R.A.A.) quoted the Prophet (S.A.W.) as saying to the people of Qaba, "How is it that Allah has spoken highly of your cleanliness?" They said that they used water after cleaning with clods of earth.

When coming out of toilet set your right foot first and say this supplicatory prayer having come out.

"O Allah! Thy forgiveness is needed."

(O Allah protecme against evil)

(*Abu Dawood, Tirmizi*).

(ii) All virtues belong to Allah who has saved me from nuisance (filth) and given me peace (*Ibn Maja*)

(iii) There is yet another supplication which the Prophet used to say:

"All praise is due to Allah who had made me taste the

delicacy of this food, sustained its energy in me and protected me against the nuisance resulting therefrom."

After coming out of toilet both the hands should be washed thoroughly with water and soap. According to a tradition quoted by Imam Nasai with reference to Hazrat Jareer bin Abdullah, the Prophet (S.A.W.) bade Hazrat Jareer to fetch clean water. Hazrat Jareer did as he was told. The Prophet cleaned his private parts after passing urine and then having rubbed his hands washed them.

B. Teaching the method of Ablution

The guardian should also teach the child how to perform ablution and acquaint him with its advantages and reward in the hereafter. He should also be told that sins are forgiven in consequence of performing ablution. Imam Muslim quotes the Holy Prophet (S.A.W.) with reference to Hazrat Abu Hurerah as saying that when the Muslim performs ablution, washing his face thoroughly all his sins relating to sight are forgiven or that when he washes his feet properly all misdeeds of his are washed away with the last drop of water which relates to walking so much so that he is completely purified after finishing with his ablution.

Supplicatory prayers to be recited after performing ablution:

1. I bear witness that there is no God worthy of worship other than Allah. He is absolutely one and has no partner and I bear witness that Muhammad (S.A.W.) is Allah's servant as well as His Messenger.

2. O Allah! Include me among those who are exceedingly repentant and include me among those who take great care in keeping themselves cleanly.

3. O Allah! Thou art Holy and Thy attributes are also Holy. I bear witness that there is none worthy of worship

except Thee. I begThy pardon and turn to Thee for forgiveness. *(Imam Nasaee)* Also offering a couple of rak'at after each ablution is also following the example of the Holy Prophet (S.A.W.). Thus *Imam Muslim* and *Imam Ahmed* quote a Tradition with reference to Hazrat A'amin Algehri (R.A.A.) wherein the Prophet (S.A.W.) is reported to have said that if a Muslim offers a couple of nafil after thoroughly performing ablution he is bound to enter the garden provided that he says the prayer in all sincerity and humility.

Nocturnal Supplications

Imam Muslim and *Abu Dawood* quote a tradition as narrated by Hazrat Abu Hurerah (R.A.A) wherein the Prophet (S.A.W.) is reported to have said, "whoever of you gets up at night should begin his salath with a couple a of rak'at (nafil). (i.e. when one gets up to offer the tahajjud prayer, should offer two short rak'ats first having perfonned ablution. The supplicatory prayer of 'tahajjud' should also be recited before offering the prayer.

The Advantages of Tahajjud

One of the advantages of Tahajjud is that the Holy Prophet (S.A.W.) has described it as the highway to the Garden. Imam Tirmizi quotes a tradition with reference to Hazrat Abdullah bin Salam (R.A.A.) wherein the Prophet (S.A.W.) is reported to have said, "O people! propagate Islam. Feed the needy and offer prayer at night when the folk are asleep. You will enter the garden safe."

The Pre-Dawn Congregation (Fajr)

The guardian is advised to teach the child the supplication said after the call to prayer. Saying of such supplication has been enjoined in the following Hadith:

According to Imam Muslim Hazrat Abdullah bin Aman

bin al A'as (R.A.A.) is reported to have heard the Prophet (S.A.W.) say: "When you hear the call for the prayer by the *Moizzin,* repeat the same words as he says in the call."

Virtues of joining congregation in the Mosque

1. *Imam Dawood* and *Imam Tirmizi* have a tradition as narrated by Hazrat Bareedah (R.A.A.) wherein the Prophet (S.A.W.) is quoted as saying "Give the tidings of being completely illumined on the Day of Judgment to those who walk up to the mosque in the darkness of night.

2. Hazrat Abu Hurerah (R.A.A.) reports the Prophet (S.A.W.) to have said "whoever performs ablution at home and leaves for one of the mosques for performing one of the religious duties, one of his sins will be forgiven at the very first step he sets and at the second step he will be elevated by one degree.

(Sahih Muslim)

The guardian is advised to acquaint the child with the following things in connection with salath (prayer):

1. No nafils are to be offered after the early morning and the evening prayers and before the *'maghrib'* prayer. Imam Bukhari and Imam Muslim quote a tradition with reference to Hazrat Abu Saeed Al Khudri (R.A.A.) wherein the Prophet (S.A.W.) is reported to have said "There is no prayer after the 'Fajr' until the sun rises above the horizon nor is there any prayer after the 'Asr' till the sun sets.

2. It is absolutely undesirable to offer any prayer at sunrise, at noontide and sunset.

According to a tradition cited by *Imam Muslim* with reference to Hazrat 'Aqaba, the Holy Prophet (S.A.W.) forbade to offer prayer or bury the dead at three particular hours (1) when the sun is rising until it is well above the horizon (2) at noontide until the shadows are lengthened and when the sun is about to set till it is out of sight.

The Morning Supplications

We are induced in the Holy Qur'an to remember Allah. Says He:

(1) "Remember Me and I will remember you."

(2:152)

(2) "And do thou (O Muhammad) remember thy Lord within thyself humbly and with awe, below thy breath, at morn and evening. And be thou not of the neglectful."

(8:205)

Similarly the verse No. 41 of Surah Al Ahzab (33) runs as follows:

"O ye who believe! Remember Allah with much remembrance."

The sayings of the Holy Prophet (S.A.W.) with regard to the Remembrance of Allah.

Says the Prophet (S.A.W.):

1. There are two expressions easy to utter but fraught with great value. The Merciful cherishes them:

Sub-han-Allah-wa bi-hamdihee, Sub-han-Allah-il-'Azeem.

Allah is pure as are also His attributes. He is pure and glorious.

(Sahih Muslim, Sahih Bukhari)

The Advantages of Reciting the Holy Qur'an

1. Recite the Qur'an. On the day of Judgment I will intercede on behalf of those who recite the Holy Qur'an. (Tradition cited by *Tirmizi* with reference to Abdullah bin Masood)

2. The best of you is he who has learnt the Qur'an and taught it to others.

(Tradition cited in *Sahih Bukhari* with reference to Hazrat Usman)

3. Whoever reads a word of Allah's Book has a good act to his credit, and a good act entails tenfold reward. I do not say that 'alif lam meem, is one word, alif is one word, lam and meem are also separate words.

(Jame' Tirmizi with reference to Hazrat Abdullah bin Masood)

The guardian is advised to recite the Qur'an himself everyday and accustom the child to its recitation. This is to be regularly done by him and the child is similarly made to do the same regularly even if one has to recite a few verses of the Holy Book, for the best act is that which is done regularly without fail, however small it may be.

Physical Exercise

After the Fajr prayer and the recitation of the Holy Qur'an the child should be habituated to do physical exercise everyday. Allah commands:

Make ready for them all thou canst of (armed) force and of horses tethered, that thereby you may dismay the enemy of Allah and your enemy, and others beside them whom you know it.

(8:60)

There is also a tradition of the Prophet (S.A.W.) to this effect:

> Stronger believer is better than a weaker one and is liked more by Allah also, although there is good in everyone.

The instructions given by the Holy Prophet (S.A.W.) with regard to sports, physical exercise and military training were translated into practice. The Prophet (S.A.W), in fact, has taken particular care to guide us in this field. This shows that he is ideal guide in all the fields of life. This point has already been dwelt upon in the earlier part of this book.

Physical training includes all kinds of exercises and athletics; for instance, race, jump, wrestling bout, weight lifting etc.

The best guardian is one who imparts to the children under his tutelage religious, military, spiritual and material training simultaneously as well as teaches them at the same time how to conduct themselves in a decorous manner in the society by being humourous and serious as the occasion demands. Such a tutor or guardian occupes a very high position in the sight of Allah as well as of the people at large, for every act of his provides proof of veracity of Islam, makes clear the facilities entailed by religion and treats youngsters with love and affection.

Study of Books Promoting Knowledge

Study is essential to increase knowledge. Says Allah:

> Say: My Lord increase me in knowledge.
>
> (20:114)

The following tradition of the Prophet (S.A.W.) means the same thing:

"Allah makes the highways to paradise easy for one who sets out in pursuit of knowledge.

(Sahih Muslim)

If the child studies in a school, he must attend to his school work so that he may be well acquainted with his lessons and subjects of study. If the child is mature enough to assimilate more knowledge, he will be well advised to study books other than those prescribed in his syllabus. This would foster his intellectual maturity and add to his knowledge. He will thus be in a better position to understand the features of Islamic culture.

If the child is employed, he should be advised to read enlightening books and literature based on Islamic culture. A little study of books on academic subjects would also be of some use.

If this is done every morning as a routine it would result in intellectual maturity and illumination of the mind.

If the parent cannot impart training to his children all alone, he may seek the help a tutor or his eldest son. If he does not have the time to guide his children at every step, he can focus attention on their education and training. His child or a tutor can help him in the task of his Children's refinement

Breakfast

The manners of eating and drinking have been dwelt upon in the second volume of this book. The parents should strictly adhere to those manners in order to demonstrate them to their children and thus to make them accustomed to them. The child may be more effectively trained if he is practically taught the manners at the dining table.

The Manners of Going out of Home

In this connection the children should be taught the following things:

1. Wearing the shoes should begin with the right foot. Similarly wearing the overcoat should begin with the right sleeve. When putting off the shoes, however, one should begin with the left foot and so on and so forth.

2. The supplication to be recited on the occasion of leaving one's home should also be taught to the child.

Traditions to this effect are as under:

1. Hazrat Abu Hurerah (R.A.A.) quotes the Prophet (S.A.W.) as saying:

"When any one of you wears his pair of shoes he should begin with his right foot and when puts it off he should begin with his left foot."

(Sahih Muslim)

2. According to a tradition narrated by Hazrat Anas bin Malik (R.A.A.) the Prophet (S.A.W.) said, "When a person goes out of his home he should say:

(In the name of Allah I trusted in Allah and there is no option and power without Allah)

Whoever says these words the angels pray for him in these words:

(Allah is enough for thee. Thou hast been shown the right path. Thou hast been provided with economically. Thou hast been saved.

Then satan will keep away from him."

The Manners of walking on the Way

1.One should walk gently or slowly. Says Allah:-
"The faithful slaves of the Beneficent are they who walk upon the earth modestly and when the foolish ones address them, answer: Peace" (25:63)

2. One should avoid catching sight of female strangers, for Allah says:

"Tell the believing men to lower their gaze and be modest. That is purer for them. Lo! Allah is Aware of what they do."

Greeting

One should say the words *"Assalamo Alekum"* when greeting and if some one else greets one should respond by saying *"walekumusalam wa rehmatullaha wa barakatuhu."*

The guardian is referred to the manners of greeting explained elsewhere in the book.

Manners of Greeting

(a) These manners also require that whoever meets you on the way you must greet him in the prescribed manner whether or not he is known to you. According to a tradition narrated by Hazrat 'Amr bin al 'Aas (R.A.A.) a man asked the Prophet (S.A.W.) "which form of *salam is* better." The Prophet (S.A.W.) said "Feeding anyone and saying *salam* to him, whether you known him or not."

(Sahih Muslim, Sahih Bukhari)

(b) If you meet a brother or friend you must shake hands with him. There is an authentic tradition to this effect quoted by Imam Abu Dawood and Imam Tirmizi with reference to Hazrat Bera'n bin A'azib (R A.A.) wherein the Prophet (S.A.W.) is quoted as saying "When two Muslims meet and shake hands praise Allah and implore Him to forgive their sins, the sins of both are forgiven."

The wording of another tradition to the same effect is "Whenever two Muslims meet and shake hands, Allah forgives their sins before they part."

4. The hazards of the roads should be avoided while passing by it, for example:

(a) One should be cautious of the passing vehicles.

(b) One should try to walk on the footpath, for says Allah:

The (faithful) slaves of the Benificent are they who walk upon the earth modestly.
(25:63)

5. Anything that is likely to hurt or injure the passersby should not be cast on the way. For instance anything on which the passerby may slip should not be thrown on the thoroughfare (e.g. the peel of a banana). Says the Prophet (S.A.W):

"Do no harm and do not be harmed"

6. If you find something lying on the road such as may injure or hurt the passerby (e.g. stone, obstruction, a nail etc.), remove it. Besides, the manholes in the streets or residental areas should be kept closed.

Imam Bukhari quotes a tradition with reference to Hazrat Abu Hurerah wherein the Prophet is reported to have said "There are more than seventy departments of faith. The highest one is to declare 'there is no God but Allah' and the lowest is to remove injurious or harmful things from the thoroughfare.

The Public Right to the Thoroughfare

The child should be familiarized with the general obligations towards the thoroughfare. According to a tradition included by *Imam Bukhari* and *Imam Muslim*, Hazrat Abu Saeed Khudri stated that the Holy Prophet (S.A.W.), asked the companions to refrain from sitting on the roads.

The companions said, "We just cannot do without these meetings. We simply sit together and have a chat with one another." The Prophet (S.A.W.) replied, "If you are not willing to give up these meetings, then you should allow the road its due right." The companions asked what the right of road was. The Prophet (S.A.W.) said, "Lowering the eyes, removing nuisance, reciprocation of greetings, enjoining mutual affection and preventing from what is forbidden."

(Sahih Bukhari, Sahih Muslim)

8. If the child is one who goes to office, school, factory or mill, he must observe his duty towards his colleague or friend e.g.

(a) Greet him when meeting

b) Visit him to inquire about his health if he falls sick

(c) If he sneezes, say *"Al hamdo lillah"*

(d) Pay visit to him on various occasions such as Eids and other festivals, vacations, holidays, Friday etc.

(e) Accept his invitation when it is extended.

We have already dwelt in this book on the rights of friends and have advanced cogent arguments in support thereof.

9. Obligations towards the teacher must be fulfilled whether he teaches at the school or provides professional guidance. The rights of the teachers are as under:

(i) He should be treated in all humility.

(ii) He should be esteemed and respected.

(iii) The pupil should never be unmindful of the teacher's superiority.

(iv) If the teacher is displeased, the pupil should tolerate his harsh behaviour.

(v) The pupil should sit before him respectfully.

(vi) The pupil should go to the tutor after seeking his permission.

(vii) When the teacher is talking the pupil should listen to him attentively.

It is also the duty of the parent to urge upon the child to remember the following things when he goes out:

(a) Fearing Allah (b) To be constantly conscious of being watched by Allah (c) offering prayer regularly (d) keeping company with the Godfearing, faithful and the righteous (e) Not to behave disrespectfully towards anyone, nor be impolite. Such a behaviour brings a person into disrepute and he loses his respect and dignity.

The Night Routine

The guardian should see to it that the child is accustomed to the following routine as well as observe it himself:

1. The dusk and the night prayers are to be offered in congregation in the mosque.

(Sahih Muslim and *Sahih Bukhari)*

2. One should be clad in neat and clean dress at the time of each prayer. Says Allah:

> O children of Adam! Look to your adornment at every place of worship.
>
> (7:31)

3. One should not go into the mosque having eaten

onion or garlic. This causes nuisance to others in the congregation. Hazrat Jabir (R.A.A.) quotes the Prophet (S.A.W) as saying "Whoever has eaten onion and garlic should keep away from our mosque."

Home Work

After the night prayer (I'sha) the parents should exhort their children to complete their school work, learn their lessons and solve complicated sums so that they may not face any difficulty the next day. In this way they will on the one hand be able to fulfil their obligations towards the trainings of children and on the other hand the children will be able to secure good position in the examination. We cite here a Hadith with regard to the completion in the most efficient manner as narrated by Hazrat Ayesha:

"When any one of you does some work Allah wishes it to be accomplished properly."

The Importance of Knowledge

The guardian is under the obligation to impress upon the child the importance of knowledge from time to time. He should in this connection draw on the Qur'anic verses, the Prophetic Traditions, the sayings of sages and achievements of great figures.

The relevant Qur'anic verses are as under:

"Are those who know equal with those who know not."

(39:9)

"Allah will exalt those who believe among you and those who have knowledge."

(58:11)

"Say my Lord increase me in knowledge."

(20:114)

"The erudite among his bondsmen fear Allah alone" (26:28)

Traditions

1. According to Hazrat Abu Hurerah the Holy Prophet (S.A.W.) said, "The world is accursed and whatever is there in the world is accursed too, with the exception of the remembrance of Allah, obedience of Allah, the scholar and the student."

(Tirmizi)

2. Hazrat Anas (R.A.A.) quotes the Prophet (S.A.W.) to have said, "Whoever sets out in quest of knowledge is in the way of Allah till he returns."

3. Hazrat Abu Umama (R.A.A.) quotes this saying of the Holy Prophet (S.A.W.), "The scholar is superior to the devout just as I am superior to a common man. Doubtless Allah and His angels and all the creatures in the heavens and earth, even the ant in its hole and the fish all shower their blessings on the people who teach morality to the people.

Words of Advice and Sagacious Saying

The guardian should for instance tell the child that knowledge enhances the esteem and value of men, raises them to the rank of great heroes and they occupy a high position in the society. The children should also be told that ignorance destroys the homes of the esteemed and honoured people, that the words of the ignorant carry no weight, that the scholars do not have a good opinion about them and that the cultured and enlightened people have no regard for the ignorant.

The guardians and parents are advised to adopt different methods to bring home to the children the merits of learning and the venerability of the ulema. Sometimes this can be done by relating instructive stories, illustrating the utility of knowledge quoting relevant verses and sayings of wise men and by the use of direct didactic method alternately.

The children should also be told of the advantages of rising early. For instance they should be told that early rising is a social virtue. Besides, they should be acquainted with the miracles of the Prophets. Stories from history should also be related to them. Historical events throwing light on the importance of knowledge should also be told, as for example the incident of the Holy Prophet's Ascension should be related to them in detail. Stories and incidents are more effective in the instruction of children than anything else.

It is incumbent upon the parents or guardians to imbibe in the children the desire for Jihad (Holy war) and impress upon their mind the necessity to liberate the Holy land of Palestine. Whenever they find time they should induce the children repeatedly to prepare themselves for *jihad* so much so that every child feels in his heart of hearts that he is under the obligation to constitute his bit towards the struggle for libeating Palestine from the clutches of the Zionists and puring its atmosphere of the diabolical presence of the Jews.

It is possible for the parents every evening to sit among the children and exhort and instruct them and establish their mental links with the society at large, provide them food for thought and enrich their minds with historical information.

In this connection the parents and guardians are advised to refer to the commentaries of the Holy Qur'an, the Prophet's Traditions as well as relevant books both old and new. Such books are also to be consulted as emphasize the importance of self-discipline; and throw light on the life of the Holy Prophet (S.A.W.). Books of history dealing with the various systems of Islam will also be useful in the instruction and moral and spiritual uplift of children.

Going to Bed Early

The parents should themselves go early to bed and accustom the children to sleep early. Going to bed late at night is harmful. It causes pain in the muscles. The greatest harm it does is that the predawn prayer is omitted and one feels lethargic when one gets up the next morning. Early to rise and early to bed is the distinguishing feature of Islamic life. This was the practice of the Holy Prophet (S.A.W.) and he has urged upon us to do so.

The children should be asked every day what they have learnt on the day and what instruction they have carried out. If the guardians feel that the education imparted to the children at the schools is not in harmony with the Islamic beliefs and ethics, they should try to correct the children's ideas and advise them to avoid misguided teachers. Nor is this all. The teachers who have turned apostate and mislead the children should be dealt with severely.

The children should be taken to parks, gardens, or the seaside at leisure time in order to refresh their minds. This would make them active and smart, and will also provide the opportunity to have a good time. They would thus be able to get a training of athletics, swimming and other sports.

Giving presents to the children, meeting their needs and buying things for them they require is also included in the obligations imposed on the parents in connection with the training of the children. May God bless the father who helps in a good act. Besides, giving presents to the child furthers his relish for worship, devotion to work and ambition for success in the examination.

These then are the principles of Islamic training and the items of daily routine. By adhering to them the parents and guardians can fulfil the Islamic requirements of training and effectively discharge their obligations in this respect.

Provision of Cultural Resources

It is incumbent upon the parents or guardians to provide the right sort of cultural means in order to discharge their obligation towards the training and education of children in a satisfactory manner. Such means would go a long way to foster the children's intellectual growth and develop their thinking on the right lines for tackling the problems of practical life.

Explanatory and Illustrative Method

Another effective method of imparting education and training to the children is to elucidate everything in detail simplify what is difficult and to make easy for them the way of learning. I think the following methods in particular would be most beneficial.

(a) The children should be acquainted with the world in general and the Islamic world in particular with the aid of atlas.

(b) All the maps of the Muslim countries showing the density of the population, the mosques, factories and the general conditions of those countries should be used.

(c) Graphs should be prepared to indicate the growth of Islamic civilization in the past bringing home to the children the achievements of their forbears in the fields of social and physical sciences and their contribution towards the development of Islamic culture.

(d) Graphs should also be prepared to bring into relief the conquest of Muslim forces and the expansion of their rule in different periods of history.

(e) Such charts should also be prepared, including the pictures of various weapons used by our forbears in the wars against the infidels and enemies of Islam, and conquered lands after land in different periods of history.

In short any picture or chart that may be conducive to the training and education of children must be used.

Visits to Museums

A most important proposal we have to present in connection with the training of children is that the parents should take them round to visit the museums in their respective countries and if possible in other Muslim countries on some suitable days. The child will thus be familiarized with academic and cultural achievements of the Muslims in history and they will have a sense of identification with the glory for which the way was paved by the Muslim heroes, whose feats are written in letters of gold in history.

Visits to archaeological sites and museums is the best method of imbibing Islamic pride and courage in the Muslim young men. It would inculcate in them self respect and real ambition for power and progress. A poet aptly describes the significance of historical sites and artefacts:

"These are signs that point to us, Ponder over these signs when we are no more.

(f) Going to public libraries during leisure hours.

The parents and guardians are advised to attach special importance to taking the children round to public libraries. This would imbibe in the children a taste for knowledge and they will get into the habit of borrowing books from the libraries to read and learn.

Besides, the libraries occupy a special position from cultural viewpoint. They help us in realizing the value of the ideological, intellectual and academic heritage of the Muslim ummah. We also learn from their stock of books the overall standpoint of Islam with regard to the universe, life and humanity. We are also acquainted with new aspects of the culture to which history bears testimony.

However, if the parents or guardians cannot spare time to take the children to libraries or cultural centres, then they should urge the children to profit by the company of the scholars so that they may learn from the latter how to benefit from the libraries and cultural centres, as well as how to gain knowledge.

Holding Competitions among Children

For instance, competitions of more reading and speed of reading during given length of time. Then they should be tested. The child securing first position in such a competition should be awarded encouraging prize. This would give an impression to the children that they are honoured and encouraged for good performance. Imam Ghazzali has this to say for the encouragement of the child:

"If the child exhibits a sterling quality or conducts himself in a polite manner, he should be given some reward in recognition thereof so that he may be pleased and honoured. He should also be praised in public to encourage him in this good commendable conduct."

(Ahyae Ullomuddin -Part III)

Encouragement of child by a reward, present or title and giving him the impression that his good behaviour has been appreciated is supported by the following traditions of the Holy Prophet (S.A.W.):

(i) Exchange presents and increase mutual affection

(Mo'jamal Tabarani)

(ii) Whoever does good to you, reciprocate it adequately.

If you are not in a position to do this, then pray for him.

Political Striving in the way of Allah

This means endeavouring to establish a government based on Islamic ideology—a government which recognizes the sovereignty of Allah alone. The Quranic injunction in this context is as follows:

> "So judge between them by that which Allah hath revealed, and follow not their desires, but beware of them lest they reduce thee from some part of that which Allah hath revealed unto thee. If they turn away, then know that Allah's Will is to smite them for some sin of theirs. Surely, many of mankind are evil-livers.
>
> Is it a judgment of the time of pagan ignorance that they are seeking? Who is better than Allah for judgment to a people who have certainty (in their belief) ?"
>
> (5:49-50)

Traditions

According to a tradition narrated by Abdullah bin Masood (R.A.A.) the Holy Prophet (S.A.W.) said, "The Messenger (S.A.W.) sent before me by Allah, he did have his disciples and companions from his Ummah who obeyed his commands. After that messenger arose some obedient people whose word and deed were contradictory. They did whatever they were forbidden. After me whoever strove against such people with his hand would be a true believer, whoever opposed them by his tongue would also be a true believer and whoever would oppose them in his heart of hearts would be a true believer too. But whoever does not do against them even this much, he would be totally faithless."

(Sahih Muslim)

Holy War

This means waging war with full strength against the rebellious elements who create hurdles in the establishment of Allah's sovereignty and striving heart and soul to disseminate the divine message all over the world. Fighting against such rebellious elements is holy war whether they are in a Muslim country or a country dominated by the infidels where war is going on such as the Indian subcontinent before its partition, Says Allah:

> "And fight them until persecution is no more and religion is all for Allah."
>
> (8:39)

Again,

> "Fight against such of those who have been given the scripture as believe not in Allah nor the Last Day, and forbid not that which Allah hath forbidden by His messenger, and follow not the religion truth, until they pay the tribute readily, being brought low."
>
> (9:29)

This is what Hazrat O bin 'Aamir declared in the dialogue which took place between the Muslims and the Iranian general Rustum. He declared, "We have been created by Allah in order that we liberate men from the bonds of men and bring them into the bondsmanship of Allah, take them out of the narrow confinement of the world and bring them into the wide and open environment of the world and deliver them from the oppression of false religions and bring them under the just system of Islam."

The result of familiarizing the children with the significance of the various forms of jihad will be that they will feel an urge to take part in jihad and will move zealously in that direction of their own accord, for they will realise that every act that conforms to Islam is nothing but jehad.

The children should be told every day the stories of the valour and achievements of the sons and successors of the Prophet's companions, that they may be impressed by them and tread in the footsteps of the forbears.

The children are to be made to learn the Qur'anic Surah by heart.

It should be ensured that the children commit to memory the Surahs Al Anfal, Al Tobah and Al Ahzab. Besides, they are to learn by heart such verses of the Qur'an which contain injunction relating to jehad. They should also be explained reasons for the revelation thereof, their meanings and significance and the position taken by the Prophet (S.A.W.) on the occasion of Battles of Badr, Khandaq, Uhud, Hunain etc. This would serve as an impulse to the thinking and understanding of children and consequently they would be turned into valiant men who would be bold enough to take the initiative and will never tolerate any one talking of Allah blasphemously. He would rather zealously march to wage the war in the way of Allah with a craving for martyrdom like his forbears and the companions of the Holy Prophet (S.A.W.).

Summary of Book

In this book we have dwelt at length on the various aspects of the training of children. The parents and guardians after going through it should have no doubts about the fact that Islam is an all-inclusive system, a unique mode and distinct way of life which adequately provides for the spiritual and moral upbringing, development of self-consistent personality and physical and social training of the children. By the adoption of this way of life a man develops balanced personality and becomes an advocate of true beliefs, moral excellence and the message of Islam. He is thus capable of discharging all the responsibilities he has to shoulder. At last he succeeds in finding a place in the paradise by securing Allah's pleasure which is the end of all ends, the *summum bonum.*

Some guardians and parents who complain of the tendency of deviation and disobedience are themselves to blame for it. No child whose father's laxity allows him to move in bad company can be disciplined and reformed. The faith of a child who reads in schools run by foreigners or Christian missionaries can be strong. If the father brings into the house a TV set for viewing obscene programmes the child can never develop good moral character. If there is obscene literature available at home like cheap romantic magazines and novels that arouse sex, it is not possible to prevent the child's behaviour against moral aberration. If the father has a liking for anti religious organizations and secular political parties, we cannot rest assured of the child's having faith in Islam. In short, if the guardian, or parents are not building the character of their children on the lines chalked out by Islam, the child cannot grow up to be a morally refined person.

Some parents think that in spite of the training they had imparted to their children, they grew up to be disobedient and deviant. This stand-point is absolutely wrong. If you probe into the matter, the parents would in the final analysis, turn out to be responsible for the misbehaviours of their children as they did not either set a good example of moral refinement by their own conduct or did not care for the Islamic methods of training at all, or gave the duties upon them by Islam.

If the child is so incorrigibly deviant and disobedient the parent or guardian is free of blame, for he will have fulfilled all the obligations imposed upon him by Allah. Hence he will not be accountable.

At the end I request the parents and guardians to make a commitment to Allah that they would bring their children according to Islamic principles and fulfil their obligation with respect to imparting comprehensive training to their children by stages with full determination.

If the parents and teachers train their children in strict conformity to the teachings of Islam, they emerge as the suns of edification in the mist of subversion, prove to be the loadstars in the dark night of deviation and misguidance and appear as moving angels in the human form. People will point to them bearing witness to the purity of their hearts, moral excellence, honesty, balance of thought and action, and refinement of social life.